This is the last page.

In keeping with the original Japanese comic format, this book reads from right to left—so action, sound effects, and word balloons are completely reversed. This preserves the orientation of the original artwork—plus, it's fun! Check out the diagram shown here to get the hang of things, and then turn to the other side of the book to get started!

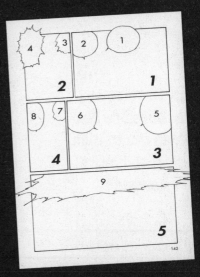

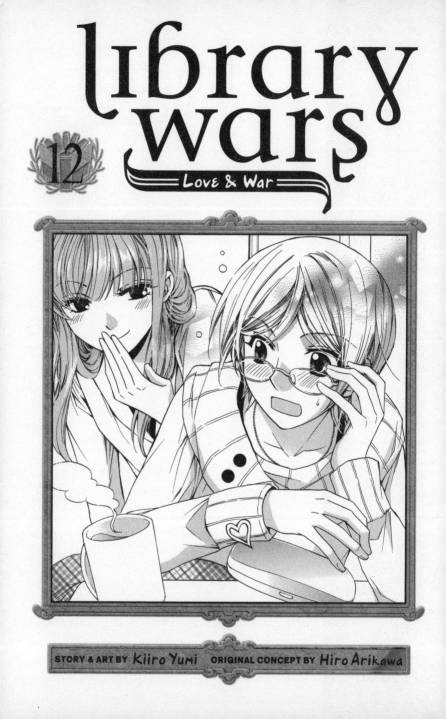

library wars

12

Love & War

STORY & ART BY Kiiro Yumi ORIGINAL CONCEPT BY Hiro Arikawa

Library Wars

Love & War

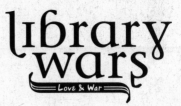

Contents

The Library Freedom Act

Libraries have the freedom to acquire their collections.

Libraries have the freedom to circulate
materials in their collections.

Libraries guarantee the privacy of their patrons.

Libraries oppose any type of censorship.

When libraries are imperiled,
librarians will join together
to secure their freedom.

library wars

Love & War

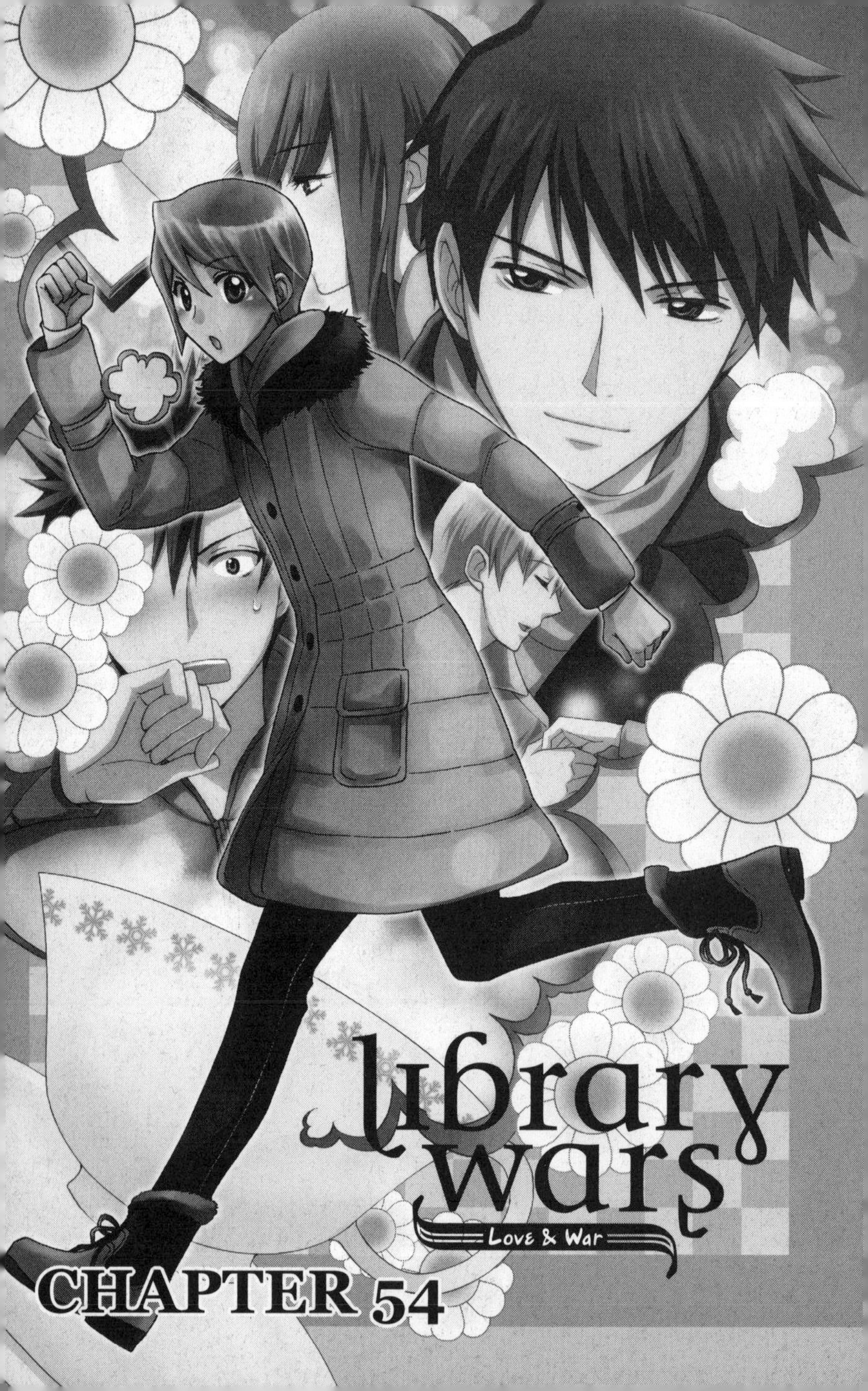
library wars
Love & War
CHAPTER 54

Library Wars: Love & War Vol. 12

Let's get started !!

Arrrgh! Graaah!

I hope you enjoy it.

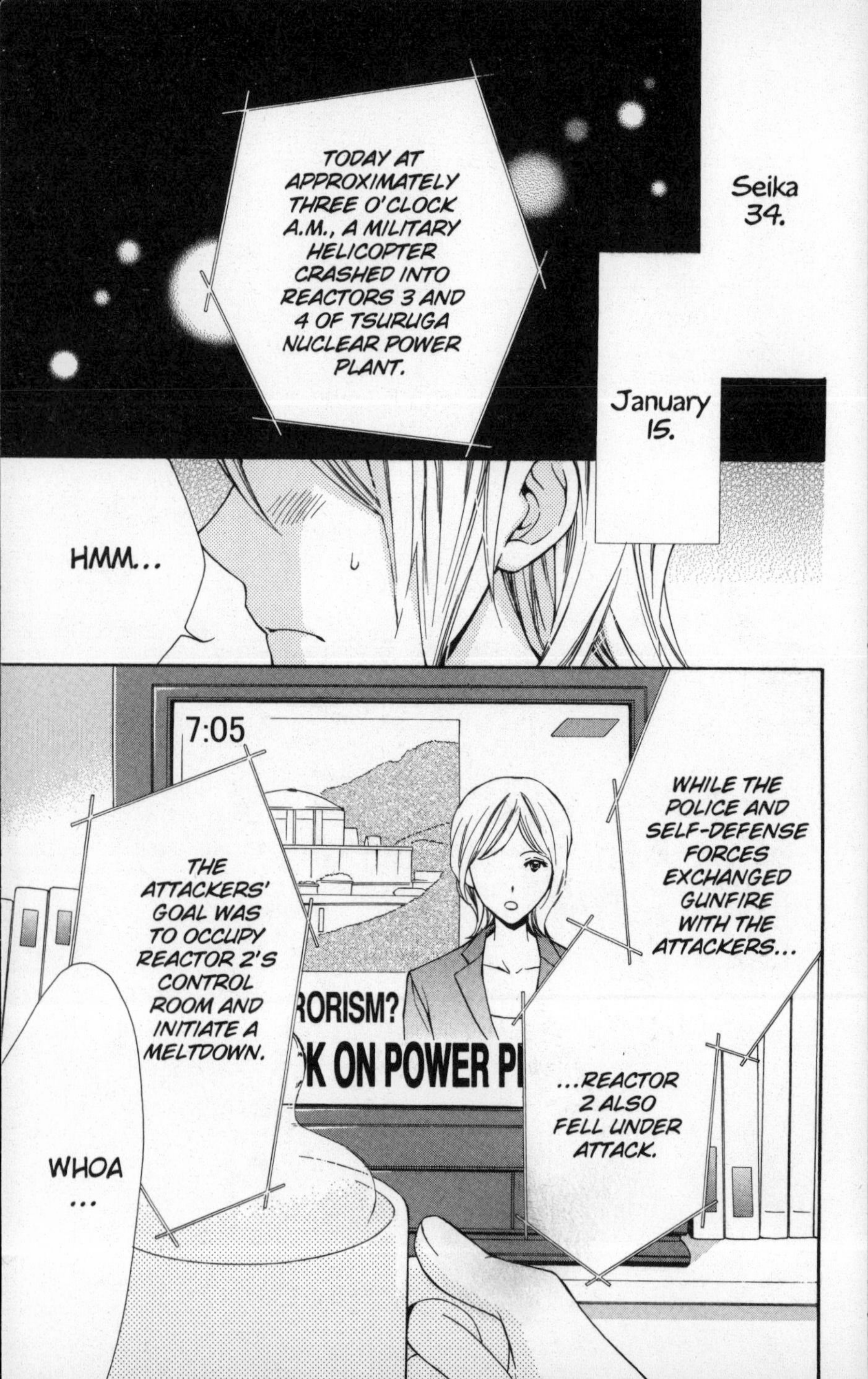
Seika 34.
January 15.
TODAY AT APPROXIMATELY THREE O'CLOCK A.M., A MILITARY HELICOPTER CRASHED INTO REACTORS 3 AND 4 OF TSURUGA NUCLEAR POWER PLANT.
HMM...
7:05
WHILE THE POLICE AND SELF-DEFENSE FORCES EXCHANGED GUNFIRE WITH THE ATTACKERS...
...REACTOR 2 ALSO FELL UNDER ATTACK.
RORISM?
K ON POWER P
THE ATTACKERS' GOAL WAS TO OCCUPY REACTOR 2'S CONTROL ROOM AND INITIATE A MELTDOWN.
WHOA ...

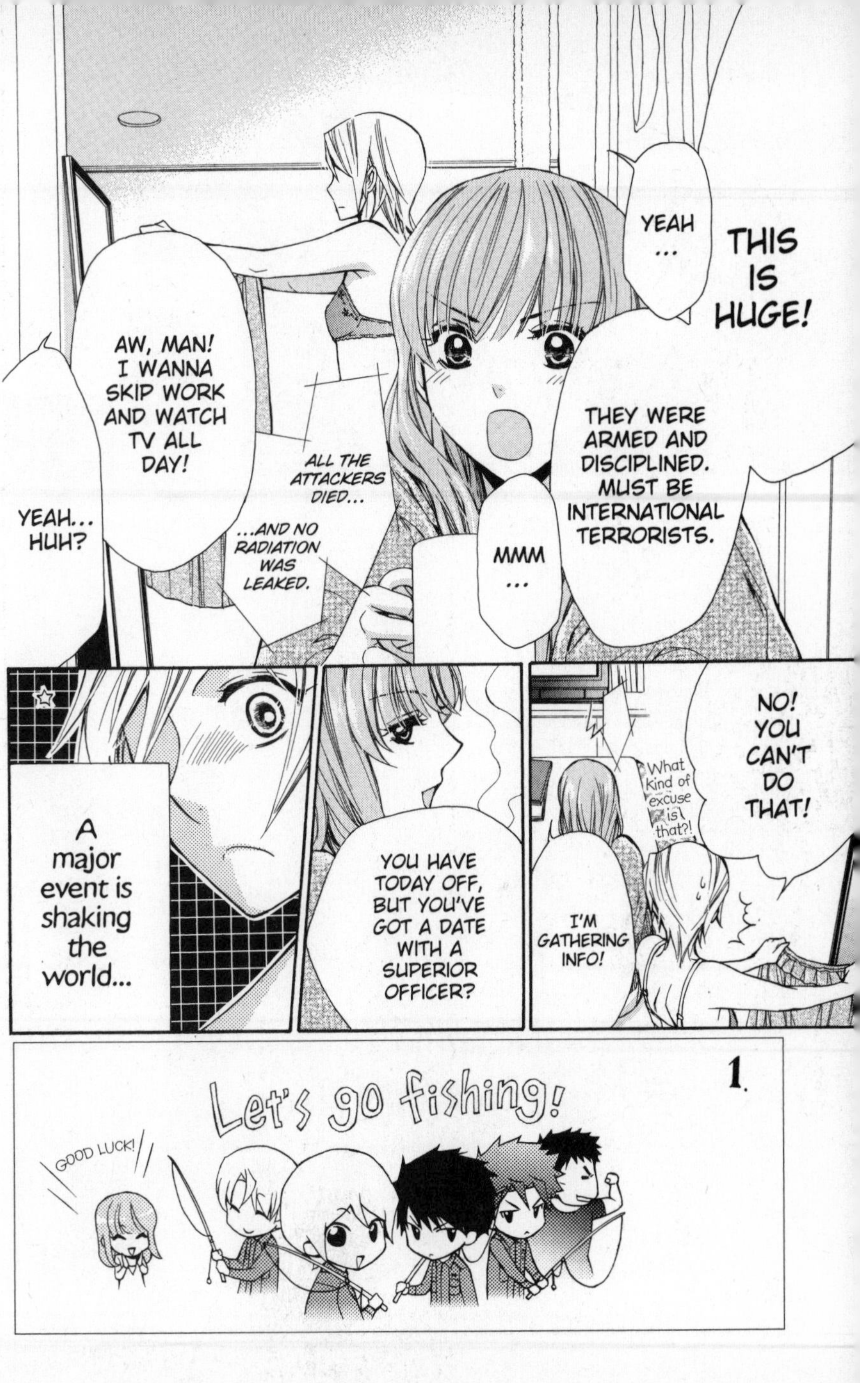
YEAH...
THIS IS HUGE!
THEY WERE ARMED AND DISCIPLINED. MUST BE INTERNATIONAL TERRORISTS.
MMM...
ALL THE ATTACKERS DIED...
...AND NO RADIATION WAS LEAKED.
AW, MAN! I WANNA SKIP WORK AND WATCH TV ALL DAY!
YEAH... HUH?
NO! YOU CAN'T DO THAT!
What kind of excuse is that?!
I'M GATHERING INFO!
YOU HAVE TODAY OFF, BUT YOU'VE GOT A DATE WITH A SUPERIOR OFFICER?
A major event is shaking the world...
1.
Let's go fishing!
GOOD LUCK!

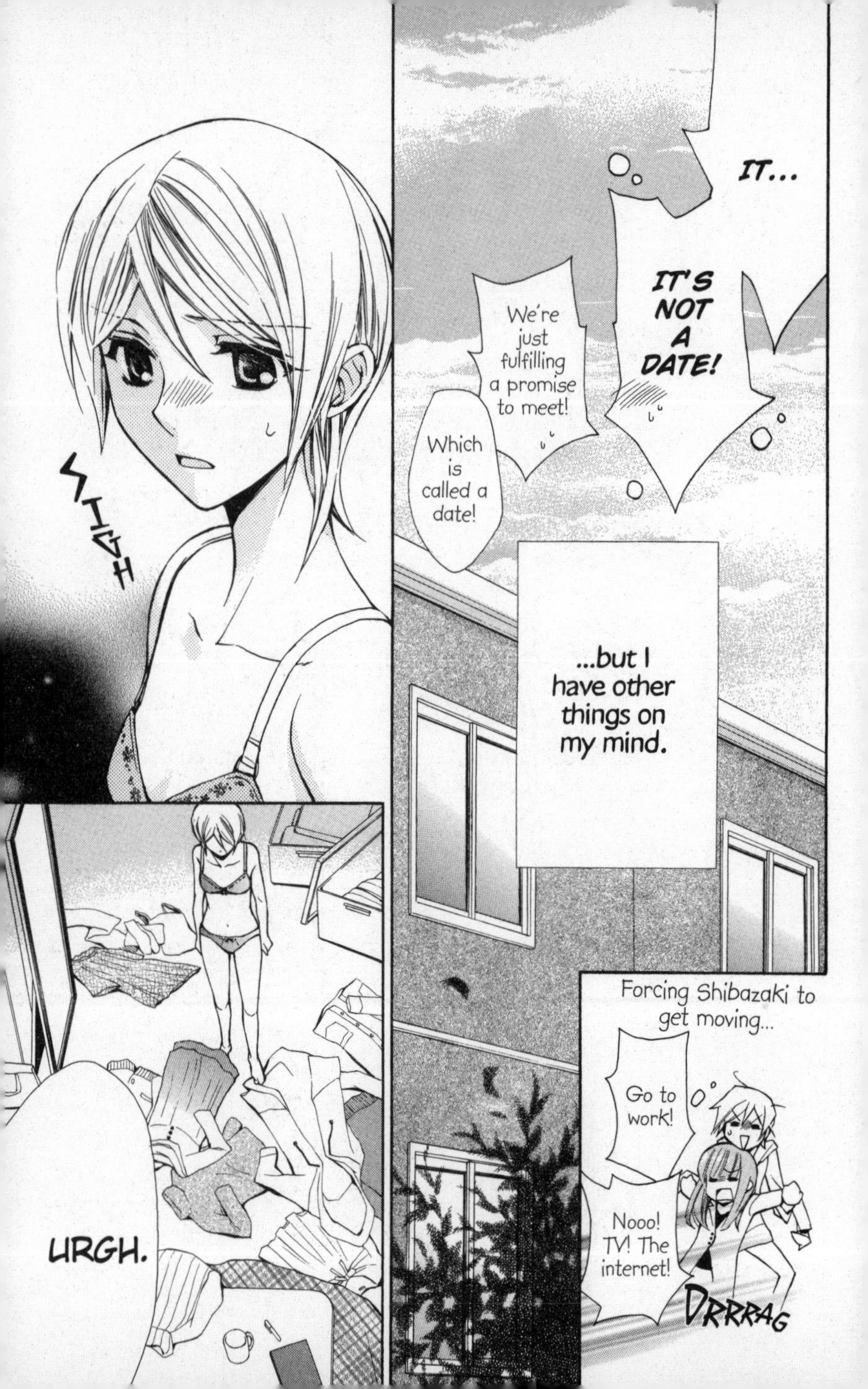
IT...
IT'S NOT A DATE!
We're just fulfilling a promise to meet!
Which is called a date!
...but I have other things on my mind.
Forcing Shibazaki to get moving...
Go to work!
Nooo! TV! The internet!
DRRRAG
SIGH
URGH.

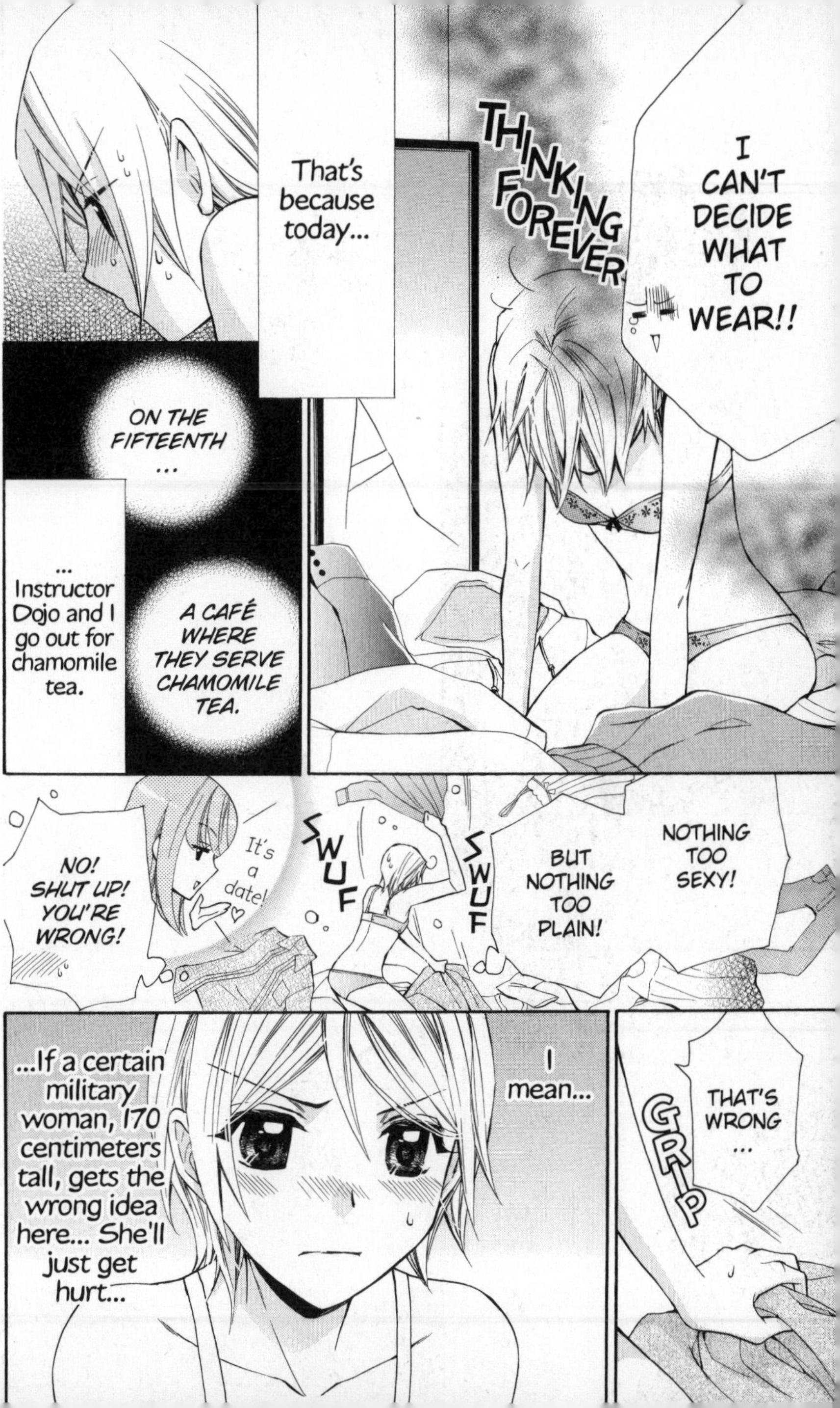

THINKING FOREVER
I CAN'T DECIDE WHAT TO WEAR!!
That's because today...
ON THE FIFTEENTH ...
... Instructor Dojo and I go out for chamomile tea.
A CAFÉ WHERE THEY SERVE CHAMOMILE TEA.
NOTHING TOO SEXY!
BUT NOTHING TOO PLAIN!
SWUF
SWUF
It's a date! ♡
NO! SHUT UP! YOU'RE WRONG!
THAT'S WRONG ...
GRIP
I mean...
...If a certain military woman, 170 centimeters tall, gets the wrong idea here... She'll just get hurt...

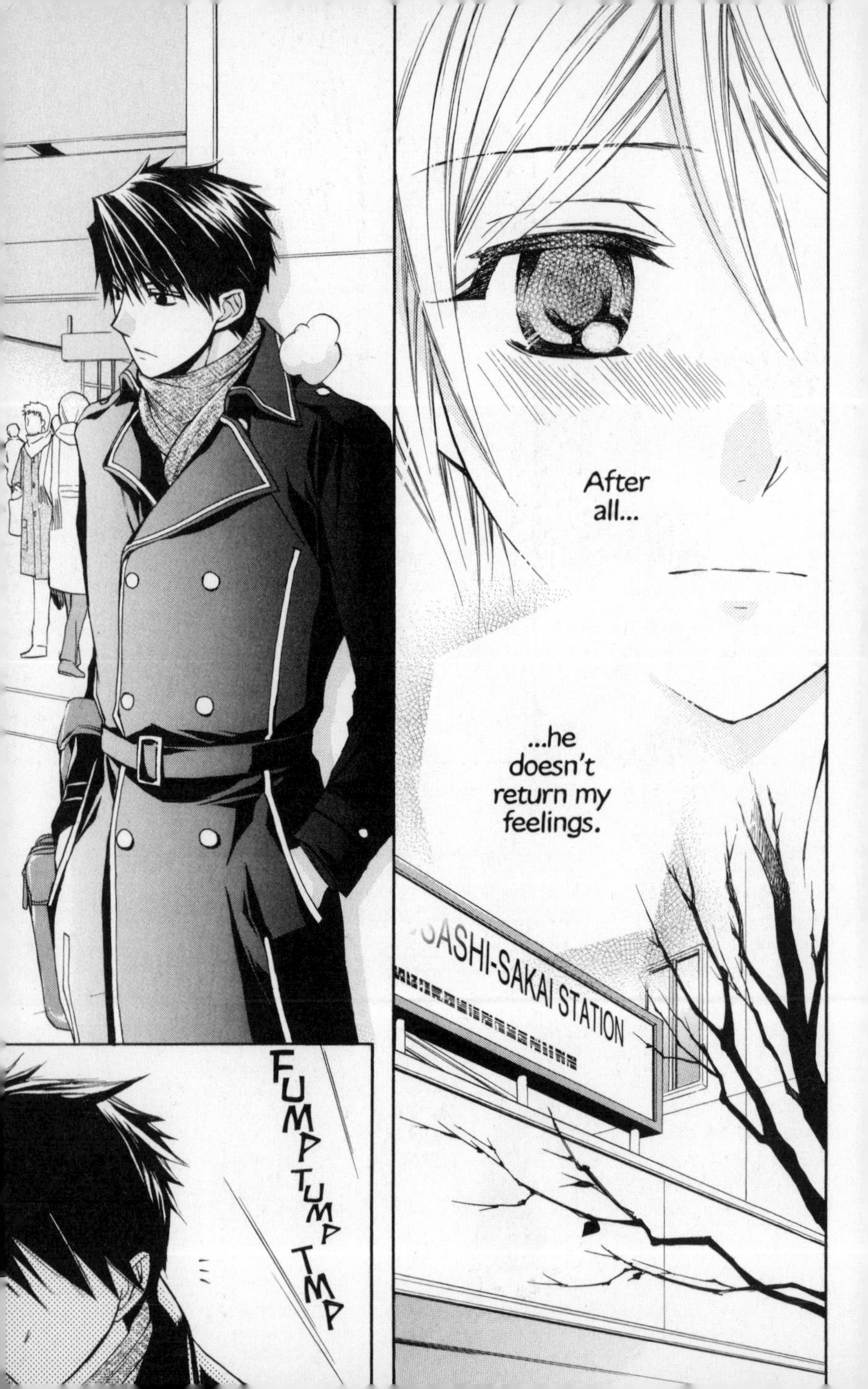
After all...
...he doesn't return my feelings.
SASHI-SAKAI STATION
FUMP TUMP TMP
...

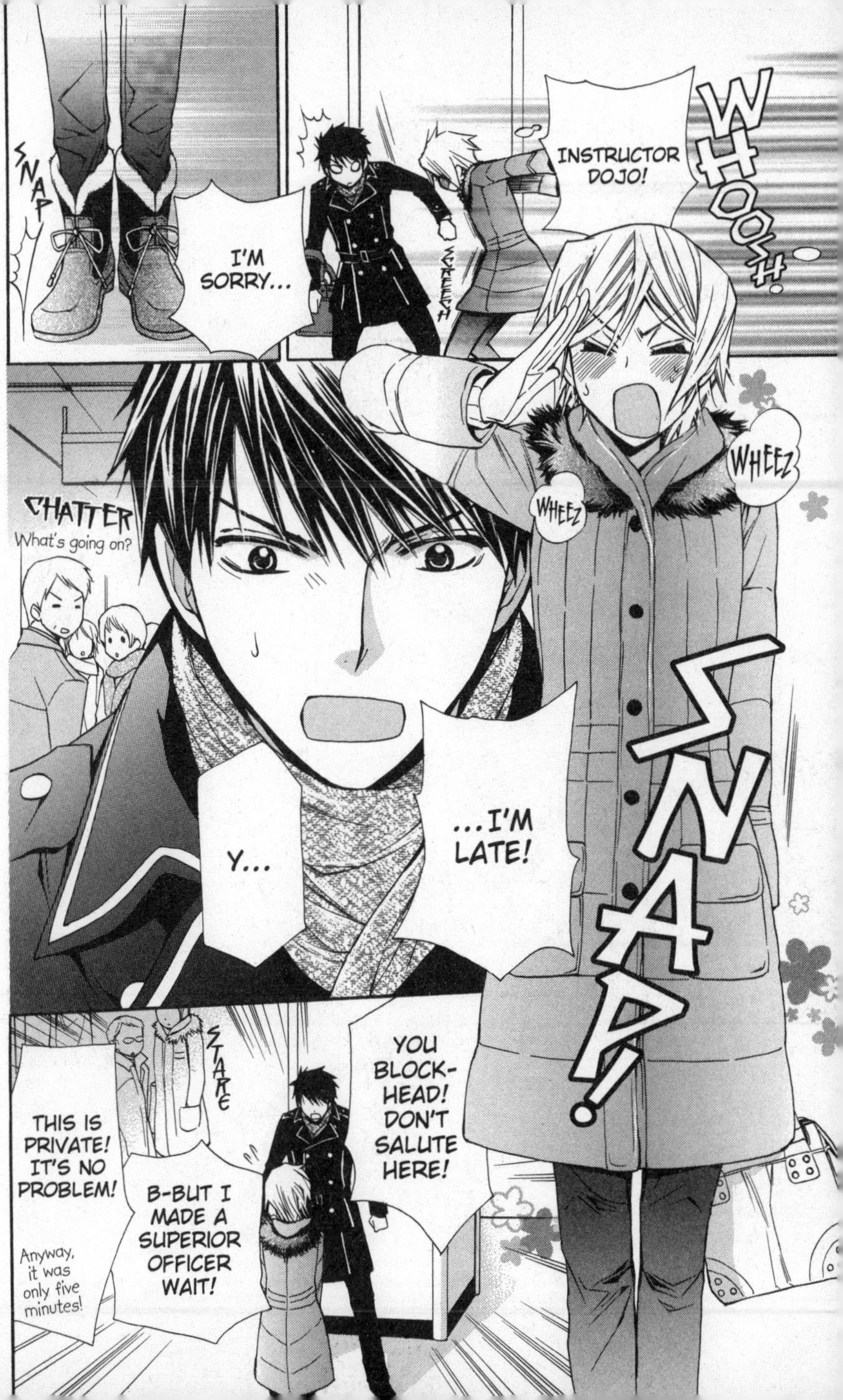
WHOOSH!
INSTRUCTOR DOJO!
SCREECH
I'M SORRY...
SNAP
WHEEZ
WHEEZ
SNAP!
Y...
...I'M LATE!
CHATTER
What's going on?
STARE
YOU BLOCK-HEAD! DON'T SALUTE HERE!
B-BUT I MADE A SUPERIOR OFFICER WAIT!
THIS IS PRIVATE! IT'S NO PROBLEM!
Anyway, it was only five minutes!

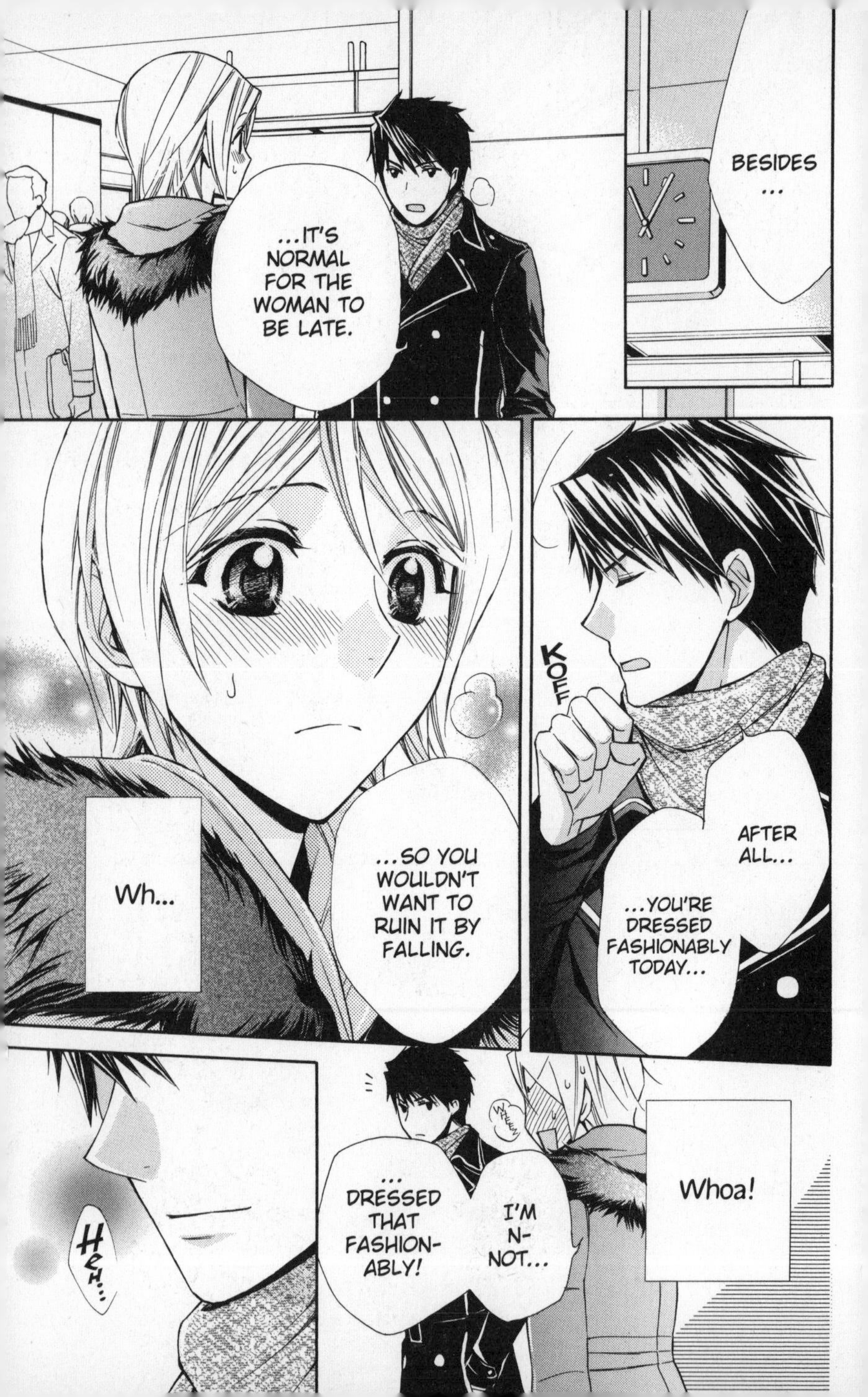

BESIDES...
...IT'S NORMAL FOR THE WOMAN TO BE LATE.
KOFF
AFTER ALL...
...YOU'RE DRESSED FASHIONABLY TODAY...
...SO YOU WOULDN'T WANT TO RUIN IT BY FALLING.
Wh...
Whoa!
I'M N-NOT...
...DRESSED THAT FASHION-ABLY!
HEH...

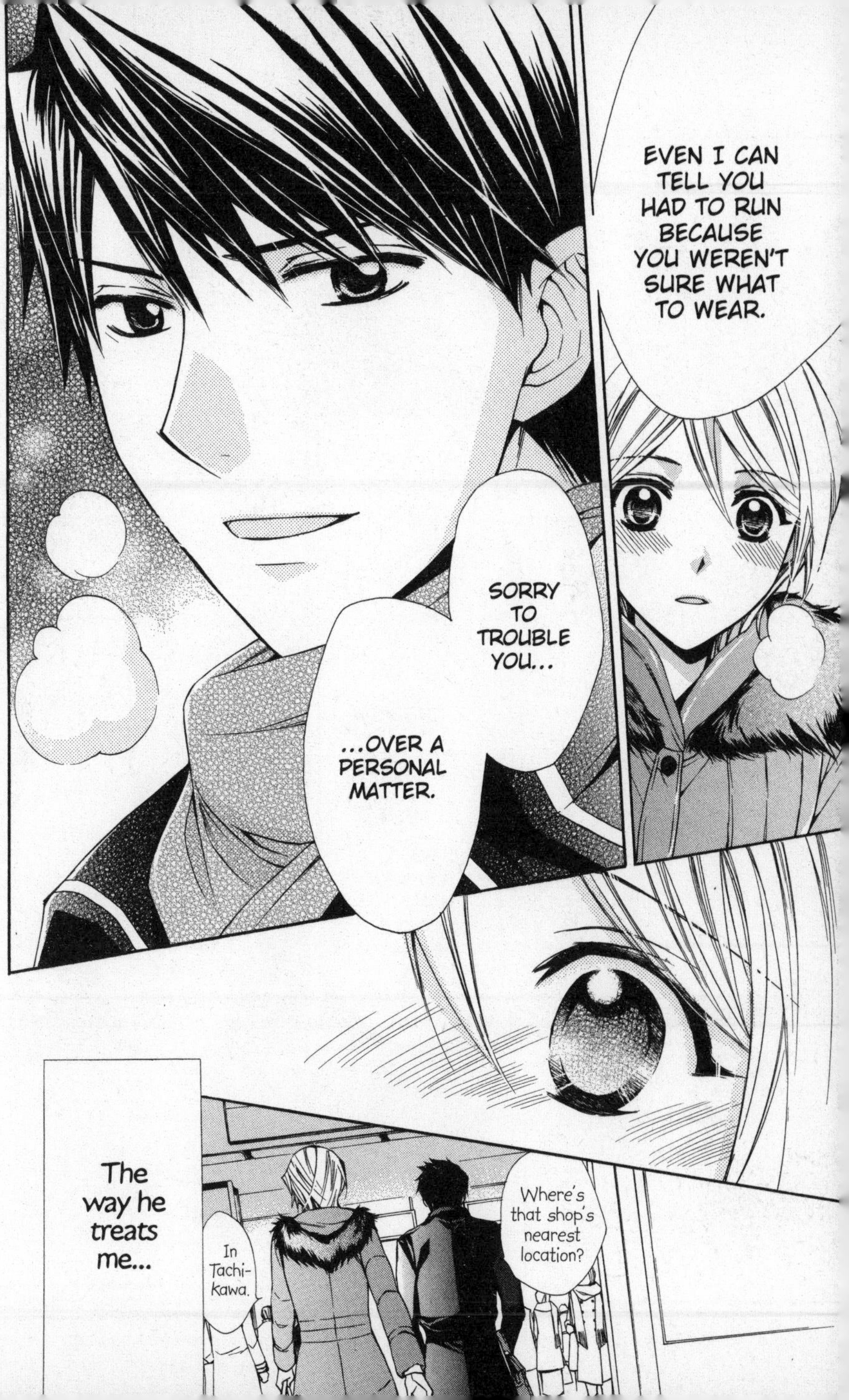
EVEN I CAN TELL YOU HAD TO RUN BECAUSE YOU WEREN'T SURE WHAT TO WEAR.
SORRY TO TROUBLE YOU...
...OVER A PERSONAL MATTER.
The way he treats me...
Where's that shop's nearest location?
In Tachi-kawa.

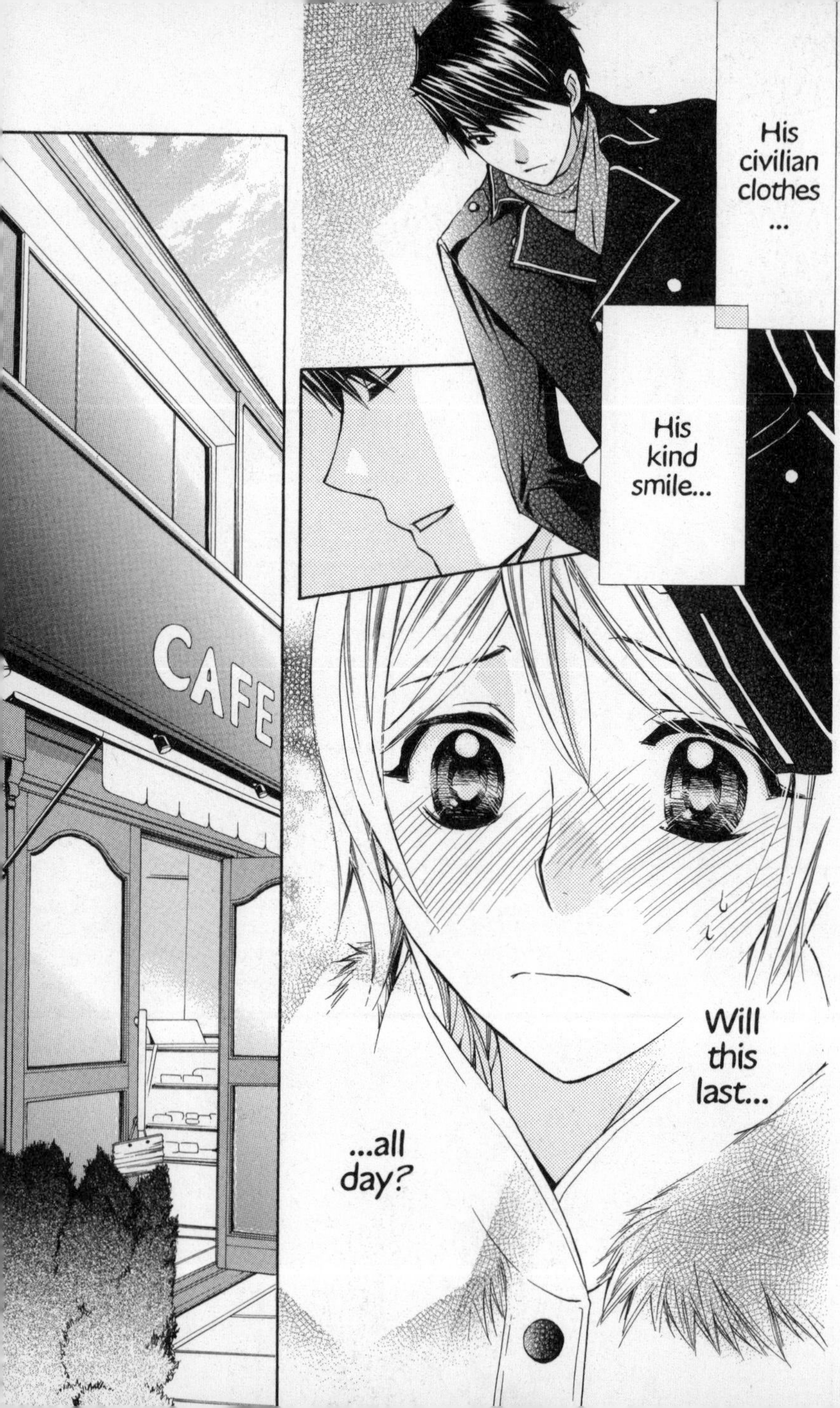
His civilian clothes ...
His kind smile...
CAFE
Will this last...
...all day?

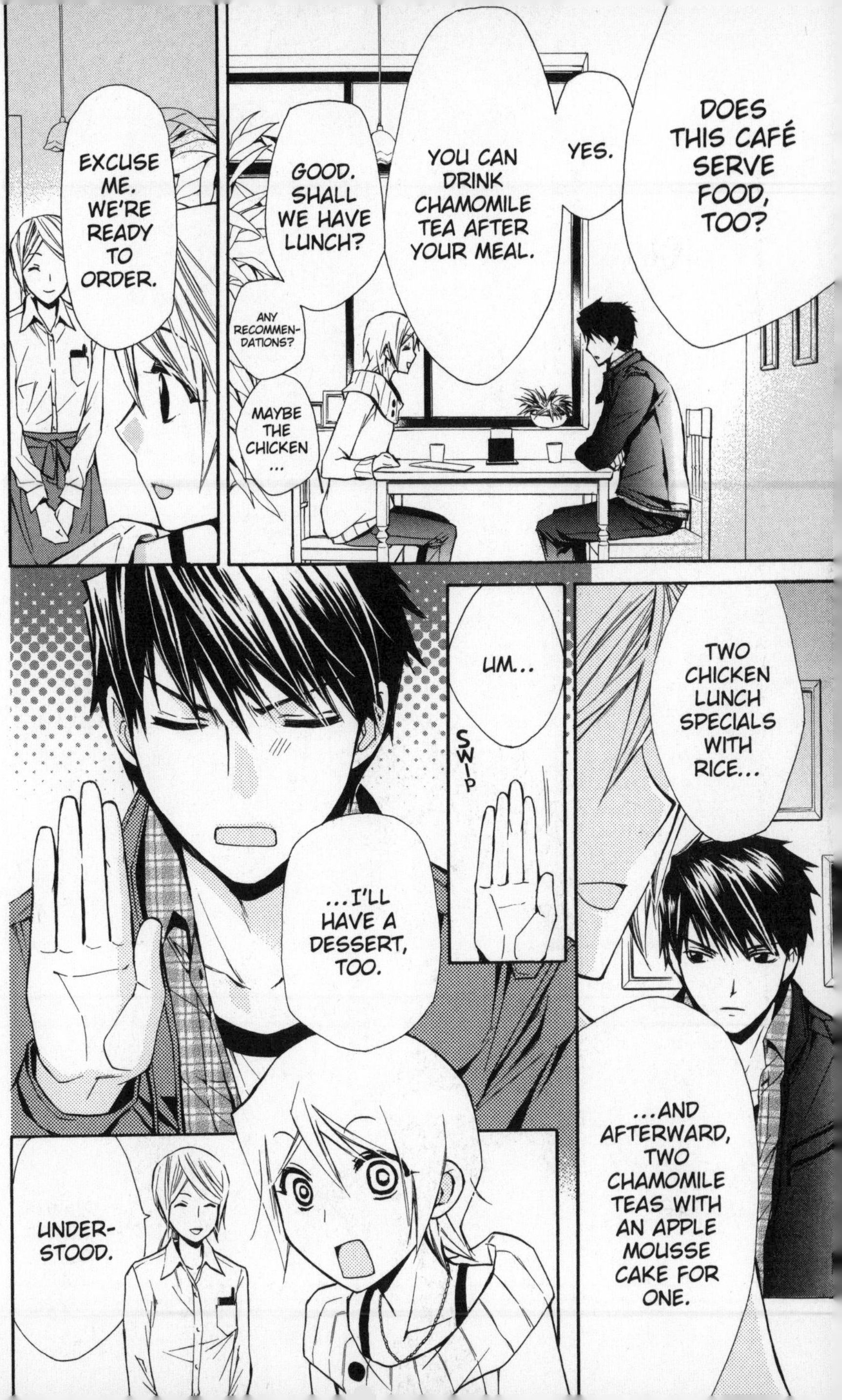
DOES THIS CAFÉ SERVE FOOD, TOO?
YES.
YOU CAN DRINK CHAMOMILE TEA AFTER YOUR MEAL.
GOOD. SHALL WE HAVE LUNCH?
ANY RECOMMENDATIONS?
MAYBE THE CHICKEN ...
EXCUSE ME. WE'RE READY TO ORDER.
TWO CHICKEN LUNCH SPECIALS WITH RICE...
...AND AFTERWARD, TWO CHAMOMILE TEAS WITH AN APPLE MOUSSE CAKE FOR ONE.
UM...
SWIP
...I'LL HAVE A DESSERT, TOO.
UNDERSTOOD.

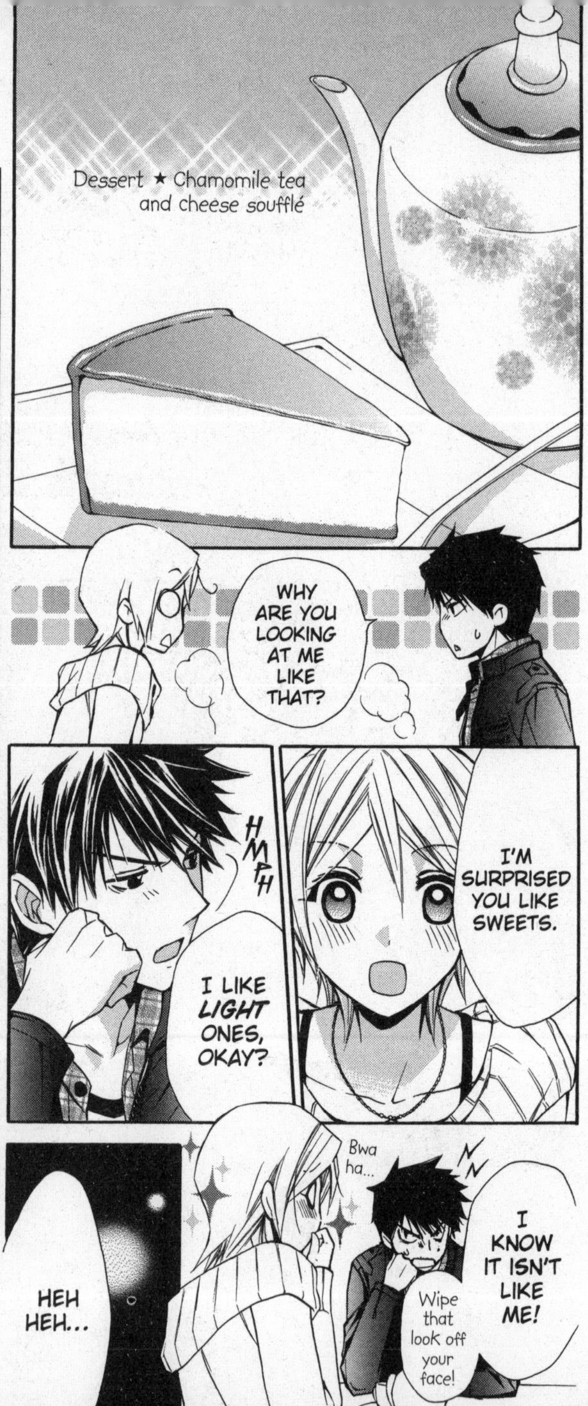
Dessert ★ Chamomile tea
and cheese soufflé
WHY ARE YOU LOOKING AT ME LIKE THAT?
I'M SURPRISED YOU LIKE SWEETS.
HMPH
I LIKE *LIGHT* ONES, OKAY?
I KNOW IT ISN'T LIKE ME!
NN
Bwa ha...
Wipe that look off your face!
HEH HEH...

1

Hi! I'm Kiiro Yumi and this is Volume 12 of *Library Wars*!

I'm so happy to have been working on this series for so long! With this volume the story enters the content of the novel *Revolution*. I'm so full of emotion! And I'm thankful for all the people involved in making this manga, for the readers, and for all of you! Thank you!

This is another clumsy volume, but I hope you enjoy it to the end.

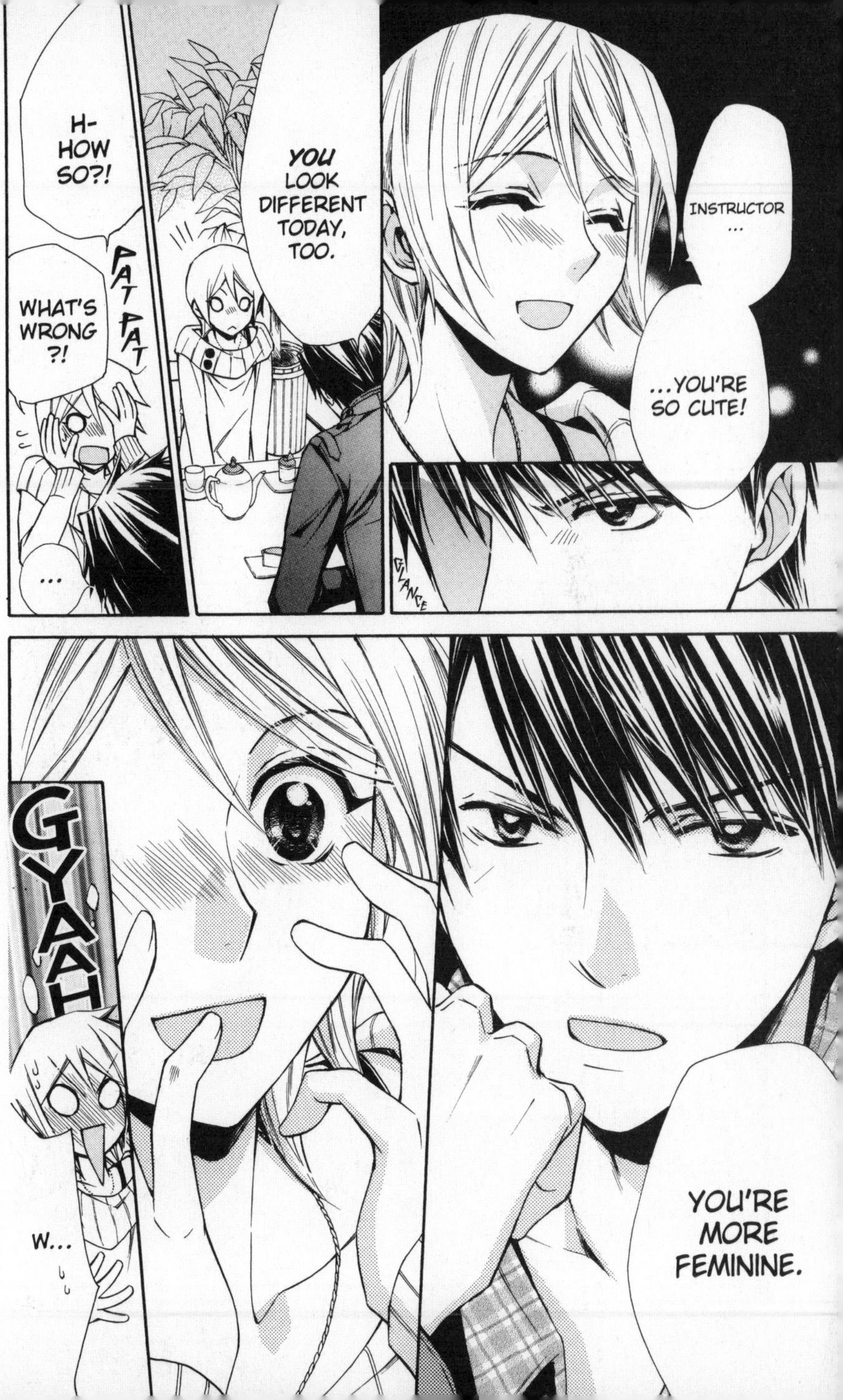
INSTRUCTOR...
...YOU'RE SO CUTE!
GLANCE
YOU LOOK DIFFERENT TODAY, TOO.
H- HOW SO?!
PAT PAT
WHAT'S WRONG?!
...
YOU'RE MORE FEMININE.
GYAAH
W...

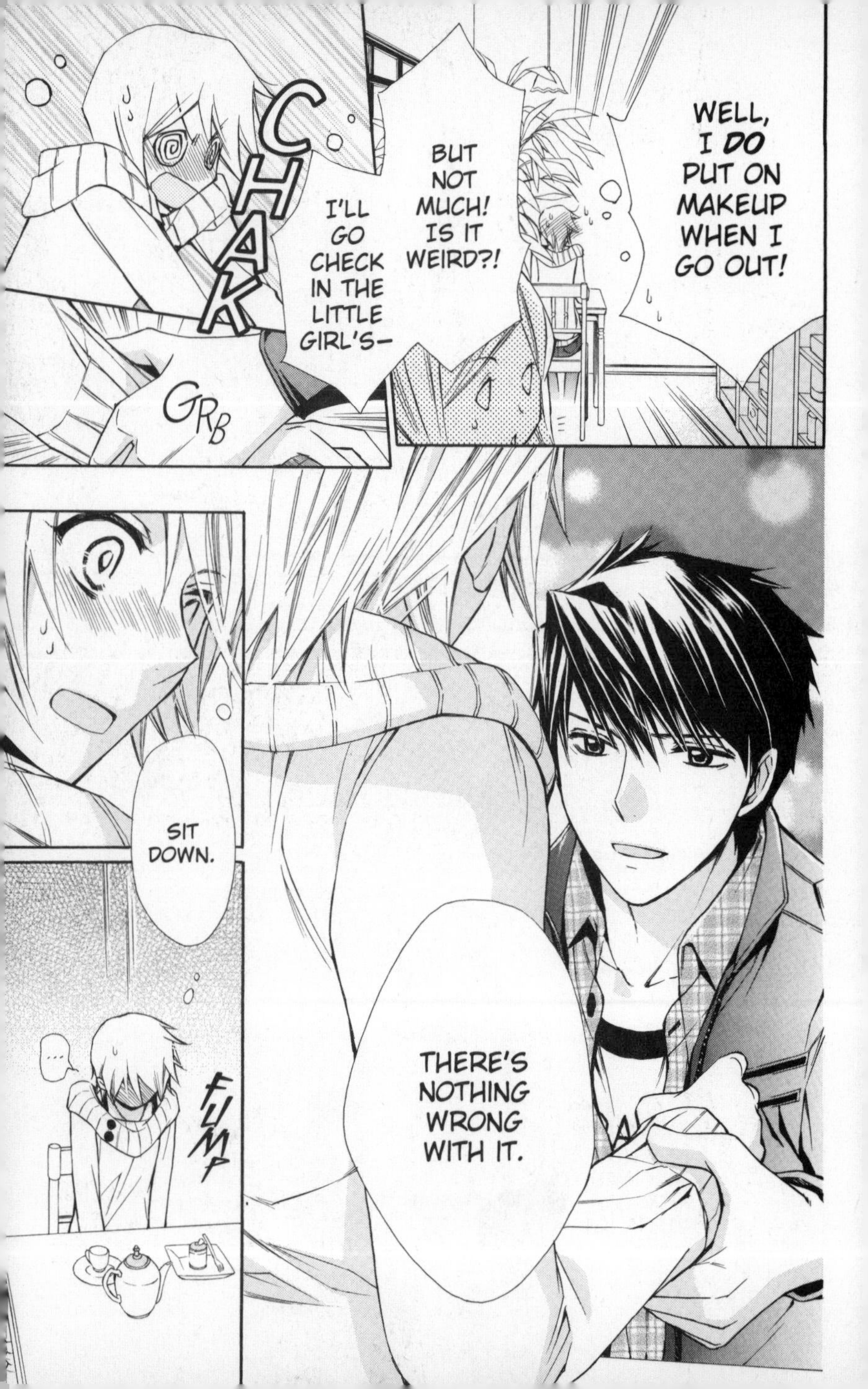
WELL, I ***DO*** PUT ON MAKEUP WHEN I GO OUT!
BUT NOT MUCH! IS IT WEIRD?!
I'LL GO CHECK IN THE LITTLE GIRL'S—
CHAK
GRB
THERE'S NOTHING WRONG WITH IT.
SIT DOWN.
...
FUMP

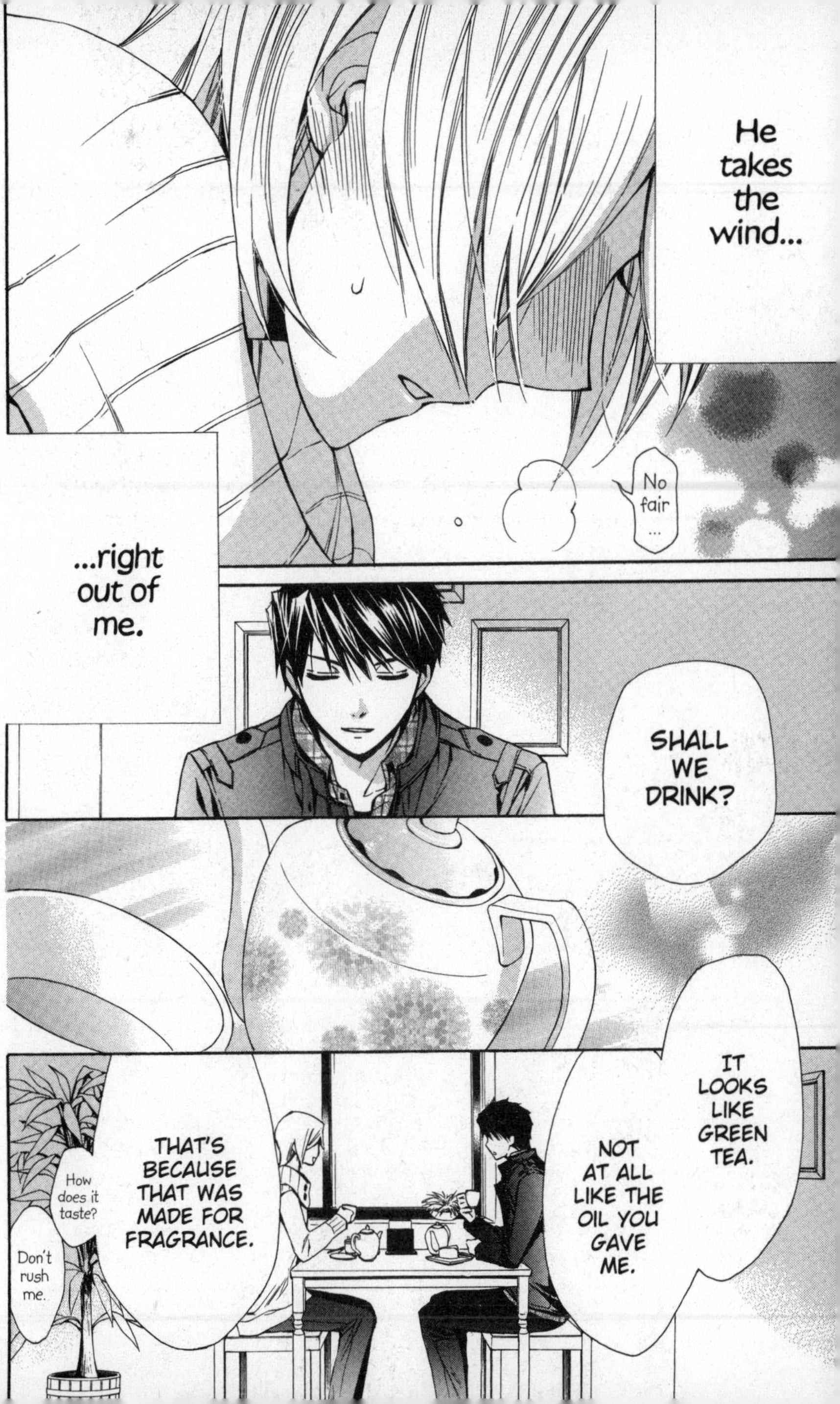
He takes the wind...
No fair...
...right out of me.
SHALL WE DRINK?
IT LOOKS LIKE GREEN TEA.
NOT AT ALL LIKE THE OIL YOU GAVE ME.
THAT'S BECAUSE THAT WAS MADE FOR FRAGRANCE.
How does it taste?
Don't rush me.

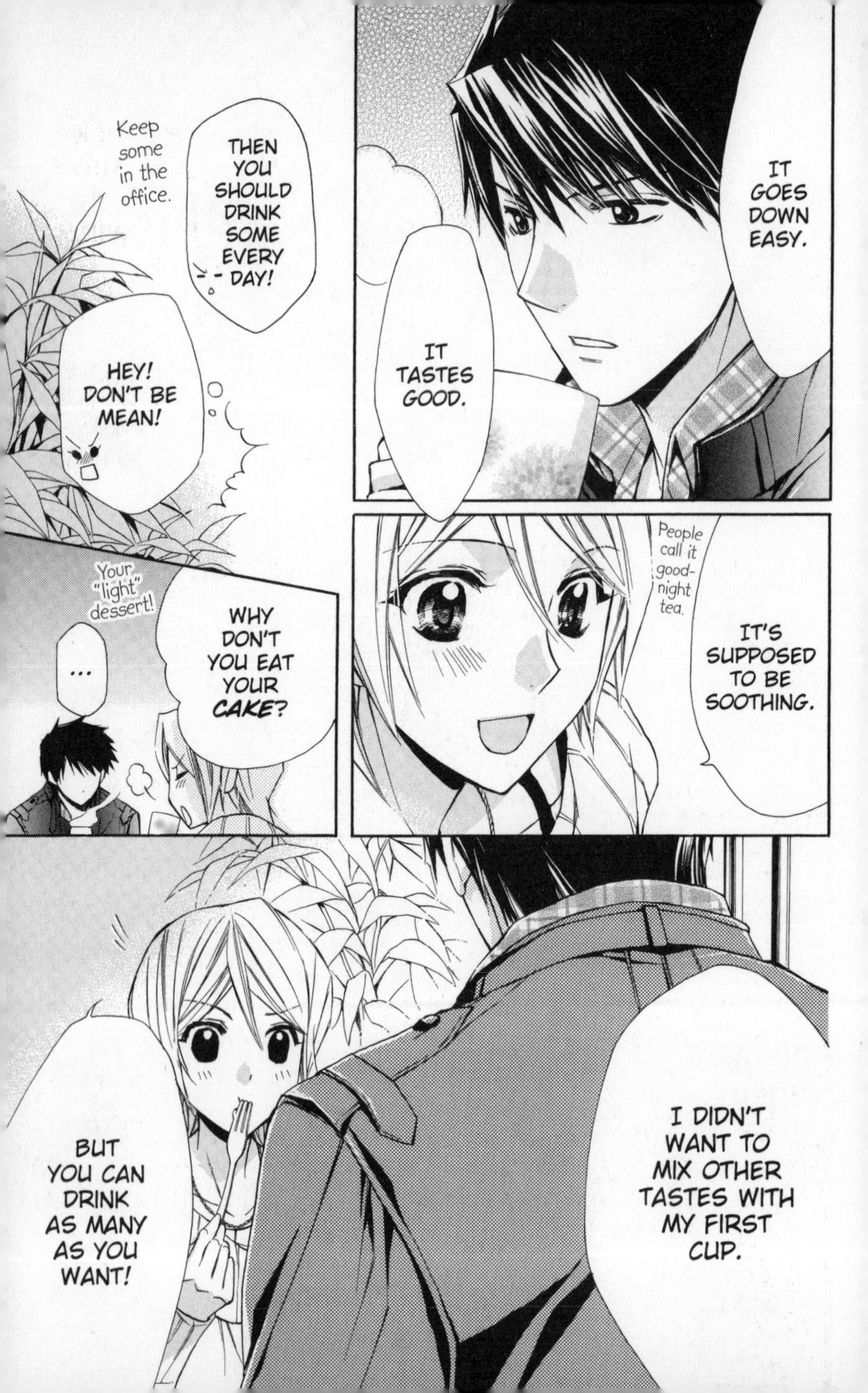
IT GOES DOWN EASY.
IT TASTES GOOD.
THEN YOU SHOULD DRINK SOME EVERY DAY!
Keep some in the office.
HEY! DON'T BE MEAN!
IT'S SUPPOSED TO BE SOOTHING.
People call it good-night tea.
WHY DON'T YOU EAT YOUR CAKE?
Your "light" dessert!
...
I DIDN'T WANT TO MIX OTHER TASTES WITH MY FIRST CUP.
BUT YOU CAN DRINK AS MANY AS YOU WANT!

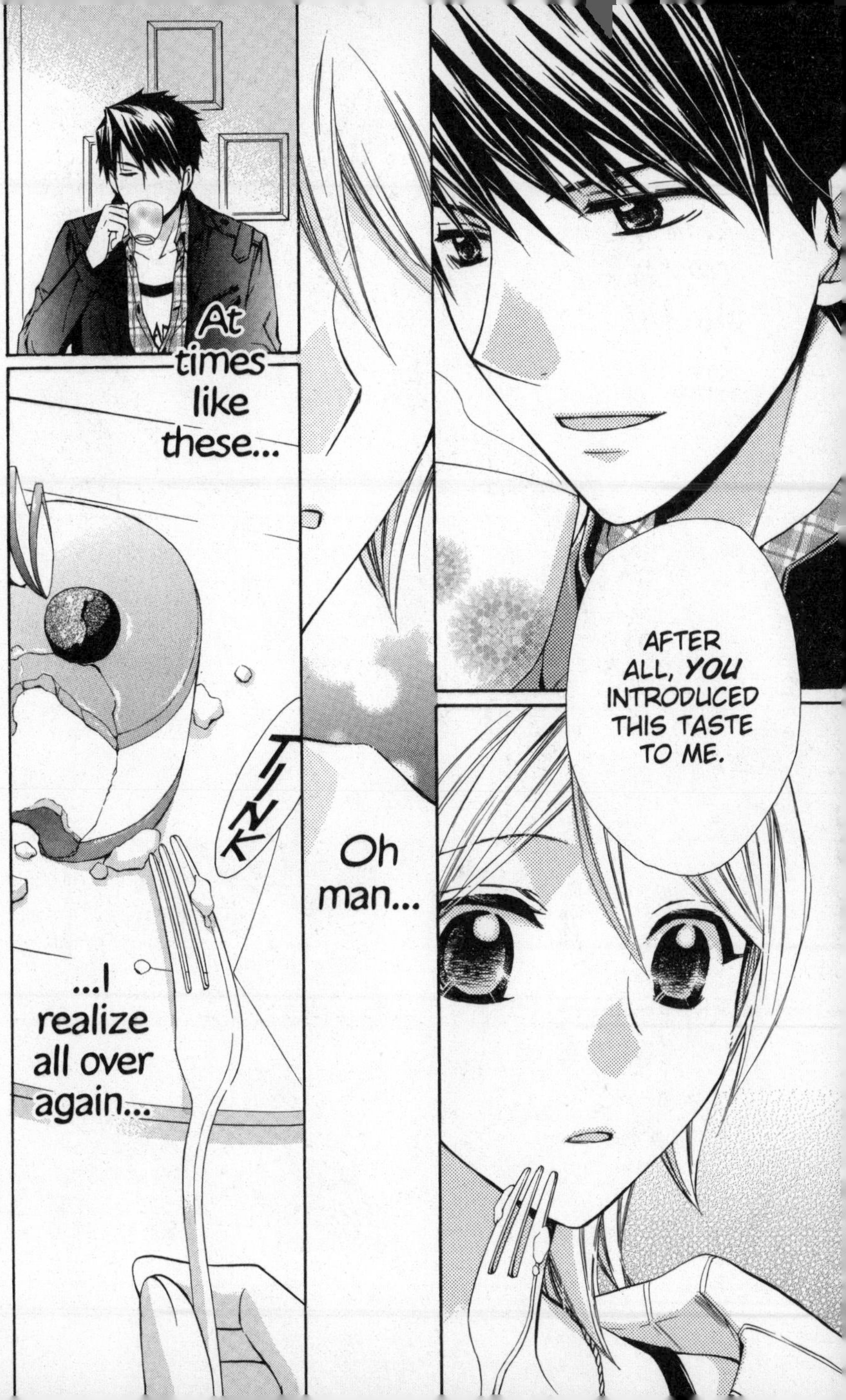
AFTER ALL, *YOU* INTRODUCED THIS TASTE TO ME.
Oh man...
At times like these...
TINK
...I realize all over again...

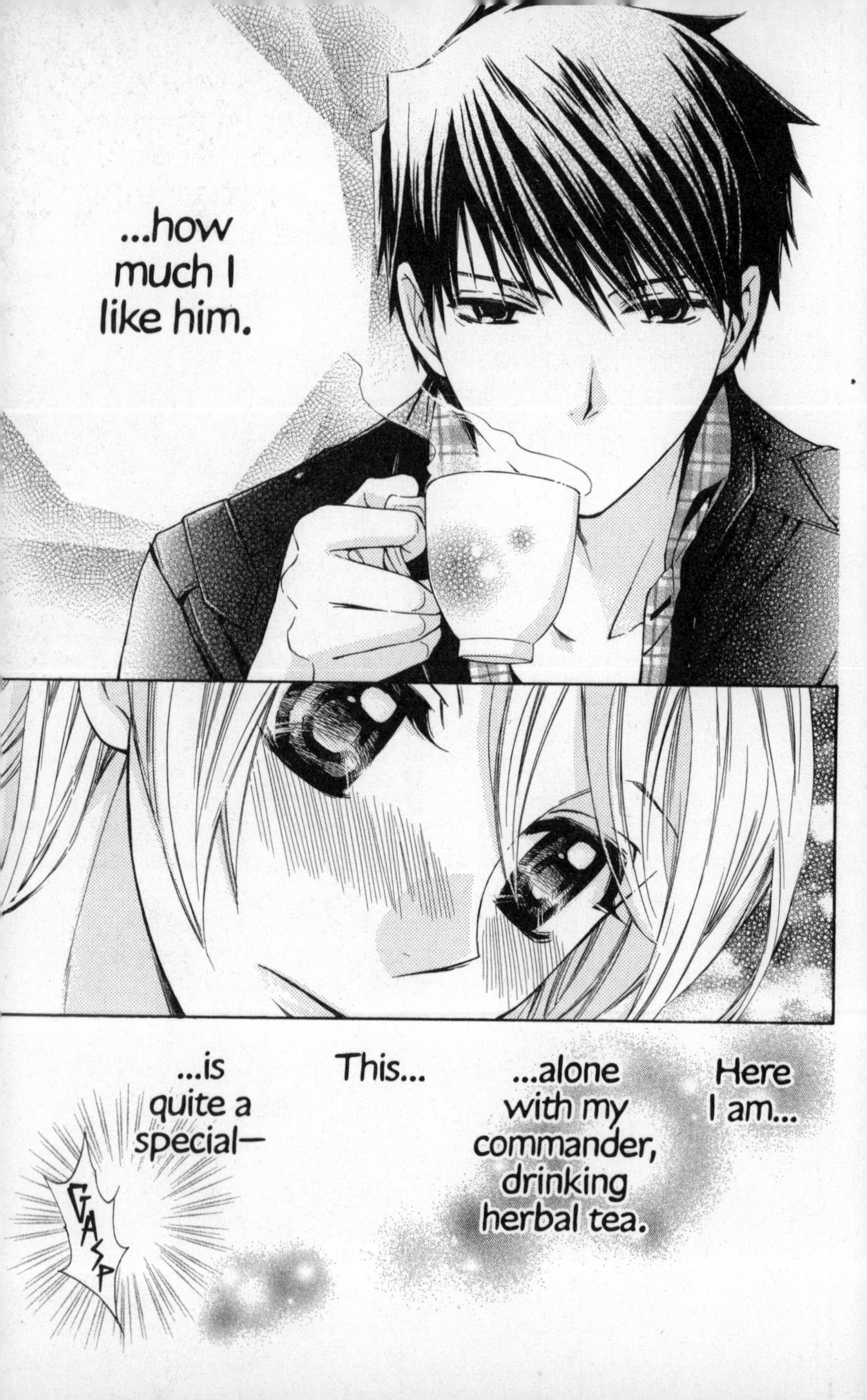
...how much I like him.
Here I am...
...alone with my commander, drinking herbal tea.
This...
...is quite a special—
GASP

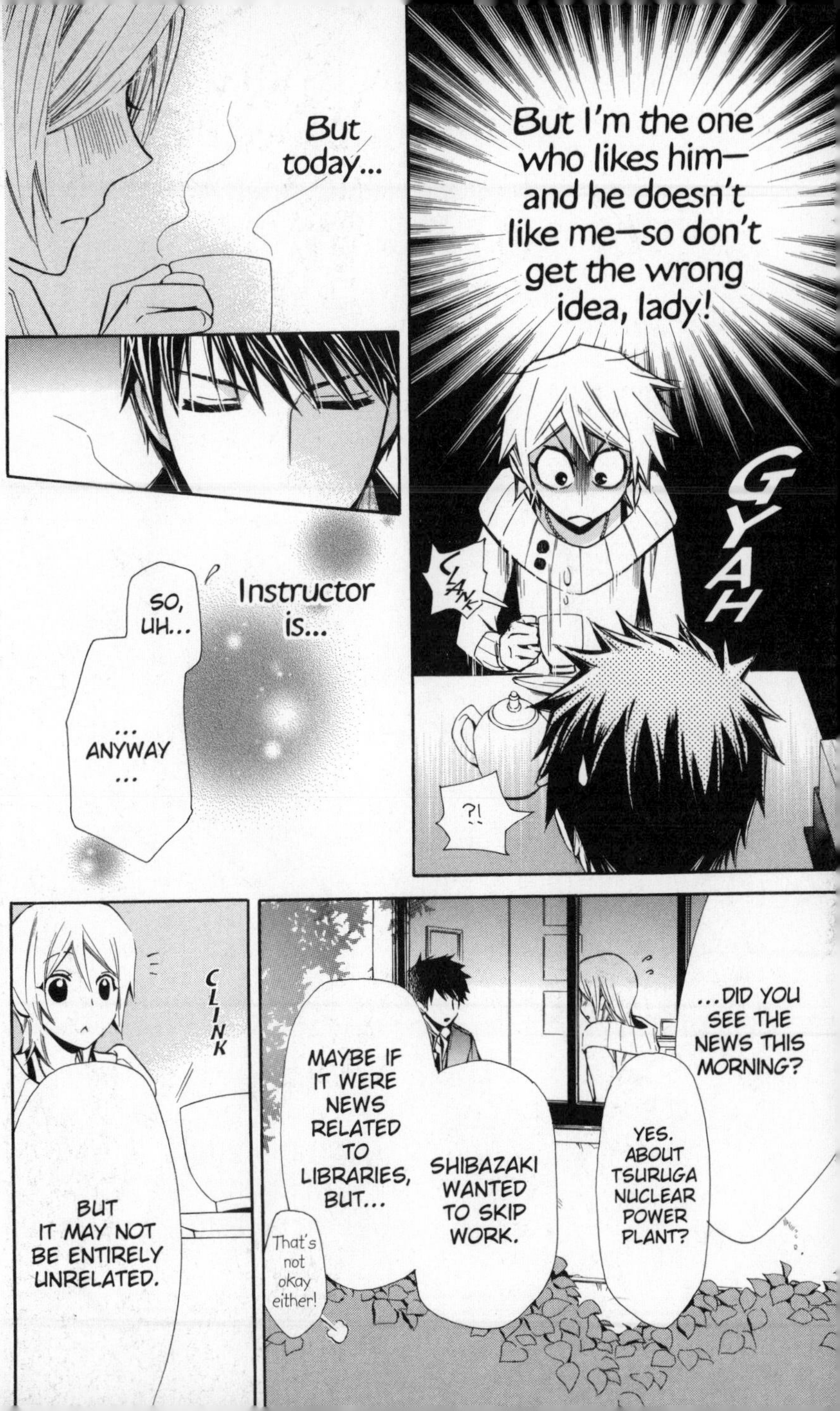
But I'm the one who likes him—and he doesn't like me—so don't get the wrong idea, lady!
GYAH
CLANK
?!
But today...
Instructor is...
SO, UH...
...ANYWAY...
...DID YOU SEE THE NEWS THIS MORNING?
YES. ABOUT TSURUGA NUCLEAR POWER PLANT?
SHIBAZAKI WANTED TO SKIP WORK.
MAYBE IF IT WERE NEWS RELATED TO LIBRARIES, BUT...
That's not okay either!
CLINK
BUT IT MAY NOT BE ENTIRELY UNRELATED.

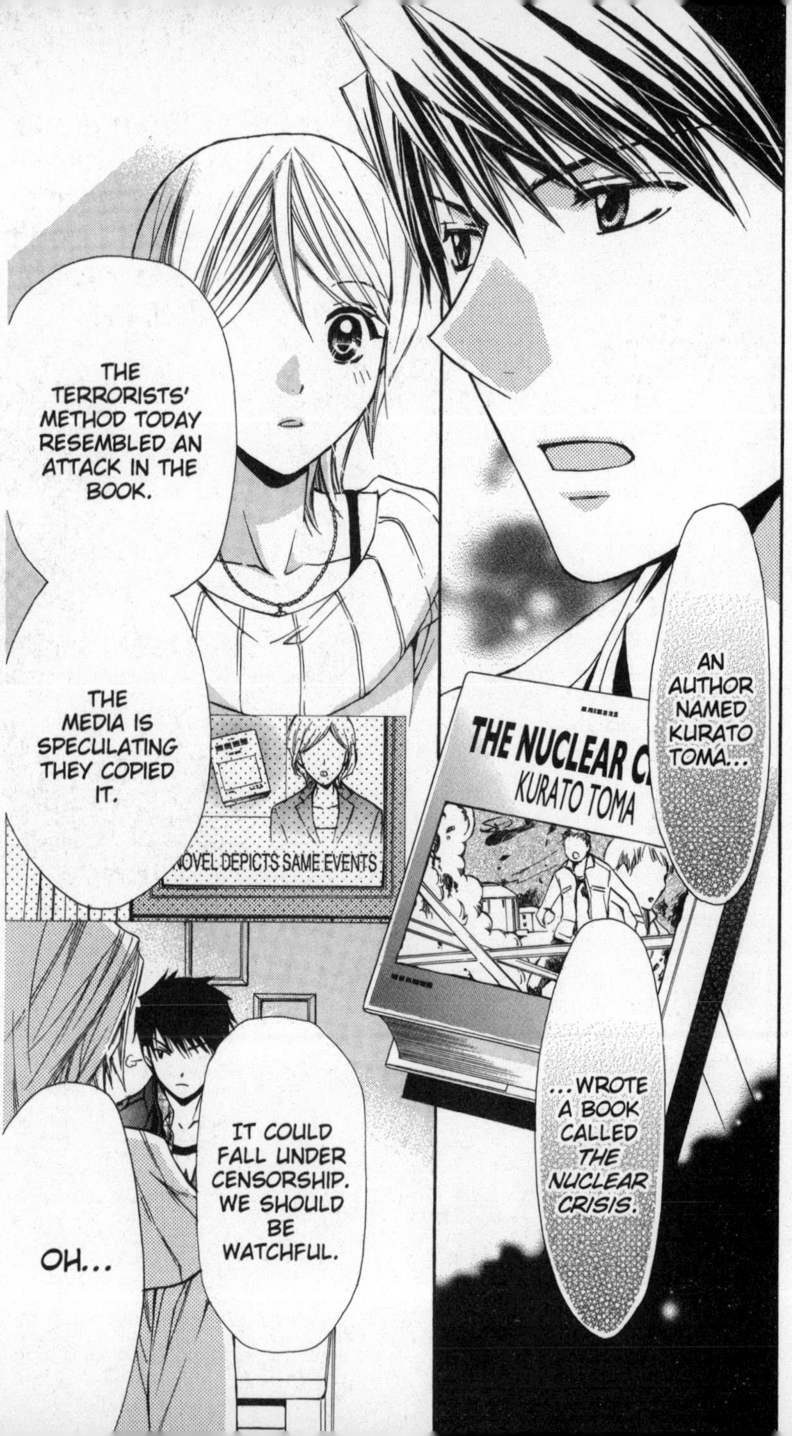
THE NUCLEAR CR
KURATO TOMA
AN AUTHOR NAMED KURATO TOMA...
...WROTE A BOOK CALLED THE NUCLEAR CRISIS.
THE TERRORISTS' METHOD TODAY RESEMBLED AN ATTACK IN THE BOOK.
THE MEDIA IS SPECULATING THEY COPIED IT.
NOVEL DEPICTS SAME EVENTS
IT COULD FALL UNDER CENSORSHIP. WE SHOULD BE WATCHFUL.
OH...

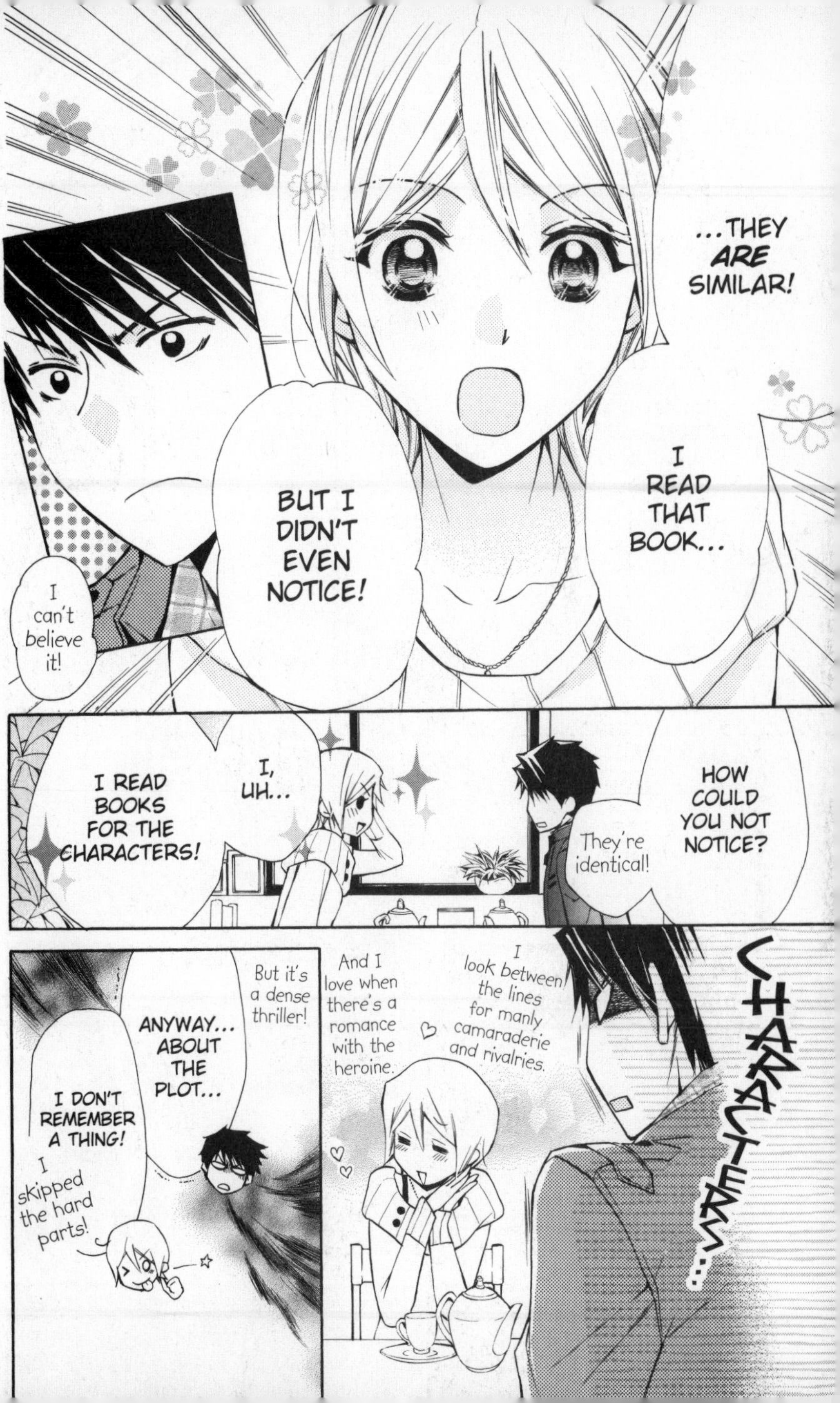
...THEY *ARE* SIMILAR!
I READ THAT BOOK...
BUT I DIDN'T EVEN NOTICE!
I can't believe it!
HOW COULD YOU NOT NOTICE?
They're identical!
I, UH...
I READ BOOKS FOR THE CHARACTERS!
CHARACTERS...
I look between the lines for manly camaraderie and rivalries.
And I love when there's a romance with the heroine.
But it's a dense thriller!
ANYWAY... ABOUT THE PLOT...
I DON'T REMEMBER A THING!
I skipped the hard parts!

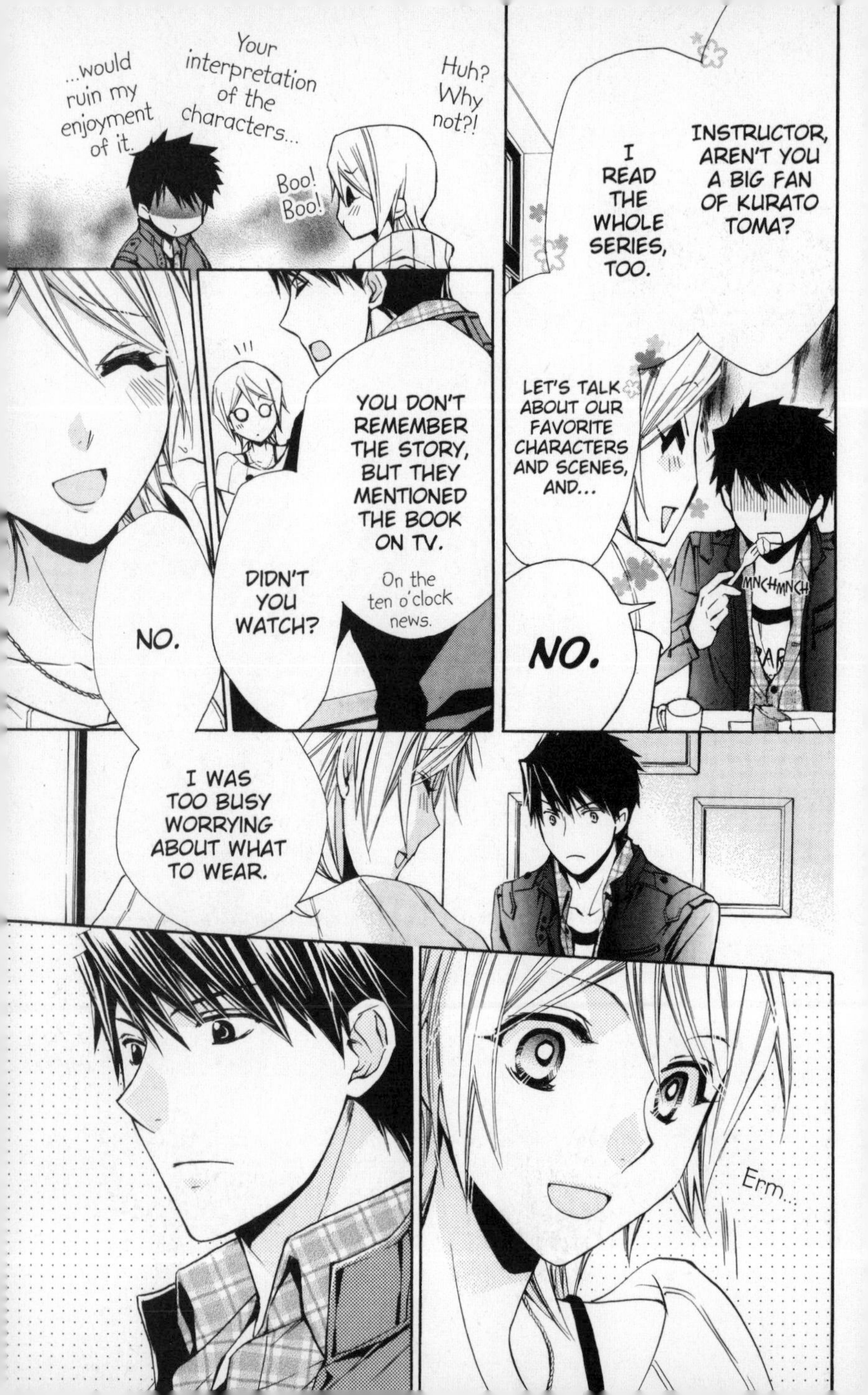
INSTRUCTOR, AREN'T YOU A BIG FAN OF KURATO TOMA?
I READ THE WHOLE SERIES, TOO.
LET'S TALK ABOUT OUR FAVORITE CHARACTERS AND SCENES, AND...
NO.
MNCH MNCH
Huh? Why not?!
Your interpretation of the characters...
...would ruin my enjoyment of it.
Boo! Boo!
YOU DON'T REMEMBER THE STORY, BUT THEY MENTIONED THE BOOK ON TV.
DIDN'T YOU WATCH?
On the ten o'clock news.
NO.
I WAS TOO BUSY WORRYING ABOUT WHAT TO WEAR.
Erm...

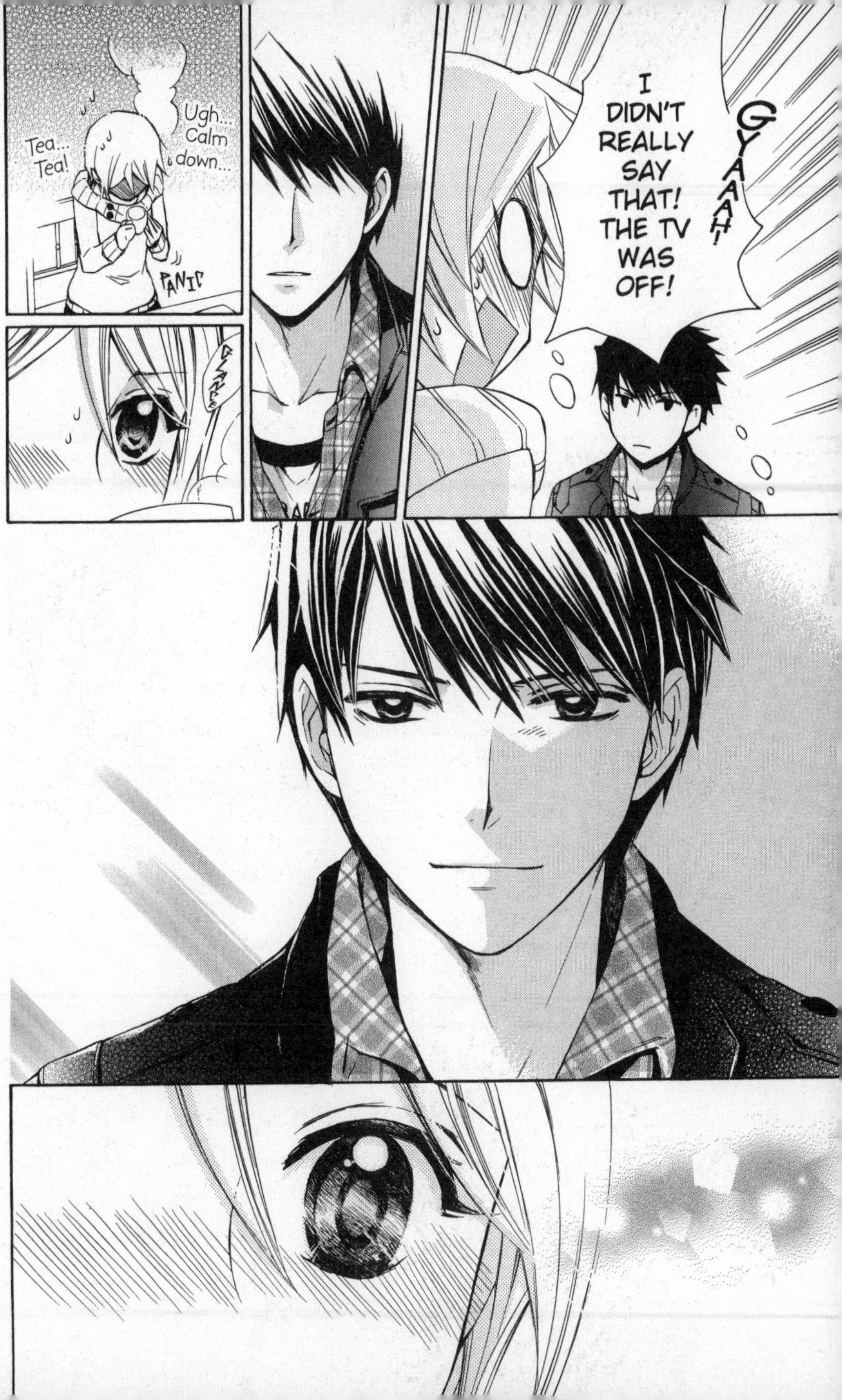
GYAAAH!
I DIDN'T REALLY SAY THAT! THE TV WAS OFF!
Ugh... Calm down...
Tea... Tea!
PANIC
GLANCE

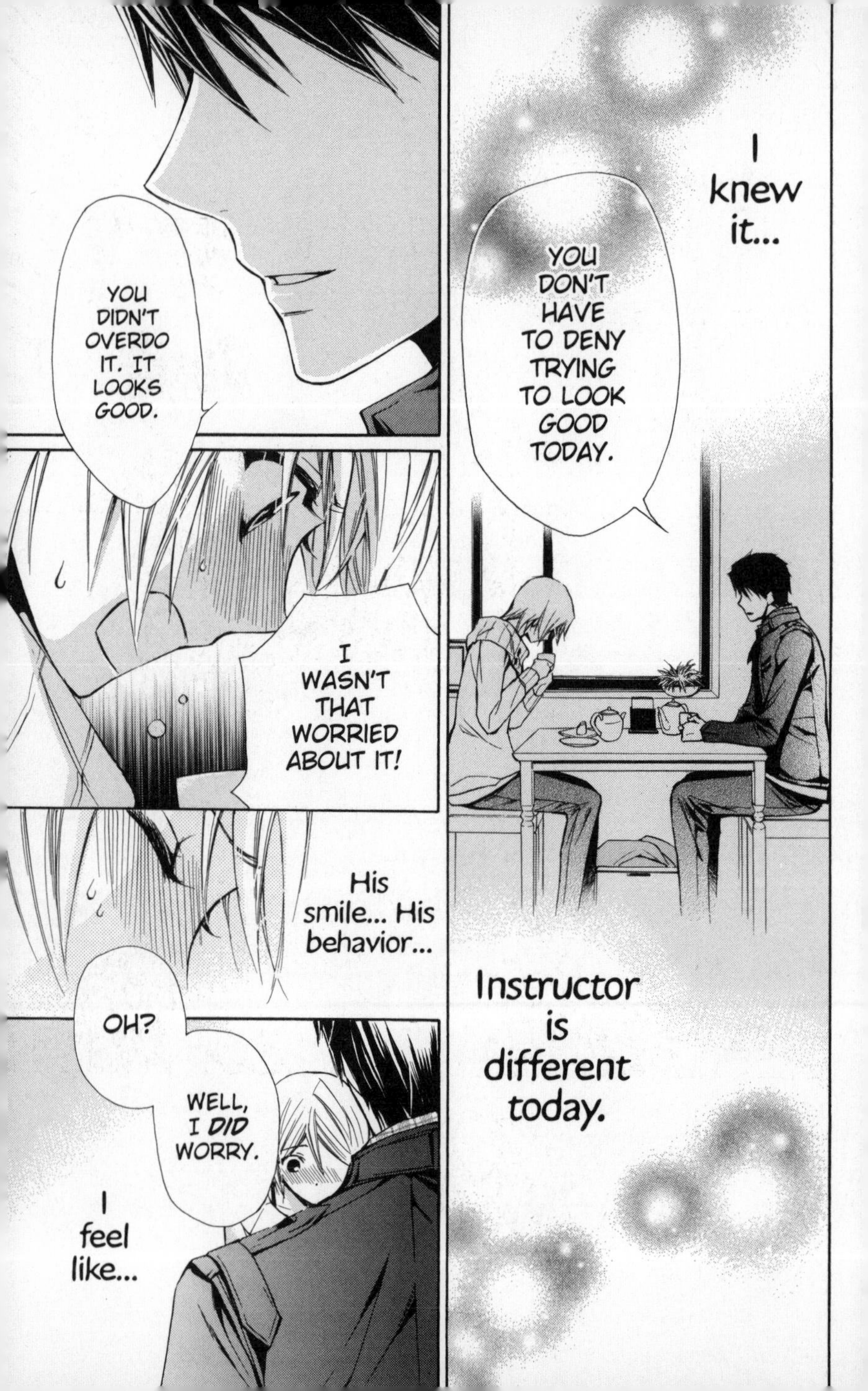
I knew it...
YOU DON'T HAVE TO DENY TRYING TO LOOK GOOD TODAY.
Instructor is different today.
YOU DIDN'T OVERDO IT. IT LOOKS GOOD.
I WASN'T THAT WORRIED ABOUT IT!
His smile... His behavior...
OH?
WELL, I *DID* WORRY.
I feel like...

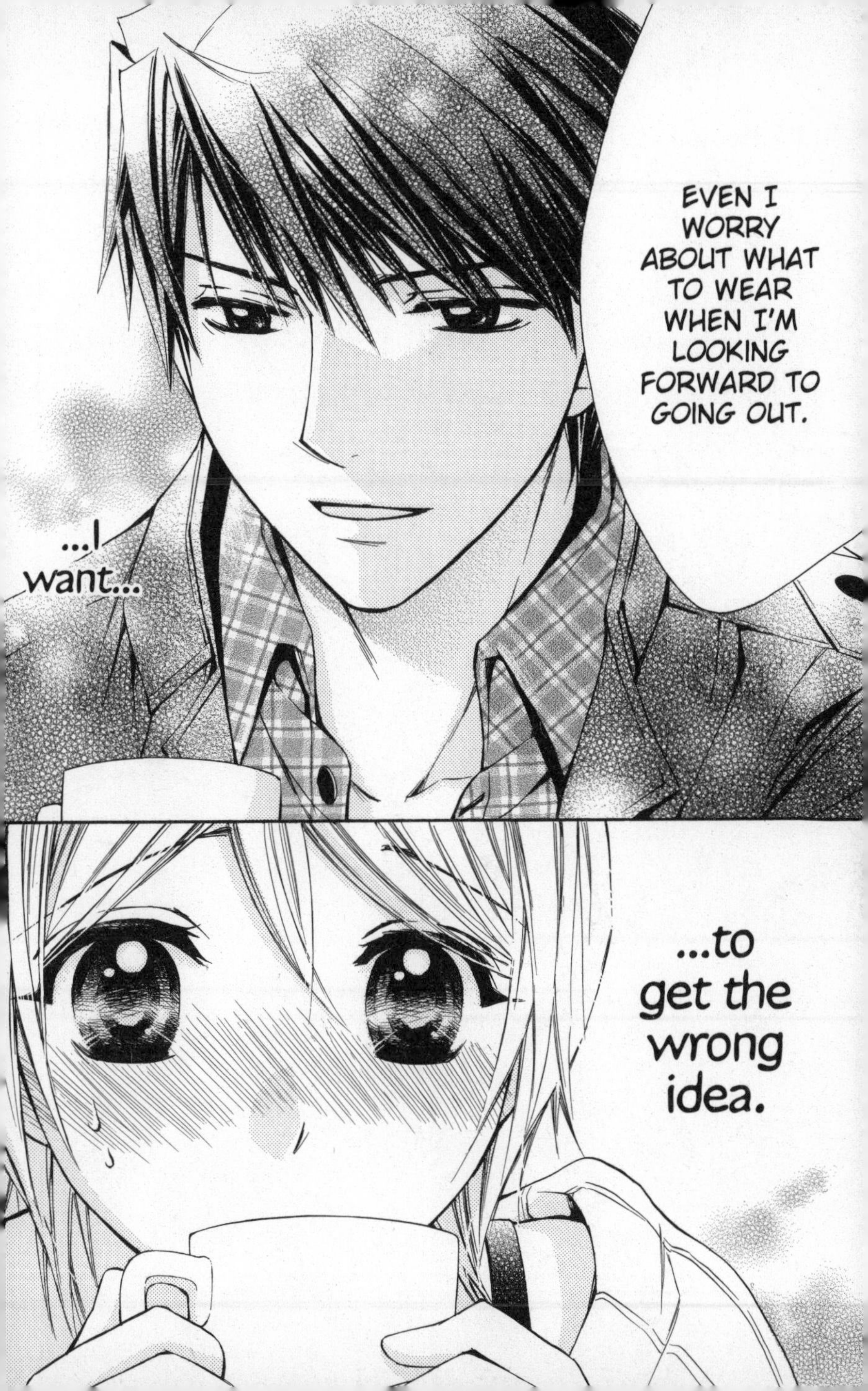
EVEN I WORRY ABOUT WHAT TO WEAR WHEN I'M LOOKING FORWARD TO GOING OUT.
...I want...
...to get the wrong idea.

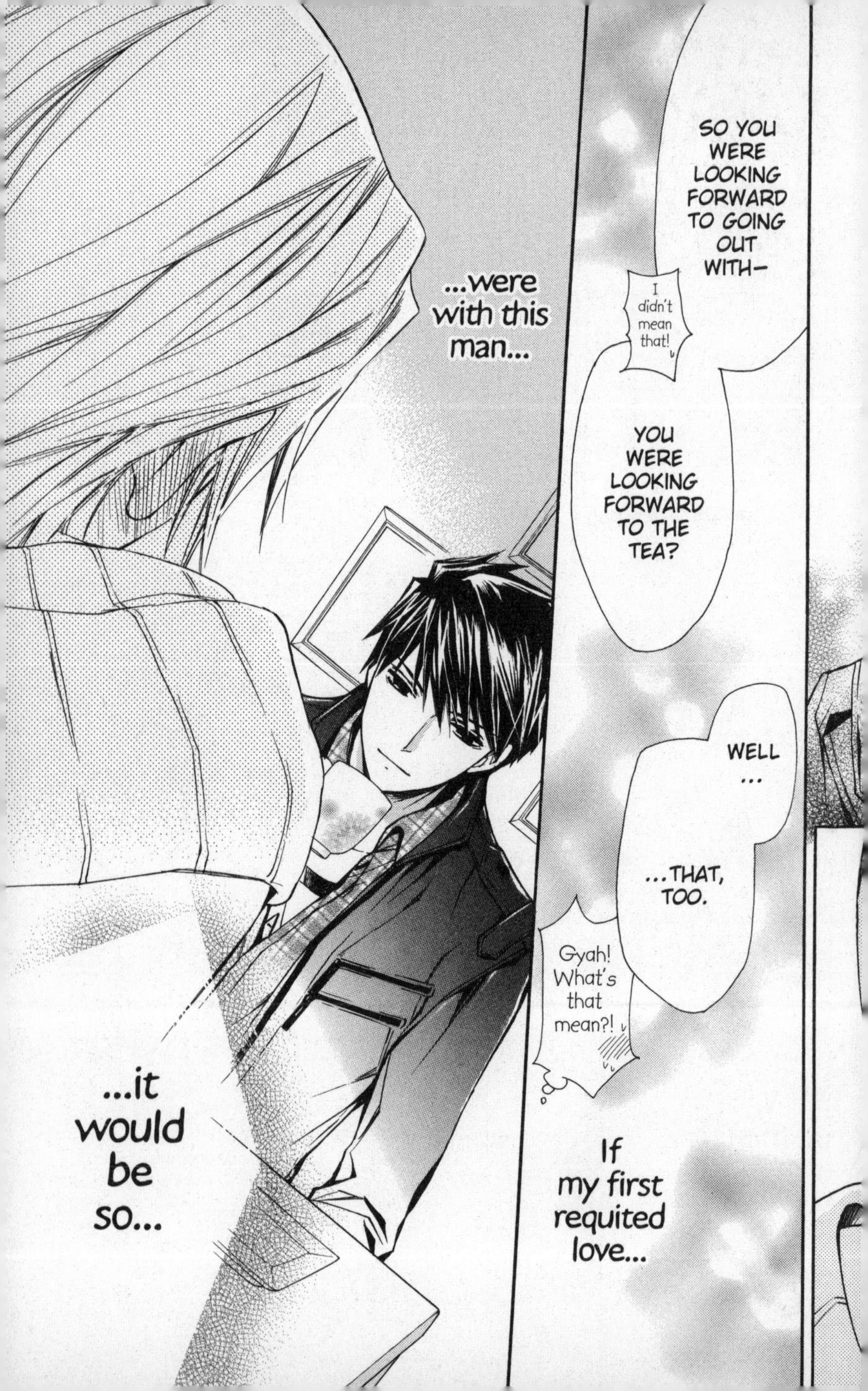
SO YOU WERE LOOKING FORWARD TO GOING OUT WITH—
I didn't mean that!
YOU WERE LOOKING FORWARD TO THE TEA?
WELL ...
...THAT, TOO.
Gyah! What's that mean?!
If my first requited love...
...were with this man...
...it would be so...

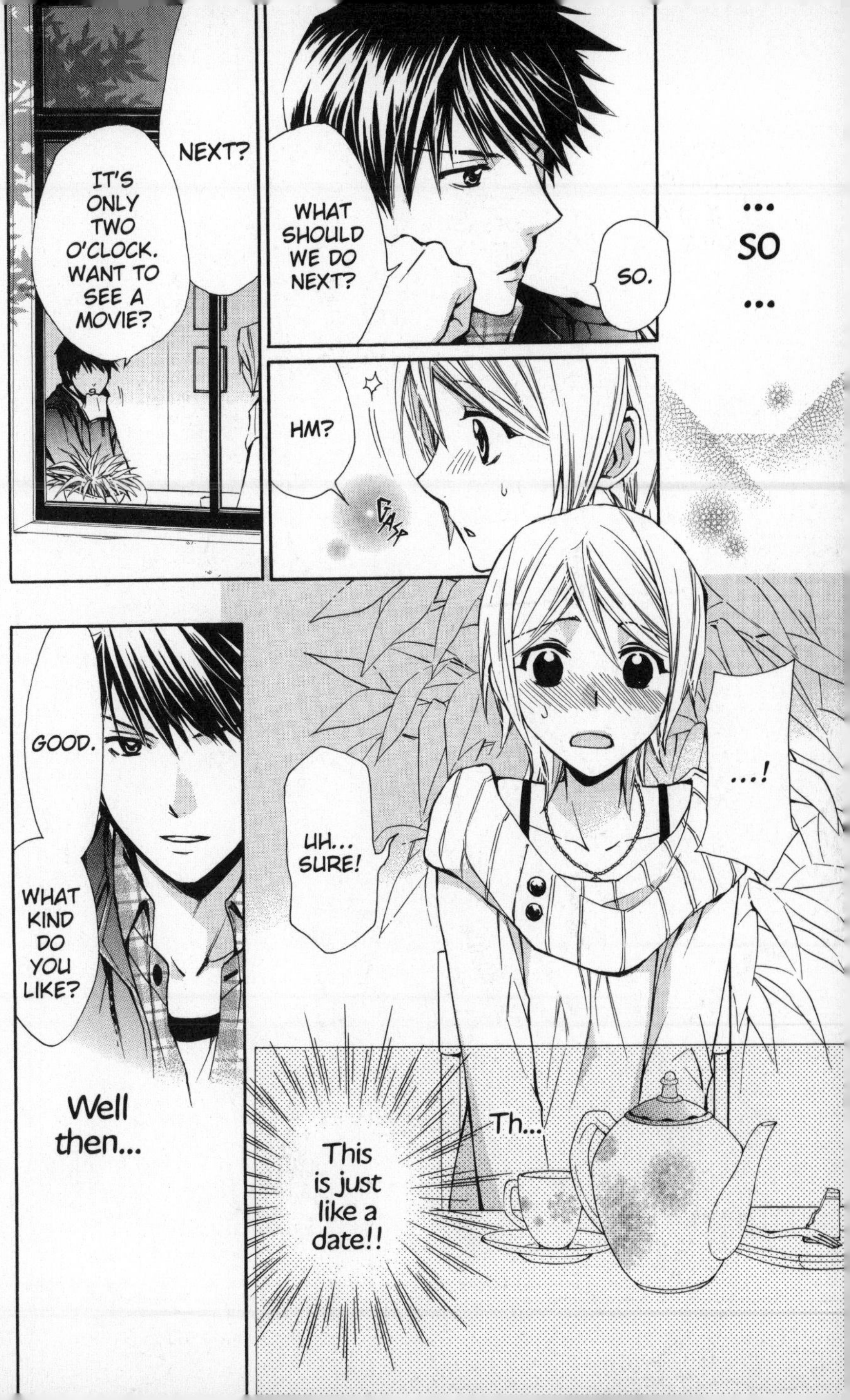
... SO ...
SO.
WHAT SHOULD WE DO NEXT?
NEXT?
IT'S ONLY TWO O'CLOCK. WANT TO SEE A MOVIE?
HM?
GASP
...!
UH... SURE!
GOOD.
WHAT KIND DO YOU LIKE?
Th...
This is just like a date!!
Well then...

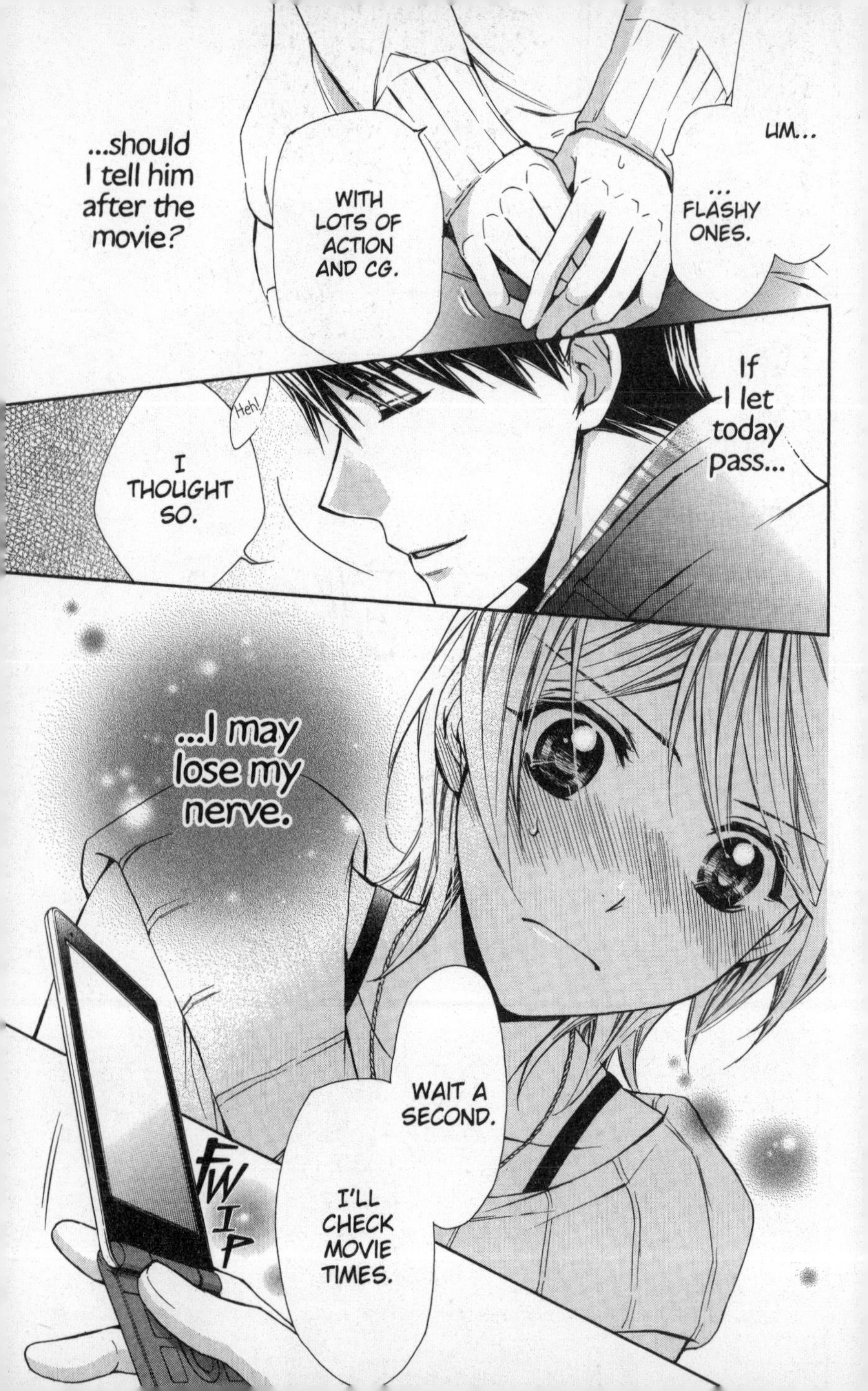
UM...
...FLASHY ONES.
WITH LOTS OF ACTION AND CG.
...should I tell him after the movie?
If I let today pass...
Heh!
I THOUGHT SO.
...I may lose my nerve.
WAIT A SECOND.
FWIP
I'LL CHECK MOVIE TIMES.

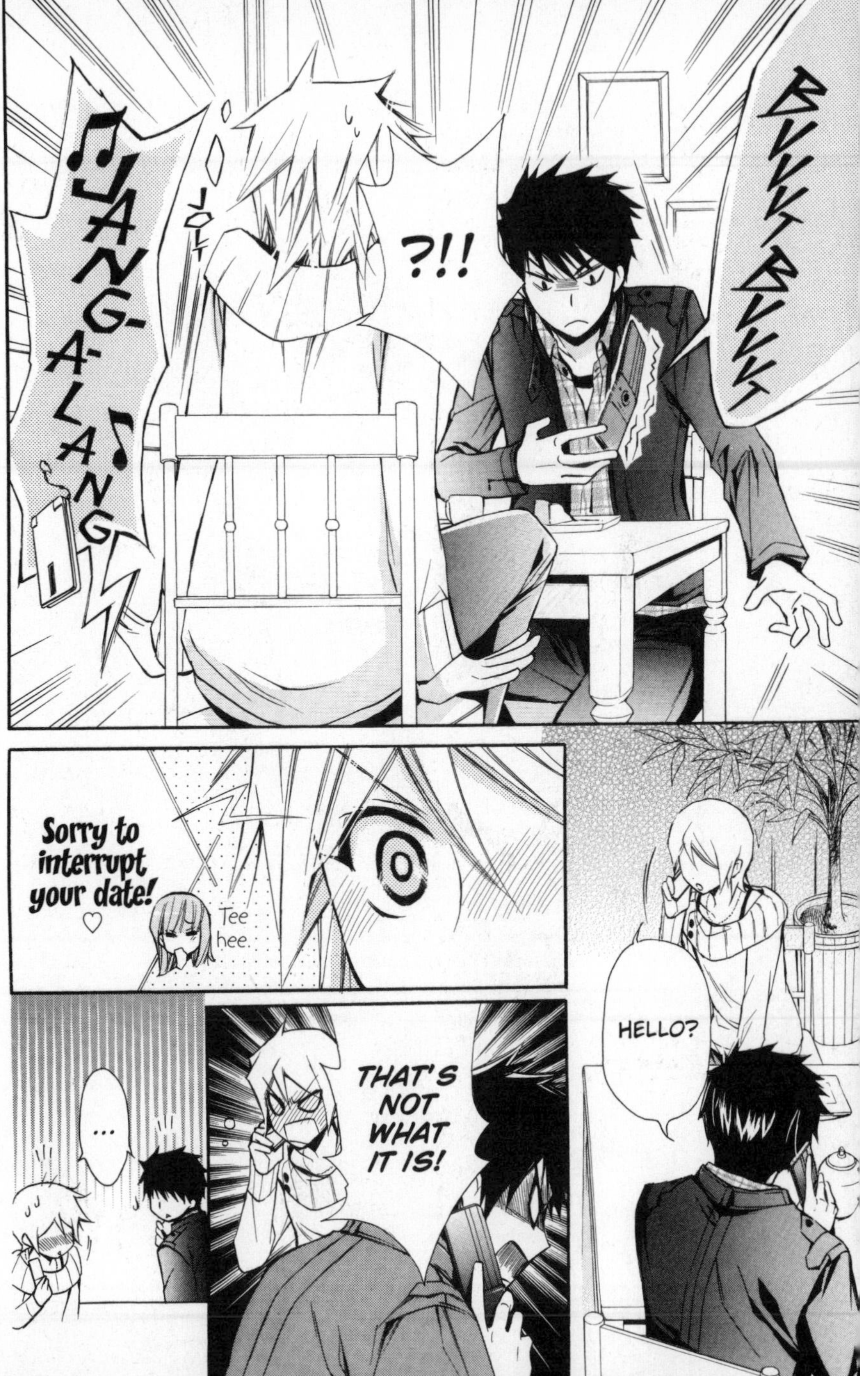
BVVVT BVVVT
?!!
JOLT
♫JANG-A-LANG♪
HELLO?
Sorry to interrupt your date! ♡
Tee hee.
THAT'S NOT WHAT IT IS!
...

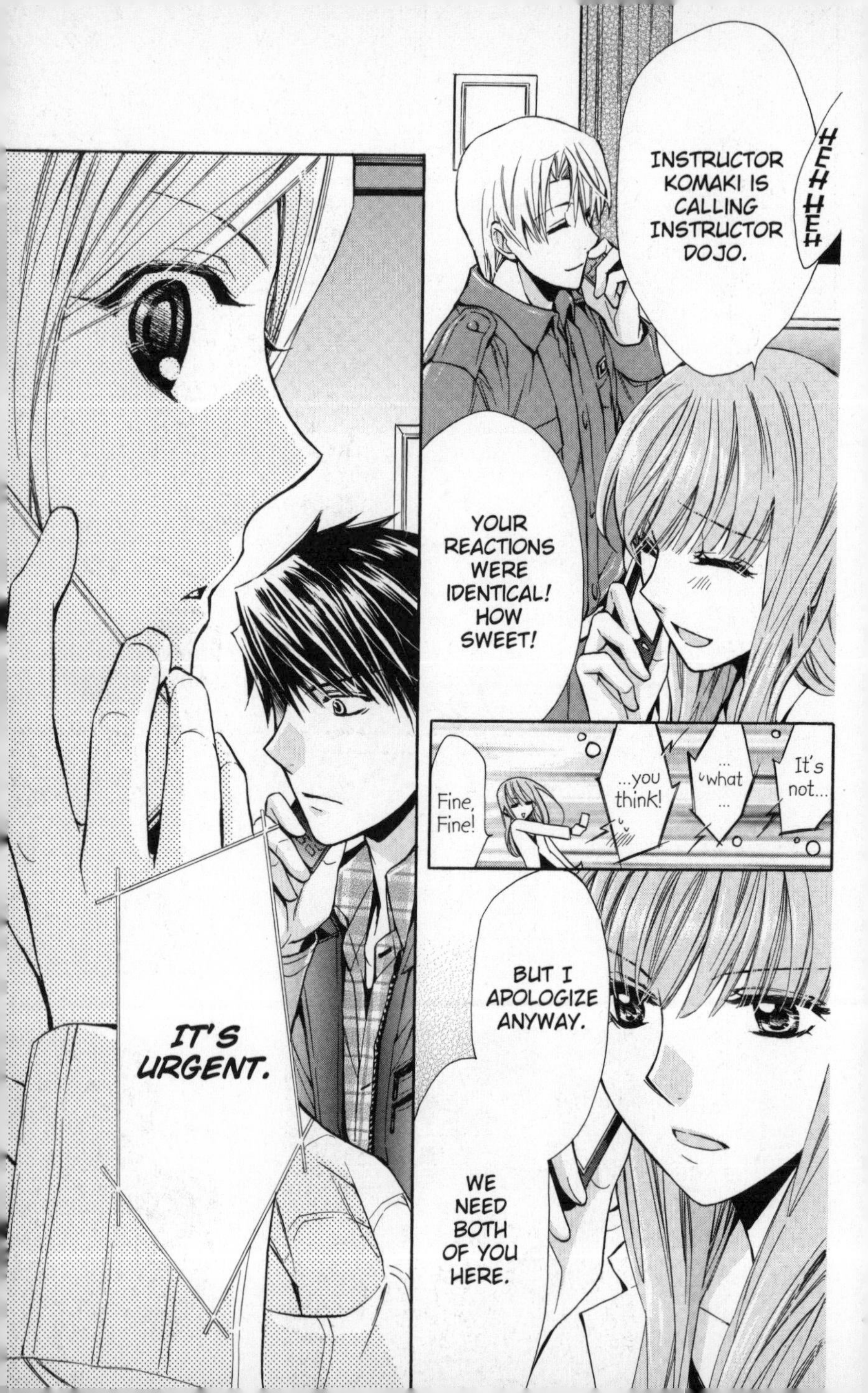
HEHHEH
INSTRUCTOR KOMAKI IS CALLING INSTRUCTOR DOJO.
YOUR REACTIONS WERE IDENTICAL! HOW SWEET!
It's not...
...what...
...you think!
Fine, Fine!
BUT I APOLOGIZE ANYWAY.
WE NEED BOTH OF YOU HERE.
IT'S URGENT.

Preparation Makes for No Regrets...

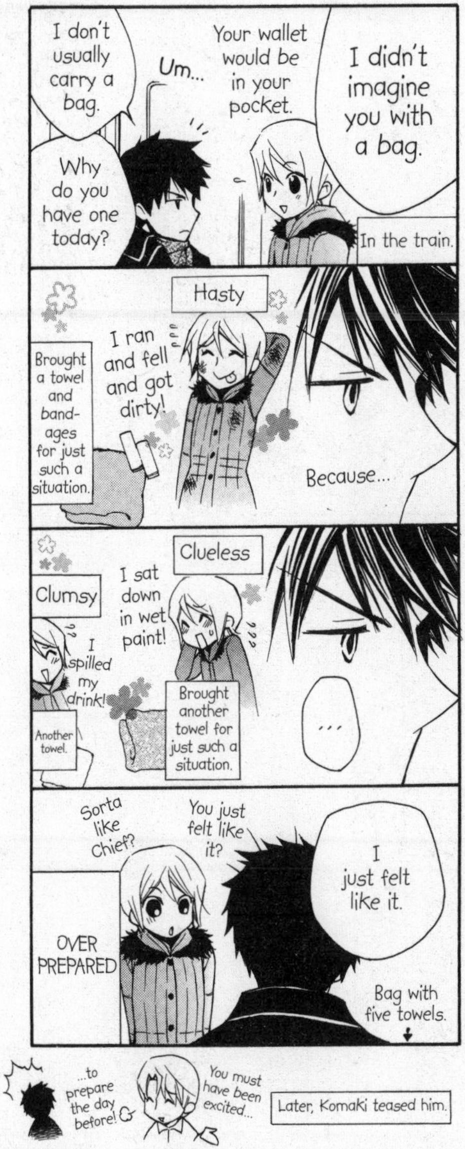
I didn't imagine you with a bag.
Your wallet would be in your pocket.
Um...
I don't usually carry a bag.
Why do you have one today?
In the train.
Because...
Hasty
I ran and fell and got dirty!
Brought a towel and band-ages for just such a situation.
...
Clueless
I sat down in wet paint!
Brought another towel for just such a situation.
Clumsy
I spilled my drink!
Another towel.
I just felt like it.
You just felt like it?
Sorta like Chief?
Bag with five towels.
OVER PREPARED
Later, Komaki teased him.
You must have been excited...
...to prepare the day before!

CHAPTER 55

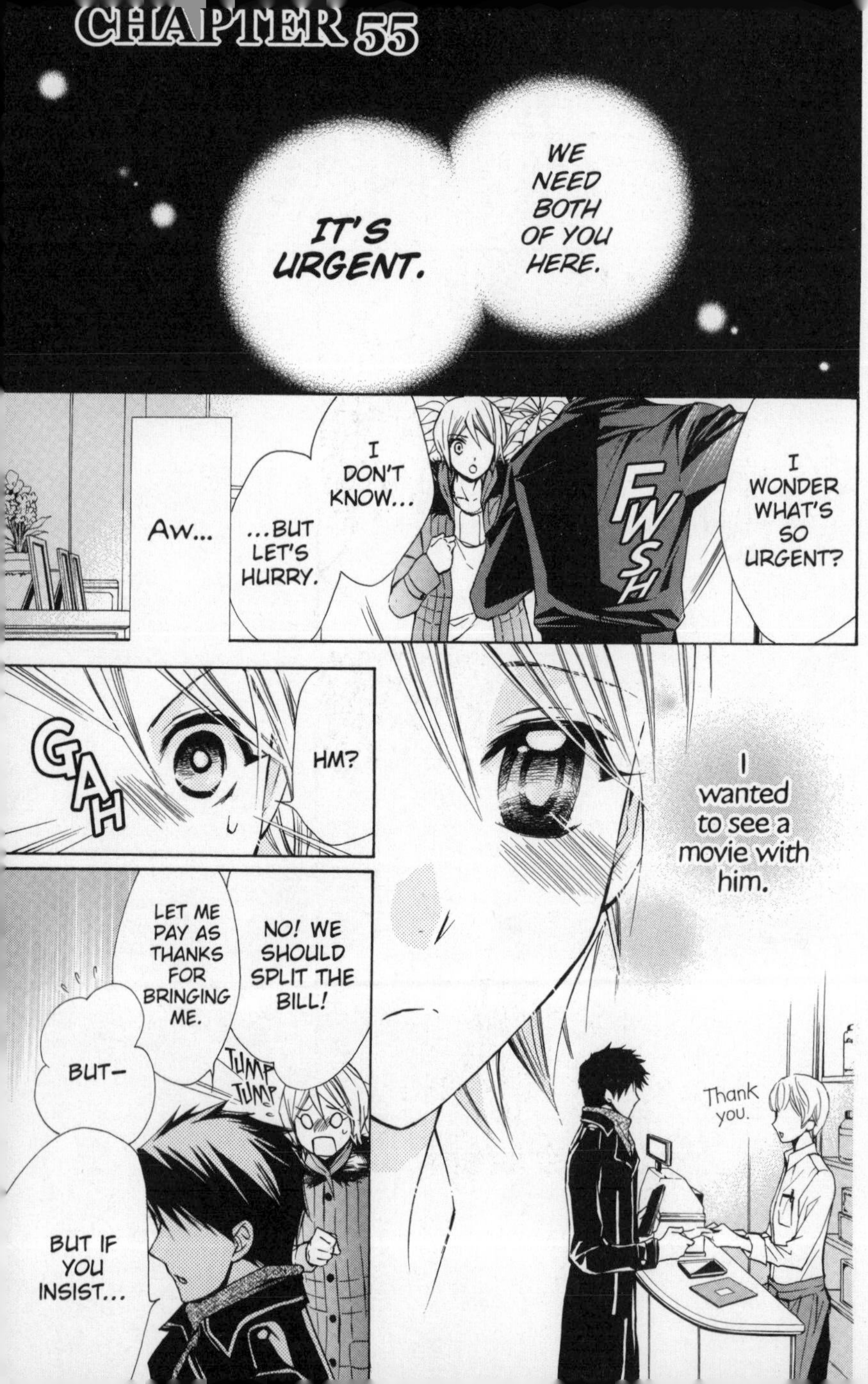

WE NEED BOTH OF YOU HERE.
IT'S URGENT.
I WONDER WHAT'S SO URGENT?
FWSH
I DON'T KNOW...
...BUT LET'S HURRY.
Aw...
I wanted to see a movie with him.
Thank you.
HM?
GAH
NO! WE SHOULD SPLIT THE BILL!
LET ME PAY AS THANKS FOR BRINGING ME.
BUT—
TUMP TUMP
BUT IF YOU INSIST...

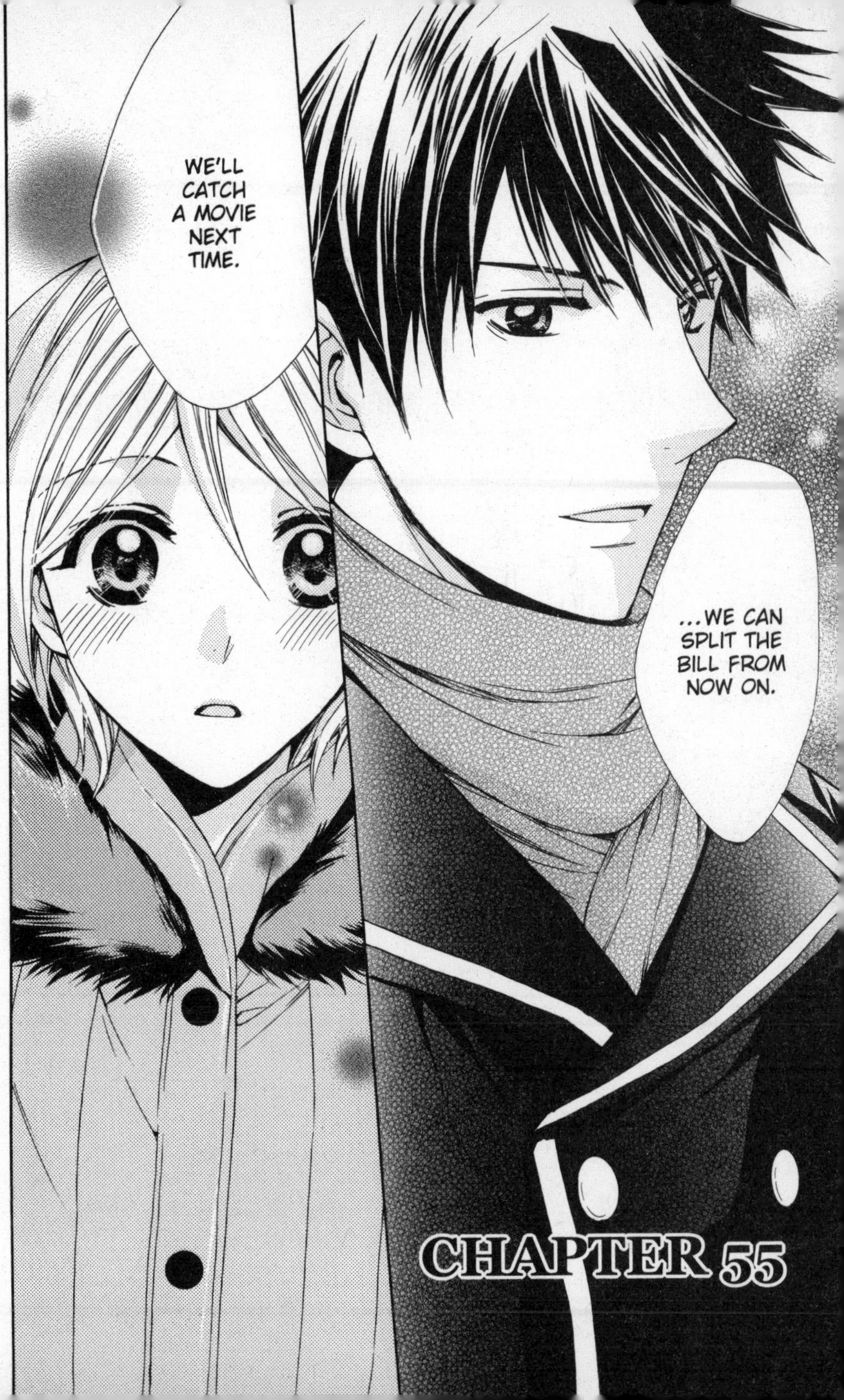
WE'LL CATCH A MOVIE NEXT TIME.
...WE CAN SPLIT THE BILL FROM NOW ON.
CHAPTER 55

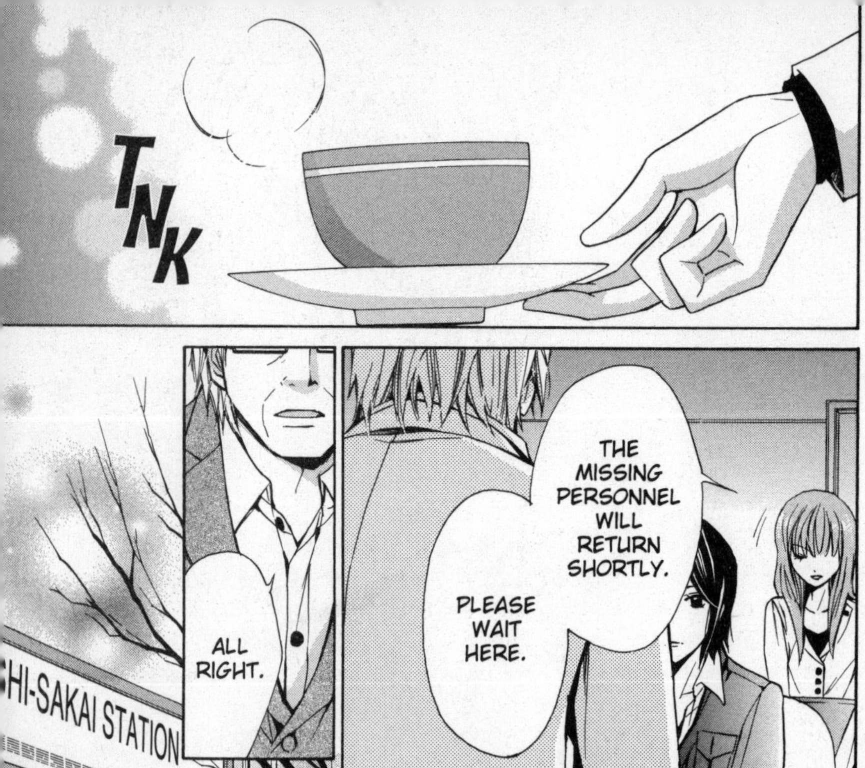
TNK
THE MISSING PERSONNEL WILL RETURN SHORTLY.
PLEASE WAIT HERE.
ALL RIGHT.
HI-SAKAI STATION

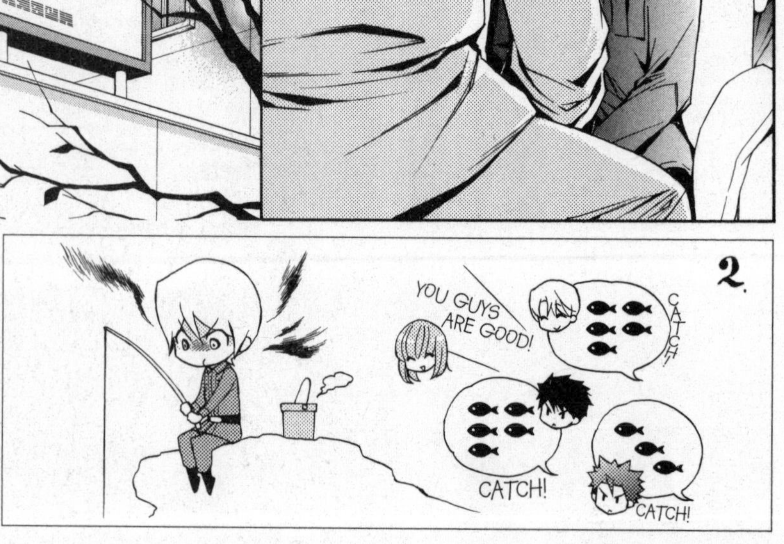
2.
CATCH!
YOU GUYS ARE GOOD!
CATCH!
CATCH!

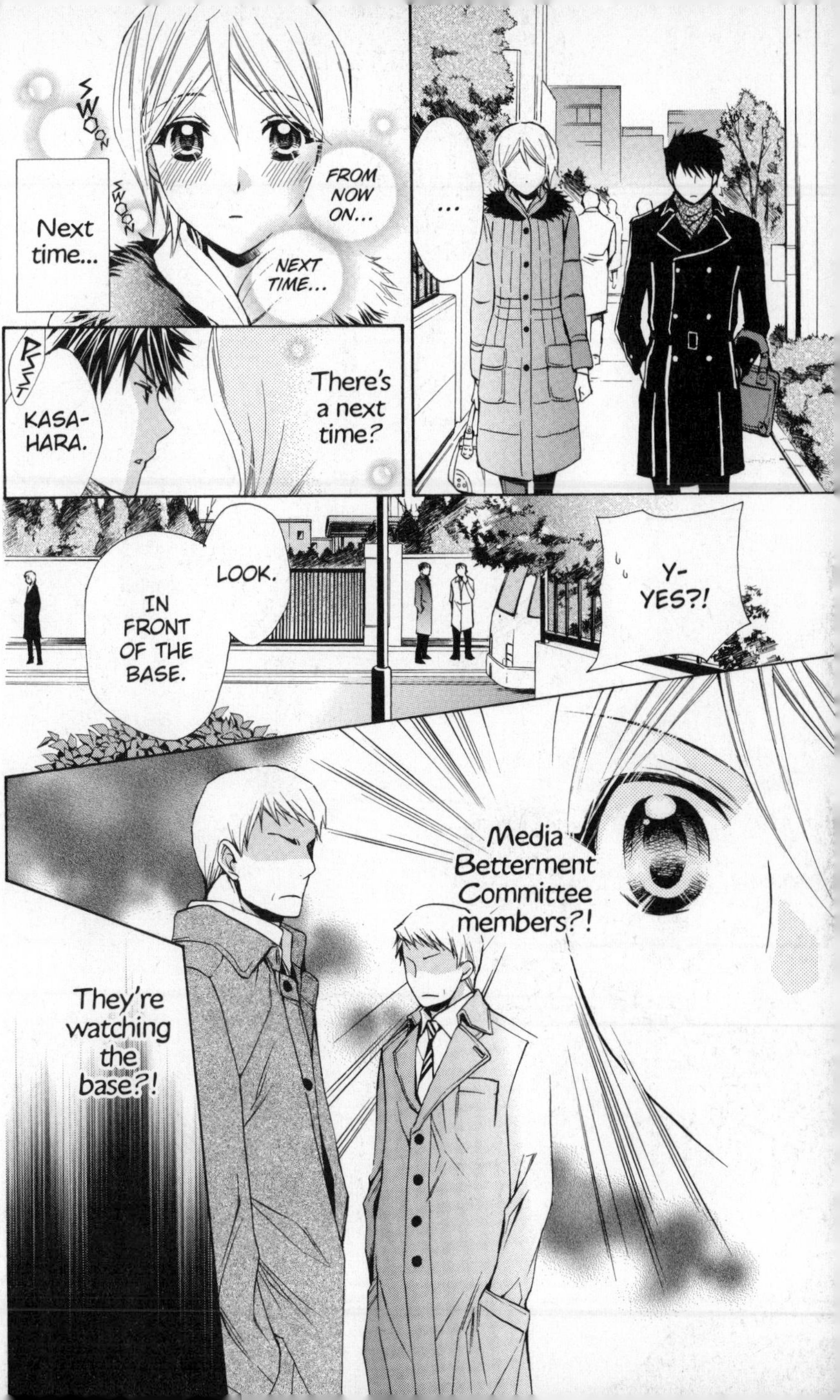
...
FROM NOW ON...
NEXT TIME...
SWOON
SWOON
Next time...
There's a next time?
PSST
KASA-HARA.
Y-YES?!
LOOK.
IN FRONT OF THE BASE.
Media Betterment Committee members?!
They're watching the base?!

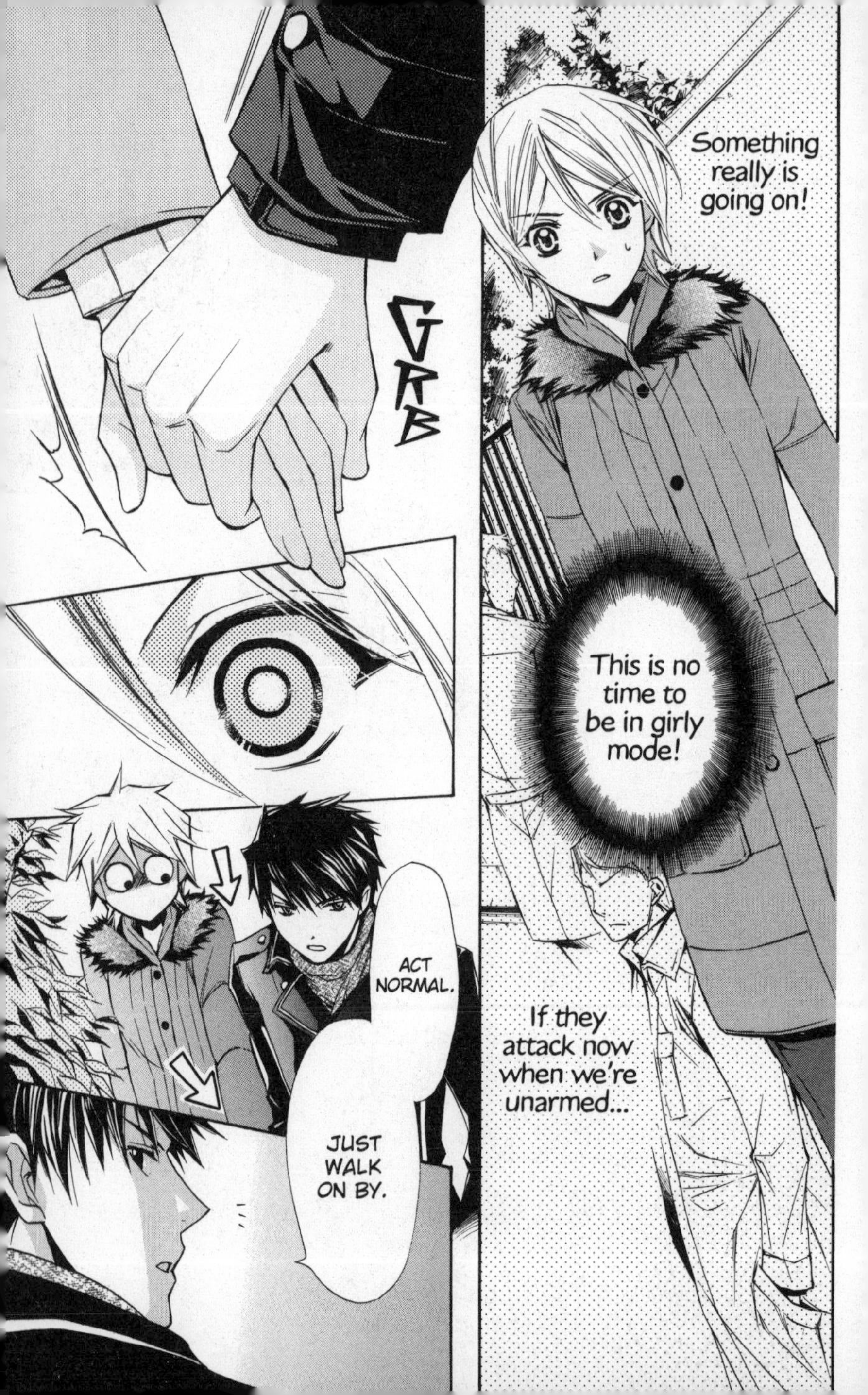
Something really is going on!
This is no time to be in girly mode!
If they attack now when we're unarmed...
GRB
ACT NORMAL.
JUST WALK ON BY.

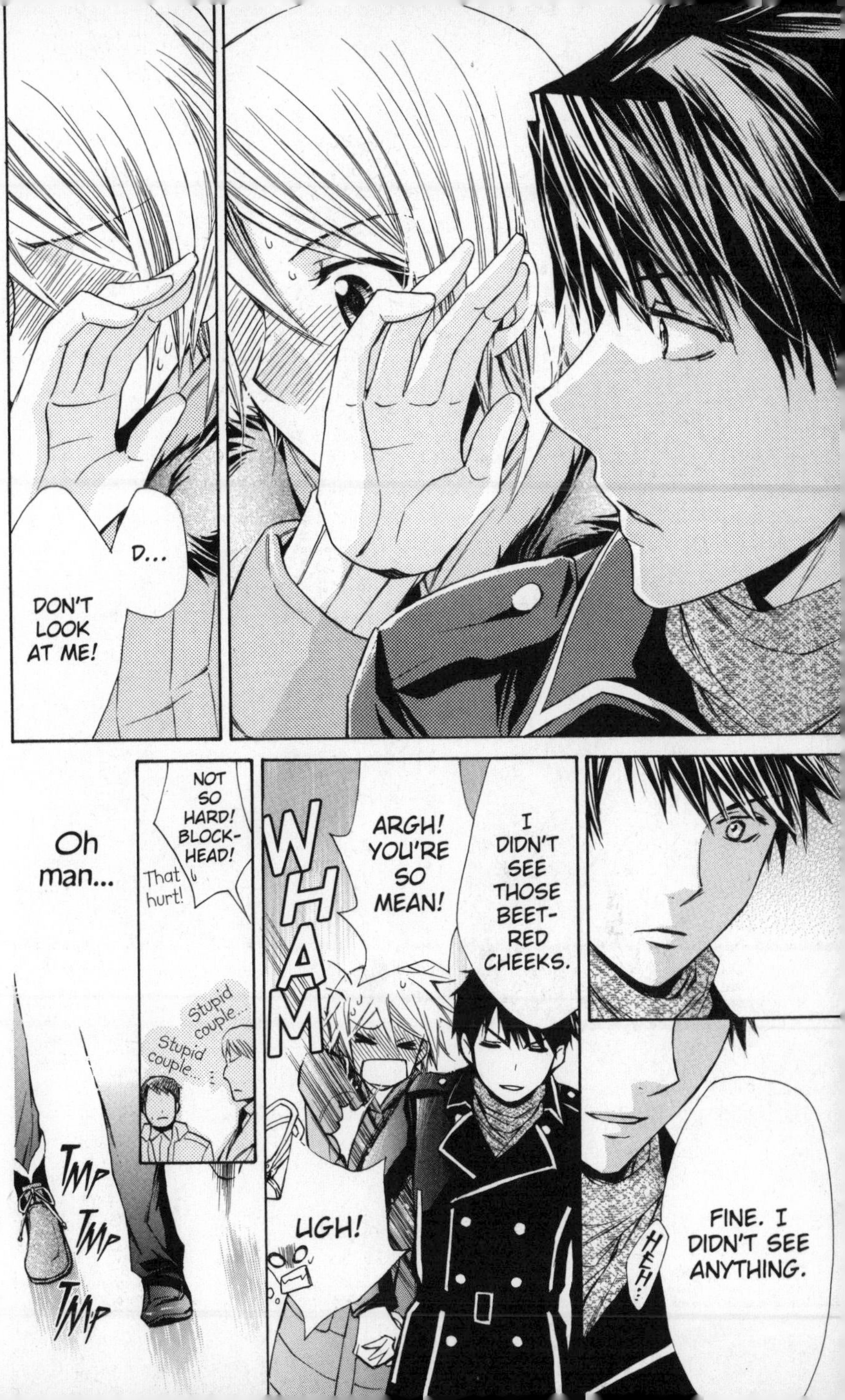
D...
DON'T LOOK AT ME!
HEH...
FINE. I DIDN'T SEE ANYTHING.
I DIDN'T SEE THOSE BEET-RED CHEEKS.
ARGH! YOU'RE SO MEAN!
WHAM
UGH!
NOT SO HARD! BLOCK-HEAD!
That hurt!
Stupid couple...
Stupid couple...
Oh man...
TMP TMP TMP

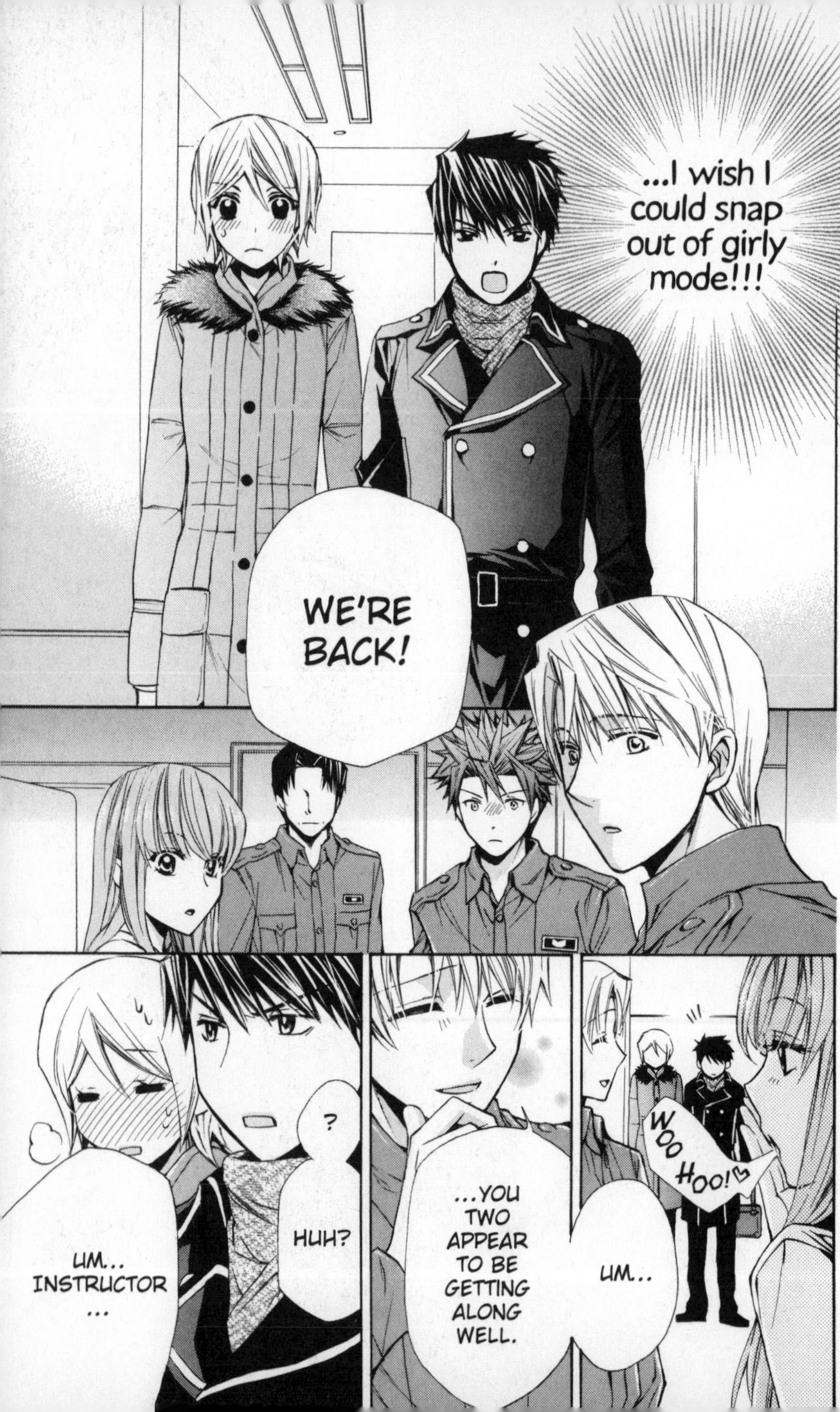
...I wish I could snap out of girly mode!!!
WE'RE BACK!
WOO HOO!
UM...
...YOU TWO APPEAR TO BE GETTING ALONG WELL.
?
HUH?
UM... INSTRUCTOR ...

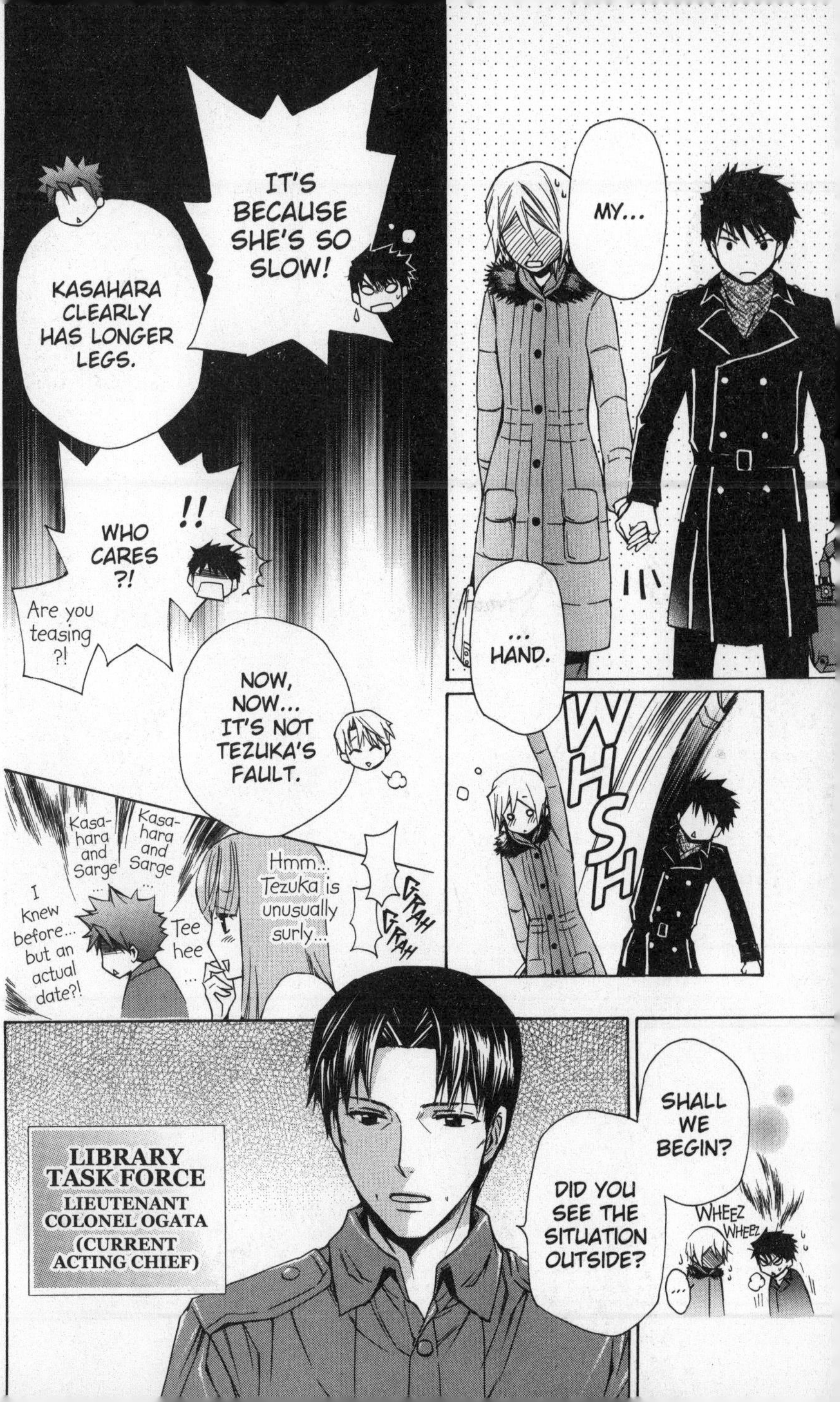
MY...
... HAND.
WHSH
IT'S BECAUSE SHE'S SO SLOW!
KASAHARA CLEARLY HAS LONGER LEGS.
!!
WHO CARES ?!
Are you teasing ?!
NOW, NOW... IT'S NOT TEZUKA'S FAULT.
GRAH GRAH
Hmm... Tezuka is unusually surly...
Tee hee ...
Kasa-hara and Sarge ...
Kasa-hara and Sarge ...
I knew before... but an actual date?!
SHALL WE BEGIN?
DID YOU SEE THE SITUATION OUTSIDE?
WHEEZ WHEEZ
...
LIBRARY TASK FORCE
LIEUTENANT COLONEL OGATA
(CURRENT ACTING CHIEF)

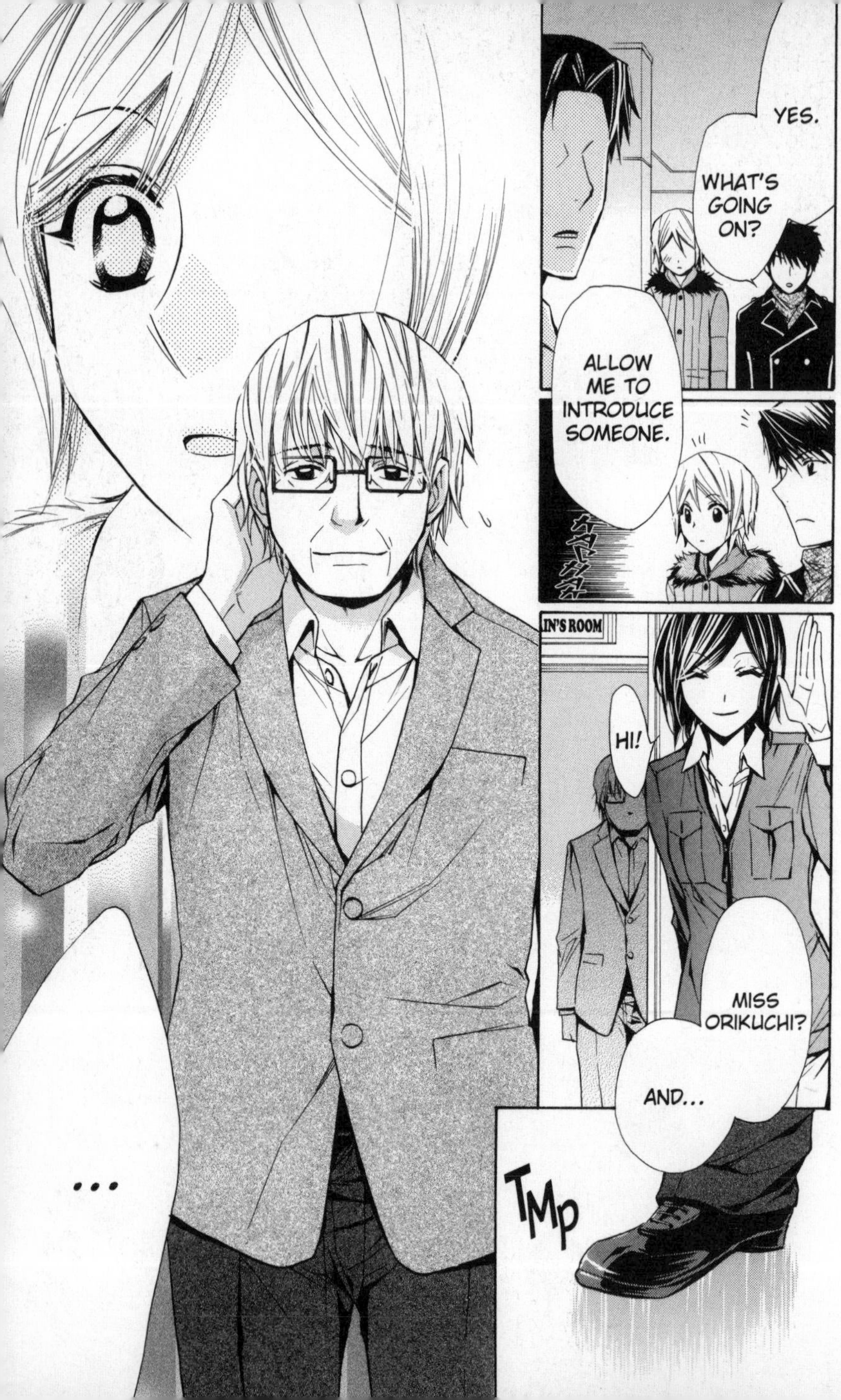
YES.
WHAT'S GOING ON?
ALLOW ME TO INTRODUCE SOMEONE.
IN'S ROOM
HI!
MISS ORIKUCHI?
AND...
TMP
...

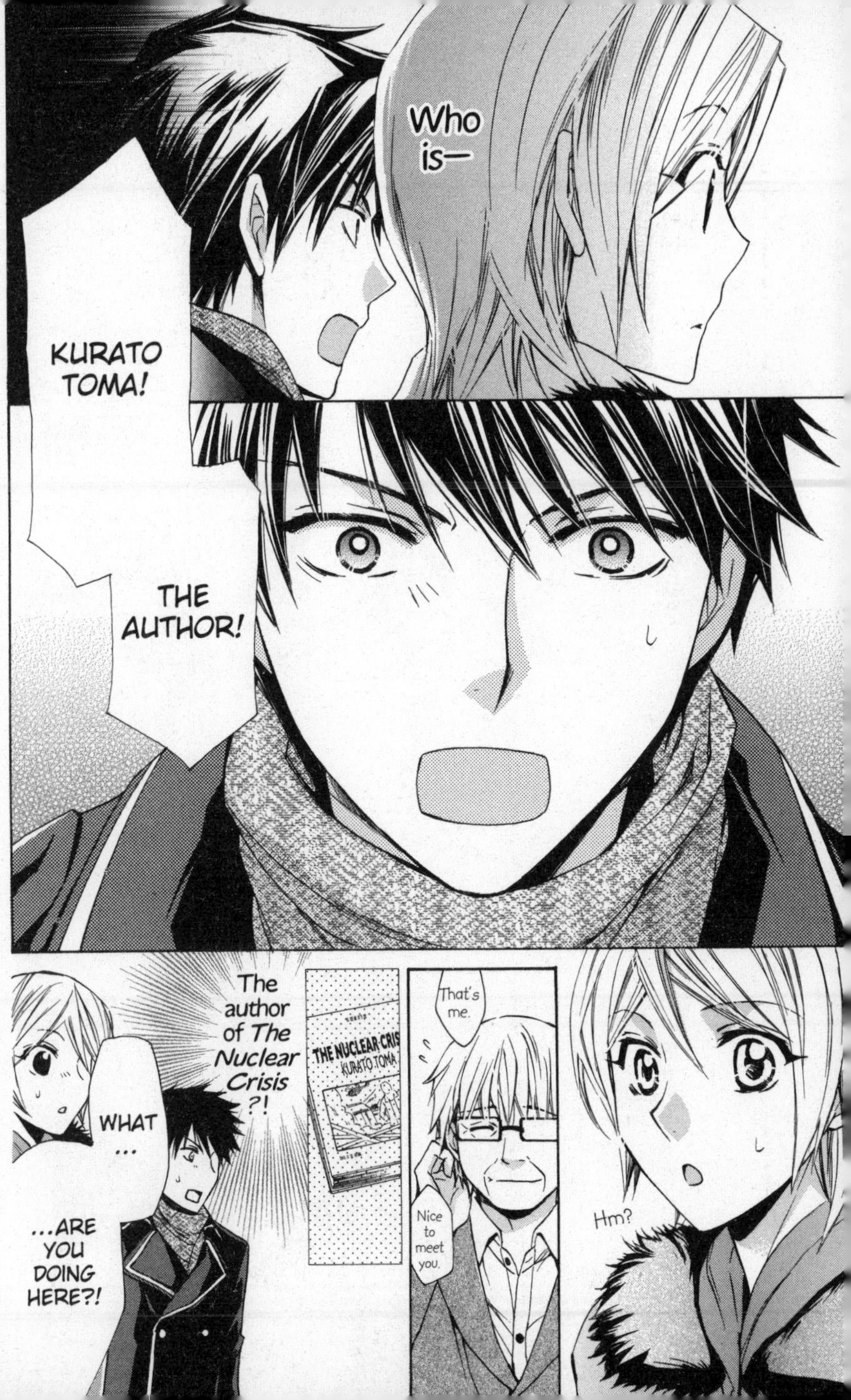
Who is—
KURATO TOMA!
THE AUTHOR!
Hm?
That's me.
Nice to meet you.
THE NUCLEAR CRIS
KURATO TOMA
The author of *The Nuclear Crisis* ?!
WHAT ...
...ARE YOU DOING HERE?!

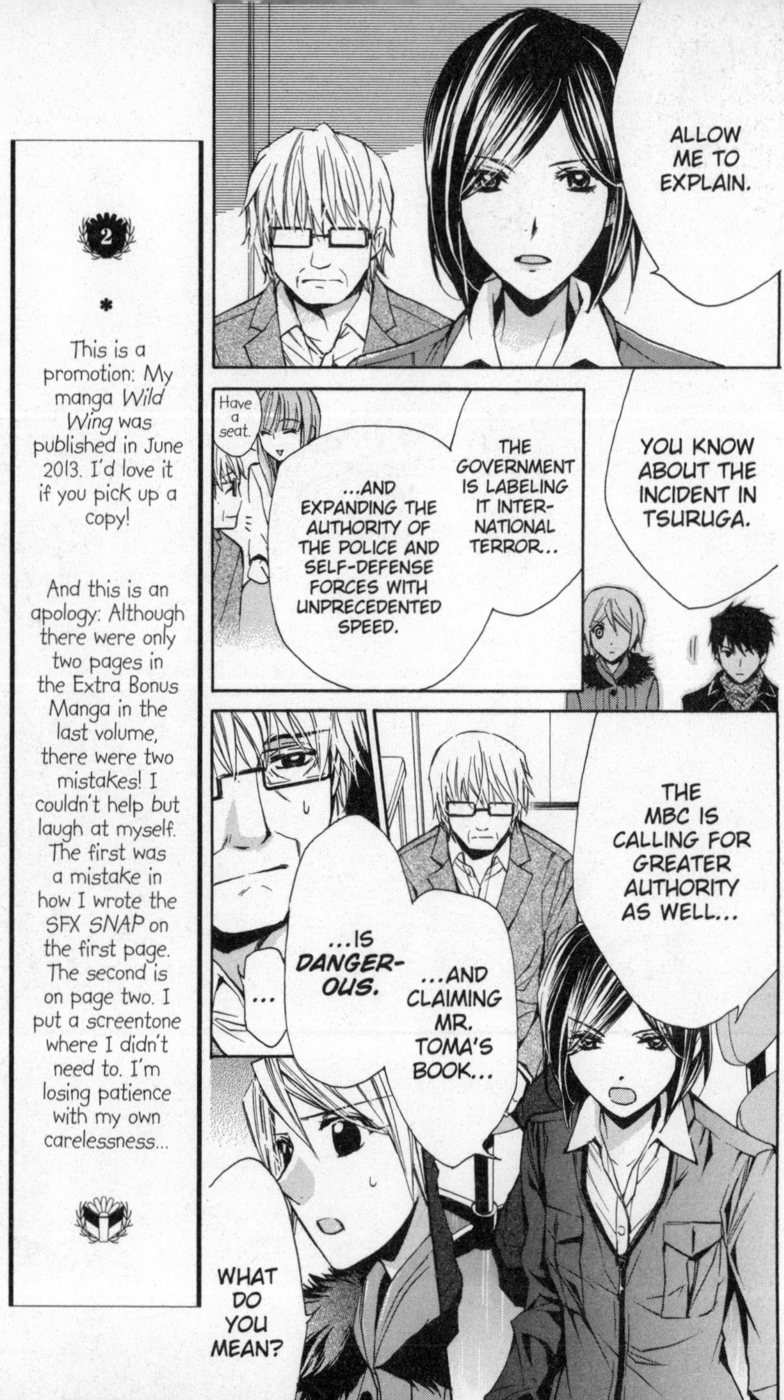
ALLOW ME TO EXPLAIN.
YOU KNOW ABOUT THE INCIDENT IN TSURUGA.
THE GOVERNMENT IS LABELING IT INTER-NATIONAL TERROR...
...AND EXPANDING THE AUTHORITY OF THE POLICE AND SELF-DEFENSE FORCES WITH UNPRECEDENTED SPEED.
Have a seat.
THE MBC IS CALLING FOR GREATER AUTHORITY AS WELL...
...AND CLAIMING MR. TOMA'S BOOK...
...IS ***DANGER-OUS.***
...
WHAT DO YOU MEAN?

2

*

This is a promotion: My manga *Wild Wing* was published in June 2013. I'd love it if you pick up a copy!

And this is an apology: Although there were only two pages in the Extra Bonus Manga in the last volume, there were two mistakes! I couldn't help but laugh at myself. The first was a mistake in how I wrote the SFX *SNAP* on the first page. The second is on page two. I put a screentone where I didn't need to. I'm losing patience with my own carelessness...

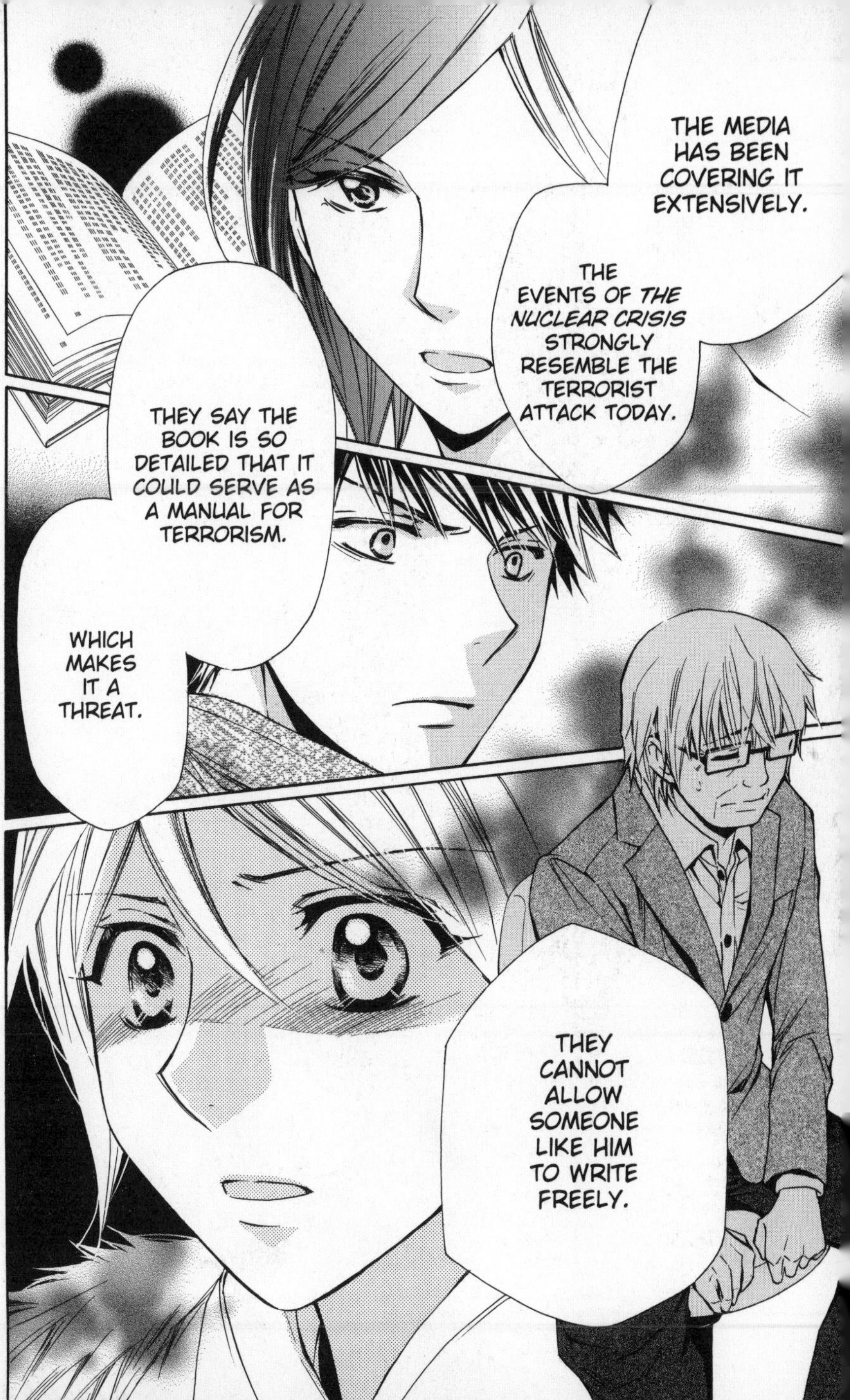
THE MEDIA HAS BEEN COVERING IT EXTENSIVELY.
THE EVENTS OF *THE NUCLEAR CRISIS* STRONGLY RESEMBLE THE TERRORIST ATTACK TODAY.
THEY SAY THE BOOK IS SO DETAILED THAT IT COULD SERVE AS A MANUAL FOR TERRORISM.
WHICH MAKES IT A THREAT.
THEY CANNOT ALLOW SOMEONE LIKE HIM TO WRITE FREELY.

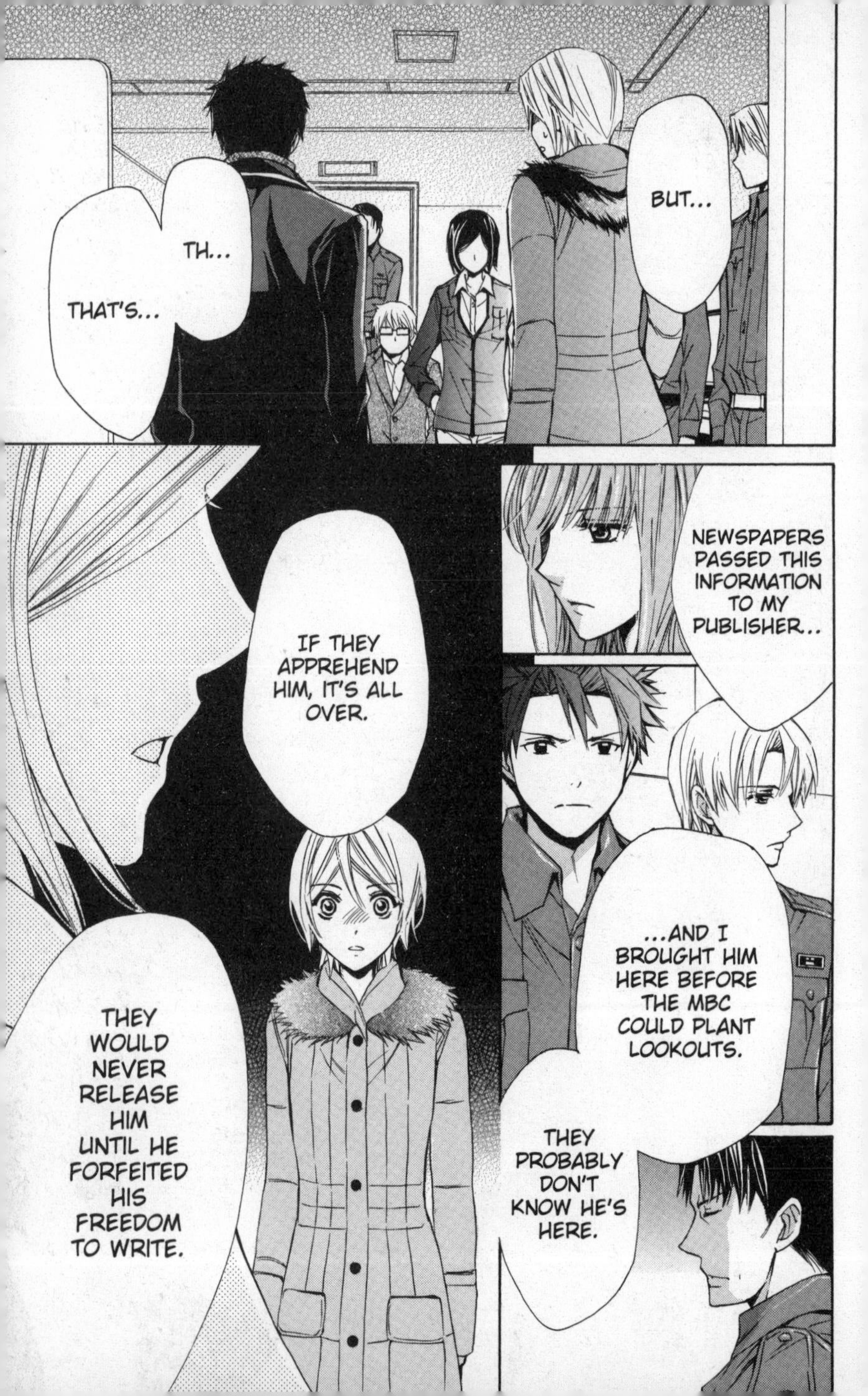
BUT...
TH...
THAT'S...
NEWSPAPERS PASSED THIS INFORMATION TO MY PUBLISHER...
...AND I BROUGHT HIM HERE BEFORE THE MBC COULD PLANT LOOKOUTS.
THEY PROBABLY DON'T KNOW HE'S HERE.
IF THEY APPREHEND HIM, IT'S ALL OVER.
THEY WOULD NEVER RELEASE HIM UNTIL HE FORFEITED HIS FREEDOM TO WRITE.

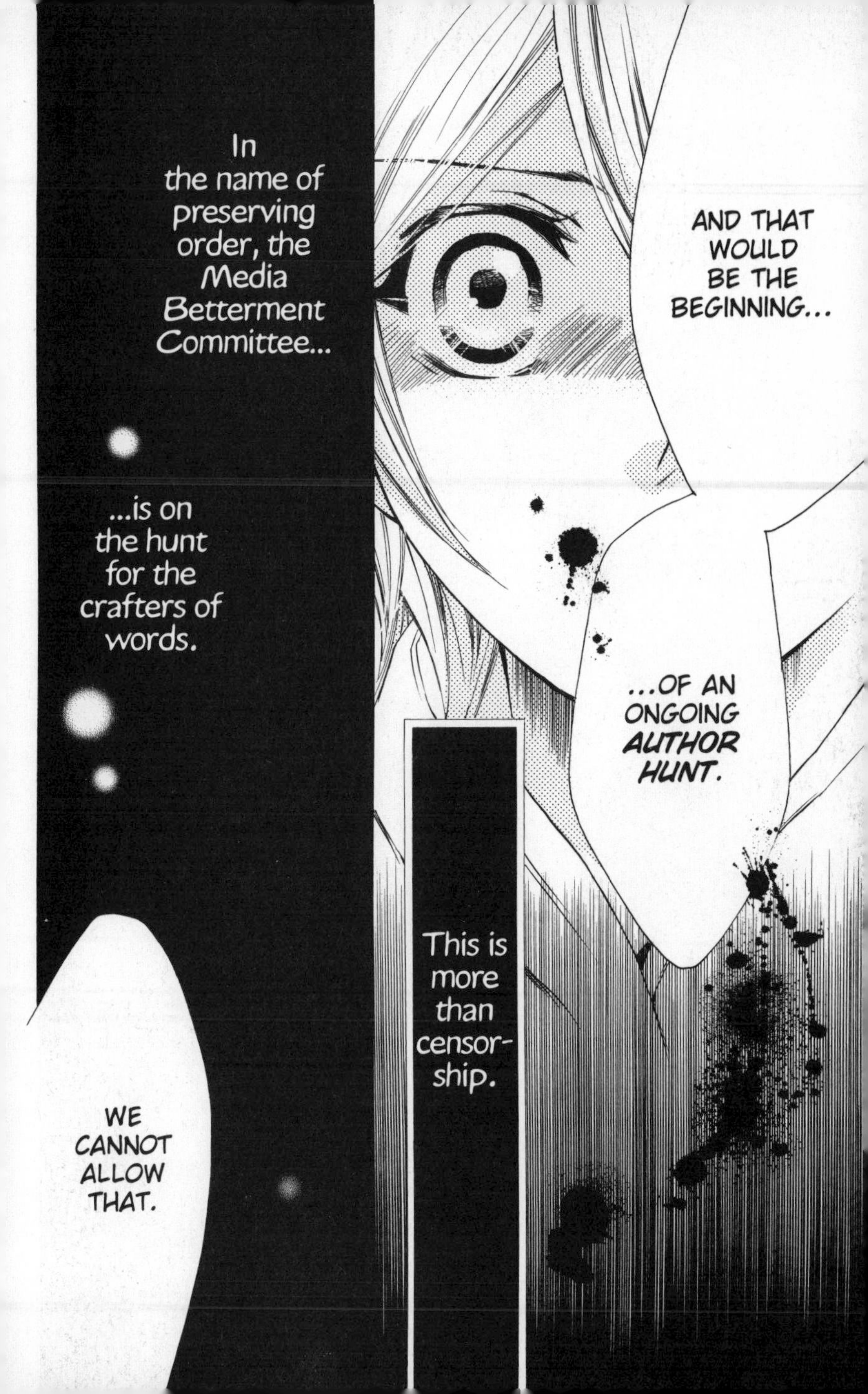
AND THAT WOULD BE THE BEGINNING...
...OF AN ONGOING AUTHOR HUNT.
This is more than censorship.
In the name of preserving order, the Media Betterment Committee...
...is on the hunt for the crafters of words.
WE CANNOT ALLOW THAT.

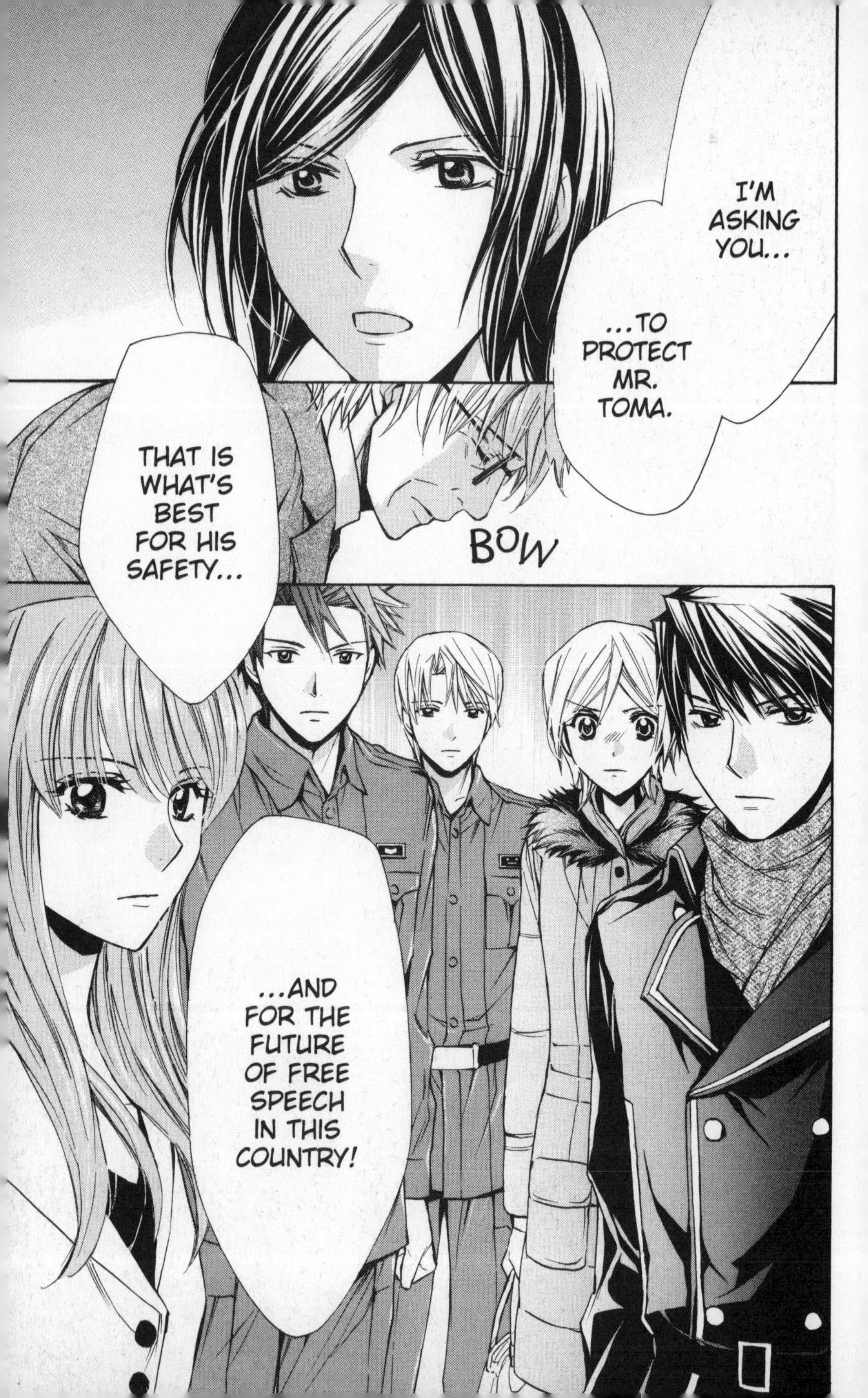
I'M ASKING YOU...
...TO PROTECT MR. TOMA.
BOW
THAT IS WHAT'S BEST FOR HIS SAFETY...
...AND FOR THE FUTURE OF FREE SPEECH IN THIS COUNTRY!

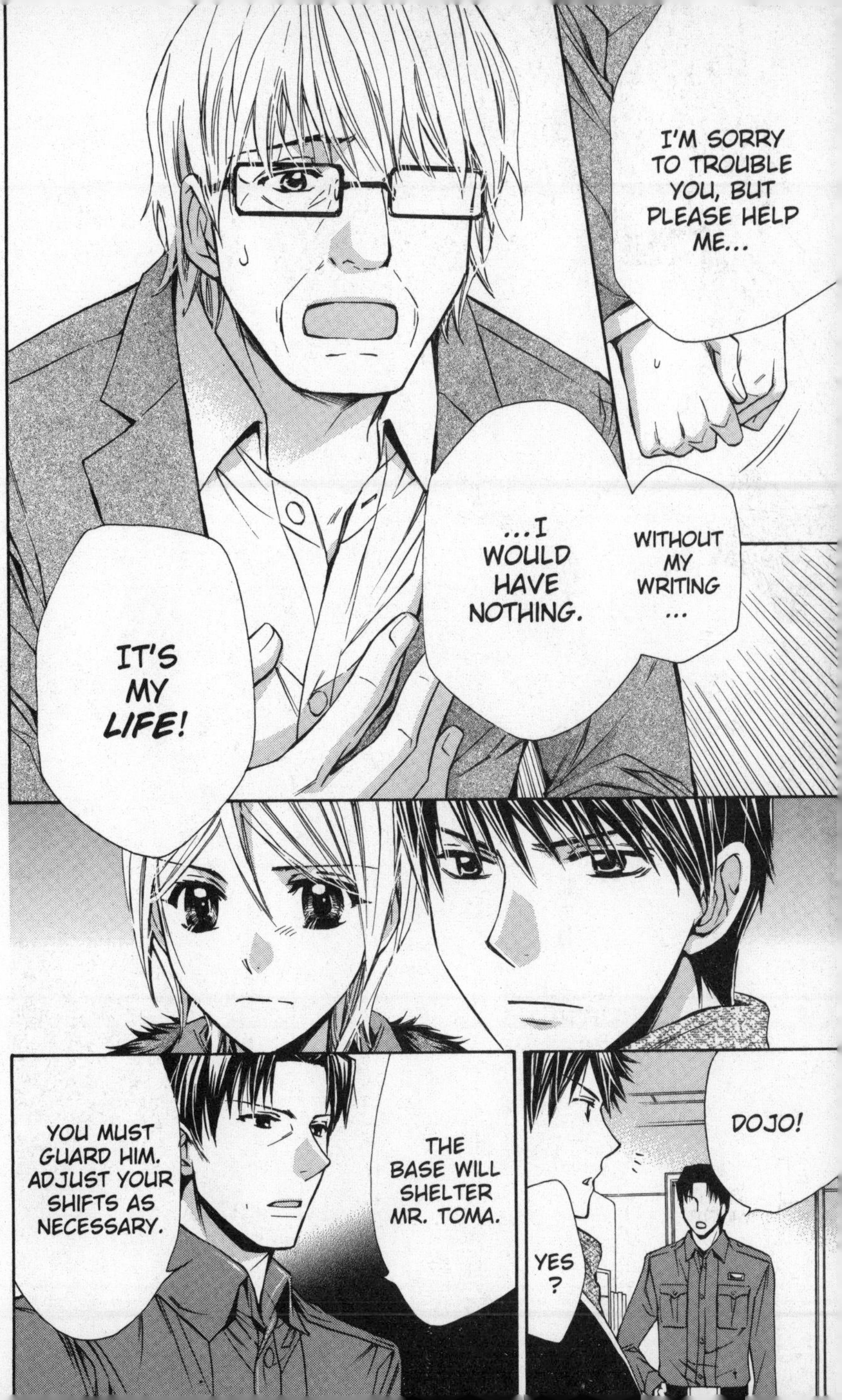
I'M SORRY TO TROUBLE YOU, BUT PLEASE HELP ME...
WITHOUT MY WRITING ...
...I WOULD HAVE NOTHING.
IT'S MY *LIFE*!
DOJO!
YES?
THE BASE WILL SHELTER MR. TOMA.
YOU MUST GUARD HIM. ADJUST YOUR SHIFTS AS NECESSARY.

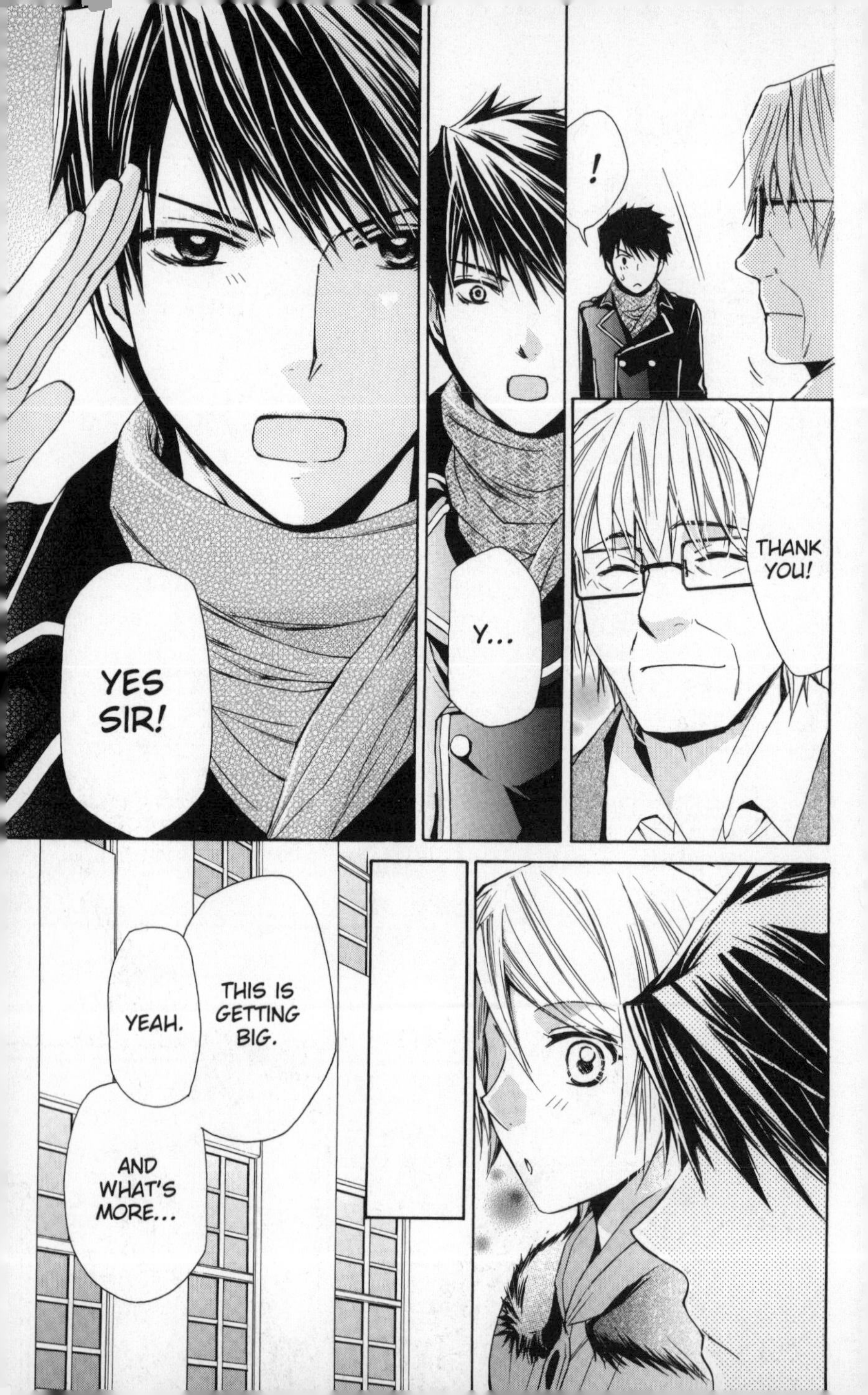
!
THANK YOU!
Y...
YES SIR!
THIS IS GETTING BIG.
YEAH.
AND WHAT'S MORE...

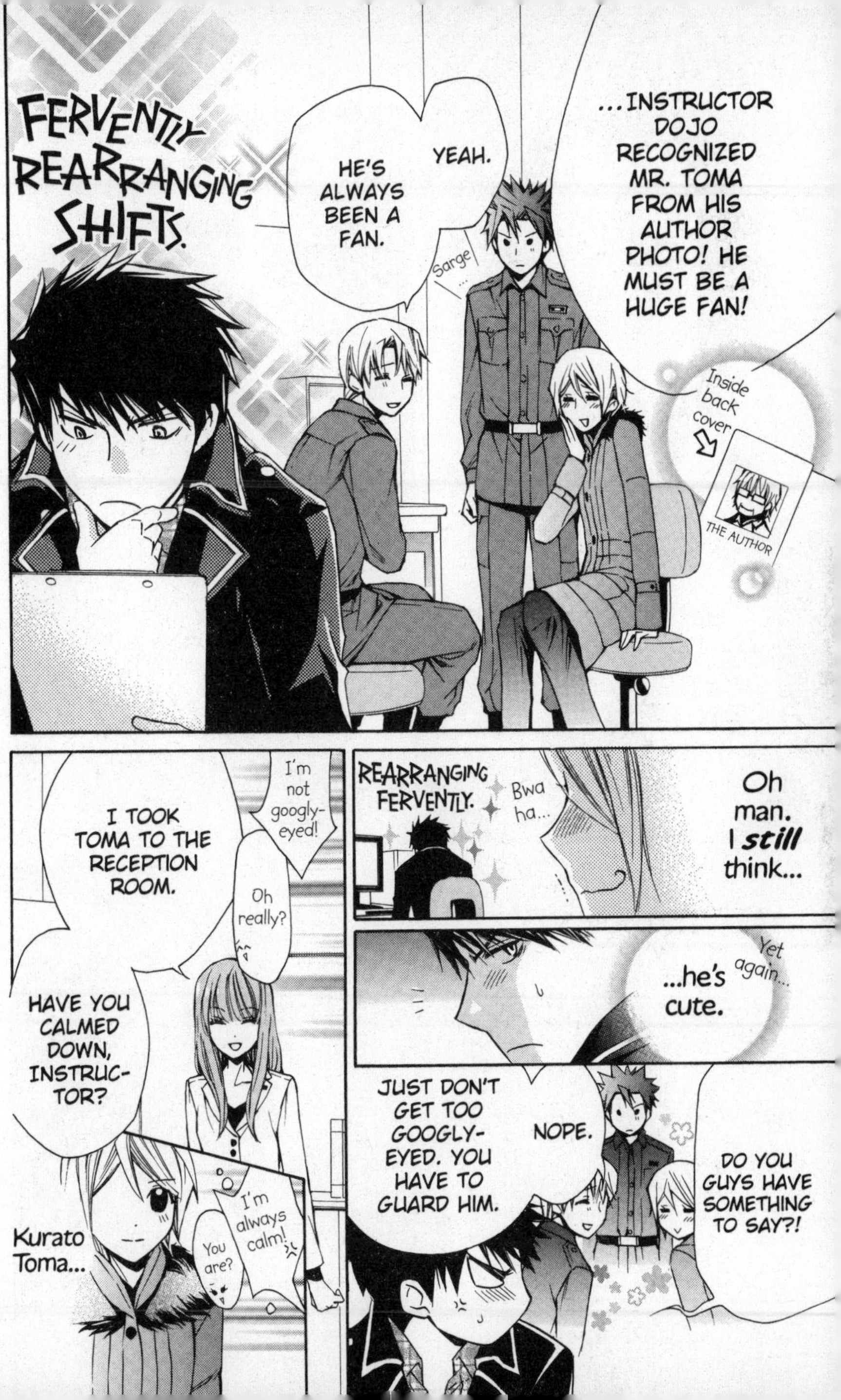
...INSTRUCTOR DOJO RECOGNIZED MR. TOMA FROM HIS AUTHOR PHOTO! HE MUST BE A HUGE FAN!
Inside back cover
THE AUTHOR
YEAH.
HE'S ALWAYS BEEN A FAN.
Sarge ...
FERVENTLY REARRANGING SHIFTS.
Oh man. I *still* think...
Bwa ha...
REARRANGING FERVENTLY.
...he's cute.
Yet again...
DO YOU GUYS HAVE SOMETHING TO SAY?!
NOPE.
JUST DON'T GET TOO GOOGLY-EYED. YOU HAVE TO GUARD HIM.
I TOOK TOMA TO THE RECEPTION ROOM.
I'm not googly-eyed!
Oh really?
HAVE YOU CALMED DOWN, INSTRUCTOR?
I'm always calm!
You are?
Kurato Toma...

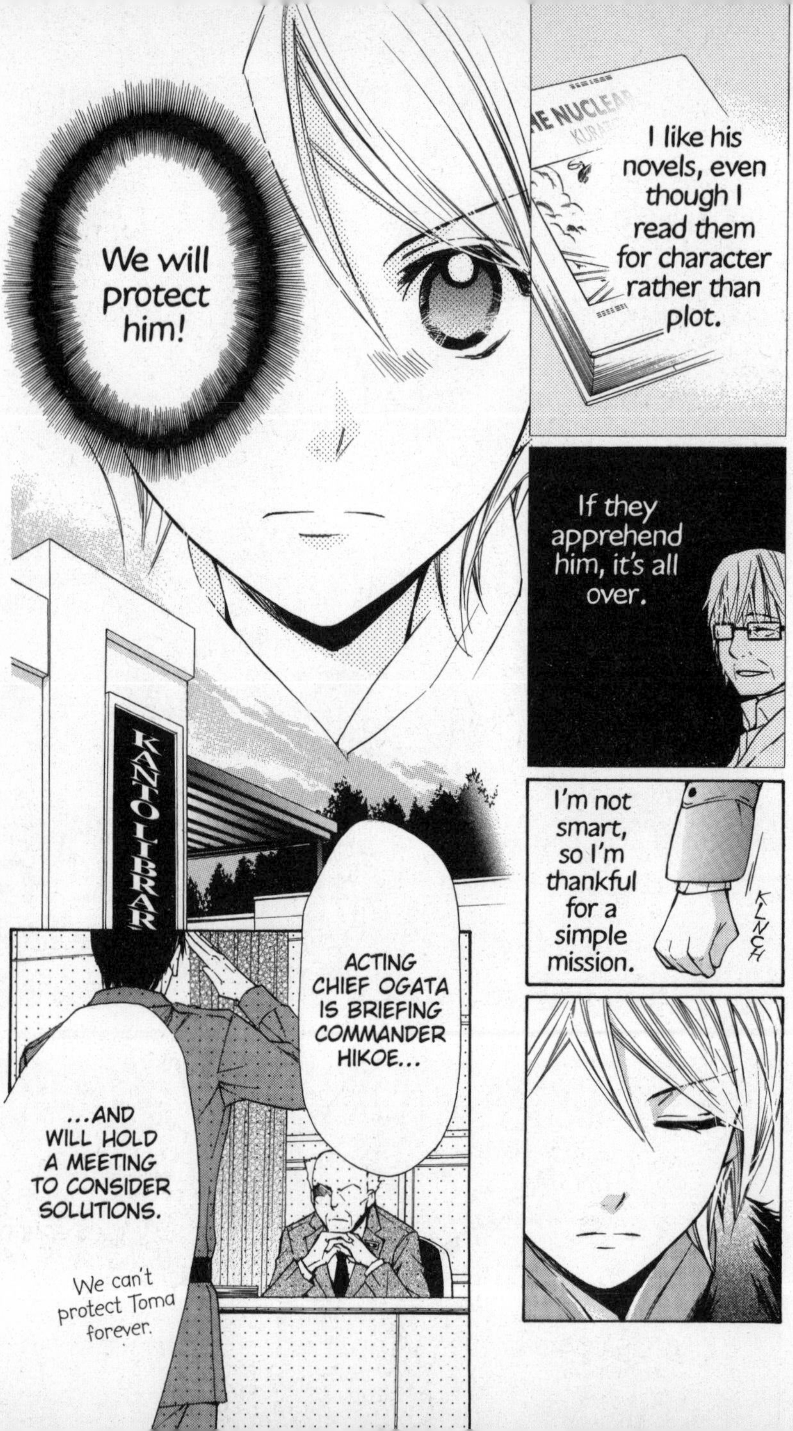
I like his novels, even though I read them for character rather than plot.
If they apprehend him, it's all over.
I'm not smart, so I'm thankful for a simple mission.
KLNCH
We will protect him!
KANTO LIBRAR
ACTING CHIEF OGATA IS BRIEFING COMMANDER HIKOE...
...AND WILL HOLD A MEETING TO CONSIDER SOLUTIONS.
We can't protect Toma forever.

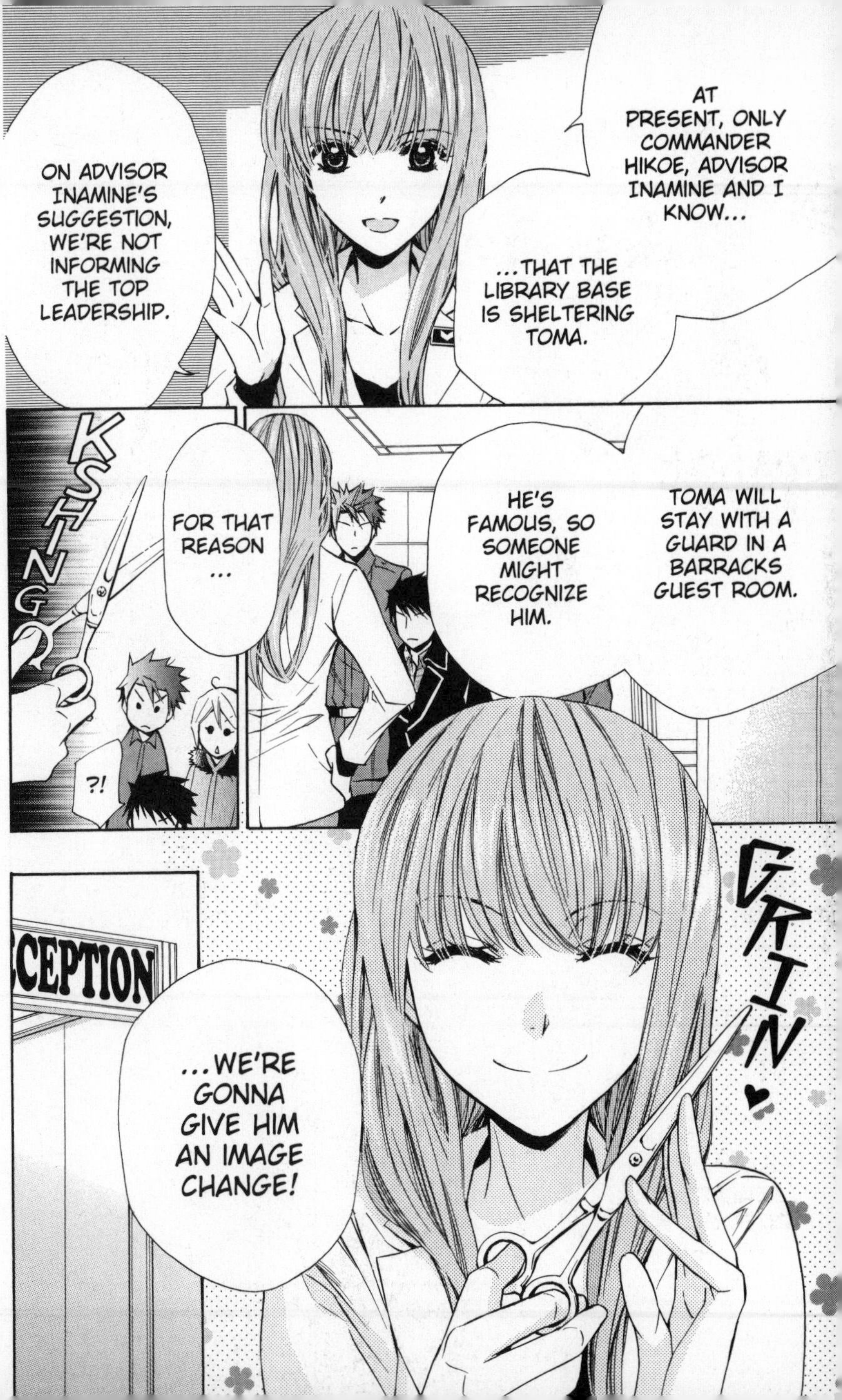
AT PRESENT, ONLY COMMANDER HIKOE, ADVISOR INAMINE AND I KNOW...
...THAT THE LIBRARY BASE IS SHELTERING TOMA.
ON ADVISOR INAMINE'S SUGGESTION, WE'RE NOT INFORMING THE TOP LEADERSHIP.
TOMA WILL STAY WITH A GUARD IN A BARRACKS GUEST ROOM.
HE'S FAMOUS, SO SOMEONE MIGHT RECOGNIZE HIM.
FOR THAT REASON ...
KSHING
?!
GRIN♥
CEPTION
...WE'RE GONNA GIVE HIM AN IMAGE CHANGE!

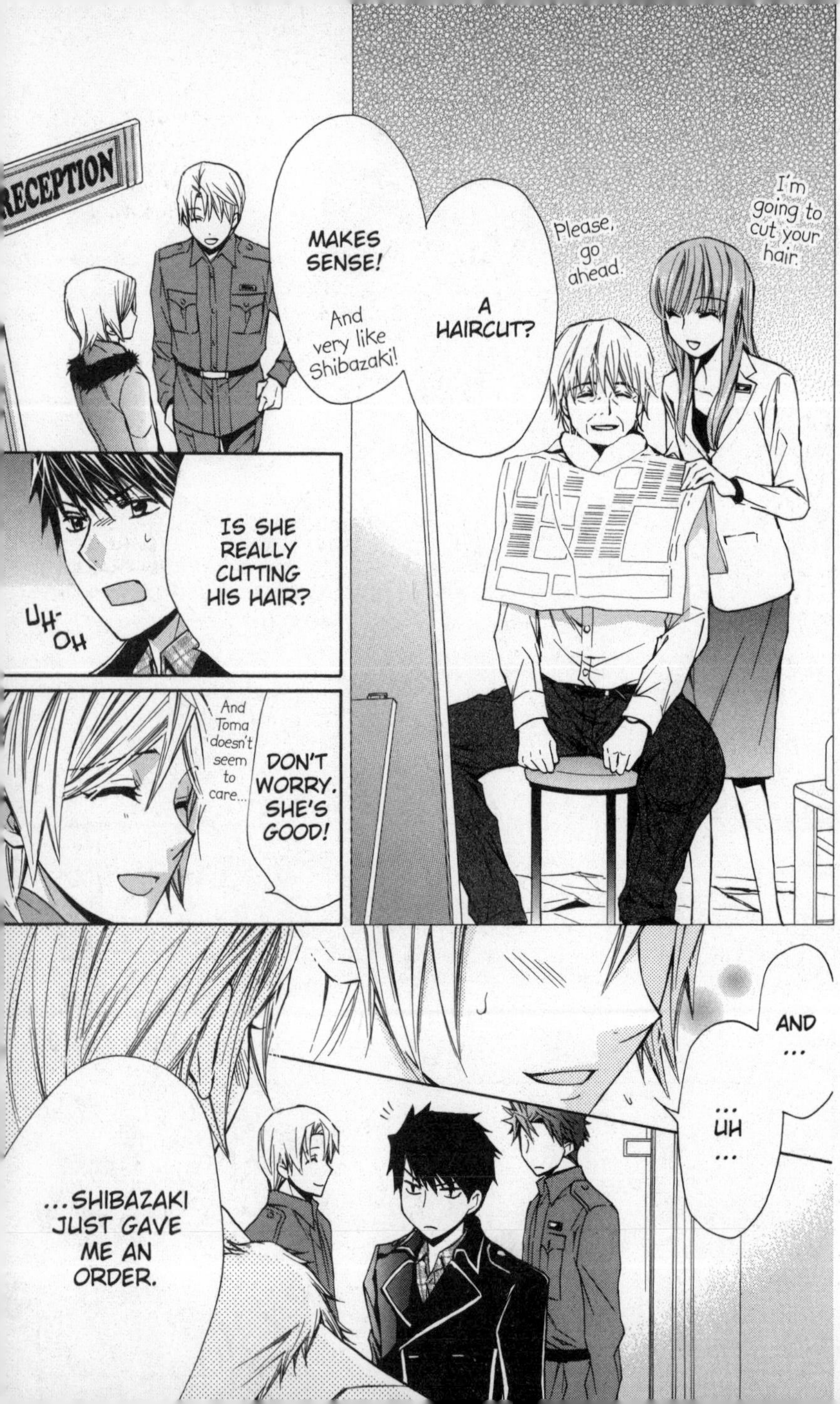
I'm going to cut your hair.
Please, go ahead.
A HAIRCUT?
MAKES SENSE!
And very like Shibazaki!
RECEPTION
IS SHE REALLY CUTTING HIS HAIR?
UH-OH
DON'T WORRY. SHE'S GOOD!
And Toma doesn't seem to care...
AND ...
... UH ...
...SHIBAZAKI JUST GAVE ME AN ORDER.

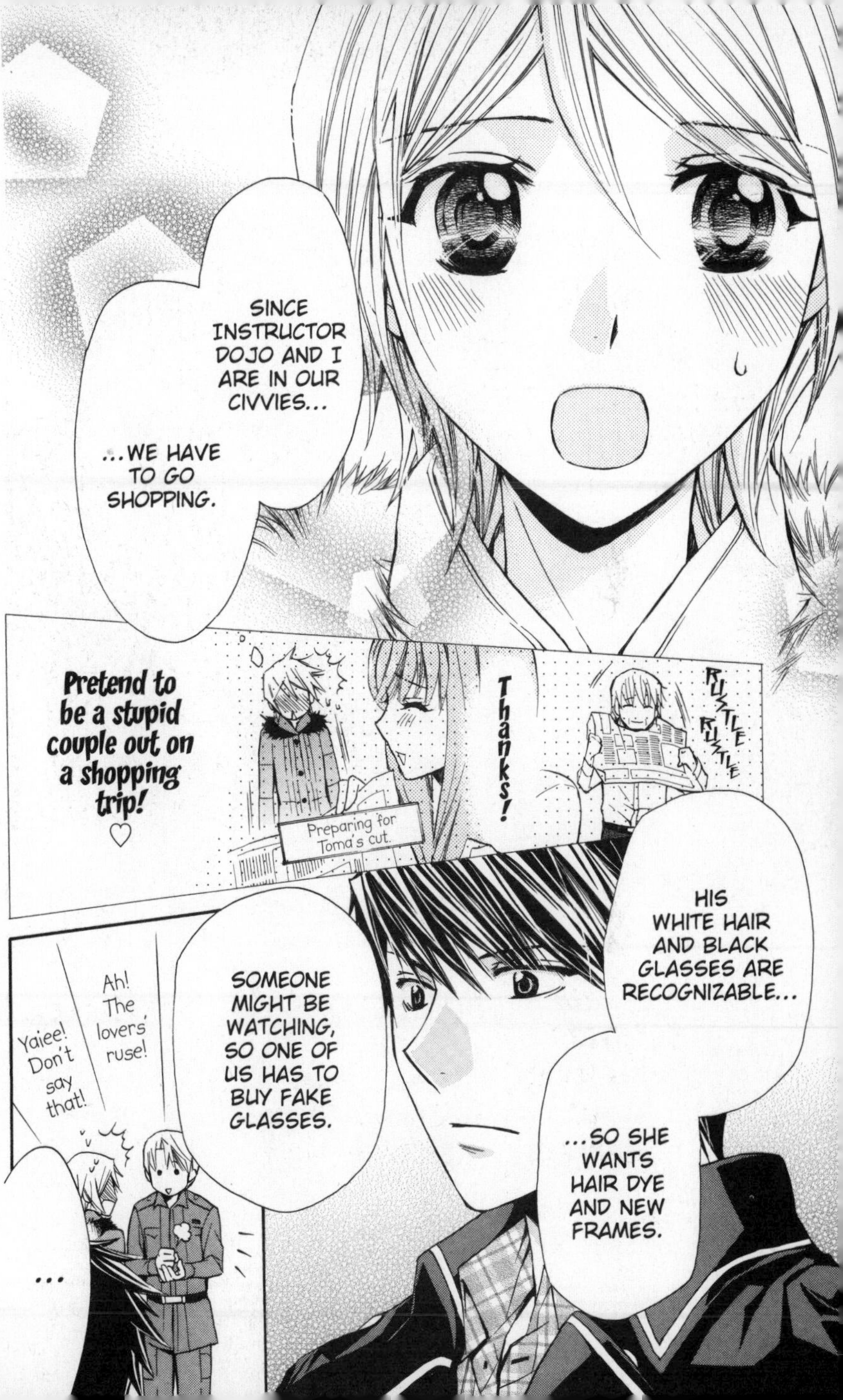
SINCE INSTRUCTOR DOJO AND I ARE IN OUR CIVVIES...
...WE HAVE TO GO SHOPPING.
RUSTLE RUSTLE
Thanks!
Preparing for Toma's cut.
Pretend to be a stupid couple out on a shopping trip! ♡
HIS WHITE HAIR AND BLACK GLASSES ARE RECOGNIZABLE...
...SO SHE WANTS HAIR DYE AND NEW FRAMES.
SOMEONE MIGHT BE WATCHING, SO ONE OF US HAS TO BUY FAKE GLASSES.
Ah! The lovers' ruse!
Yaiee! Don't say that!
...

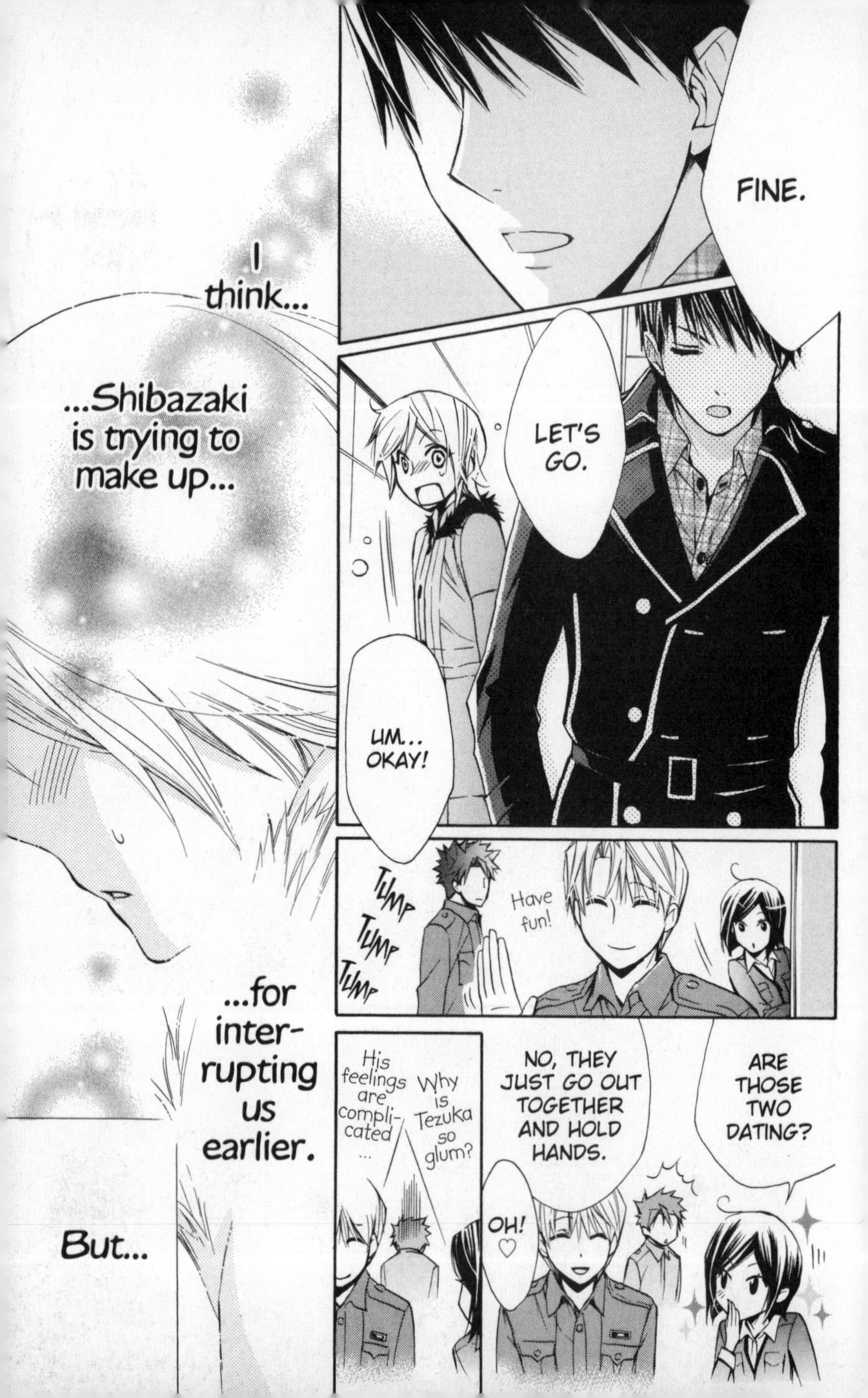
FINE.
LET'S GO.
UM... OKAY!
Have fun!
TUMP TUMP TUMP
ARE THOSE TWO DATING?
NO, THEY JUST GO OUT TOGETHER AND HOLD HANDS.
OH! ♡
Why is Tezuka so glum?
His feelings are compli-cated...
I think...
...Shibazaki is trying to make up...
...for inter-rupting us earlier.
But...

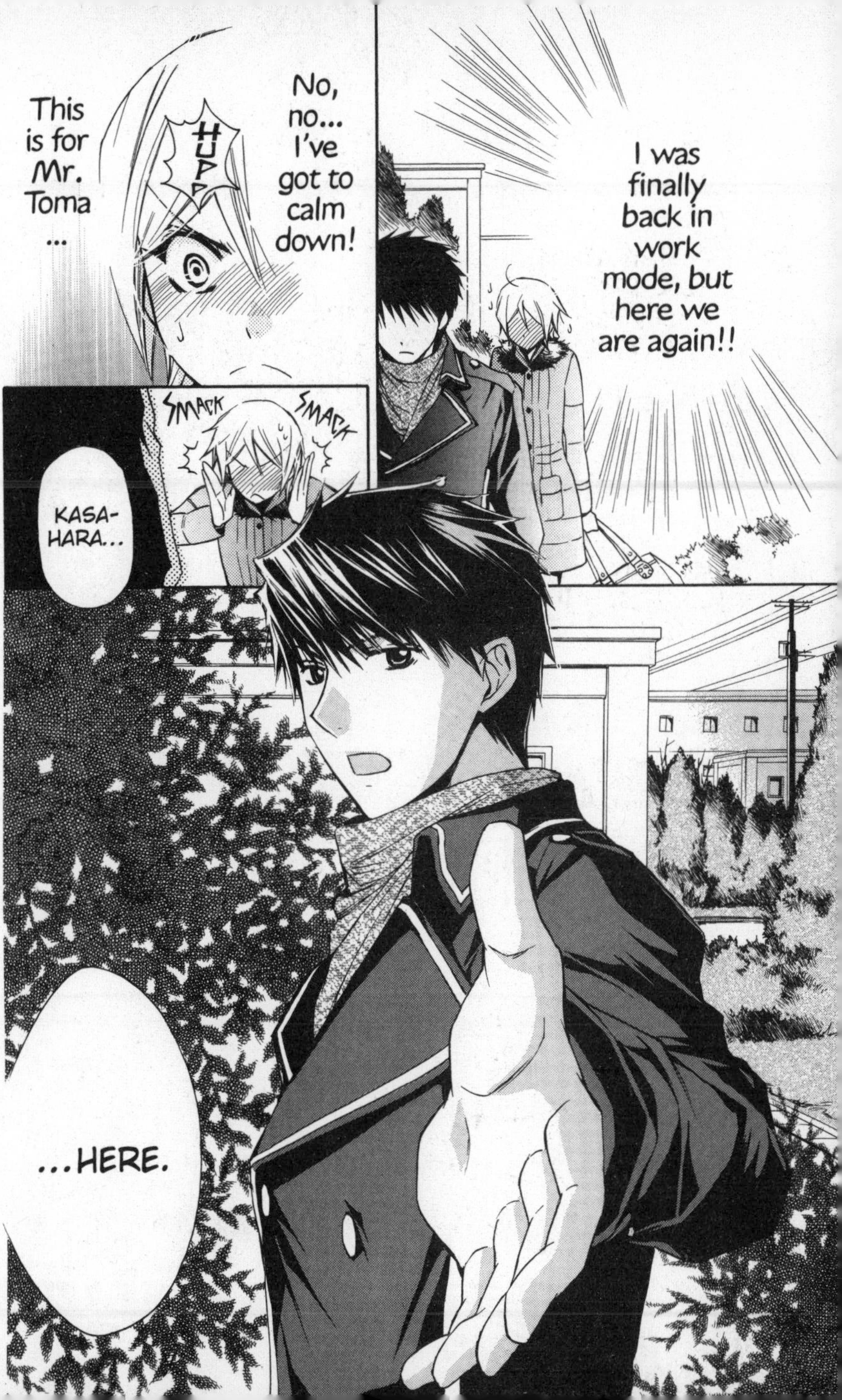
I was finally back in work mode, but here we are again!!
No, no... I've got to calm down!
HUPP
This is for Mr. Toma ...
SMACK
SMACK
KASA-HARA...
...HERE.

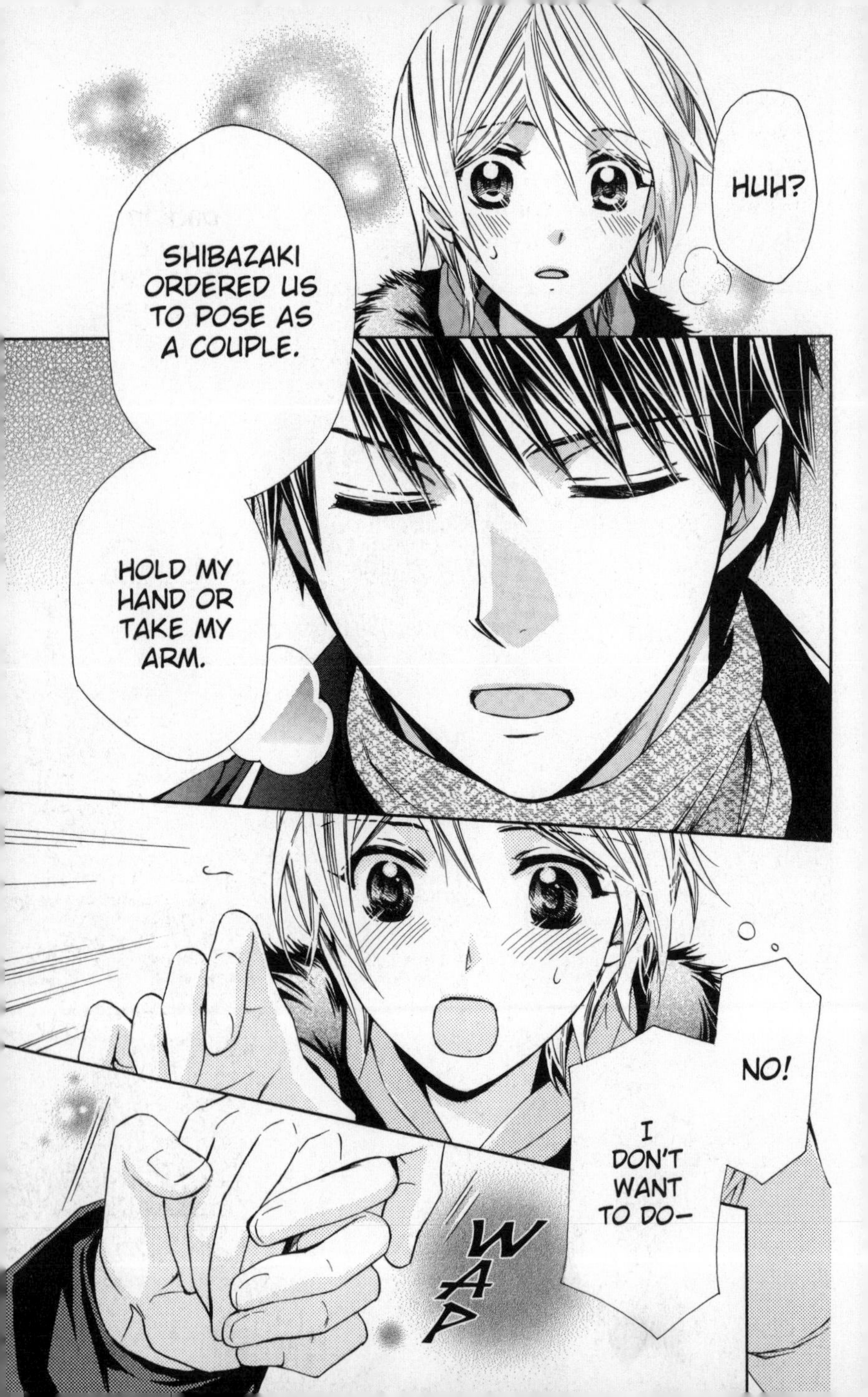
HUH?
SHIBAZAKI ORDERED US TO POSE AS A COUPLE.
HOLD MY HAND OR TAKE MY ARM.
NO!
I DON'T WANT TO DO—
WAP

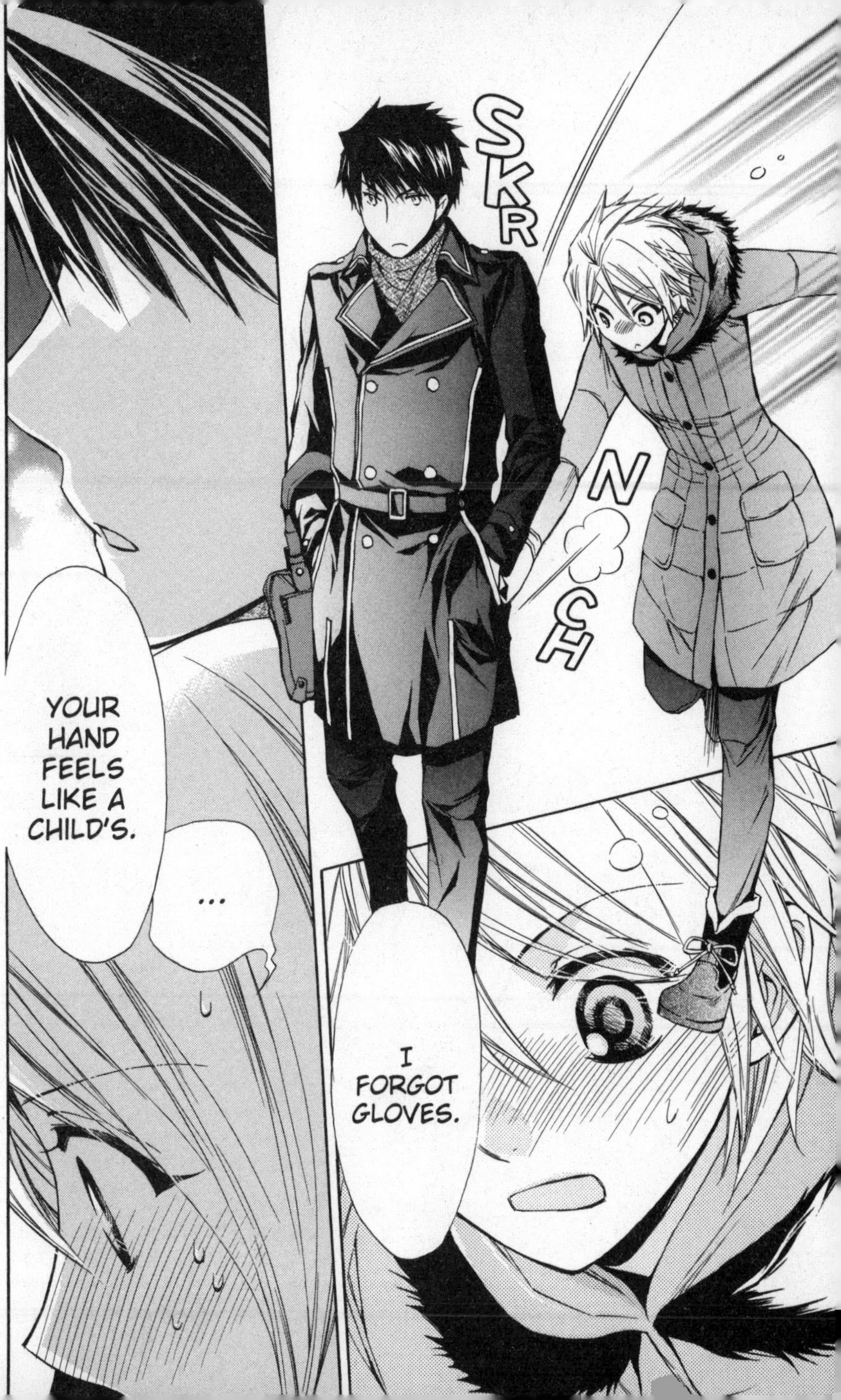
SKRNCH
I FORGOT GLOVES.
YOUR HAND FEELS LIKE A CHILD'S.
...

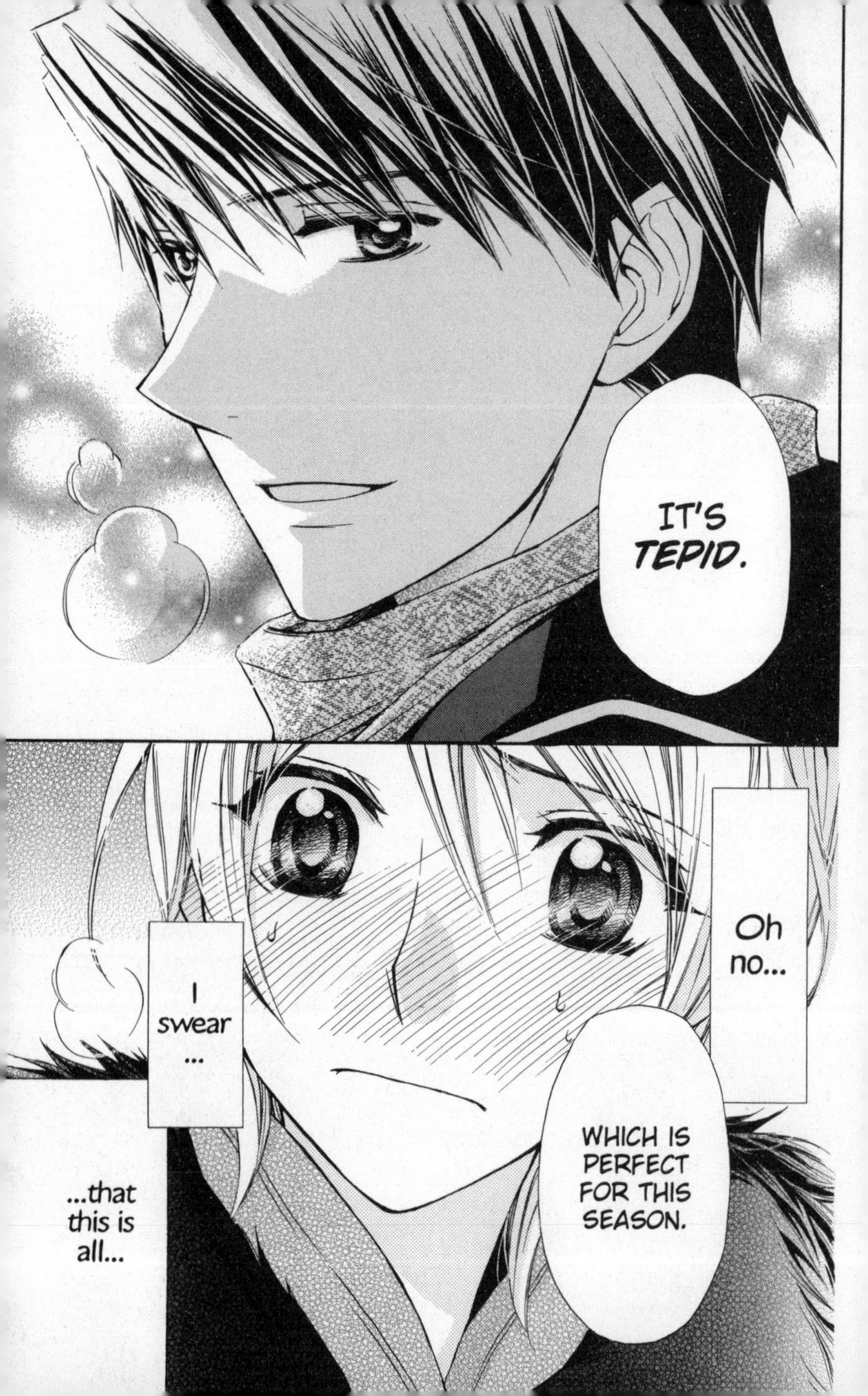
IT'S *TEPID.*
Oh no...
WHICH IS PERFECT FOR THIS SEASON.
I swear ...
...that this is all...

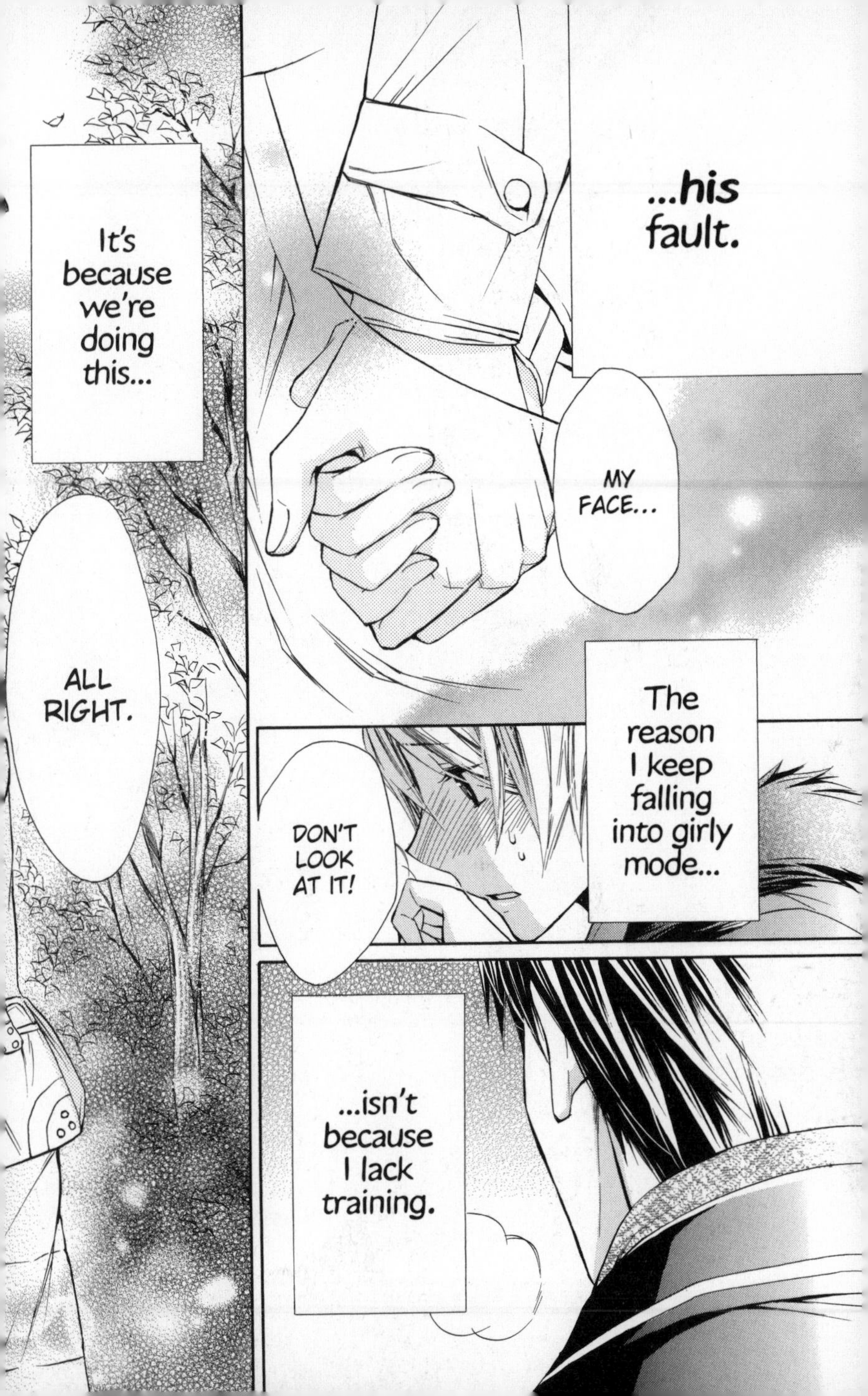
...his fault.
MY FACE...
The reason I keep falling into girly mode...
DON'T LOOK AT IT!
...isn't because I lack training.
It's because we're doing this...
ALL RIGHT.

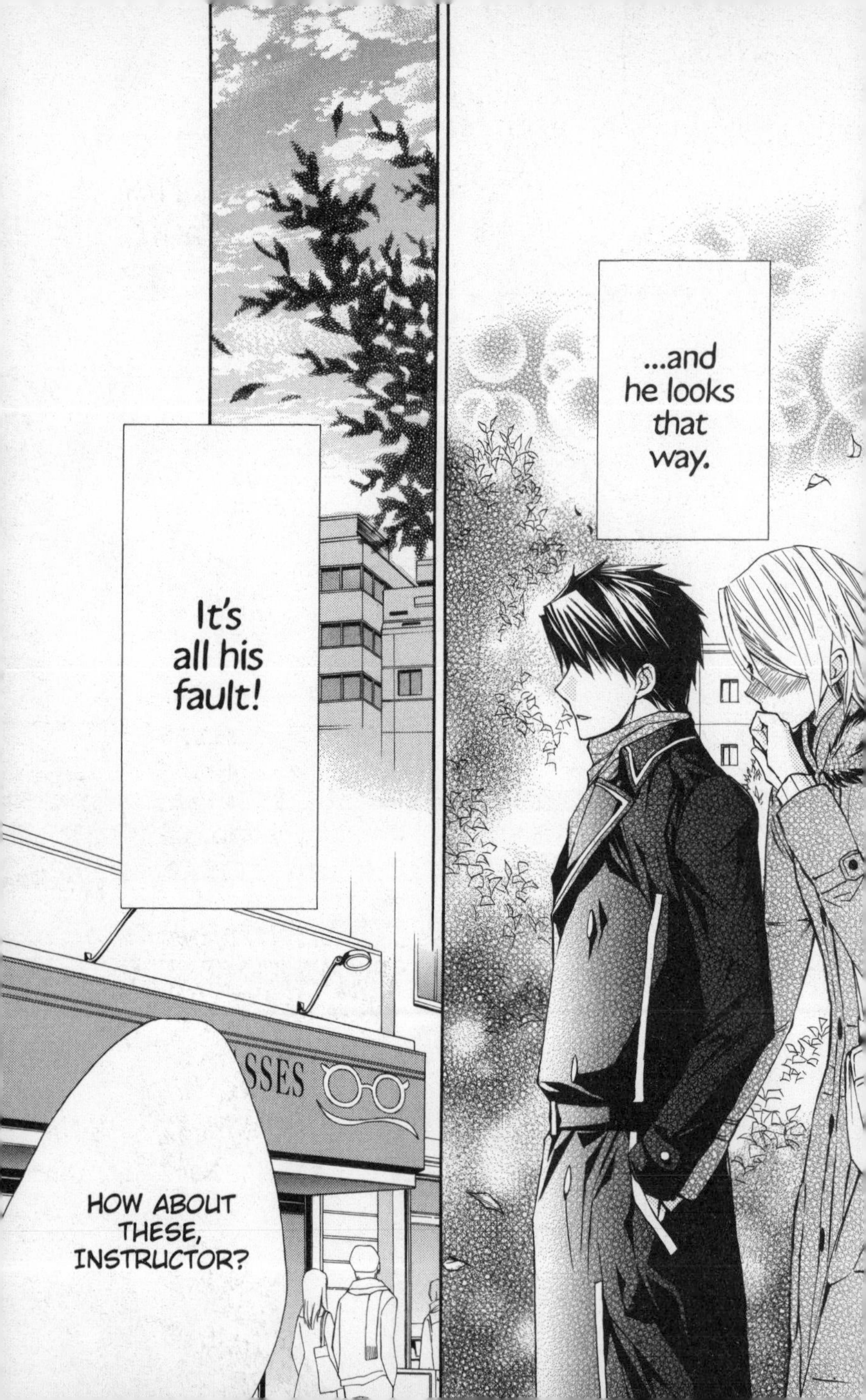
...and he looks that way.
It's all his fault!
SSES
HOW ABOUT THESE, INSTRUCTOR?

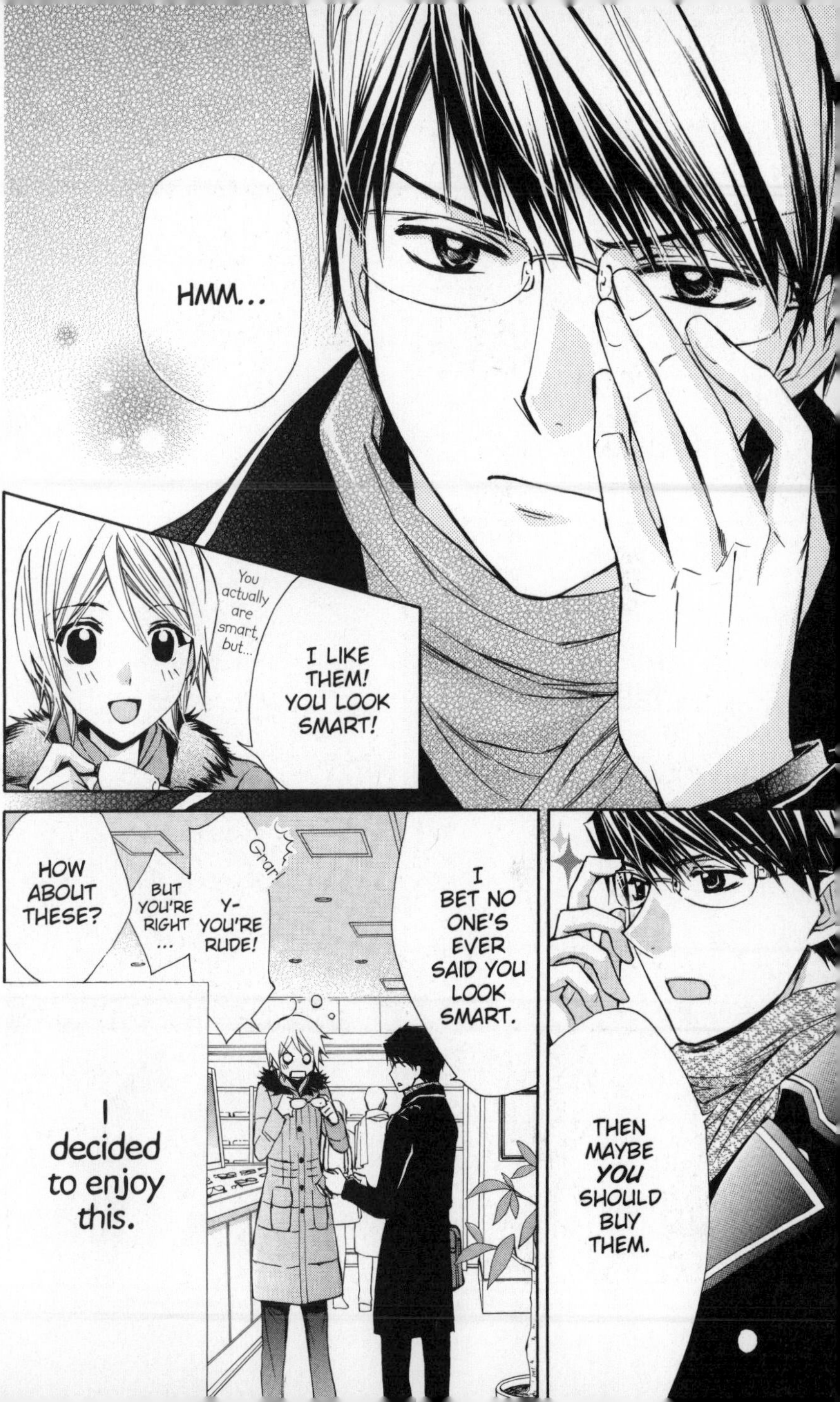
HMM...
I LIKE THEM! YOU LOOK SMART!
You actually are smart, but...
I BET NO ONE'S EVER SAID YOU LOOK SMART.
THEN MAYBE *YOU* SHOULD BUY THEM.
Y-YOU'RE RUDE!
Grar!
BUT YOU'RE RIGHT...
HOW ABOUT THESE?
I decided to enjoy this.

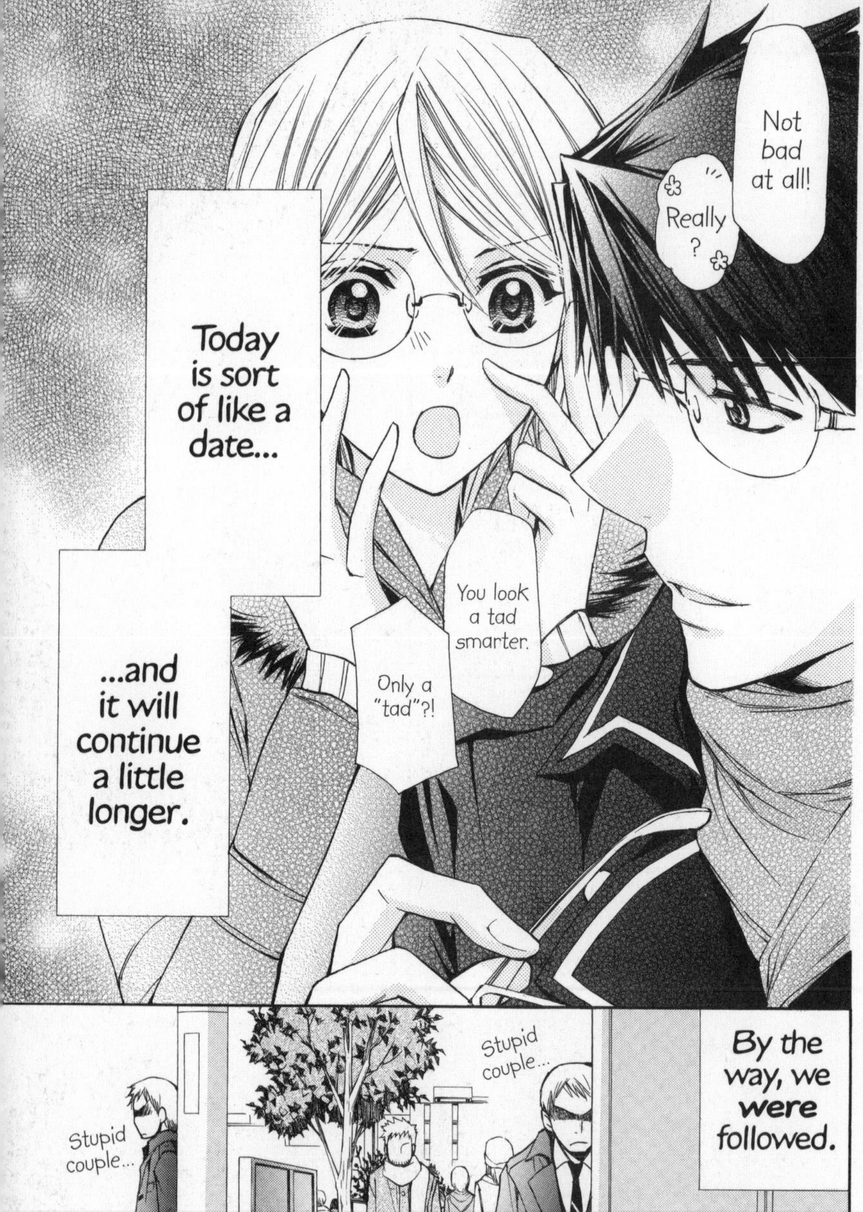
Not bad at all!
Really?
Today is sort of like a date...
You look a tad smarter.
Only a "tad"?!
...and it will continue a little longer.
By the way, we **were** followed.
Stupid couple...
Stupid couple...

Secret Admirer part II (1)

Moburo on January 15

Pre-viously on Secret Admirer...
Moburo Agohige has a crush on Iku Kasahara, but his love has no future.
He was at the station at 11 on January 15.
*Off work due to a public holiday.
Instructor Dojo!
I'm sorry I'm late!!
SNAP!
You block-head!
A date?! Are they dating?! Hold on a sec!!!
They're team-mates! And commander and subor-dinate!
They must be shopping for work or meeting to discuss something they couldn't in the office!
That's gotta be it!!
It's his little brother Mobukichi's birthday, so he's shopping for a present.
Hey, bro, I want a collectible figurine! Huh? Why're you crying?

To be continued.

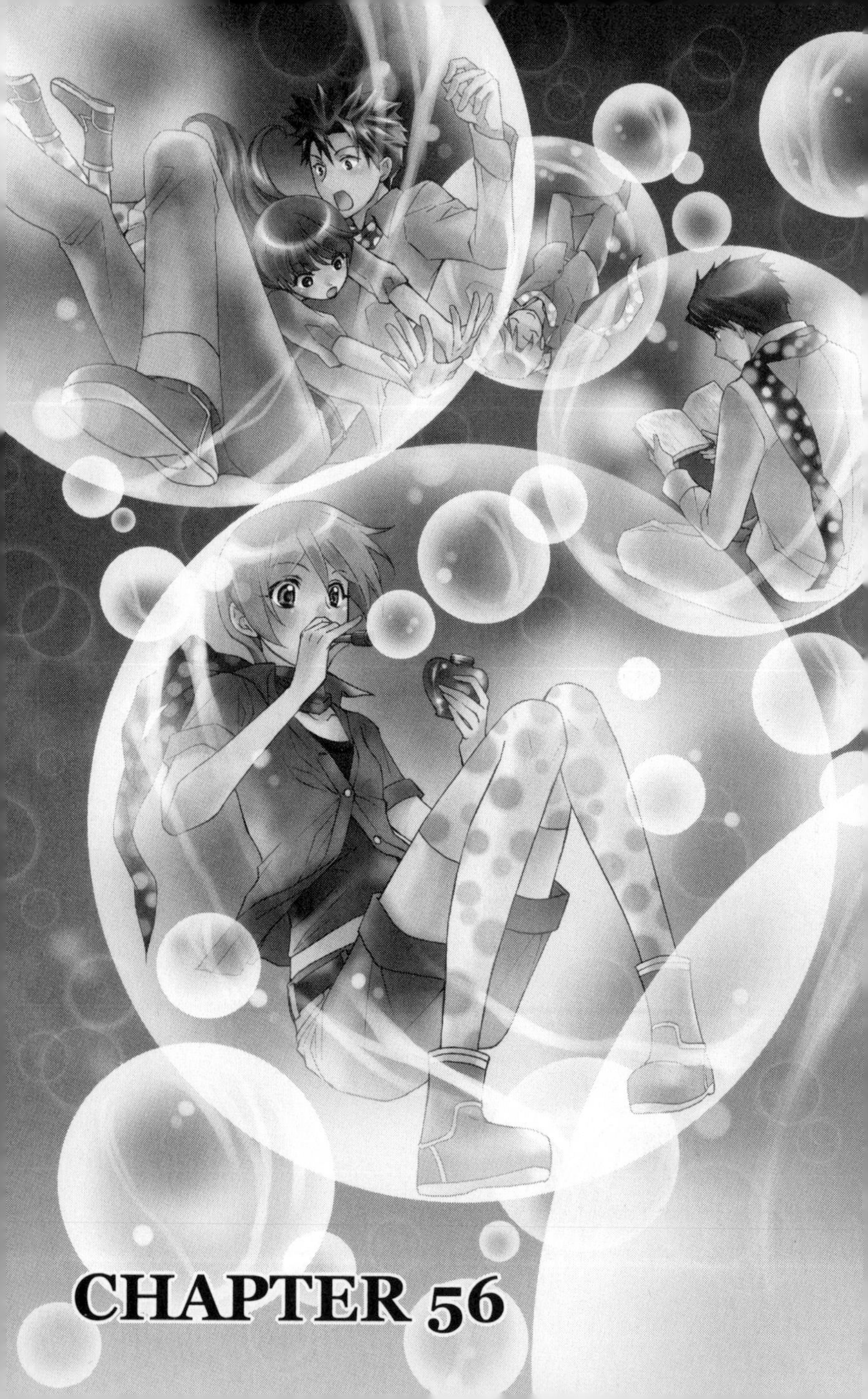

CHAPTER 56

Our first two-parter!

Secret Admirer part II (2)

Moburo on January 15

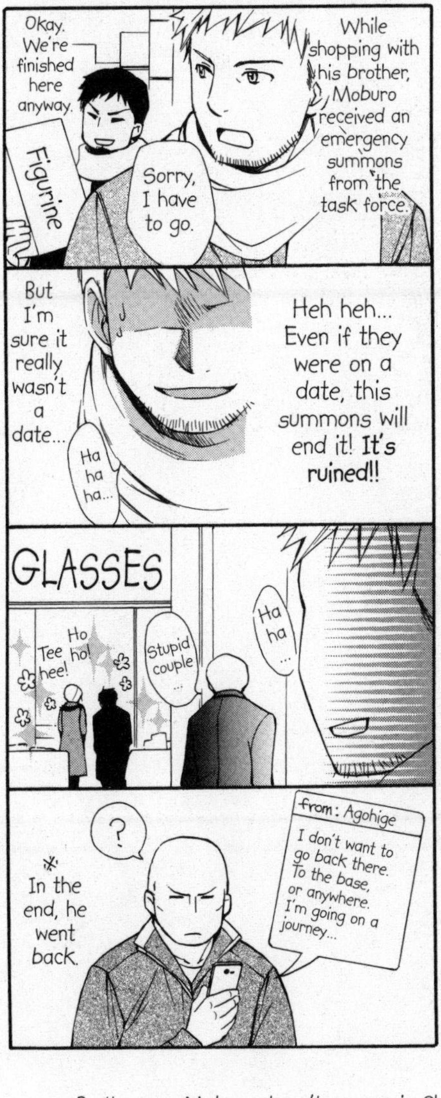

While shopping with his brother, Moburo received an emergency summons from the task force.
Okay. We're finished here anyway.
Sorry, I have to go.
Figurine
Heh heh... Even if they were on a date, this summons will end it! It's ruined!!
But I'm sure it really wasn't a date...
Ha ha ha...
Ha ha ...
Stupid couple ...
GLASSES
Ho ho!
Tee hee!
from: Agohige
I don't want to go back there. To the base, or anywhere. I'm going on a journey...
?
※ In the end, he went back.

By the way, Moburo doesn't appear in Chapter 57, so don't look for him!

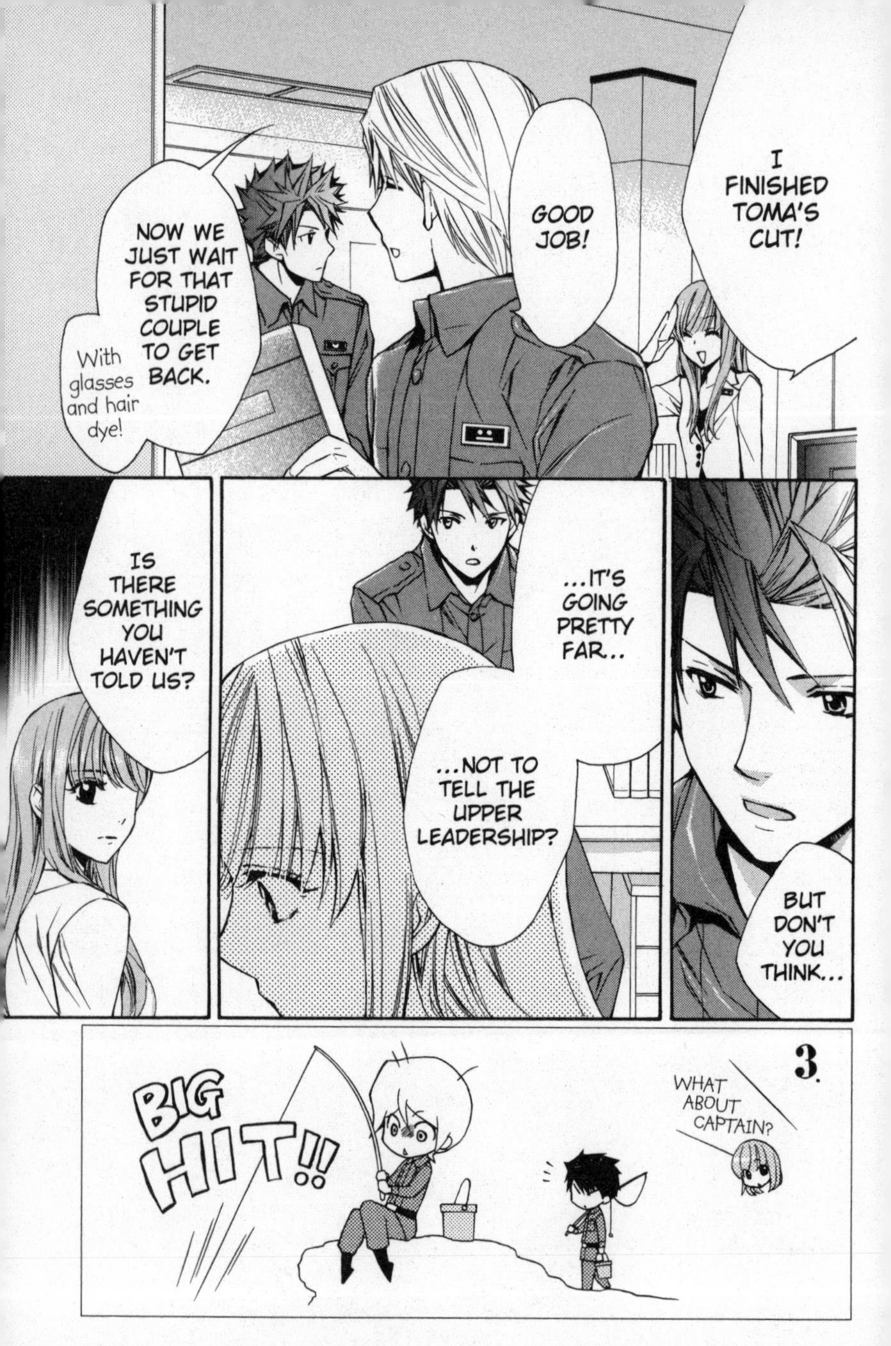
I FINISHED TOMA'S CUT!
GOOD JOB!
NOW WE JUST WAIT FOR THAT STUPID COUPLE TO GET BACK.
With glasses and hair dye!
BUT DON'T YOU THINK...
...IT'S GOING PRETTY FAR...
...NOT TO TELL THE UPPER LEADERSHIP?
IS THERE SOMETHING YOU HAVEN'T TOLD US?
3.
WHAT ABOUT CAPTAIN?
BIG HIT!!

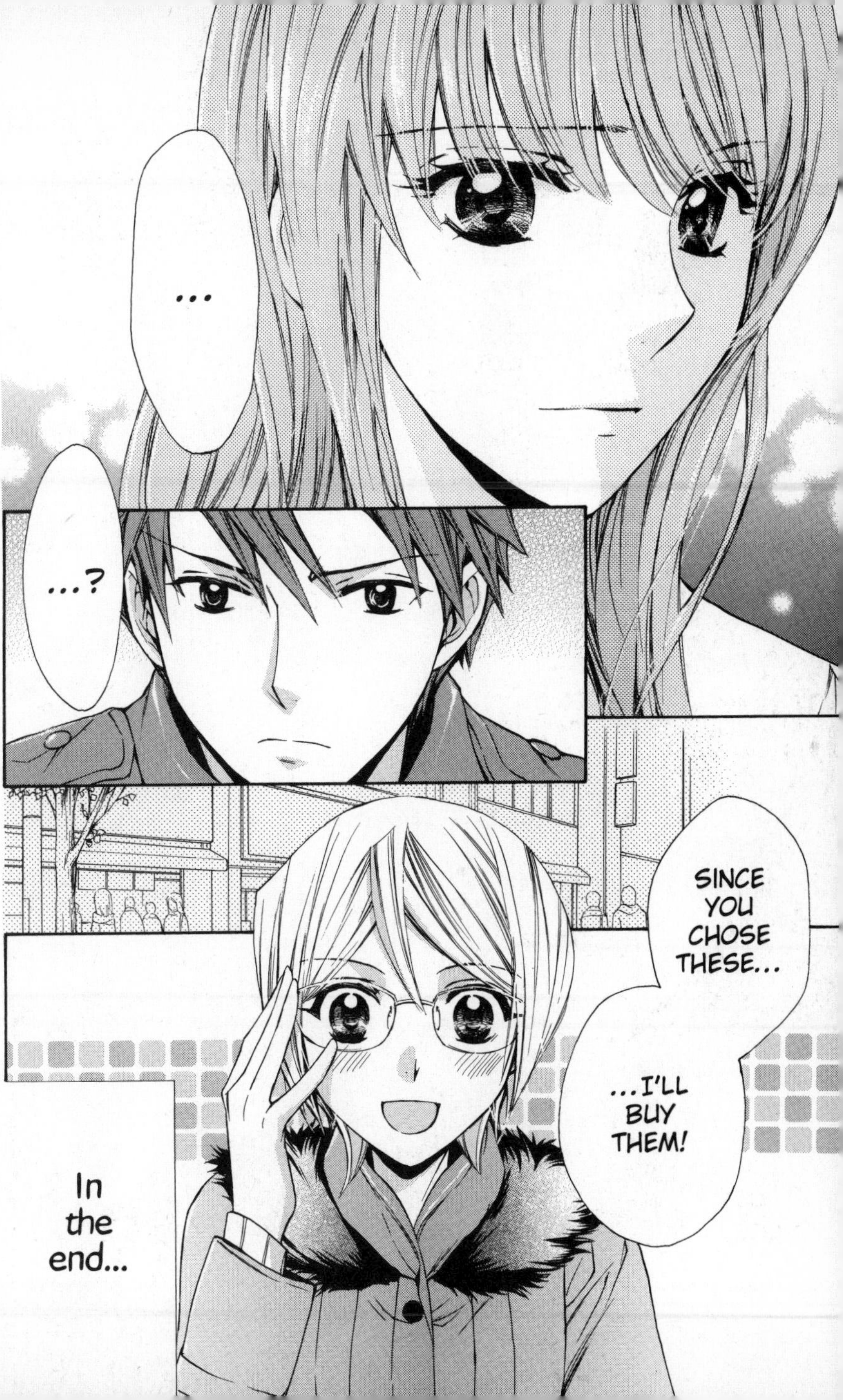
...
...?
SINCE YOU CHOSE THESE...
...I'LL BUY THEM!
In the end...

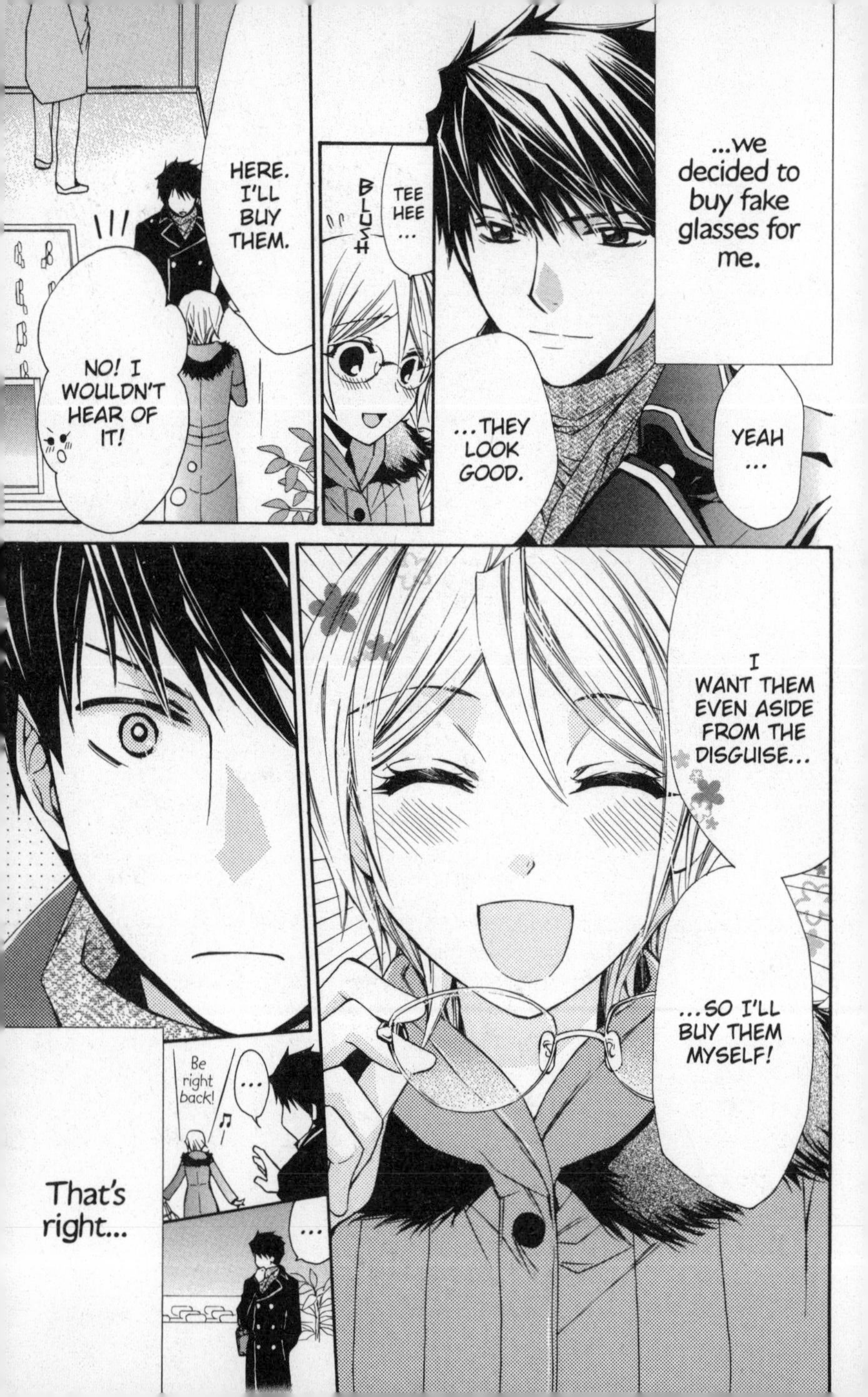
...we decided to buy fake glasses for me.
YEAH ...
...THEY LOOK GOOD.
TEE HEE ...
BLUSH
HERE. I'LL BUY THEM.
NO! I WOULDN'T HEAR OF IT!
I WANT THEM EVEN ASIDE FROM THE DISGUISE...
...SO I'LL BUY THEM MYSELF!
Be right back!
...
...
That's right...

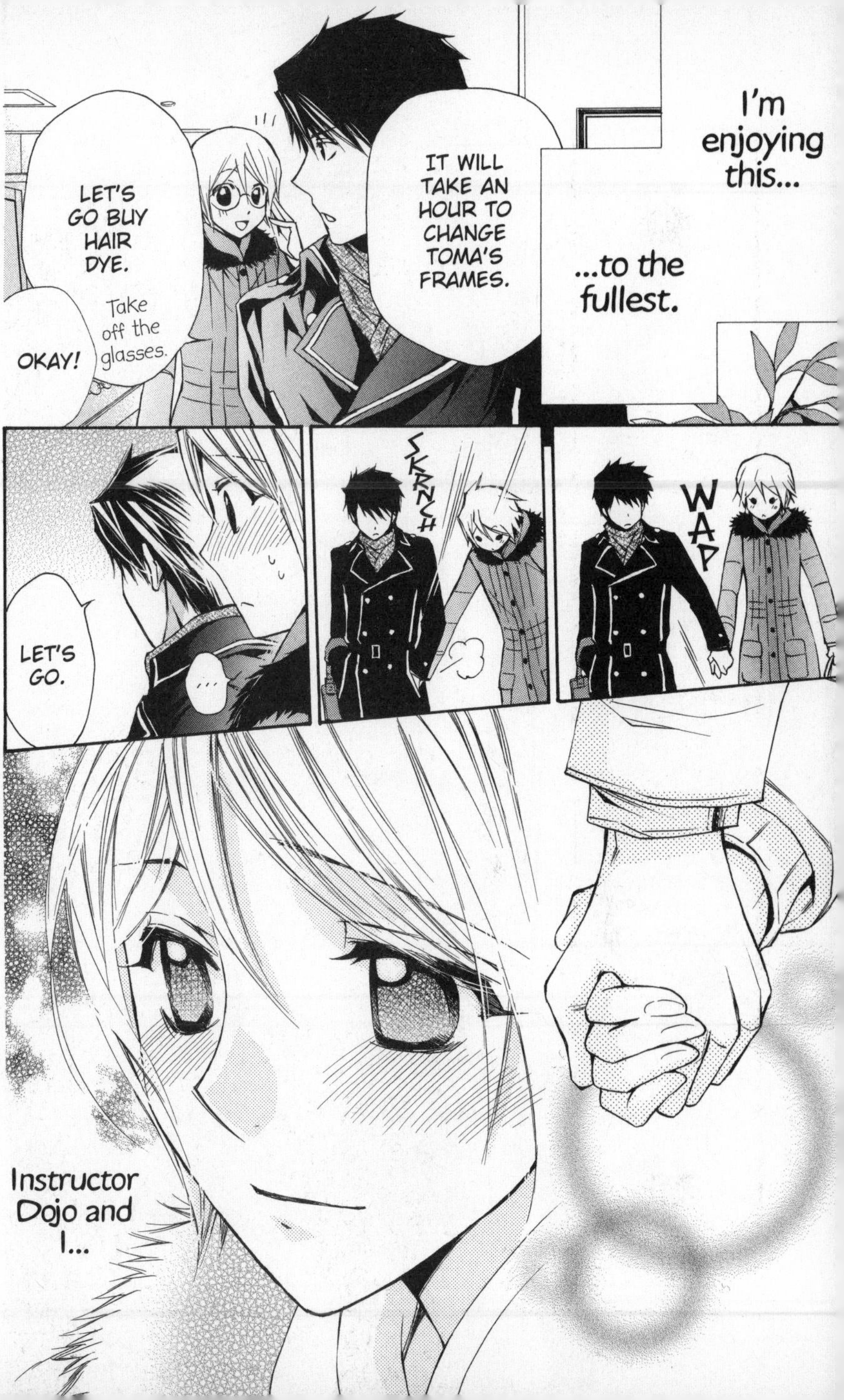
I'm enjoying this...
...to the fullest.
IT WILL TAKE AN HOUR TO CHANGE TOMA'S FRAMES.
LET'S GO BUY HAIR DYE.
Take off the glasses.
OKAY!
WAP
SKRNCH
LET'S GO.
...
Instructor Dojo and I...

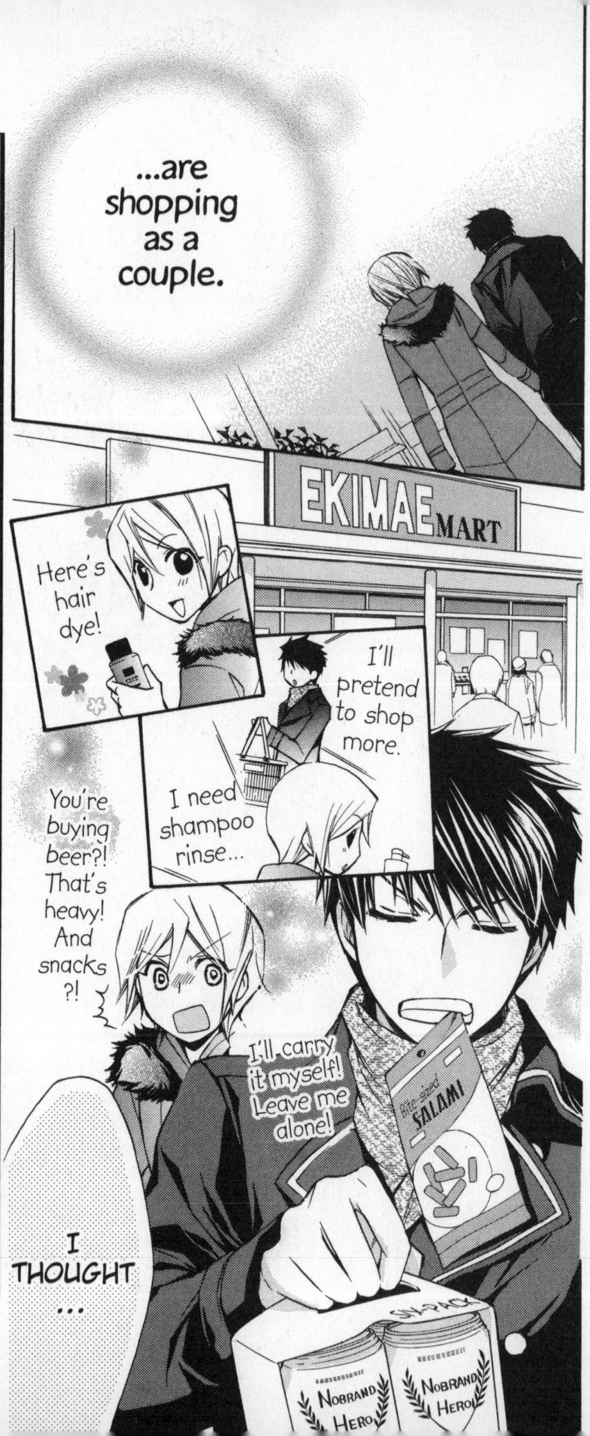
...are shopping as a couple.
EKIMAE MART
Here's hair dye!
I'll pretend to shop more.
I need shampoo rinse...
You're buying beer?! That's heavy! And snacks?!
I'll carry it myself! Leave me alone!
Bite-sized SALAMI
SIX-PACK
NOBRAND HERO
NOBRAND HERO
I THOUGHT...

3

The *Library Wars* movie finally opened in April 2013! As a fan, I enjoyed it a lot. It was great! It was thrilling and moving with perfect casting and great story development and direction. Personally, I like action movies, especially gunfights. I couldn't help but get excited (lol) to see how courageous Okada was in the last half of the movie, and I thoroughly enjoyed every bit of it!!

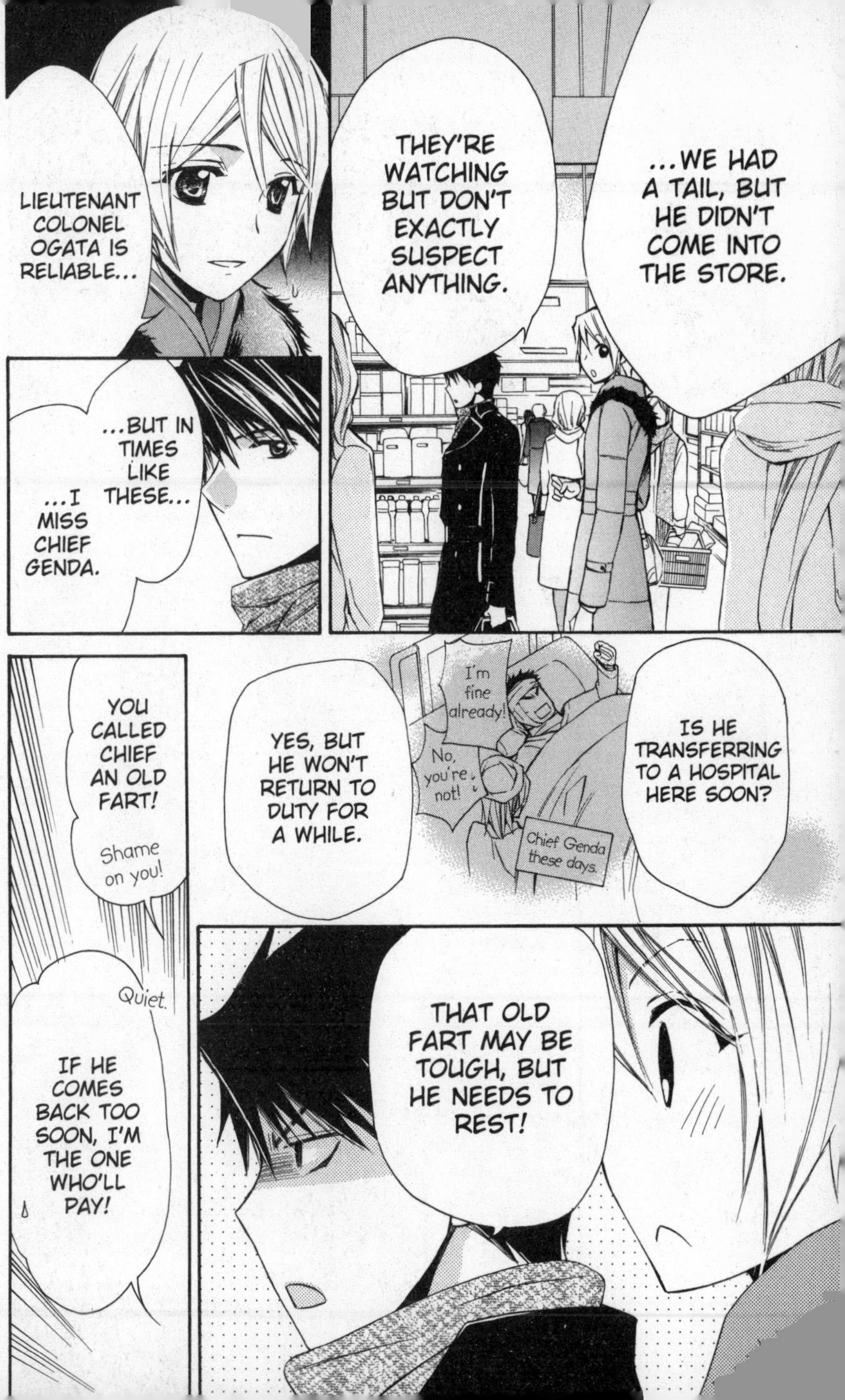
...WE HAD A TAIL, BUT HE DIDN'T COME INTO THE STORE.
THEY'RE WATCHING BUT DON'T EXACTLY SUSPECT ANYTHING.
LIEUTENANT COLONEL OGATA IS RELIABLE...
...BUT IN TIMES LIKE THESE...
...I MISS CHIEF GENDA.
IS HE TRANSFERRING TO A HOSPITAL HERE SOON?
I'm fine already!
No, you're not!
Chief Genda these days.
YES, BUT HE WON'T RETURN TO DUTY FOR A WHILE.
THAT OLD FART MAY BE TOUGH, BUT HE NEEDS TO REST!
YOU CALLED CHIEF AN OLD FART!
Shame on you!
Quiet.
IF HE COMES BACK TOO SOON, I'M THE ONE WHO'LL PAY!

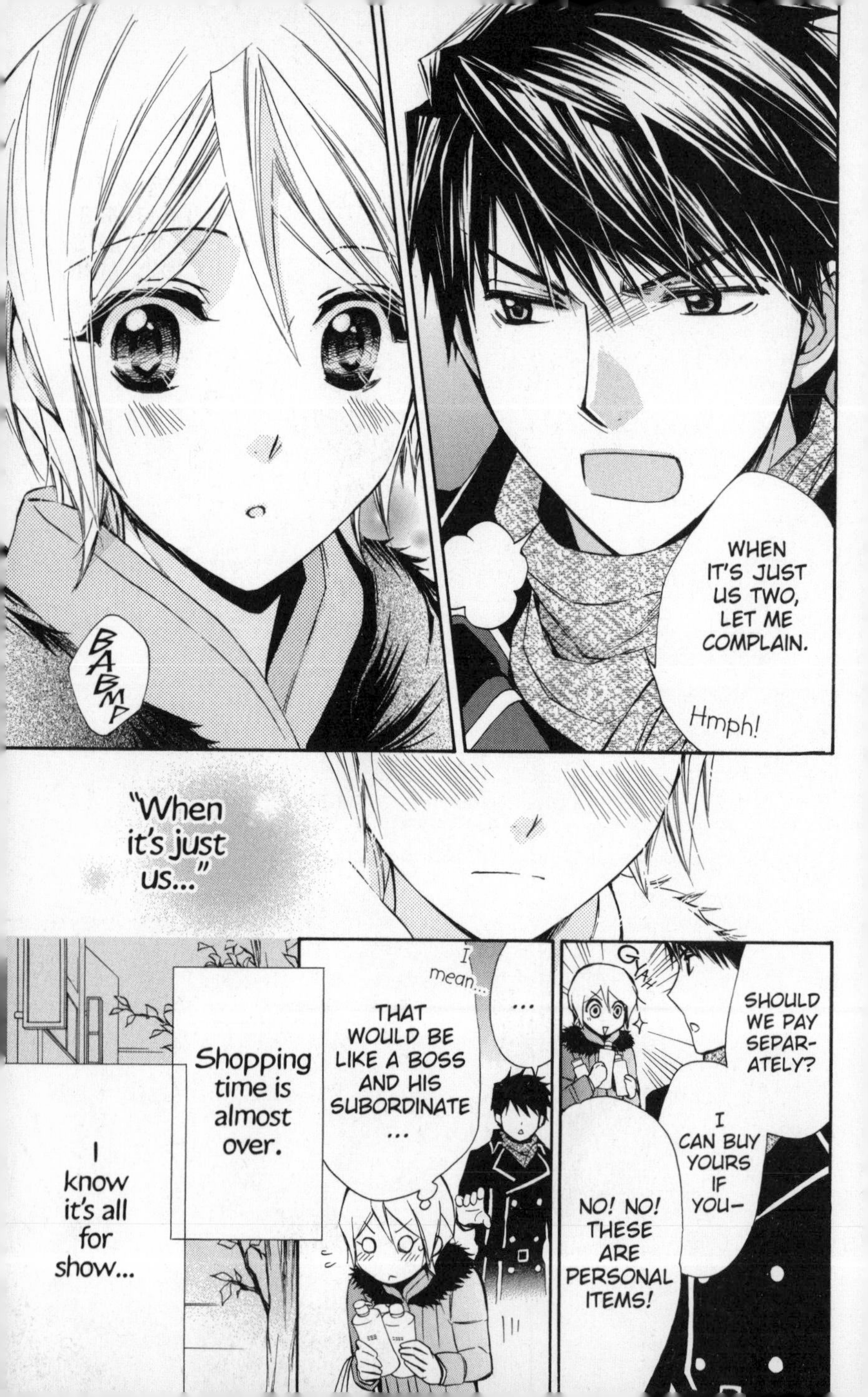
WHEN IT'S JUST US TWO, LET ME COMPLAIN.
Hmph!
BABMP
"When it's just us..."
GYAH
SHOULD WE PAY SEPARATELY?
I CAN BUY YOURS IF YOU—
NO! NO! THESE ARE PERSONAL ITEMS!
I mean...
...
THAT WOULD BE LIKE A BOSS AND HIS SUBORDINATE ...
Shopping time is almost over.
I know it's all for show...

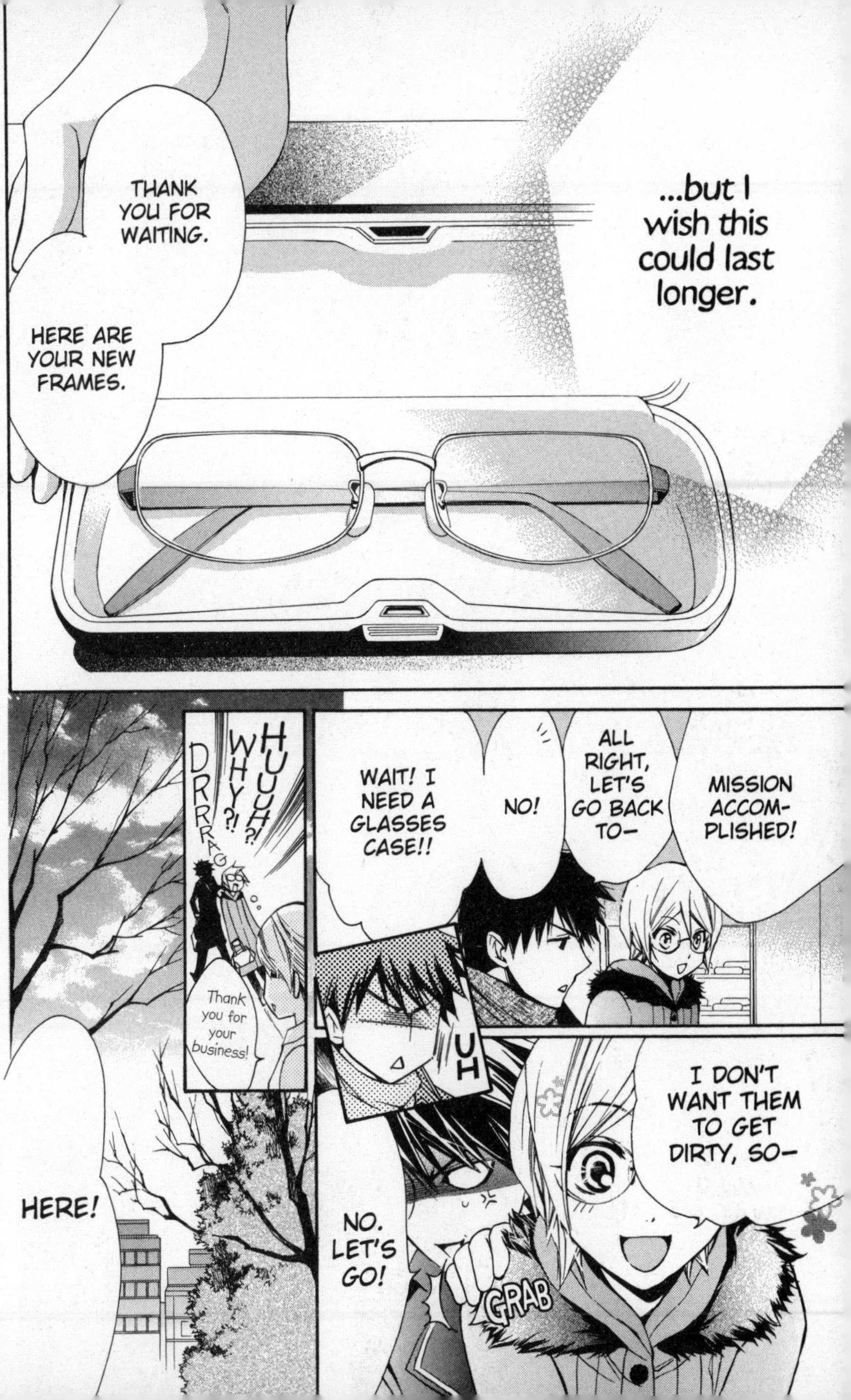
...but I wish this could last longer.
THANK YOU FOR WAITING.
HERE ARE YOUR NEW FRAMES.
MISSION ACCOMPLISHED!
ALL RIGHT, LET'S GO BACK TO—
NO!
WAIT! I NEED A GLASSES CASE!!
UH
I DON'T WANT THEM TO GET DIRTY, SO—
GRAB
NO. LET'S GO!
HUUUH?!
WHY?!
DRRRAG
Thank you for your business!
HERE!

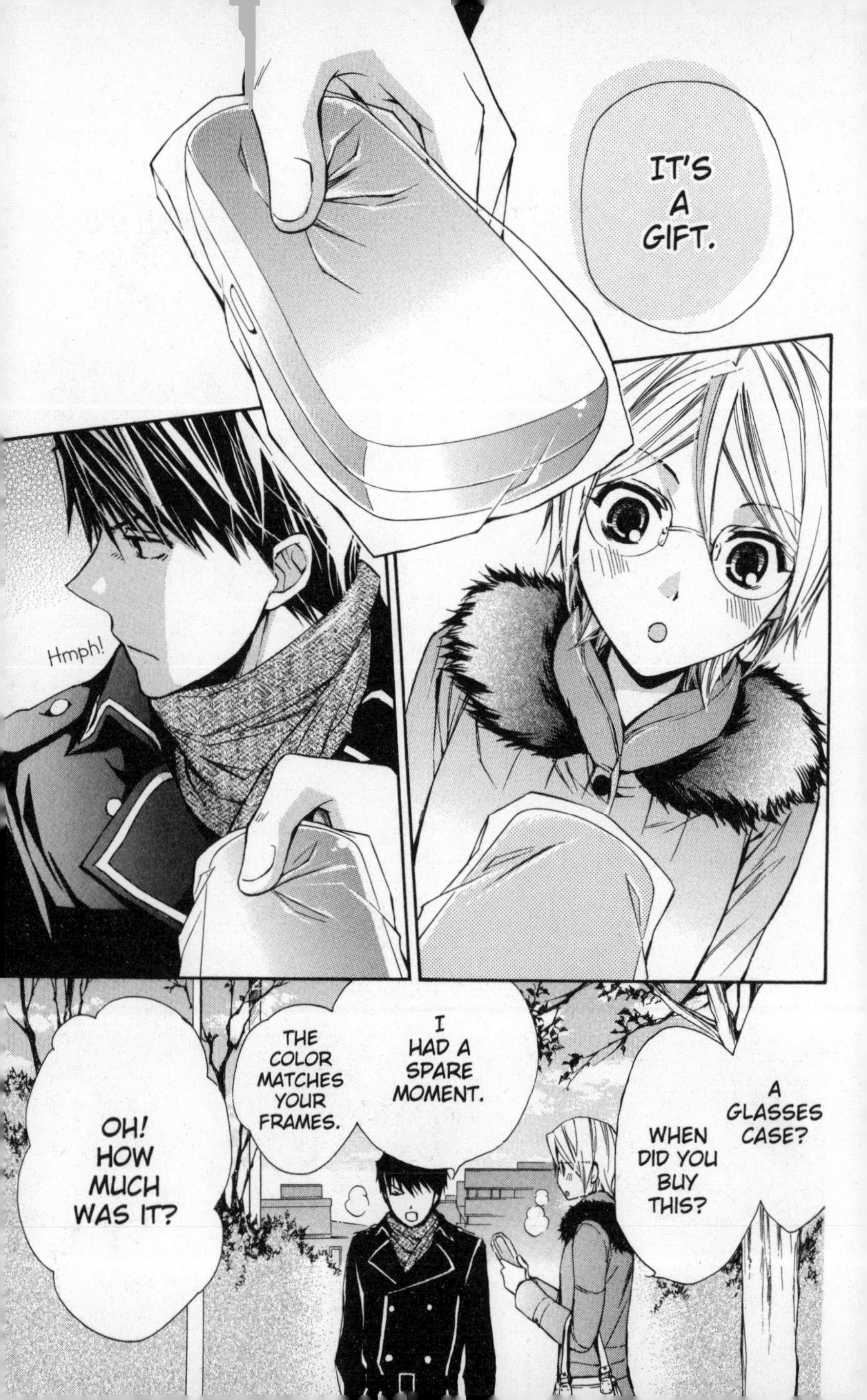
IT'S A GIFT.
Hmph!
A GLASSES CASE?
WHEN DID YOU BUY THIS?
I HAD A SPARE MOMENT.
THE COLOR MATCHES YOUR FRAMES.
OH! HOW MUCH WAS IT?

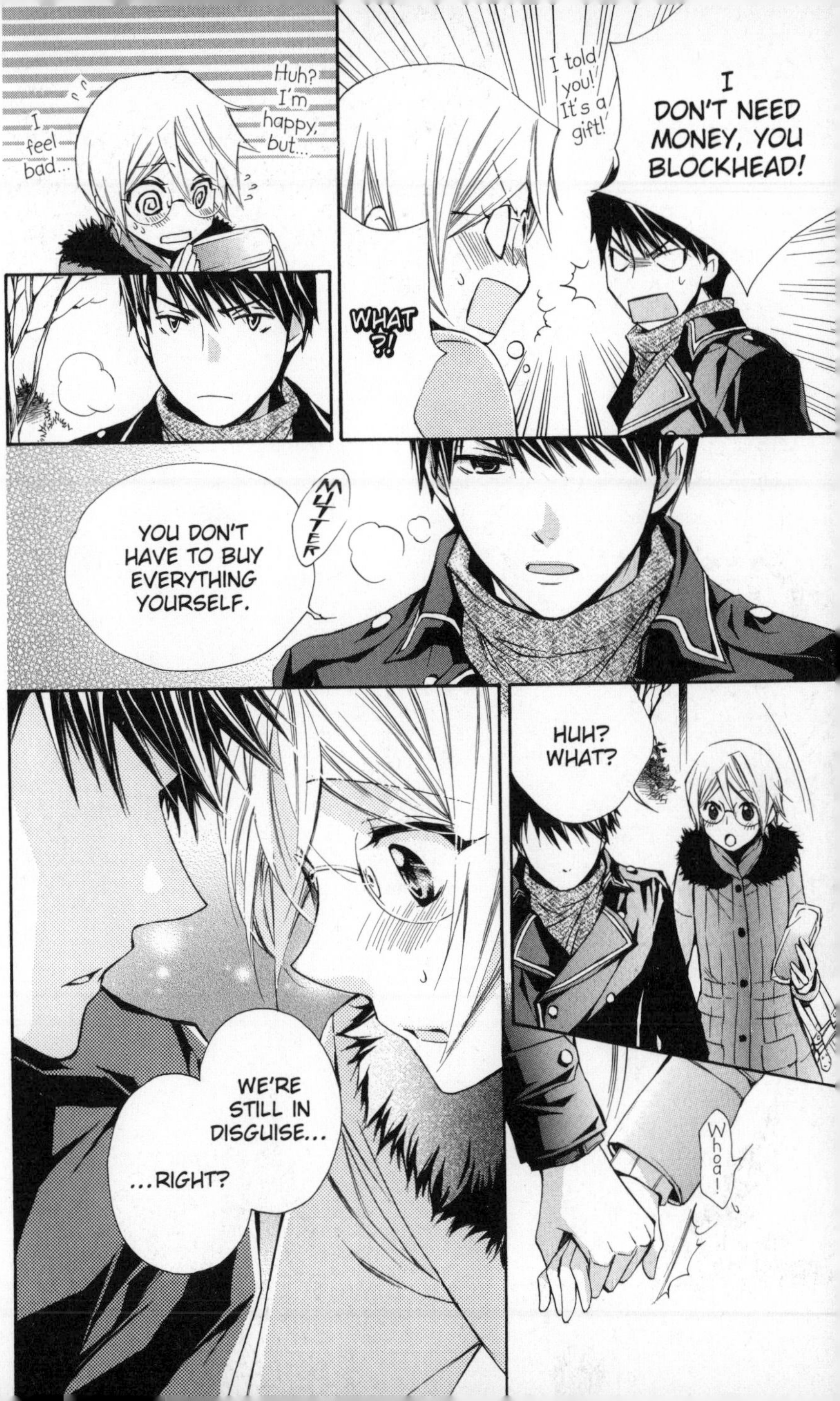
I DON'T NEED MONEY, YOU BLOCKHEAD!
I told you! It's a gift!
WHAT ?!
Huh? I'm happy, but...
I feel bad...
MUTTER
YOU DON'T HAVE TO BUY EVERYTHING YOURSELF.
HUH? WHAT?
Whoa!
WE'RE STILL IN DISGUISE...
...RIGHT?

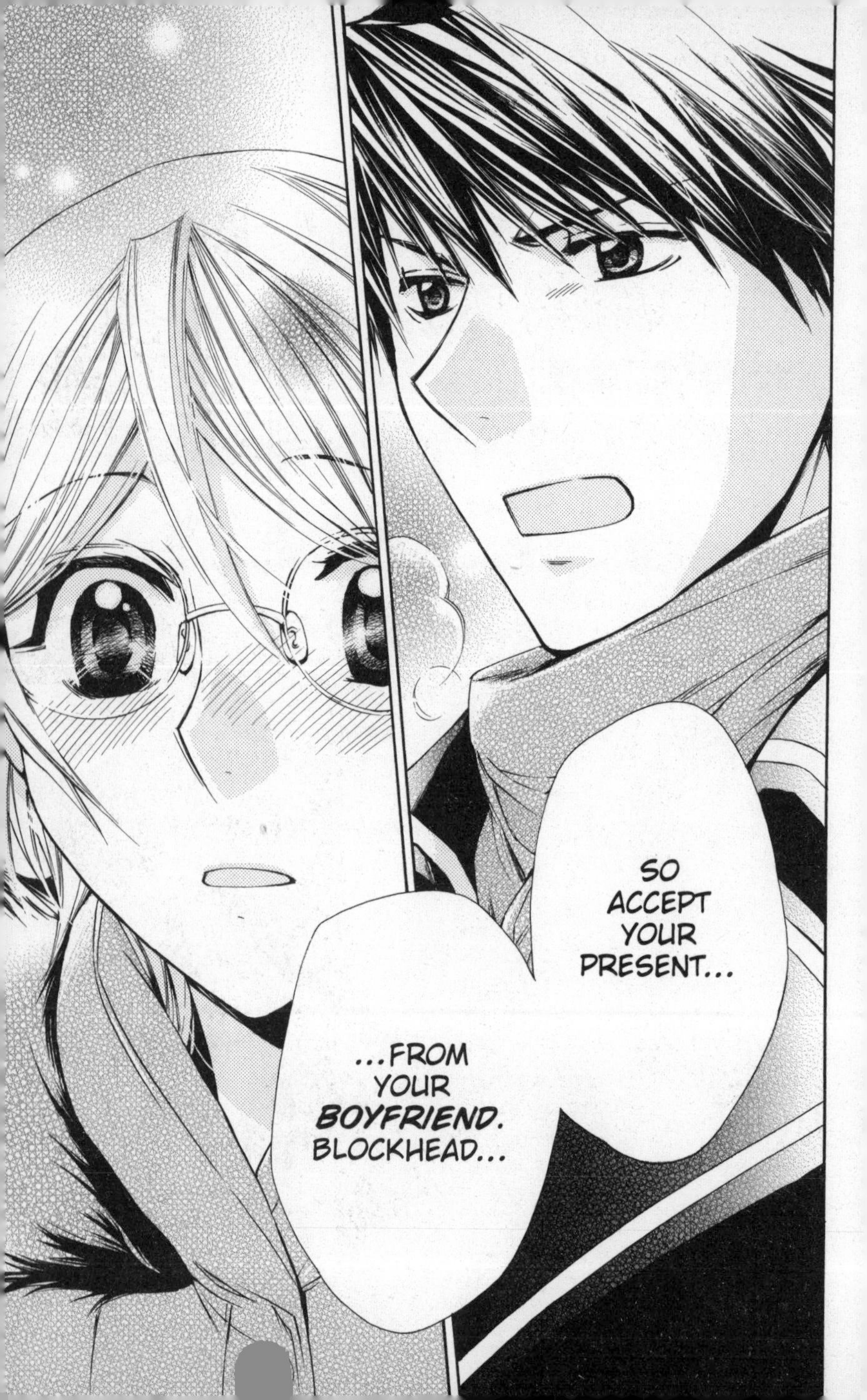
SO ACCEPT YOUR PRESENT...
...FROM YOUR *BOYFRIEND*. BLOCKHEAD...

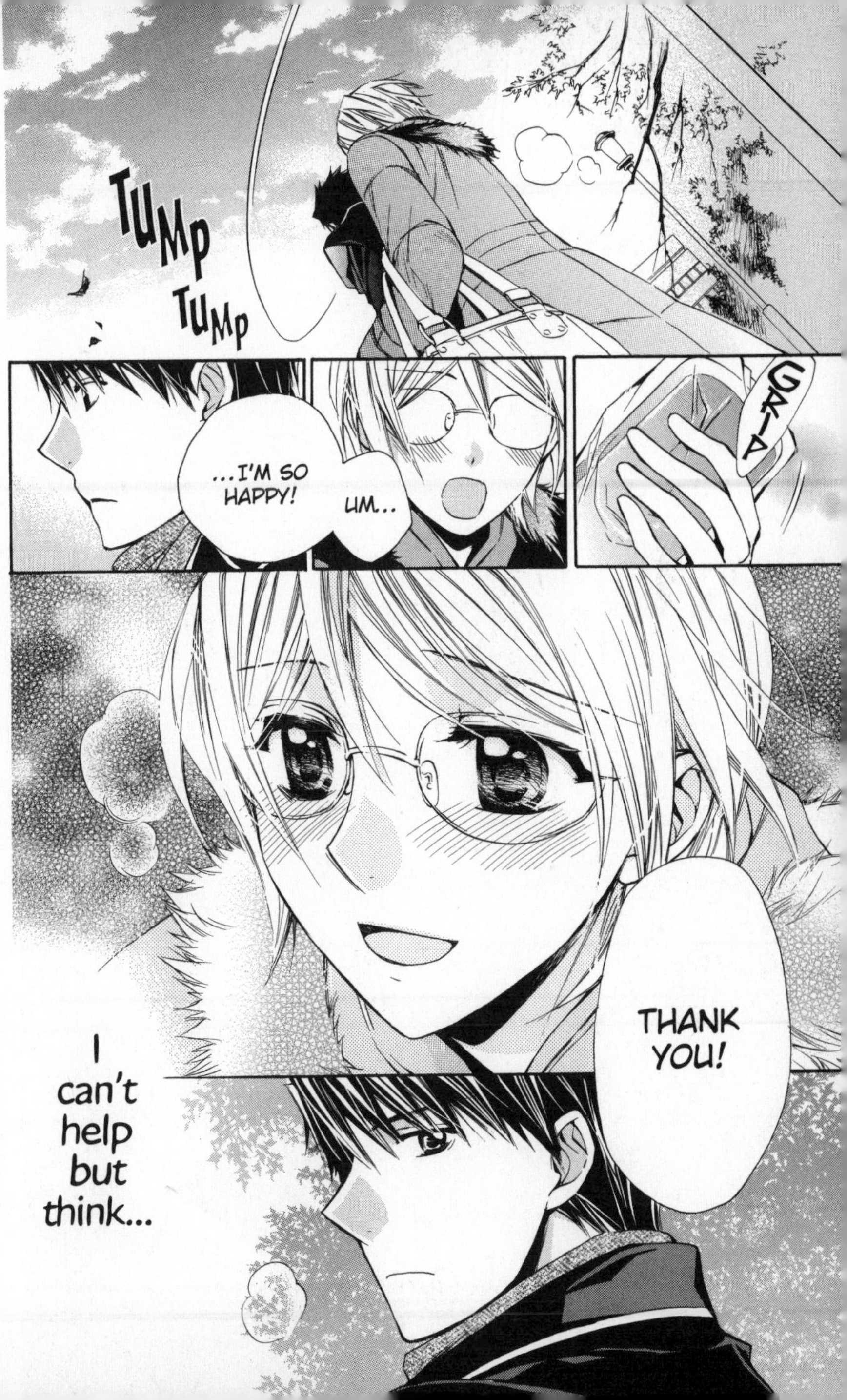
TUMP TUMP
GRIP
UM...
...I'M SO HAPPY!
THANK YOU!
I can't help but think...

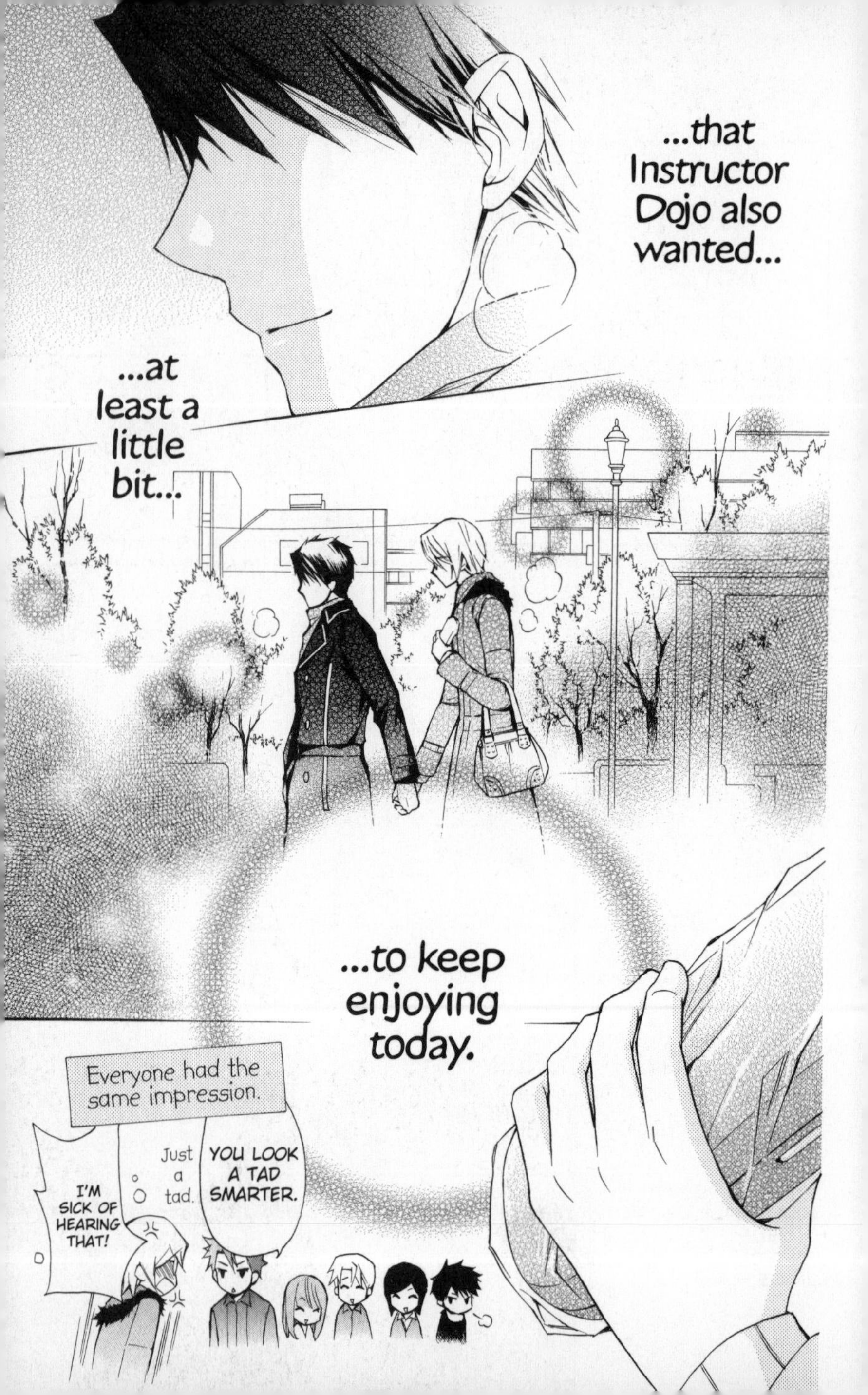
...that Instructor Dojo also wanted...
...at least a little bit...
...to keep enjoying today.
Everyone had the same impression.
YOU LOOK A TAD SMARTER.
Just a tad.
I'M SICK OF HEARING THAT!

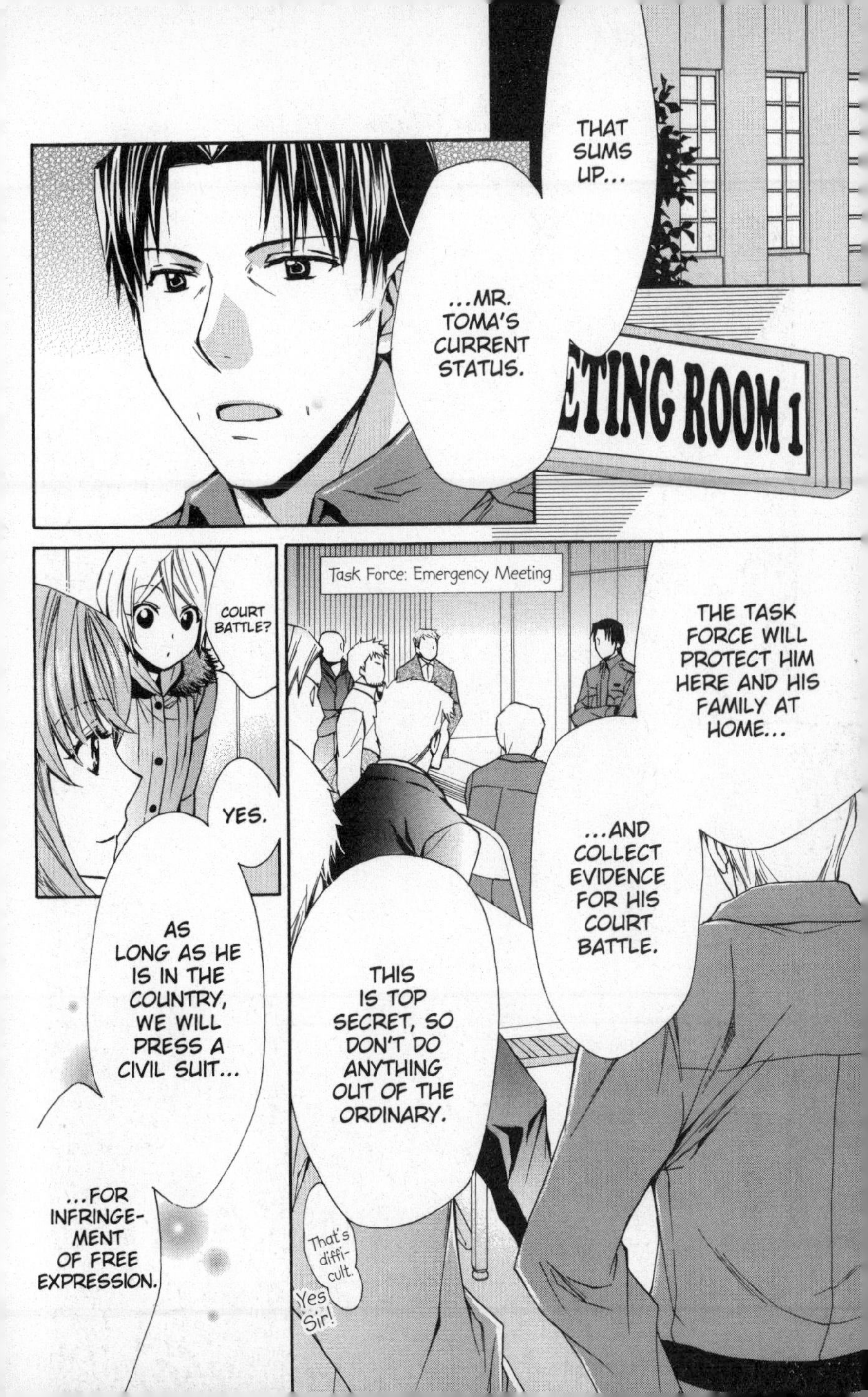
THAT SUMS UP...
ETING ROOM 1
...MR. TOMA'S CURRENT STATUS.
Task Force: Emergency Meeting
THE TASK FORCE WILL PROTECT HIM HERE AND HIS FAMILY AT HOME...
...AND COLLECT EVIDENCE FOR HIS COURT BATTLE.
THIS IS TOP SECRET, SO DON'T DO ANYTHING OUT OF THE ORDINARY.
That's diffi-cult.
Yes Sir!
COURT BATTLE?
YES.
AS LONG AS HE IS IN THE COUNTRY, WE WILL PRESS A CIVIL SUIT...
...FOR INFRINGE-MENT OF FREE EXPRESSION.

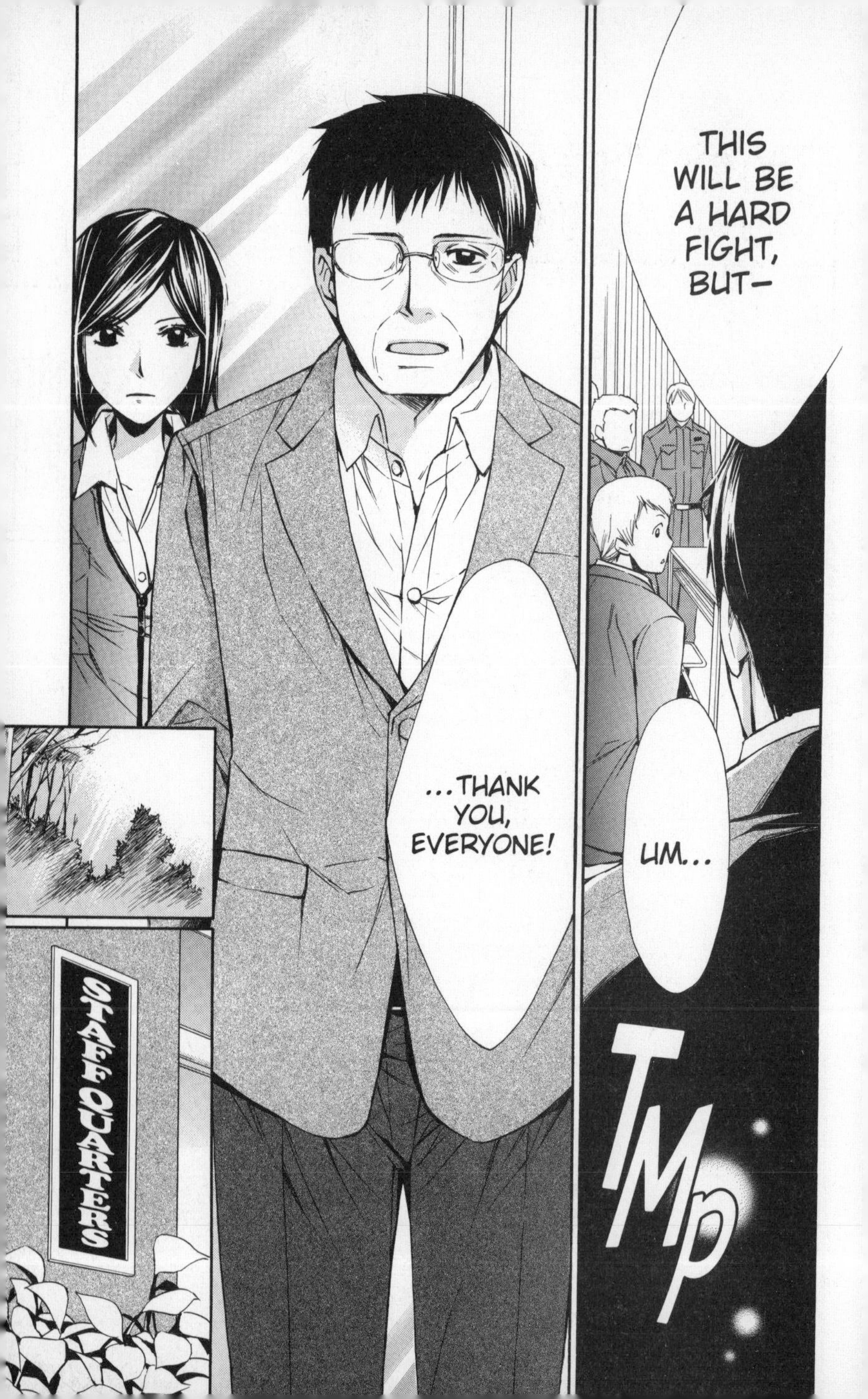
THIS WILL BE A HARD FIGHT, BUT–
UM...
TMP
...THANK YOU, EVERYONE!
STAFF QUARTERS

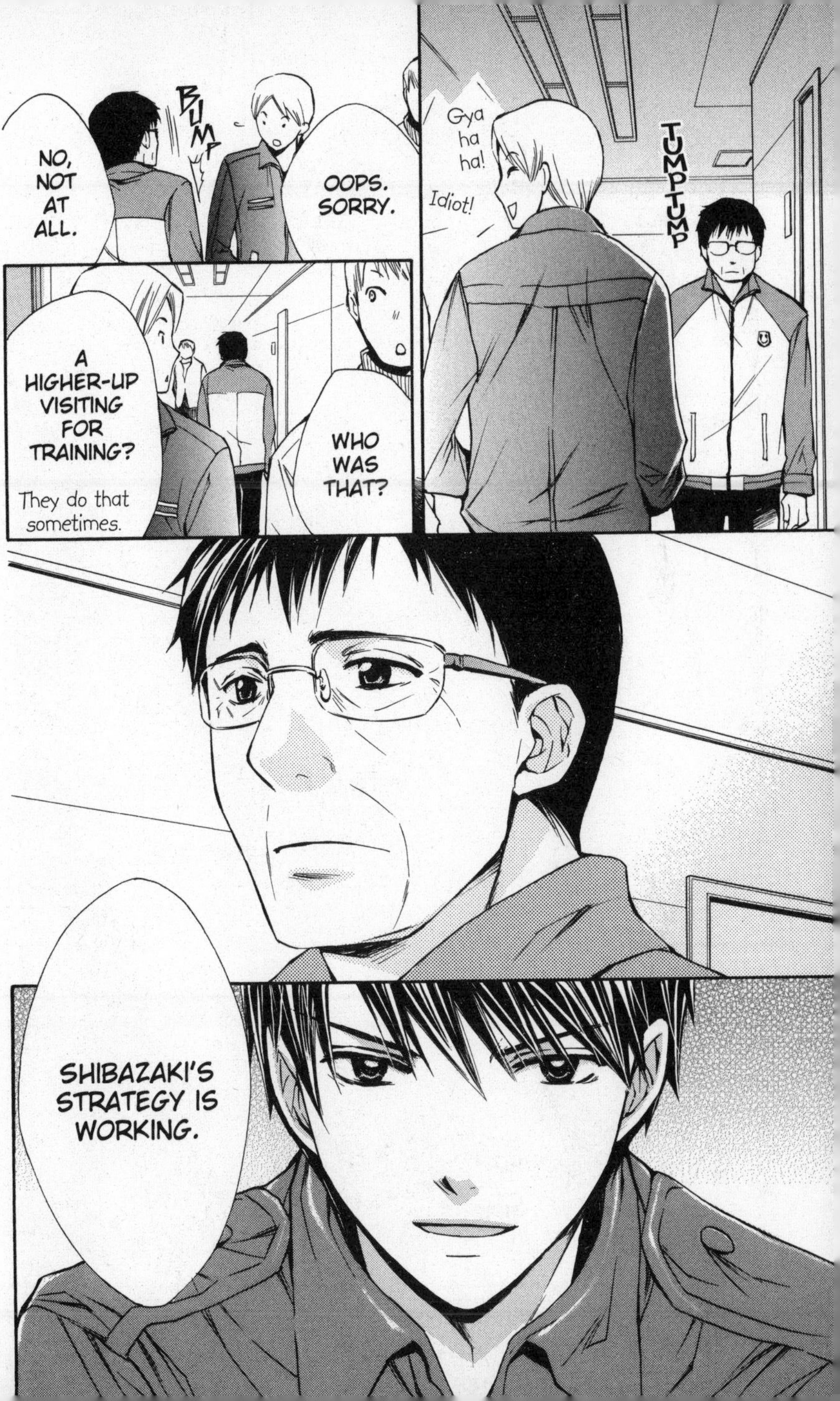
Gya ha ha!
Idiot!
TUMPTUMP
BUMP
OOPS. SORRY.
NO, NOT AT ALL.
WHO WAS THAT?
A HIGHER-UP VISITING FOR TRAINING?
They do that sometimes.
SHIBAZAKI'S STRATEGY IS WORKING.

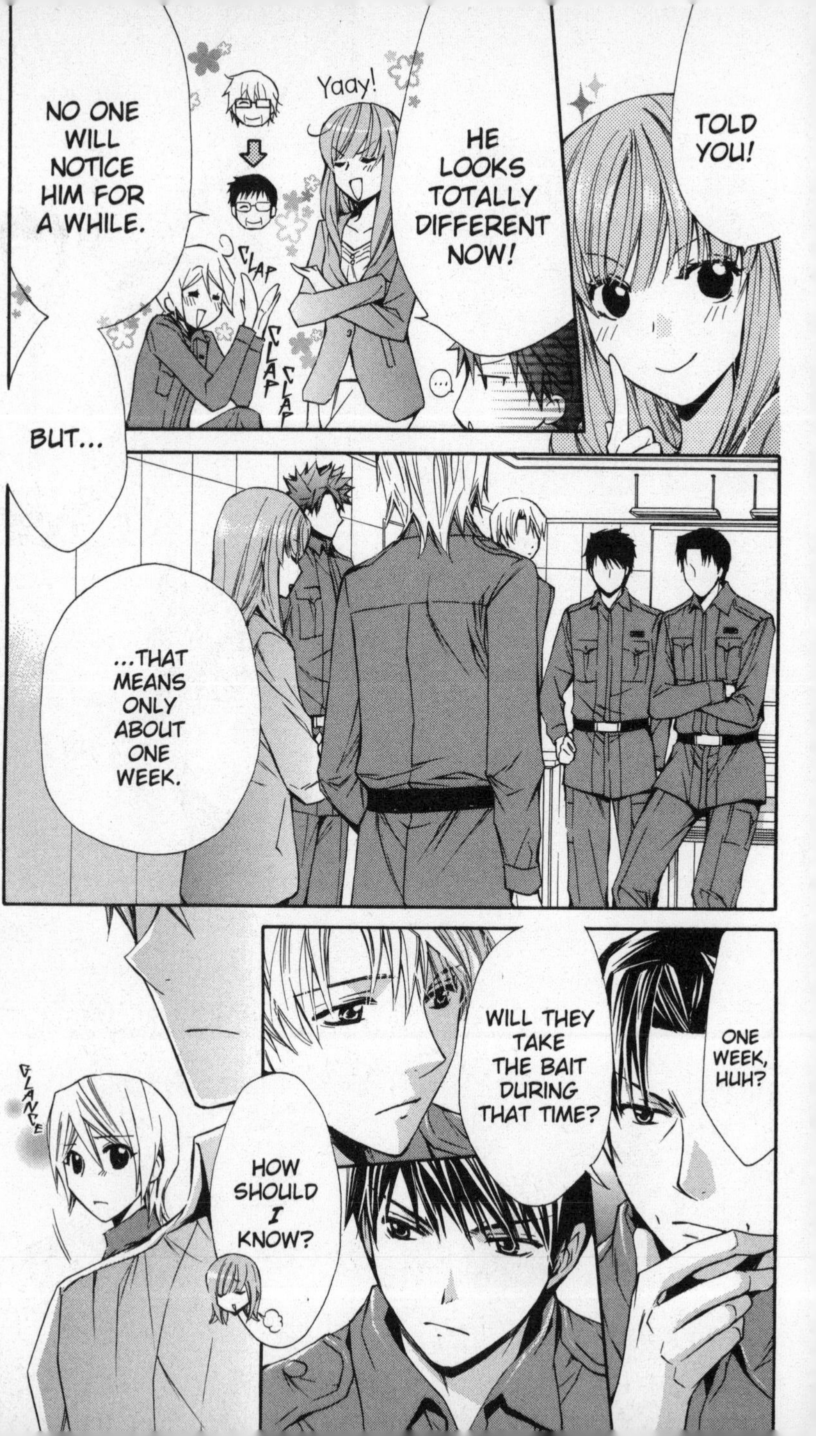
TOLD YOU!
HE LOOKS TOTALLY DIFFERENT NOW!
Yaay!
CLAP
CLAP CLAP CLAP
...
NO ONE WILL NOTICE HIM FOR A WHILE.
BUT...
...THAT MEANS ONLY ABOUT ONE WEEK.
ONE WEEK, HUH?
WILL THEY TAKE THE BAIT DURING THAT TIME?
HOW SHOULD I KNOW?
GLANCE

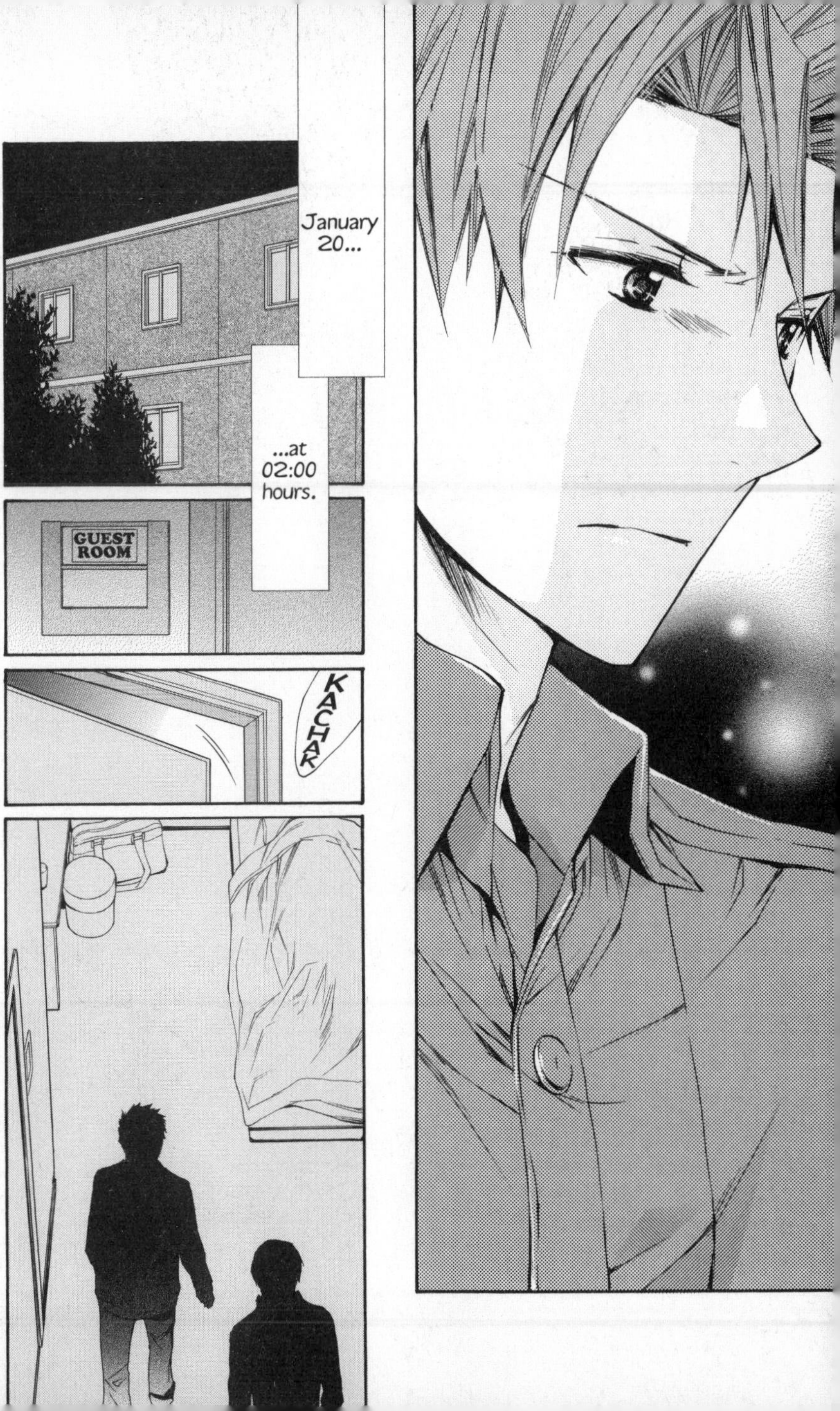
January 20...
...at 02:00 hours.
GUEST ROOM
KACHAK

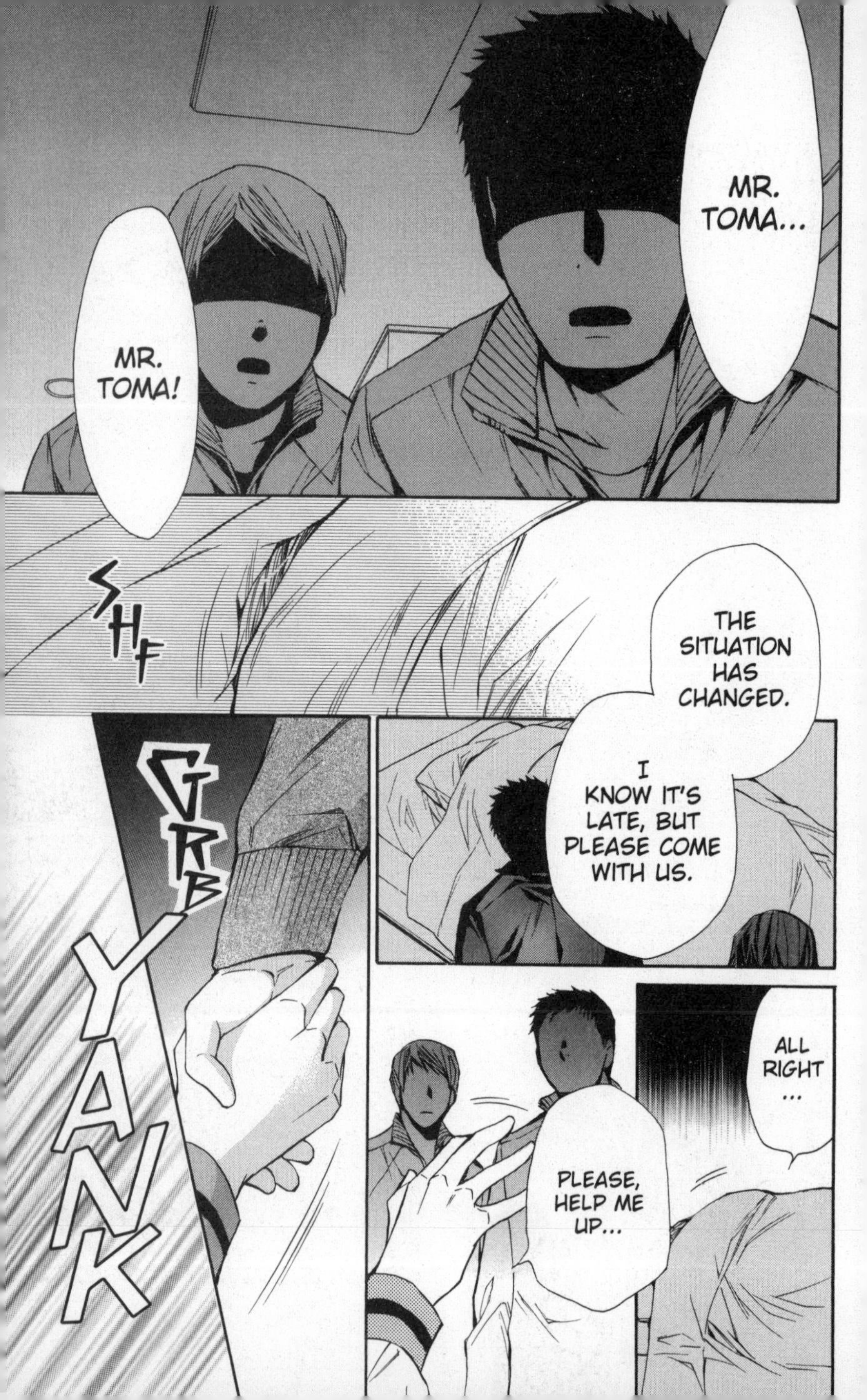
MR. TOMA...
MR. TOMA!
SHF
THE SITUATION HAS CHANGED.
I KNOW IT'S LATE, BUT PLEASE COME WITH US.
ALL RIGHT...
PLEASE, HELP ME UP...
GRB
YANK

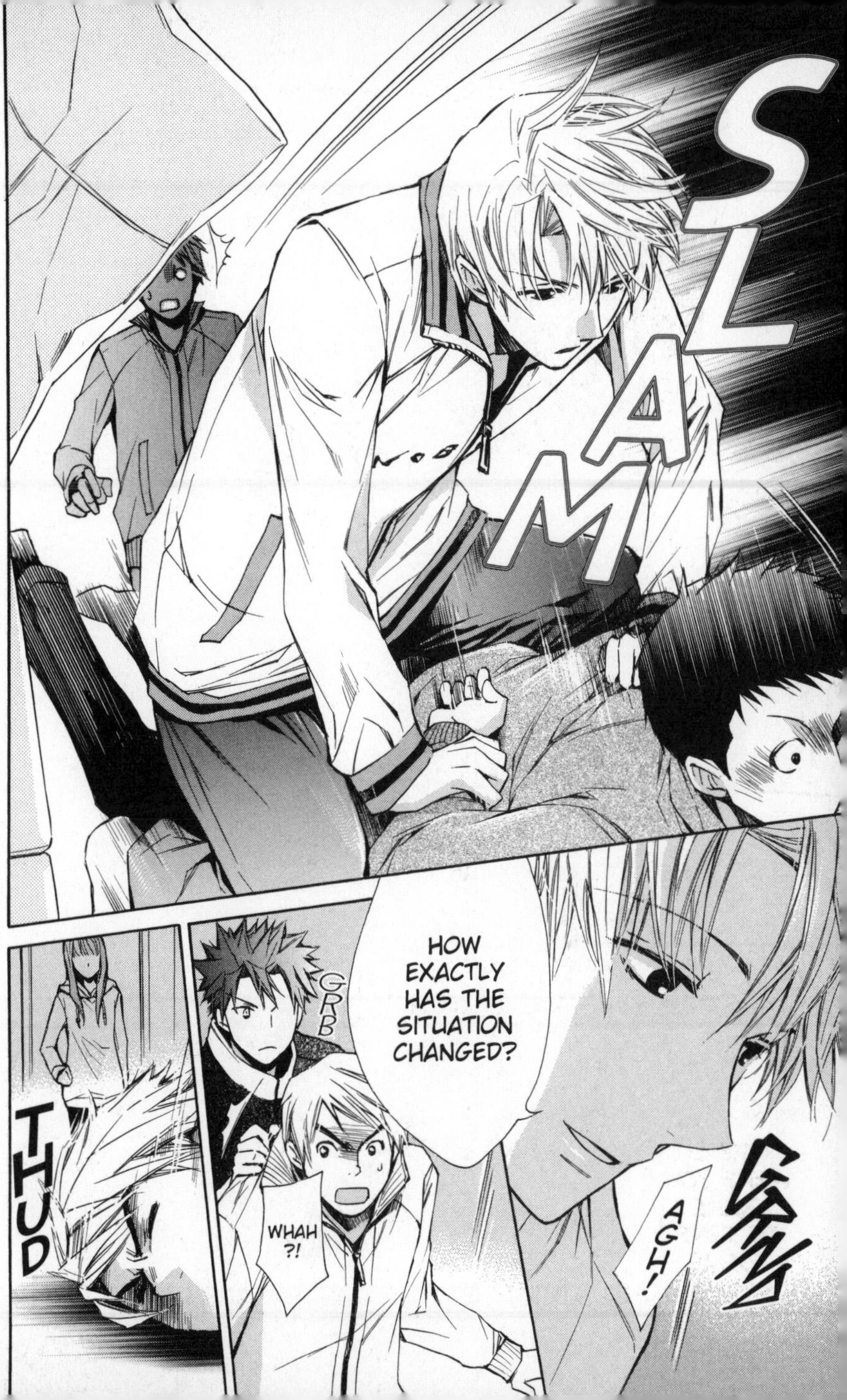
SLAM
HOW EXACTLY HAS THE SITUATION CHANGED?
AGH!
GRB
WHAH ?!
THUD

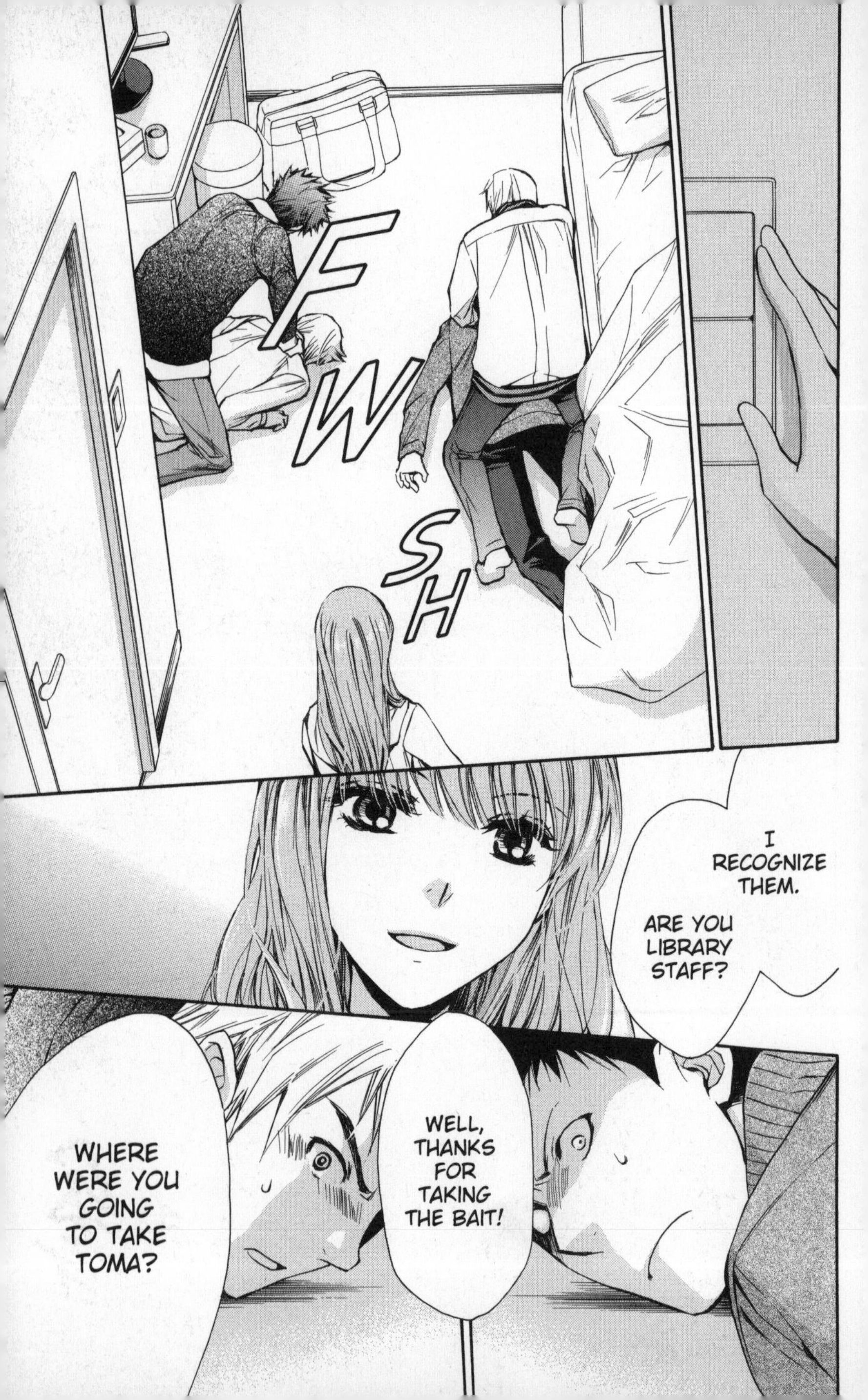
FWSH
I RECOGNIZE THEM.
ARE YOU LIBRARY STAFF?
WELL, THANKS FOR TAKING THE BAIT!
WHERE WERE YOU GOING TO TAKE TOMA?

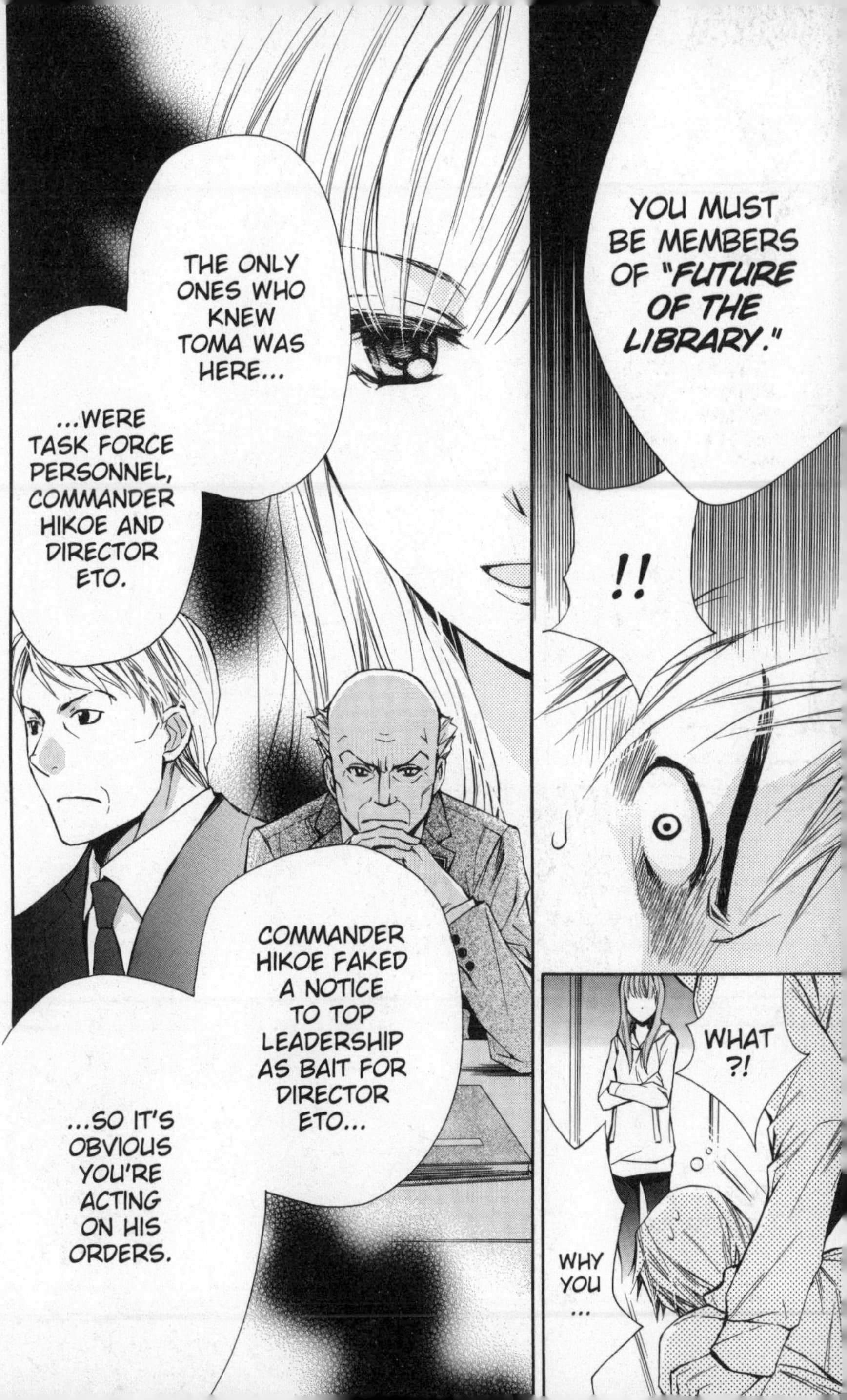
YOU MUST BE MEMBERS OF "FUTURE OF THE LIBRARY."
!!
WHAT ?!
WHY YOU ...
THE ONLY ONES WHO KNEW TOMA WAS HERE...
...WERE TASK FORCE PERSONNEL, COMMANDER HIKOE AND DIRECTOR ETO.
COMMANDER HIKOE FAKED A NOTICE TO TOP LEADERSHIP AS BAIT FOR DIRECTOR ETO...
...SO IT'S OBVIOUS YOU'RE ACTING ON HIS ORDERS.

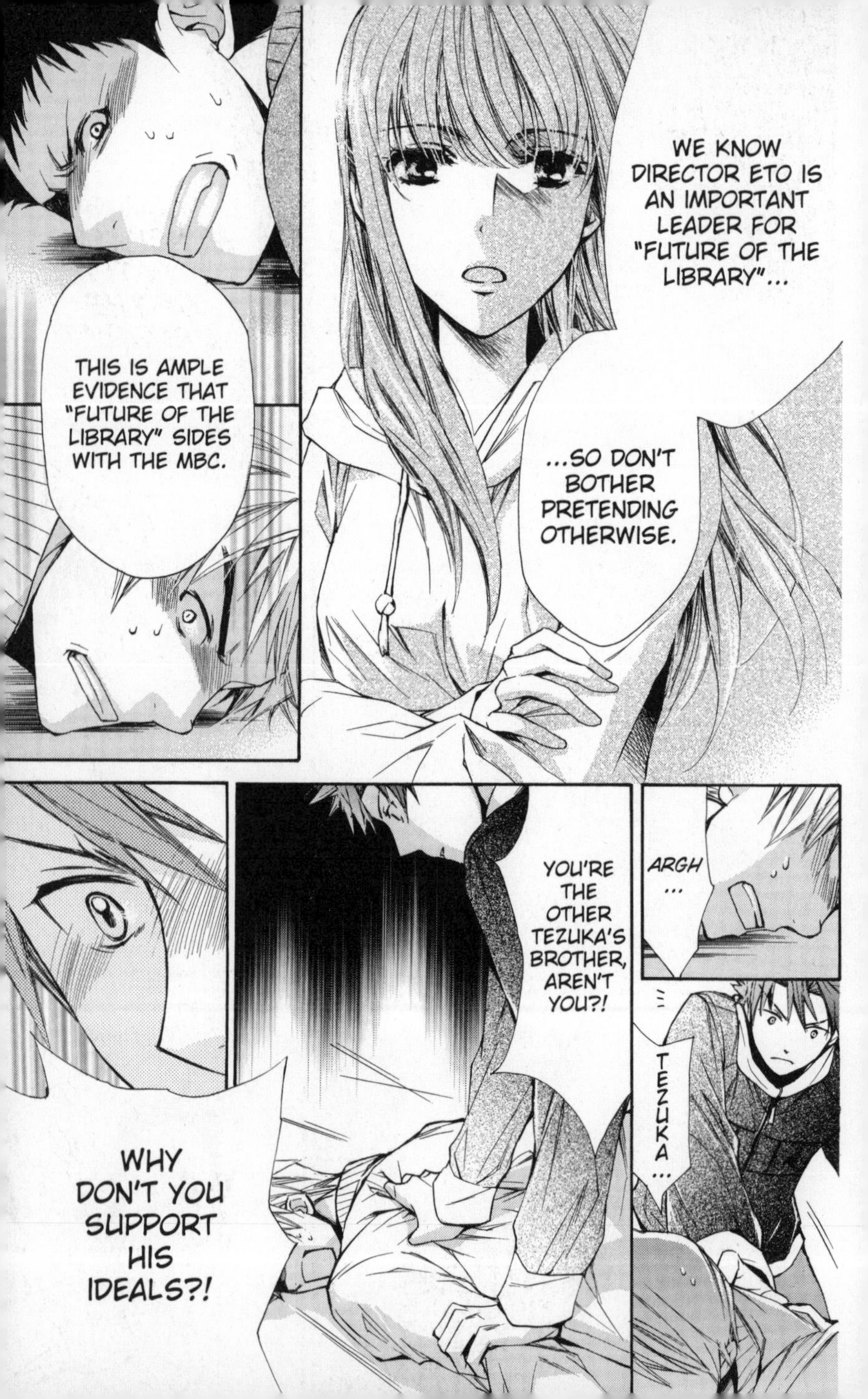
WE KNOW DIRECTOR ETO IS AN IMPORTANT LEADER FOR "FUTURE OF THE LIBRARY"...
...SO DON'T BOTHER PRETENDING OTHERWISE.
THIS IS AMPLE EVIDENCE THAT "FUTURE OF THE LIBRARY" SIDES WITH THE MBC.
ARGH...
TEZUKA...
YOU'RE THE OTHER TEZUKA'S BROTHER, AREN'T YOU?!
WHY DON'T YOU SUPPORT HIS IDEALS?!

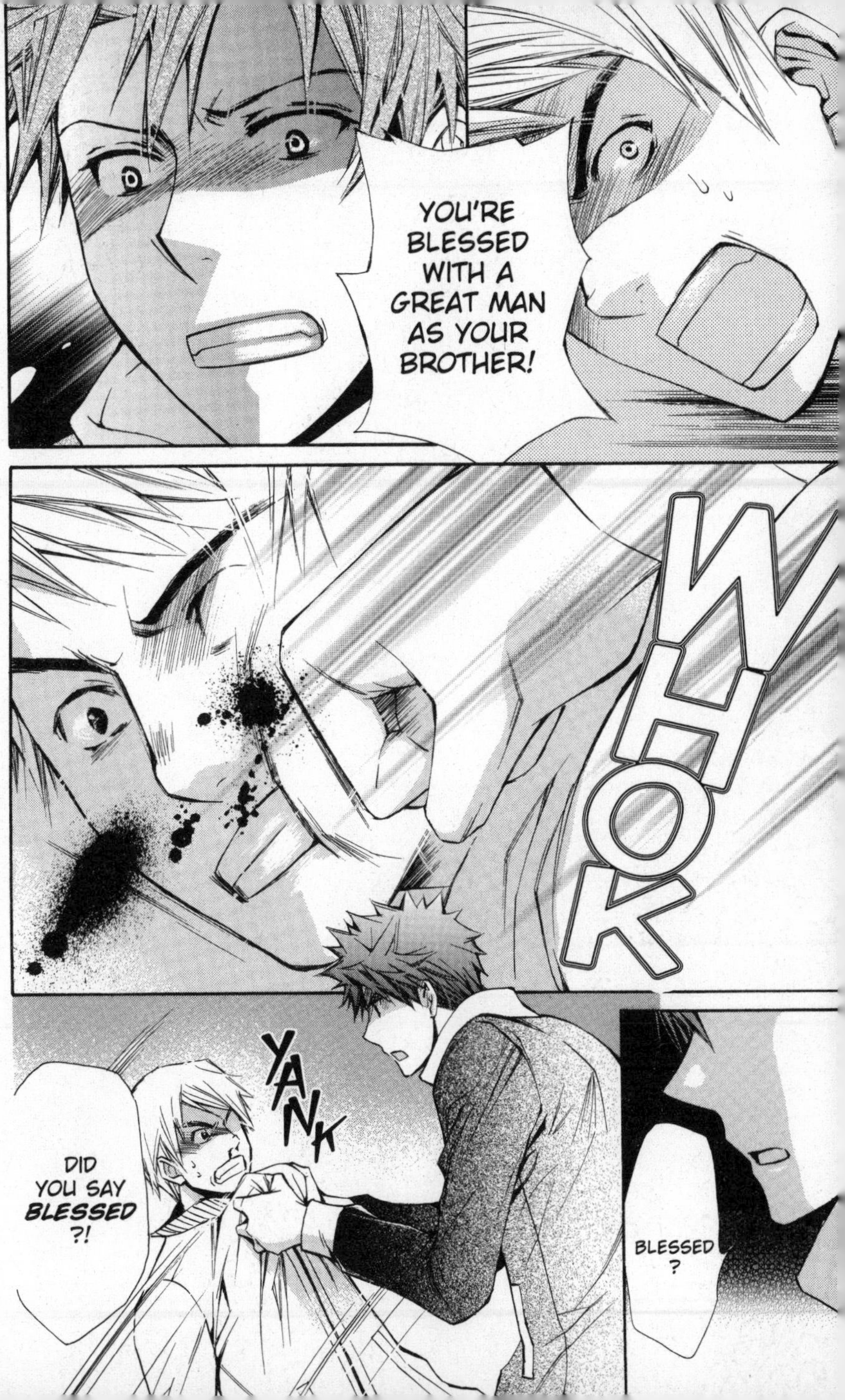
YOU'RE BLESSED WITH A GREAT MAN AS YOUR BROTHER!
WHOK
BLESSED ?
YANK
DID YOU SAY BLESSED ?!

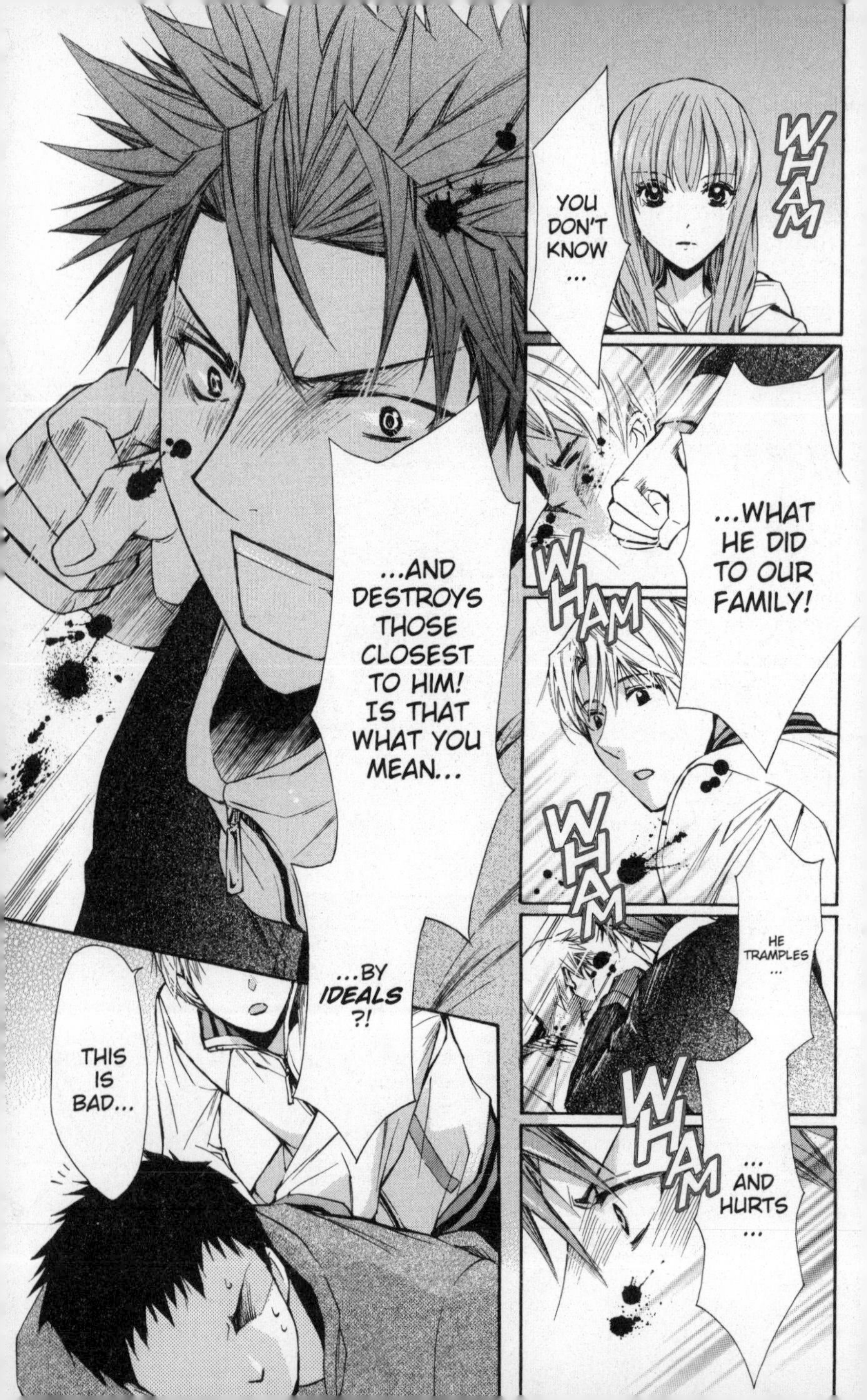
WHAM
YOU DON'T KNOW...
WHAM
...WHAT HE DID TO OUR FAMILY!
WHAM
WHAM
HE TRAMPLES...
WHAM
...AND HURTS...
...AND DESTROYS THOSE CLOSEST TO HIM! IS THAT WHAT YOU MEAN...
...BY IDEALS?!
THIS IS BAD...

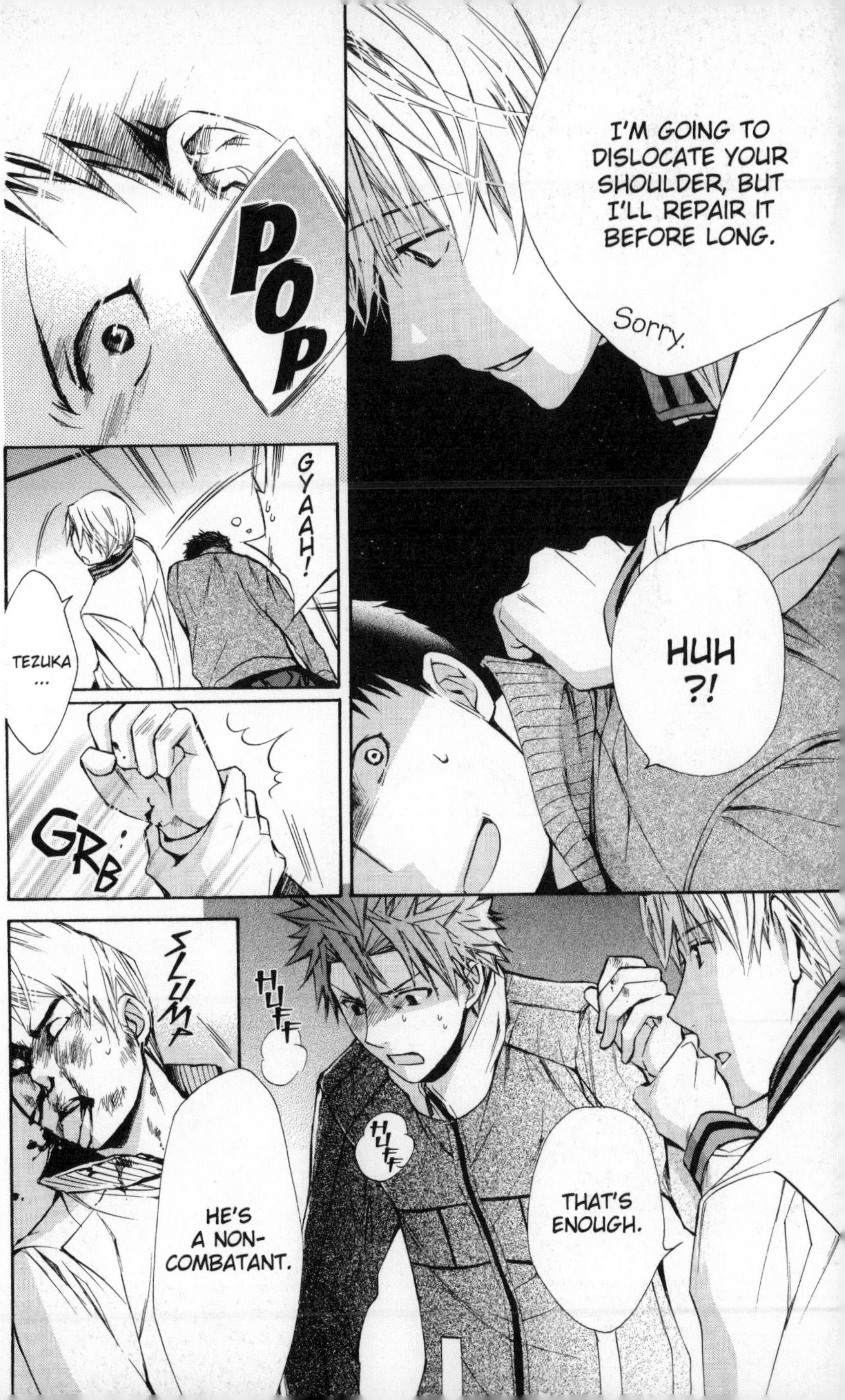

I'M GOING TO DISLOCATE YOUR SHOULDER, BUT I'LL REPAIR IT BEFORE LONG.
Sorry.
HUH ?!
POP
GYAAH!
TEZUKA ...
GRB
THAT'S ENOUGH.
HUFF
HUFF
SLUMP
HE'S A NON-COMBATANT.

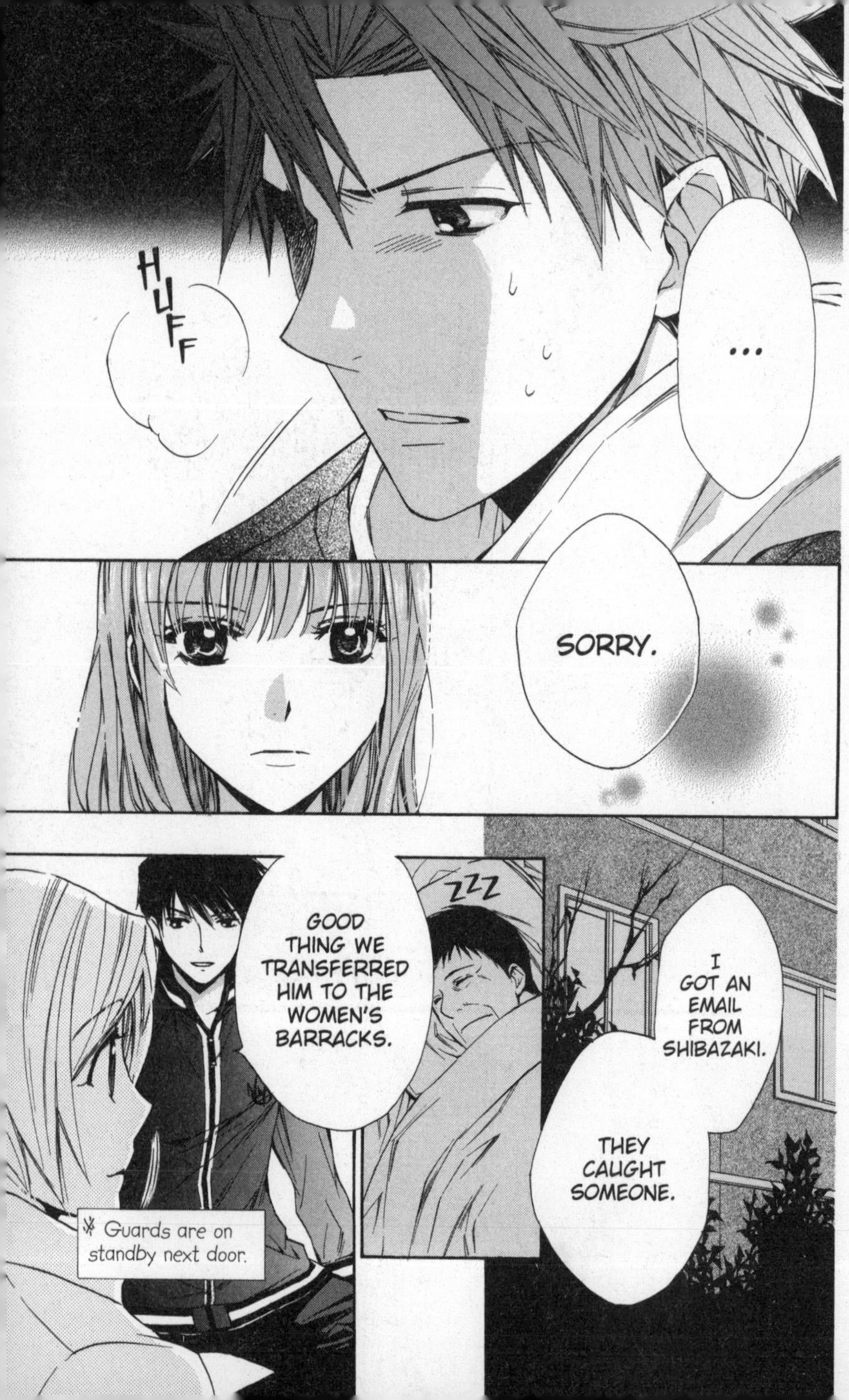
...
HUFF
SORRY.
I GOT AN EMAIL FROM SHIBAZAKI.
THEY CAUGHT SOMEONE.
ZZZ
GOOD THING WE TRANSFERRED HIM TO THE WOMEN'S BARRACKS.
Guards are on standby next door.

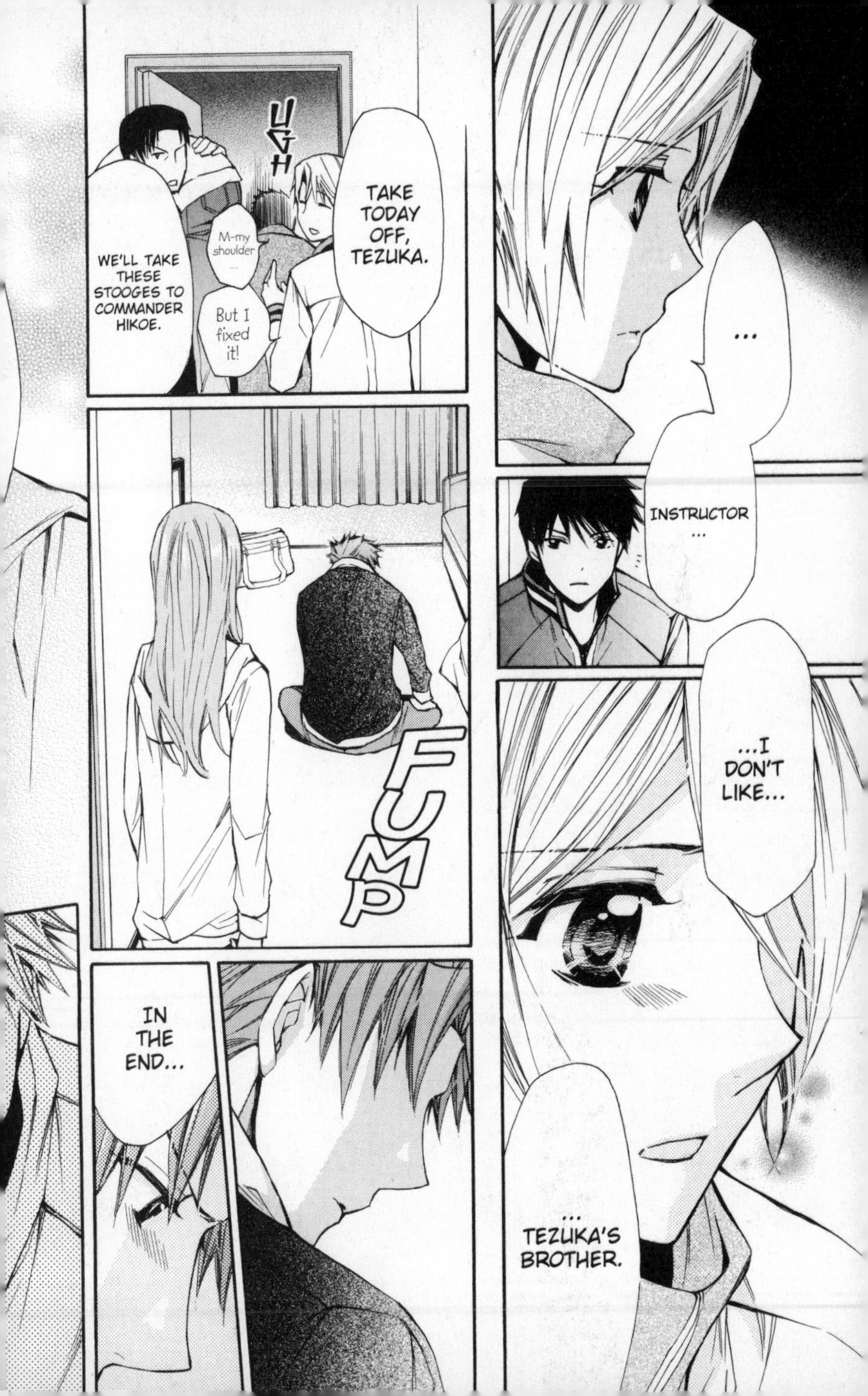
...
INSTRUCTOR...
...I DON'T LIKE...
...TEZUKA'S BROTHER.
TAKE TODAY OFF, TEZUKA.
UGH
M-my shoulder...
But I fixed it!
WE'LL TAKE THESE STOOGES TO COMMANDER HIKOE.
FUMP
IN THE END...

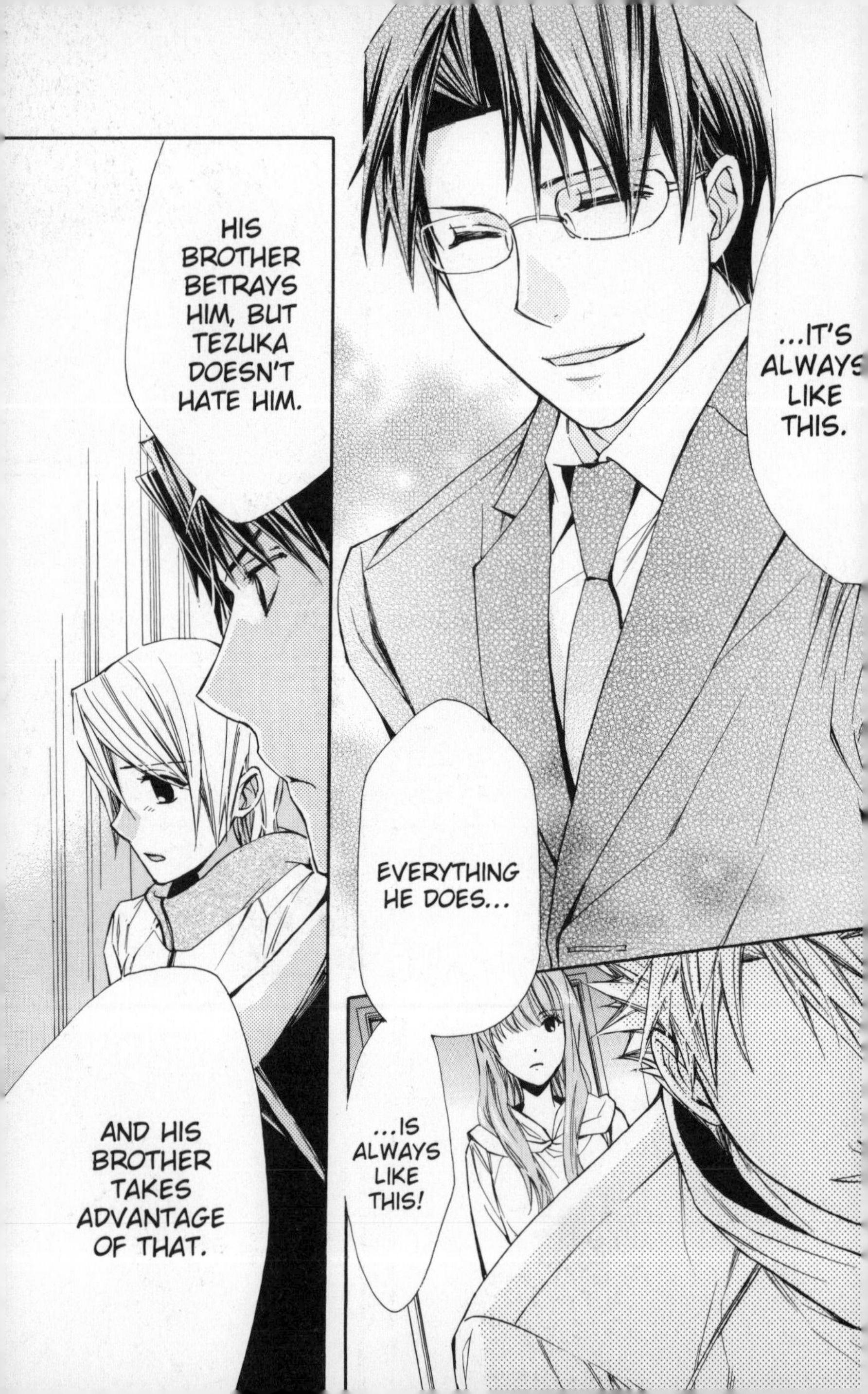
...IT'S ALWAYS LIKE THIS.
EVERYTHING HE DOES...
...IS ALWAYS LIKE THIS!
HIS BROTHER BETRAYS HIM, BUT TEZUKA DOESN'T HATE HIM.
AND HIS BROTHER TAKES ADVANTAGE OF THAT.

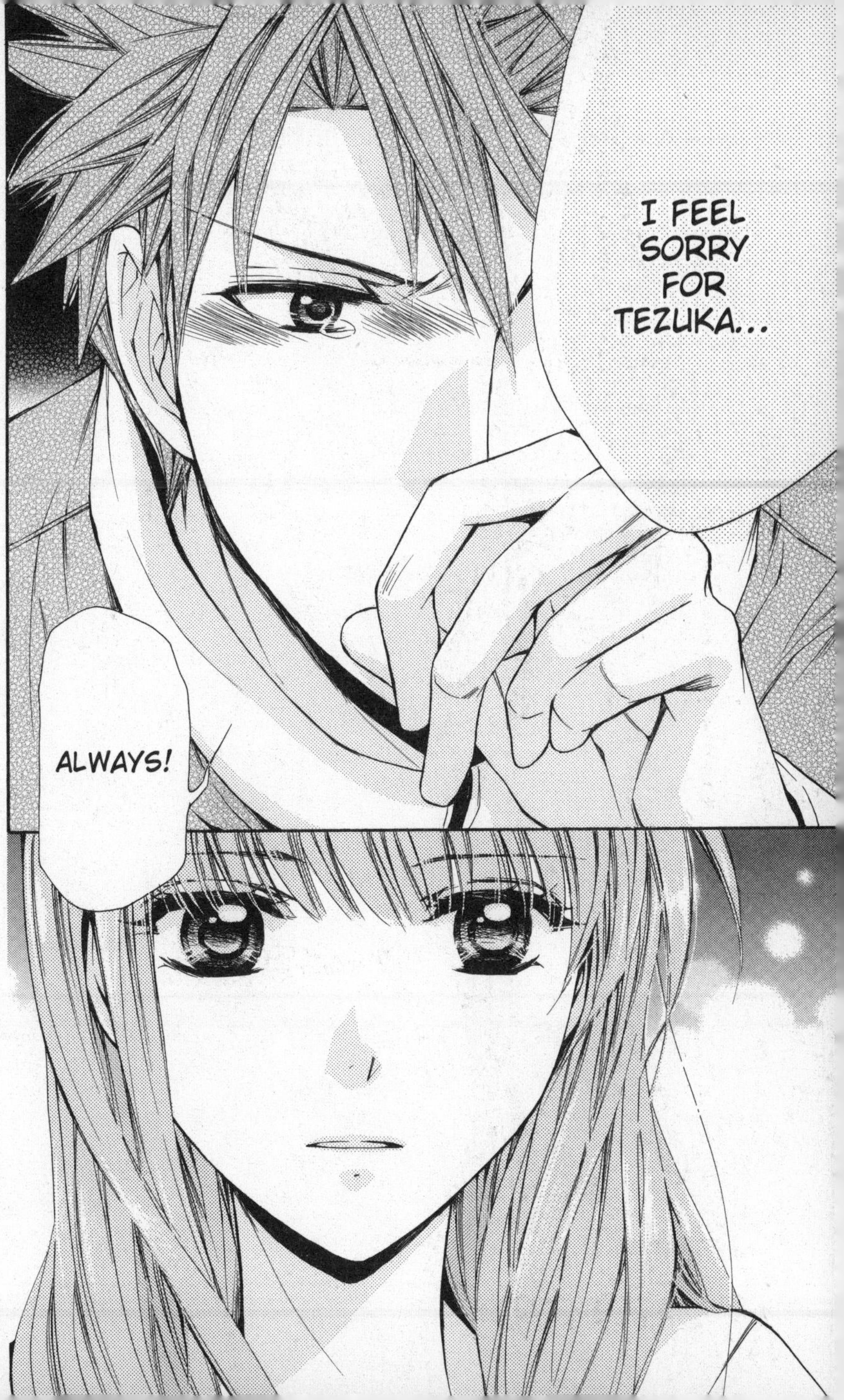
I FEEL SORRY FOR TEZUKA...
ALWAYS!

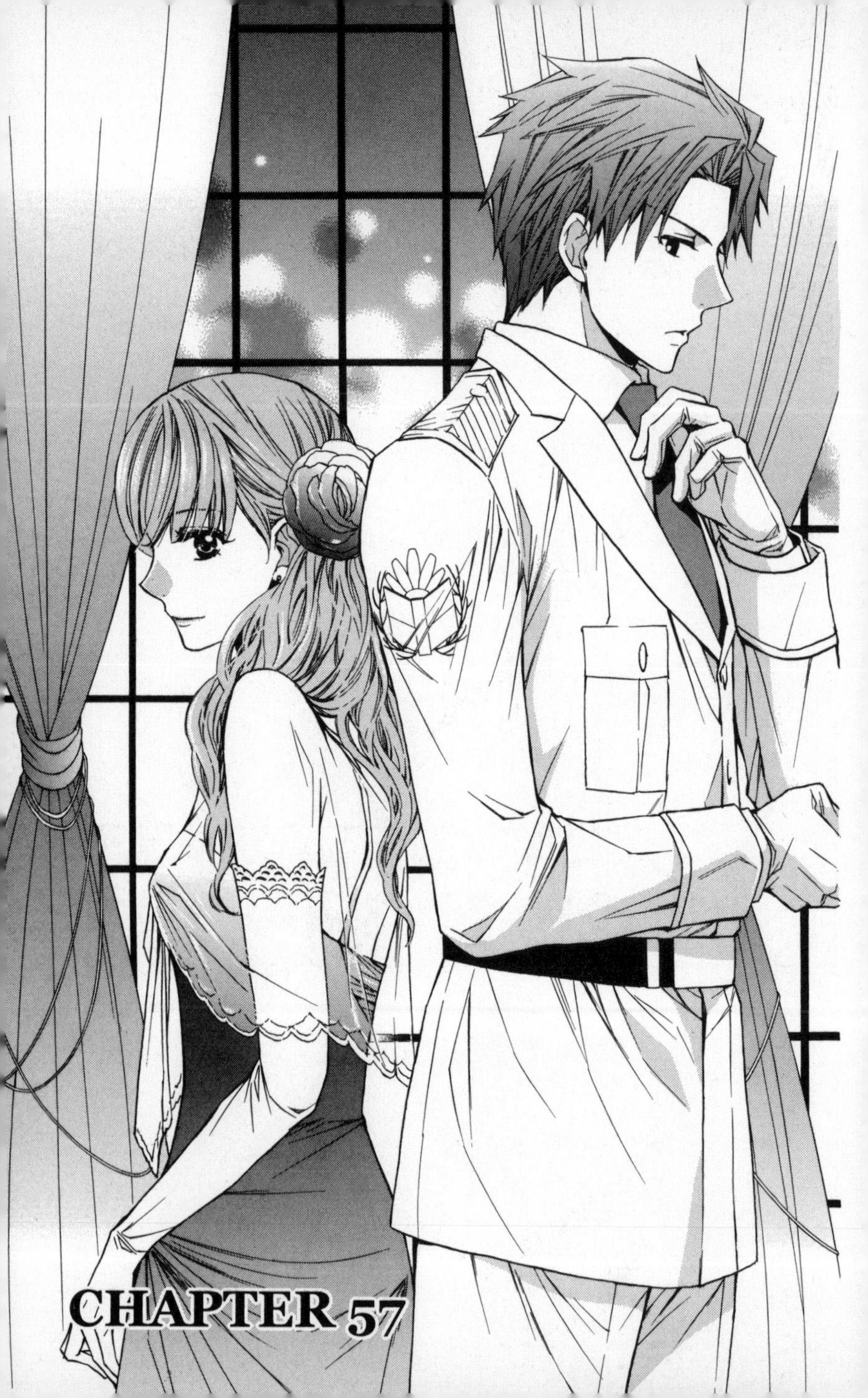
CHAPTER 57

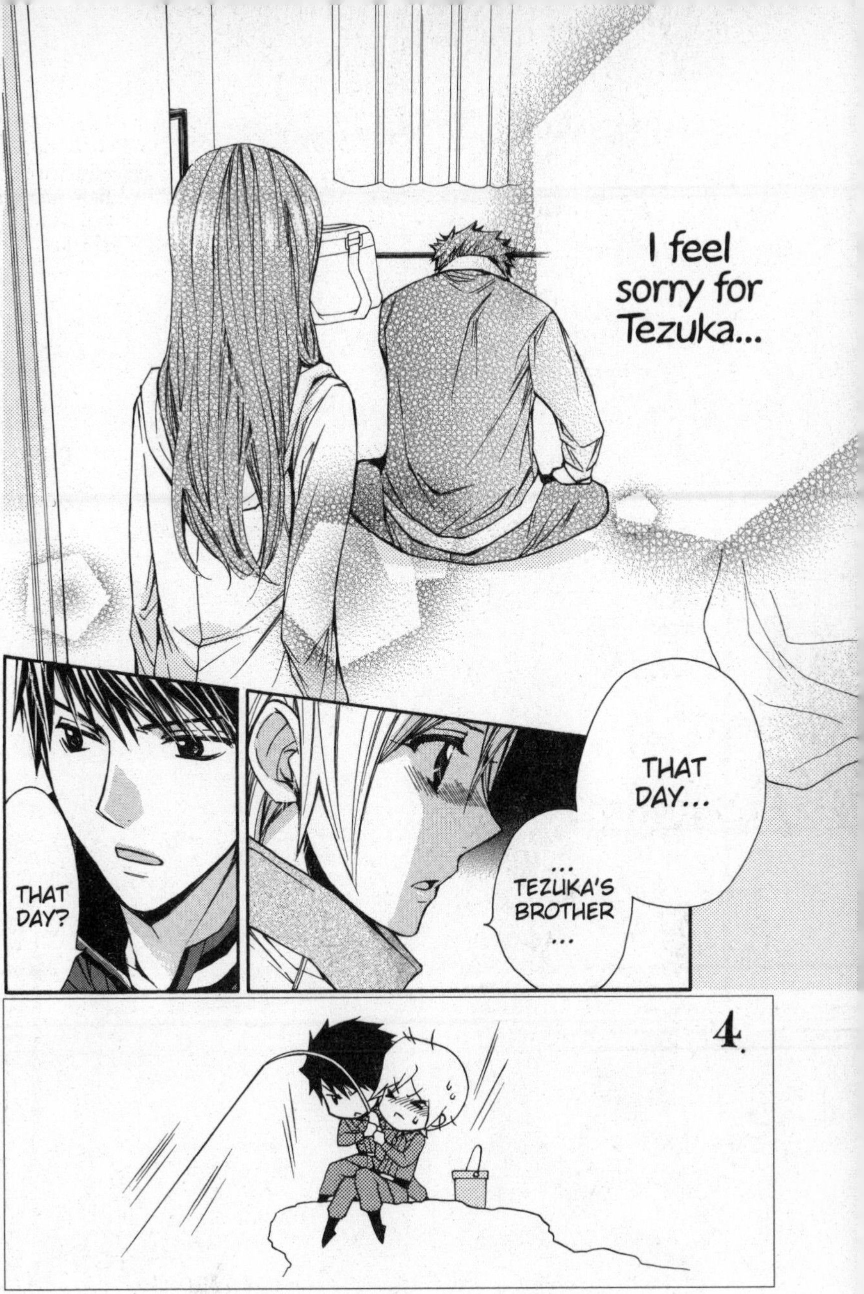
I feel sorry for Tezuka...
THAT DAY...
... TEZUKA'S BROTHER ...
THAT DAY?
4.

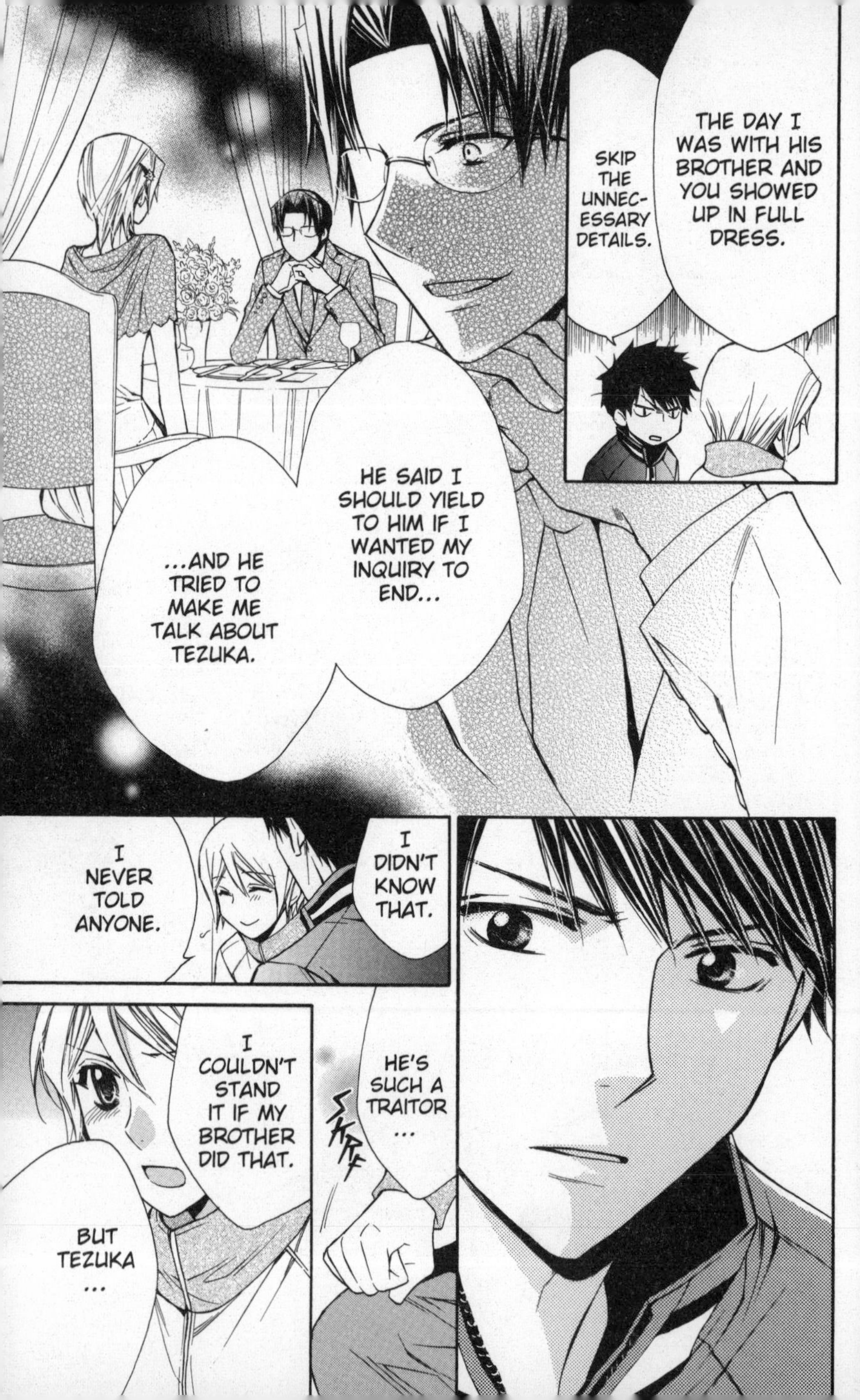
THE DAY I WAS WITH HIS BROTHER AND YOU SHOWED UP IN FULL DRESS.
SKIP THE UNNEC-ESSARY DETAILS.
HE SAID I SHOULD YIELD TO HIM IF I WANTED MY INQUIRY TO END...
...AND HE TRIED TO MAKE ME TALK ABOUT TEZUKA.
I DIDN'T KNOW THAT.
I NEVER TOLD ANYONE.
HE'S SUCH A TRAITOR ...
SKRF
I COULDN'T STAND IT IF MY BROTHER DID THAT.
BUT TEZUKA ...

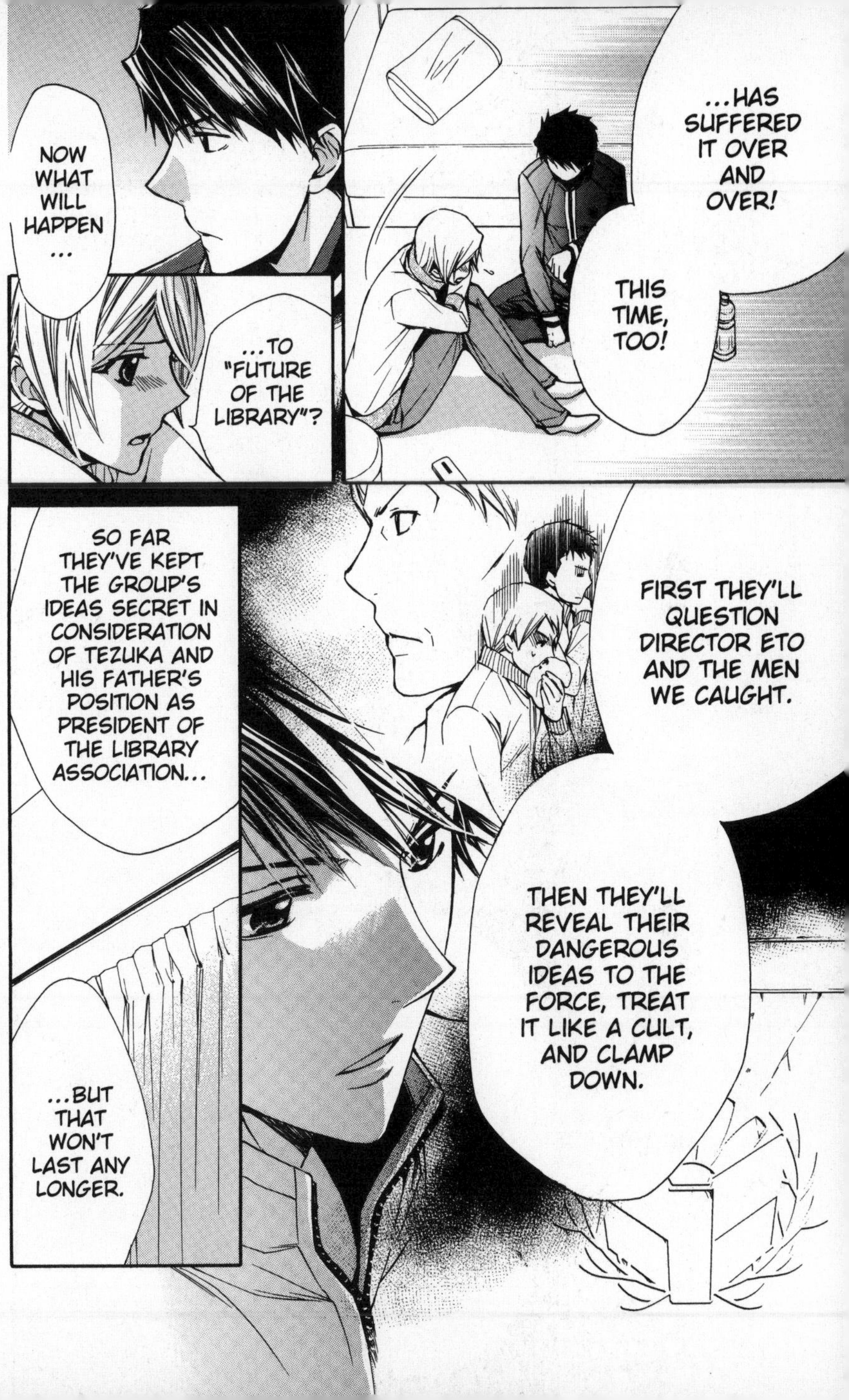
...HAS SUFFERED IT OVER AND OVER!
THIS TIME, TOO!
NOW WHAT WILL HAPPEN ...
...TO "FUTURE OF THE LIBRARY"?
FIRST THEY'LL QUESTION DIRECTOR ETO AND THE MEN WE CAUGHT.
THEN THEY'LL REVEAL THEIR DANGEROUS IDEAS TO THE FORCE, TREAT IT LIKE A CULT, AND CLAMP DOWN.
SO FAR THEY'VE KEPT THE GROUP'S IDEAS SECRET IN CONSIDERATION OF TEZUKA AND HIS FATHER'S POSITION AS PRESIDENT OF THE LIBRARY ASSOCIATION...
...BUT THAT WON'T LAST ANY LONGER.

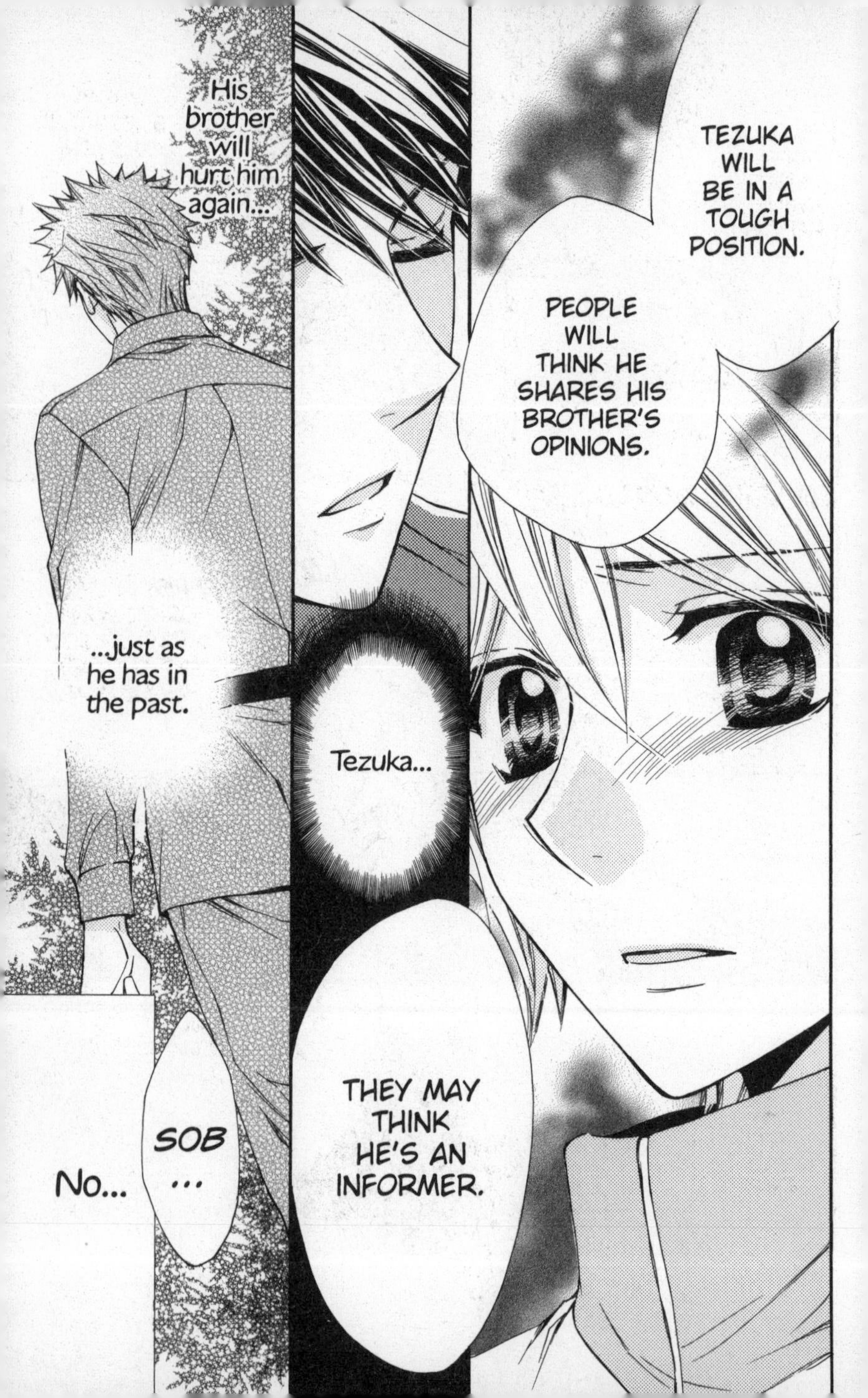
TEZUKA WILL BE IN A TOUGH POSITION.
PEOPLE WILL THINK HE SHARES HIS BROTHER'S OPINIONS.
THEY MAY THINK HE'S AN INFORMER.
Tezuka...
His brother will hurt him again...
...just as he has in the past.
SOB...
No...

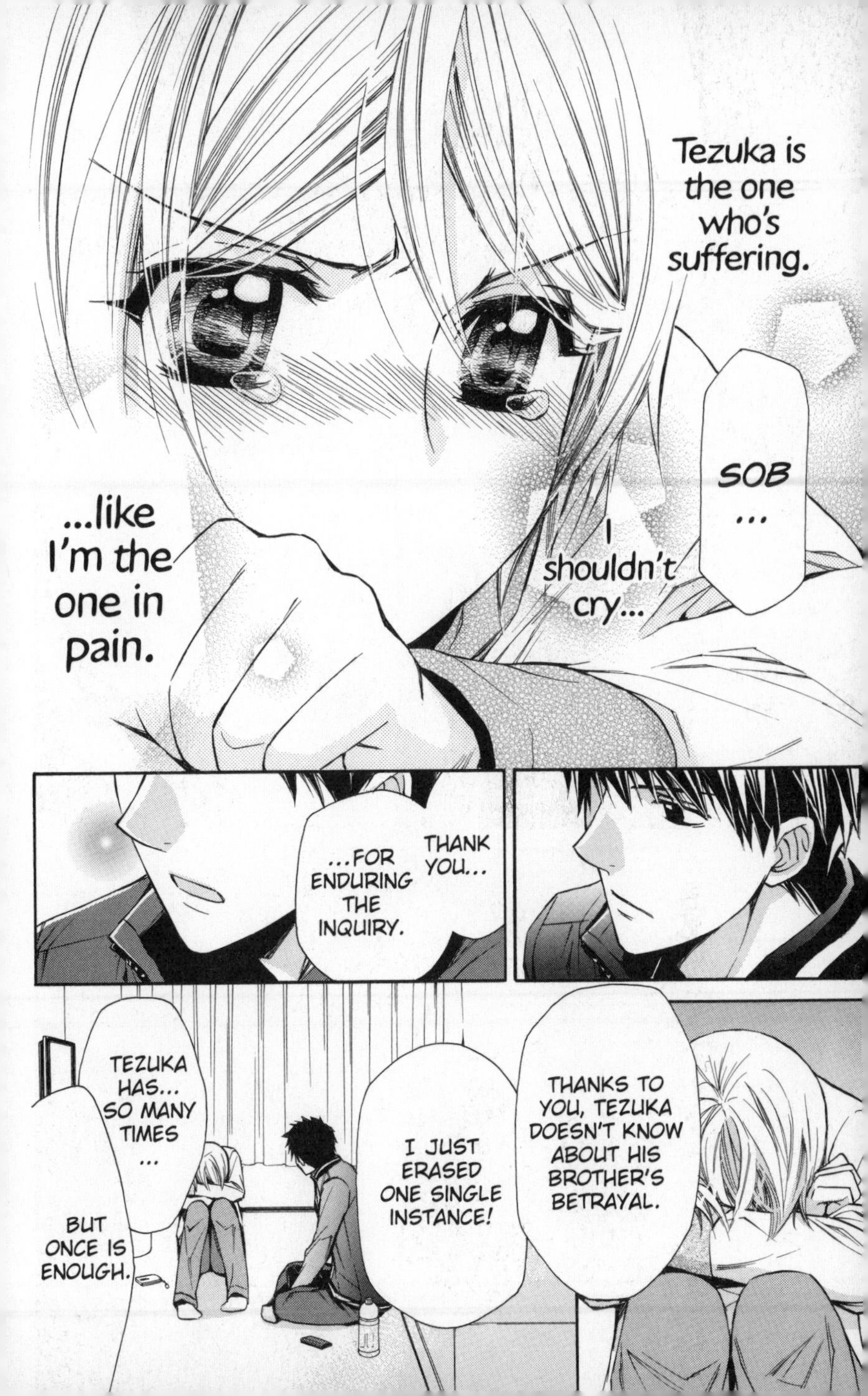
Tezuka is the one who's suffering.
SOB ...
I shouldn't cry...
...like I'm the one in pain.
THANK YOU...
...FOR ENDURING THE INQUIRY.
THANKS TO YOU, TEZUKA DOESN'T KNOW ABOUT HIS BROTHER'S BETRAYAL.
I JUST ERASED ONE SINGLE INSTANCE!
TEZUKA HAS... SO MANY TIMES ...
BUT ONCE IS ENOUGH.

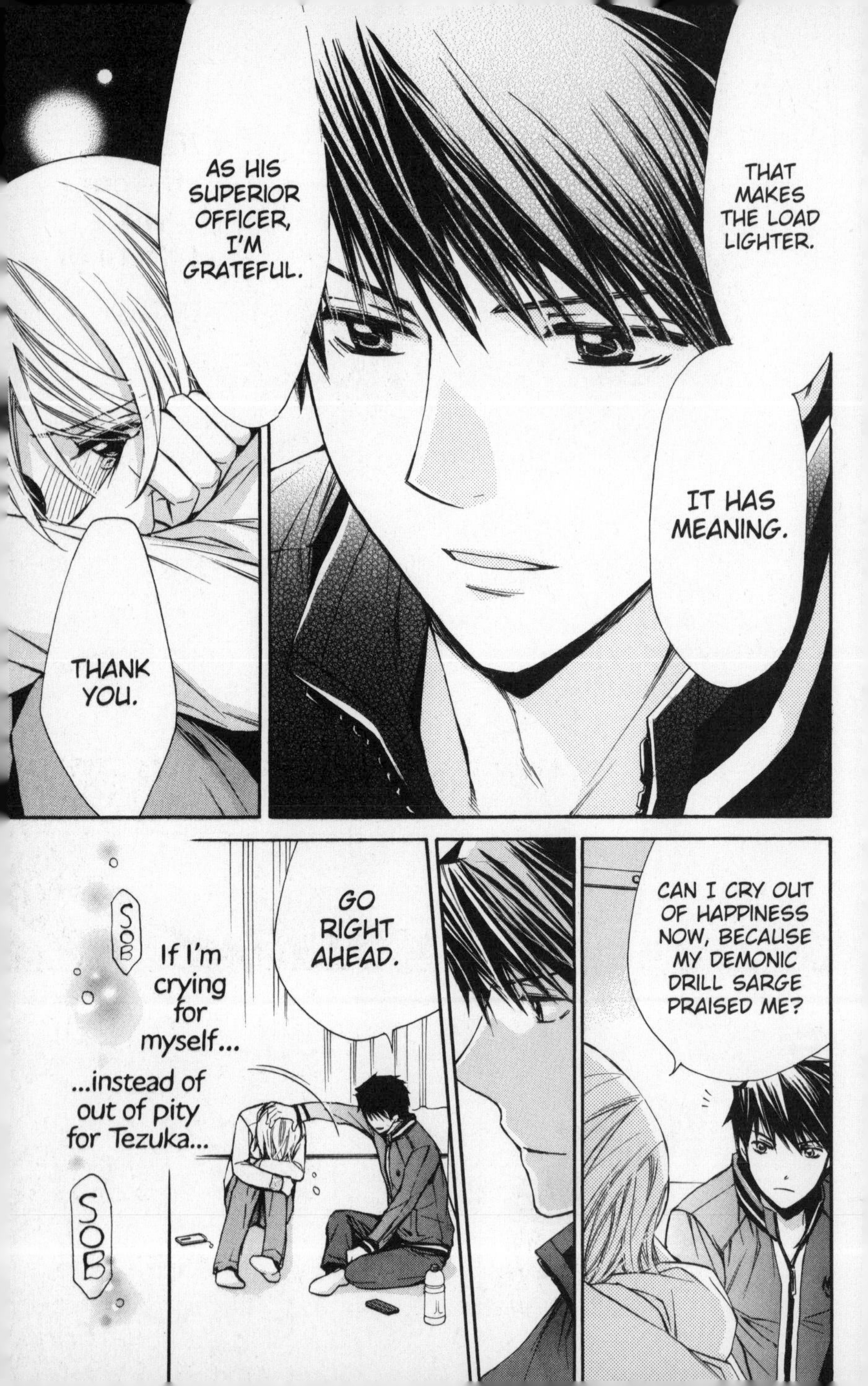
THAT MAKES THE LOAD LIGHTER.
AS HIS SUPERIOR OFFICER, I'M GRATEFUL.
IT HAS MEANING.
THANK YOU.
CAN I CRY OUT OF HAPPINESS NOW, BECAUSE MY DEMONIC DRILL SARGE PRAISED ME?
GO RIGHT AHEAD.
SOB
If I'm crying for myself...
...instead of out of pity for Tezuka...
SOB

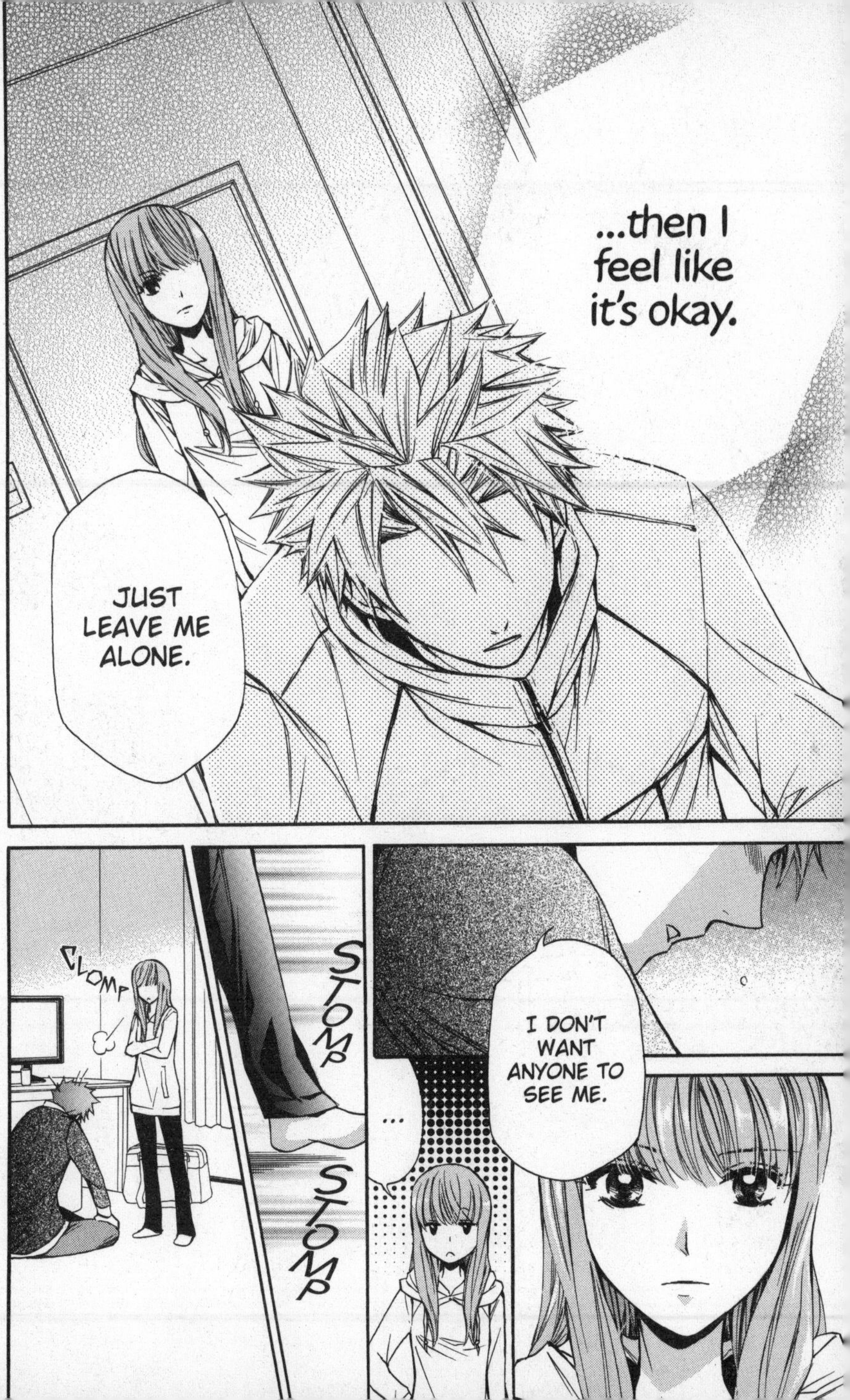
...then I feel like it's okay.
JUST LEAVE ME ALONE.
I DON'T WANT ANYONE TO SEE ME.
...
STOMP
STOMP
CLOMP

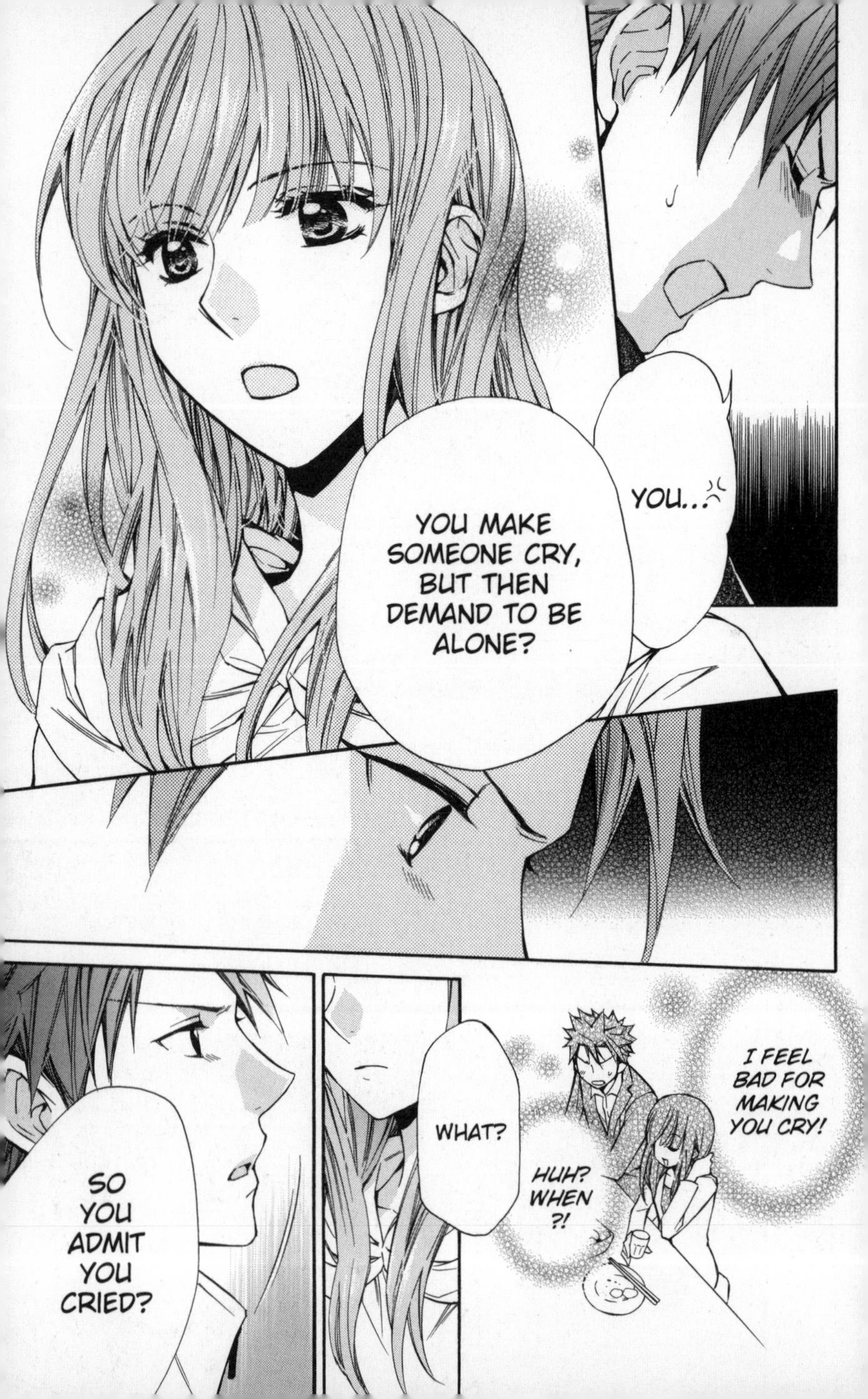
YOU...
YOU MAKE SOMEONE CRY, BUT THEN DEMAND TO BE ALONE?
I FEEL BAD FOR MAKING YOU CRY!
HUH? WHEN ?!
WHAT?
SO YOU ADMIT YOU CRIED?

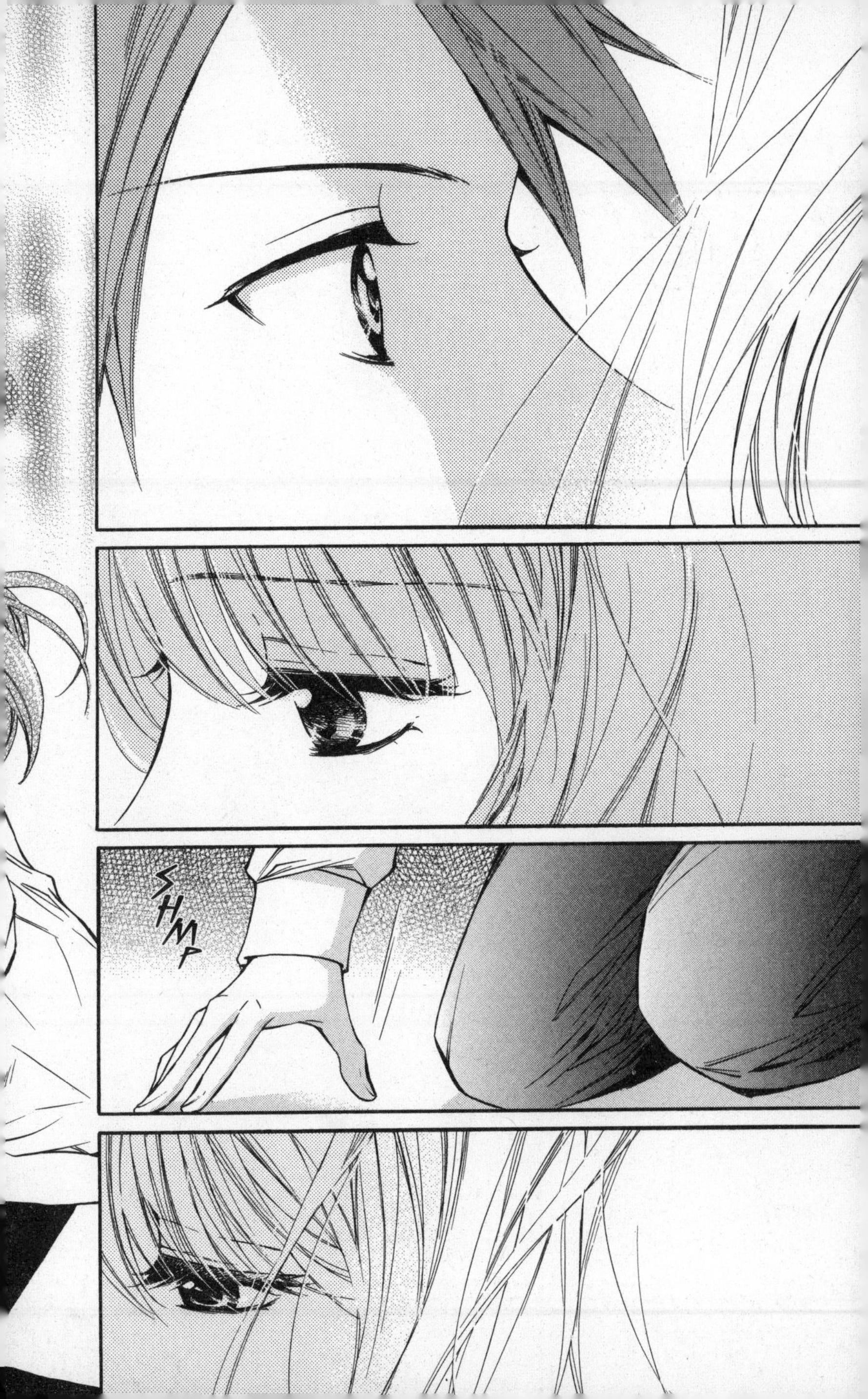
SHMP

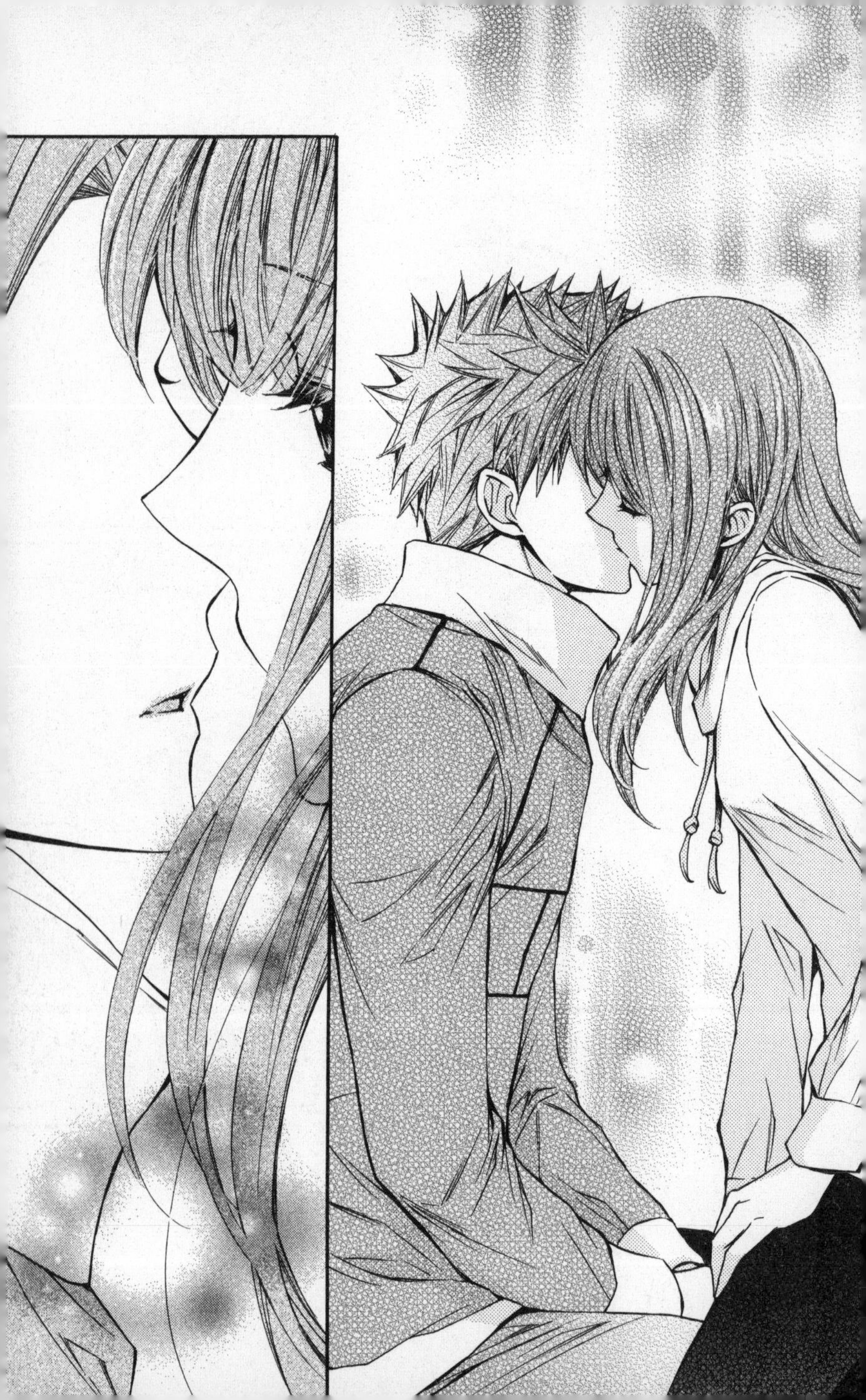

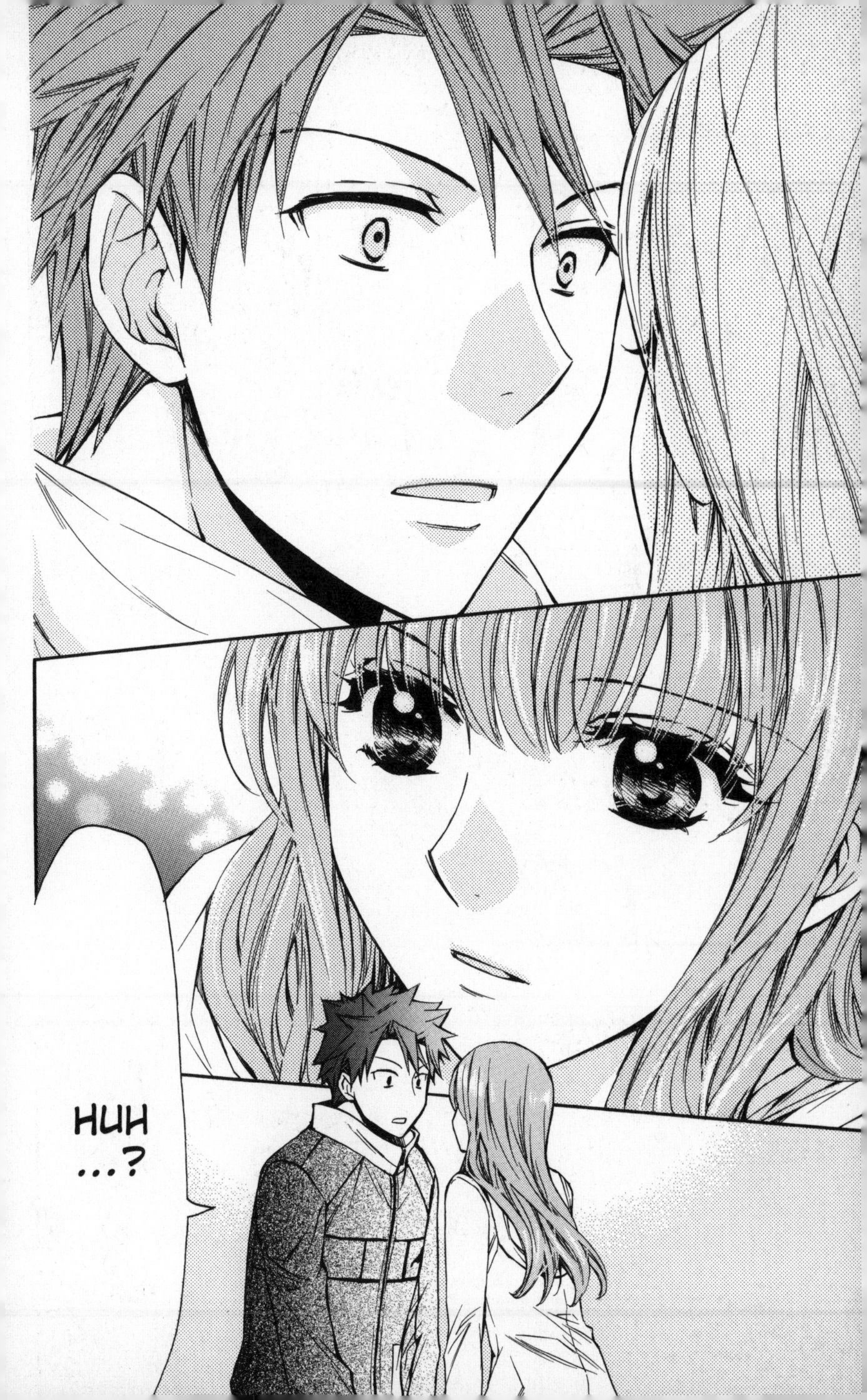
HUH ...?

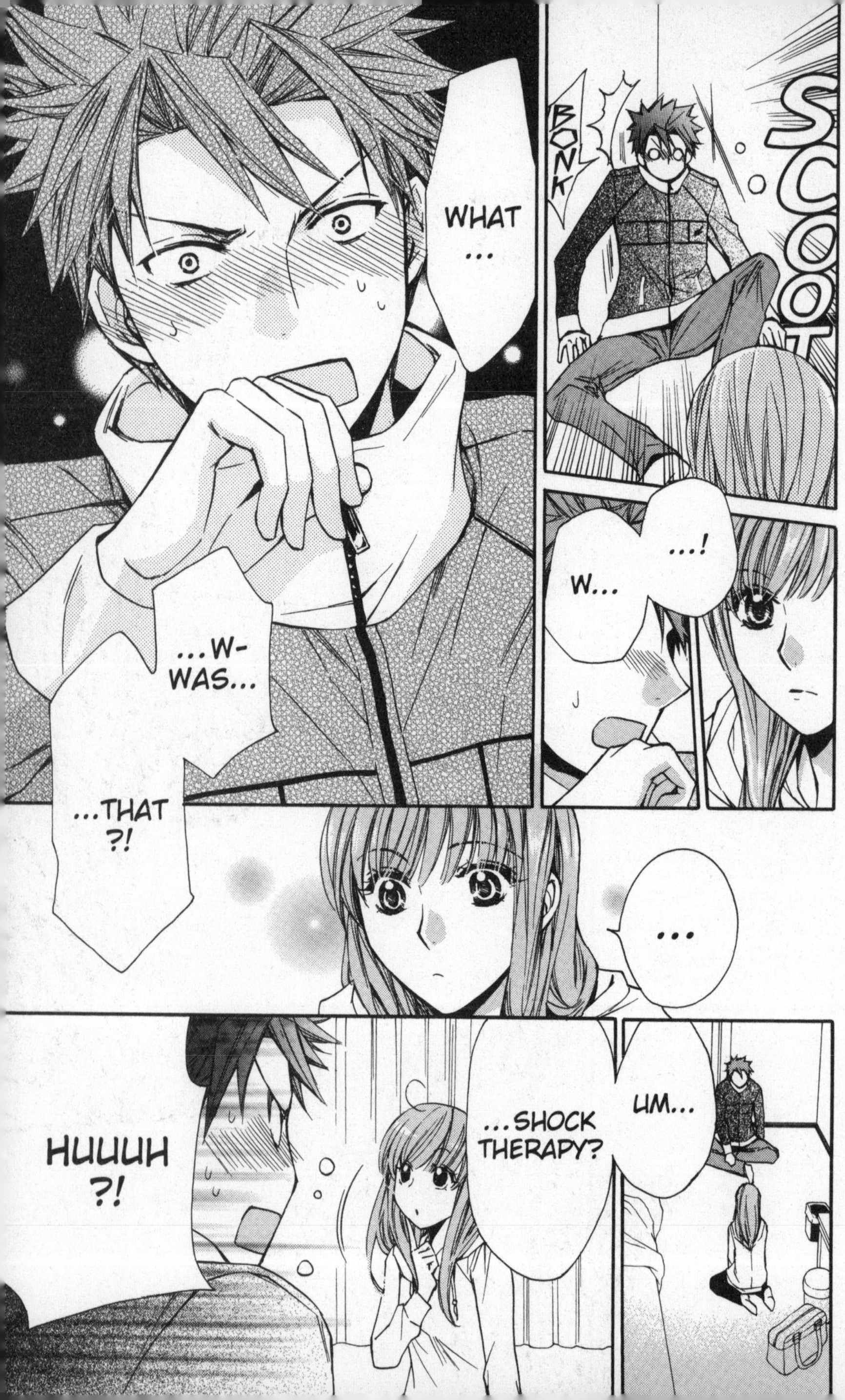
SCOOT
BONK
...!
W...
WHAT...
...W-WAS...
...THAT?!
...
UM...
...SHOCK THERAPY?
HUUUH?!

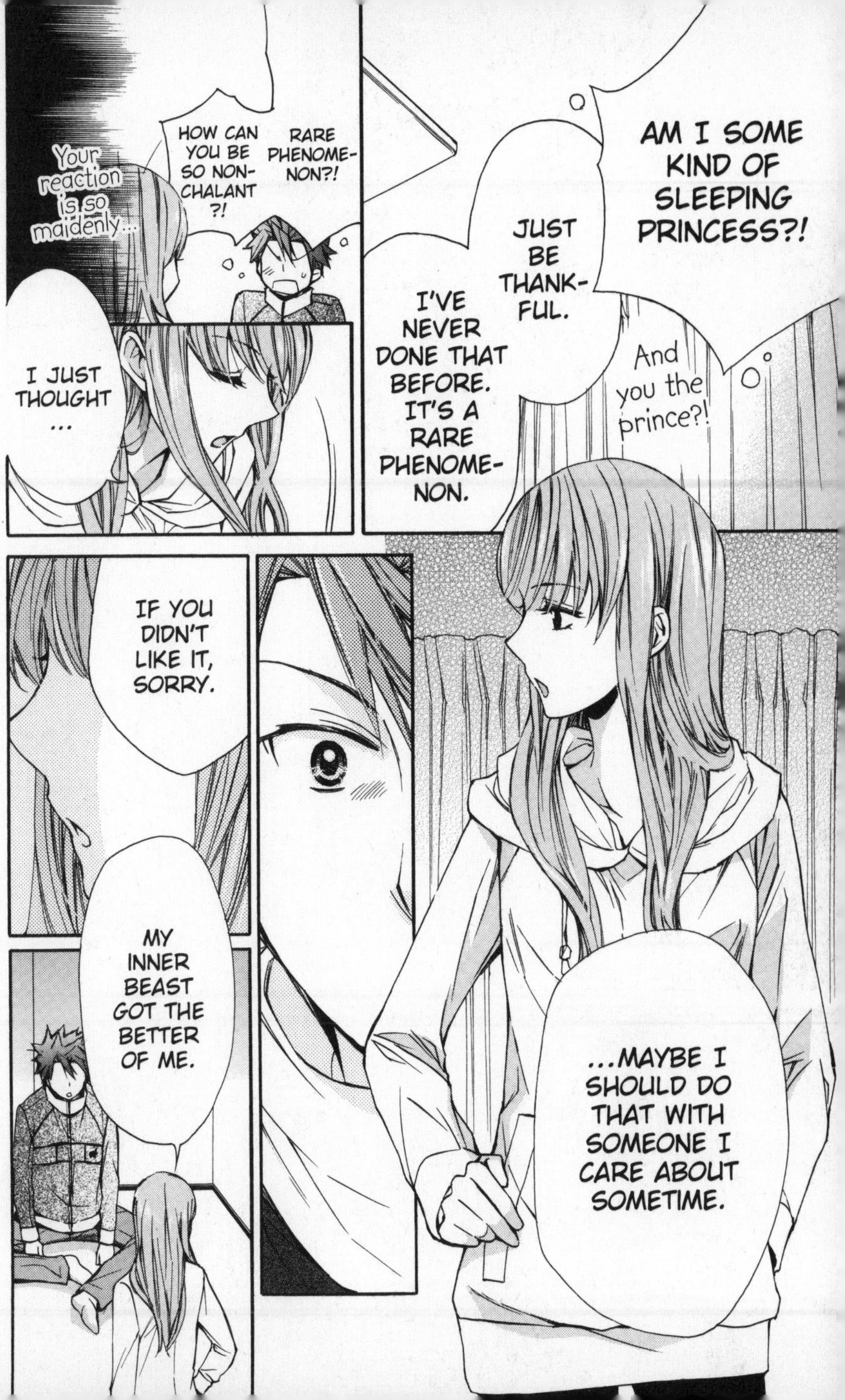
AM I SOME KIND OF SLEEPING PRINCESS?!
And you the prince?!
JUST BE THANKFUL.
I'VE NEVER DONE THAT BEFORE. IT'S A RARE PHENOMENON.
RARE PHENOMENON?!
HOW CAN YOU BE SO NONCHALANT?!
Your reaction is so maidenly...
I JUST THOUGHT...
...MAYBE I SHOULD DO THAT WITH SOMEONE I CARE ABOUT SOMETIME.
IF YOU DIDN'T LIKE IT, SORRY.
MY INNER BEAST GOT THE BETTER OF ME.

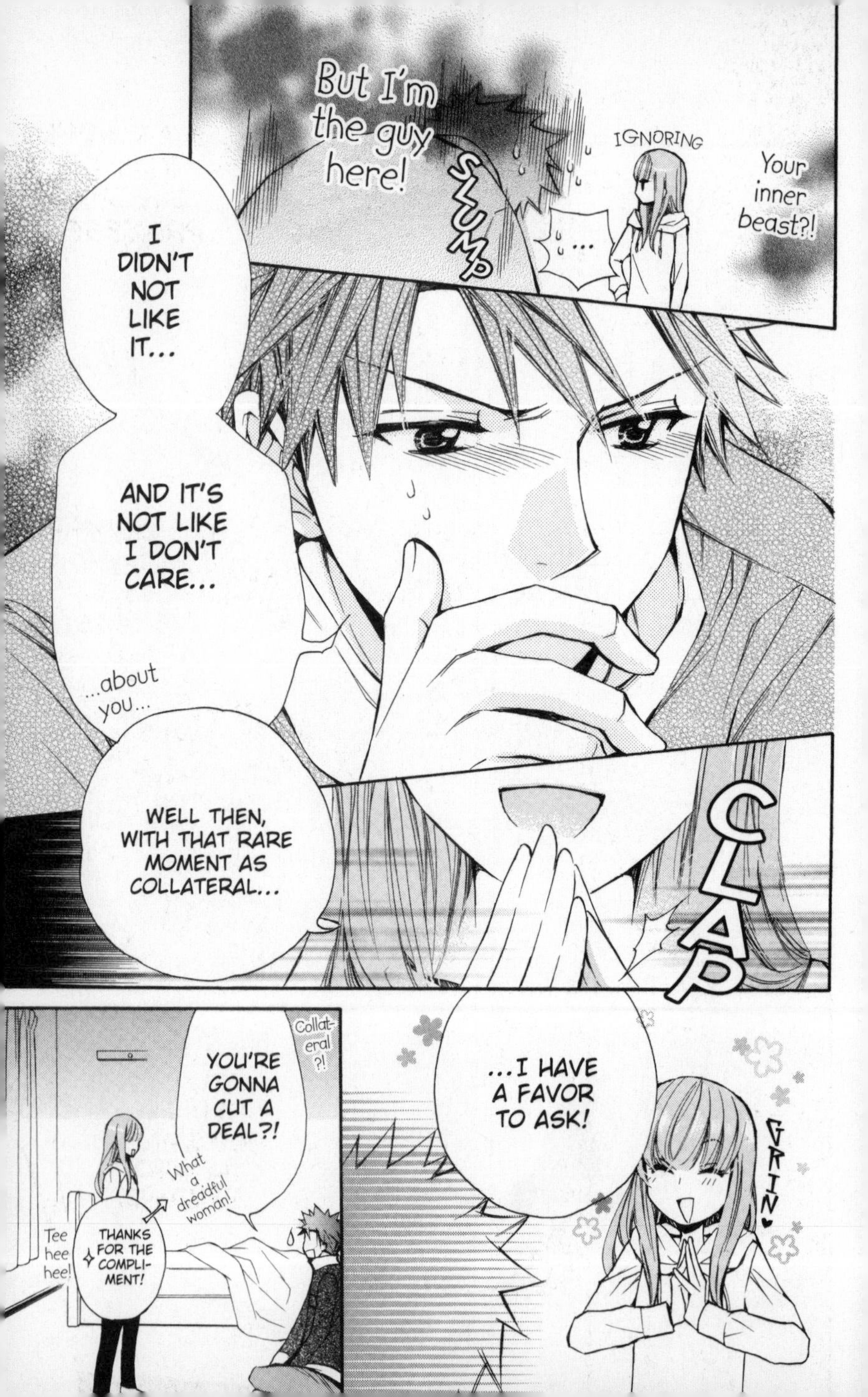

Your inner beast?!
IGNORING
...
SLUMP
But I'm the guy here!
I DIDN'T NOT LIKE IT...
AND IT'S NOT LIKE I DON'T CARE...
...about you...
CLAP
WELL THEN, WITH THAT RARE MOMENT AS COLLATERAL...
...I HAVE A FAVOR TO ASK!
GRIN
Collat-eral?!
YOU'RE GONNA CUT A DEAL?!
What a dreadful woman!
THANKS FOR THE COMPLI-MENT!
Tee hee hee!

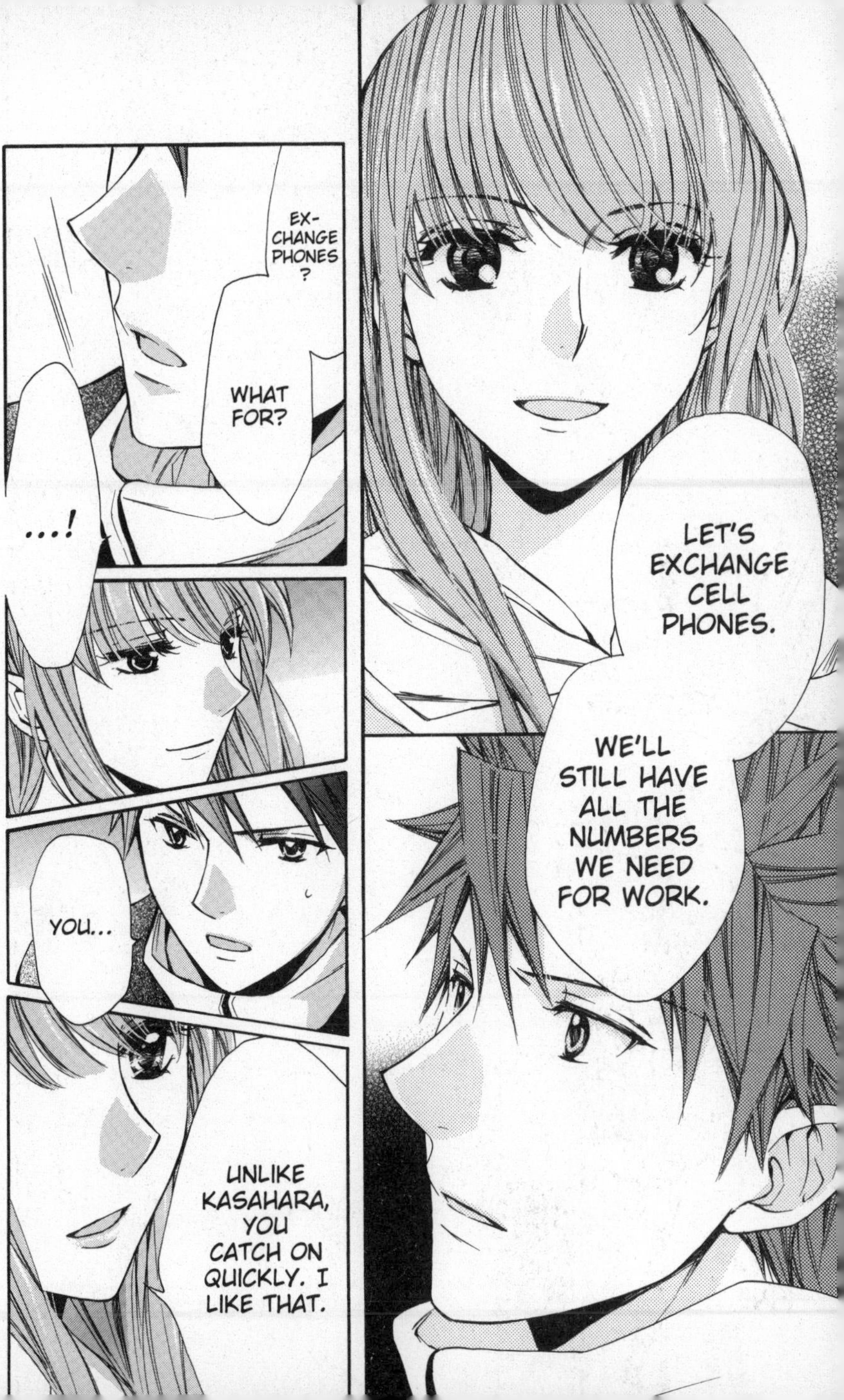
LET'S EXCHANGE CELL PHONES.
WE'LL STILL HAVE ALL THE NUMBERS WE NEED FOR WORK.
EX-CHANGE PHONES?
WHAT FOR?
...!
YOU...
UNLIKE KASAHARA, YOU CATCH ON QUICKLY. I LIKE THAT.

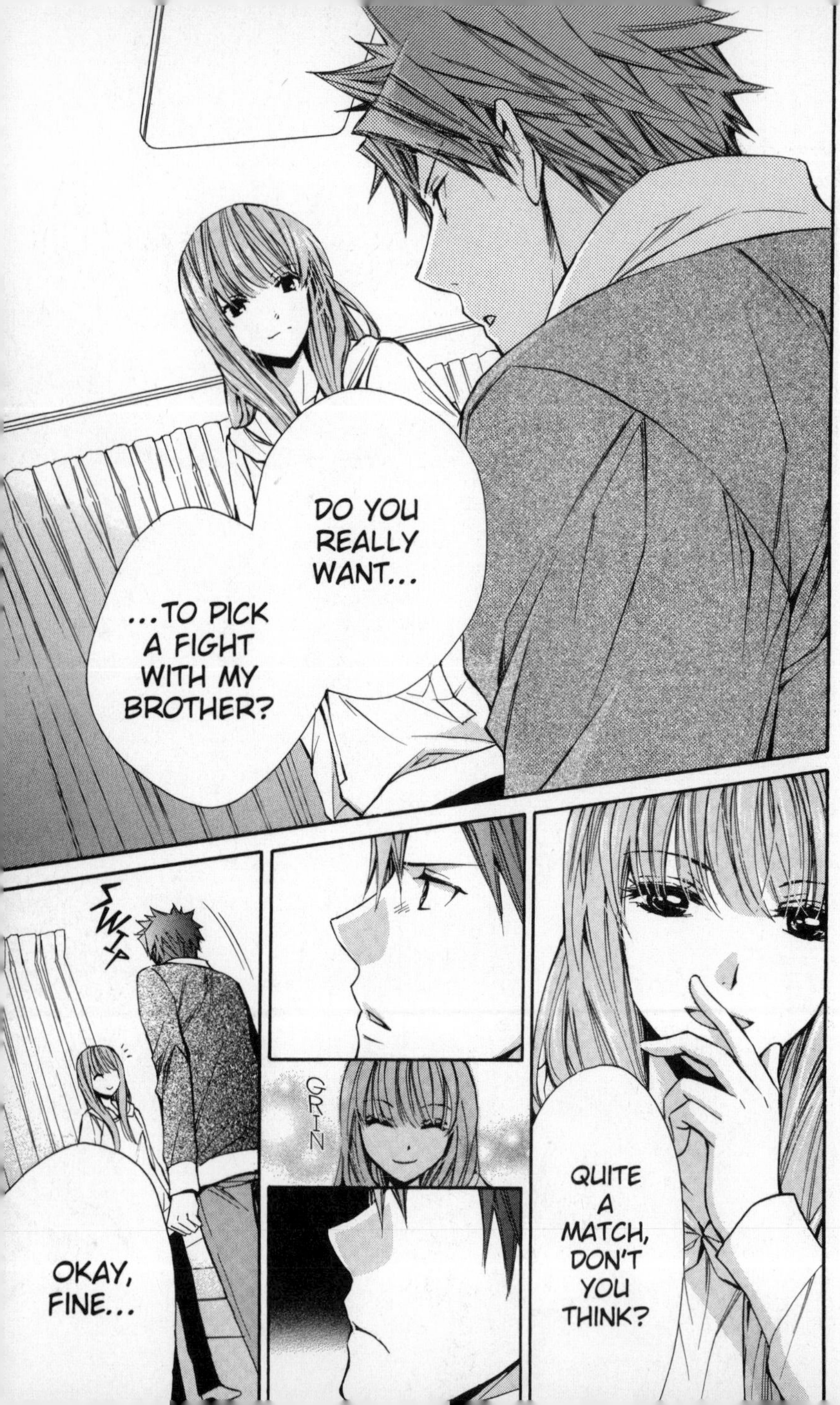
DO YOU REALLY WANT...
...TO PICK A FIGHT WITH MY BROTHER?
QUITE A MATCH, DON'T YOU THINK?
GRIN
SWIP
OKAY, FINE...

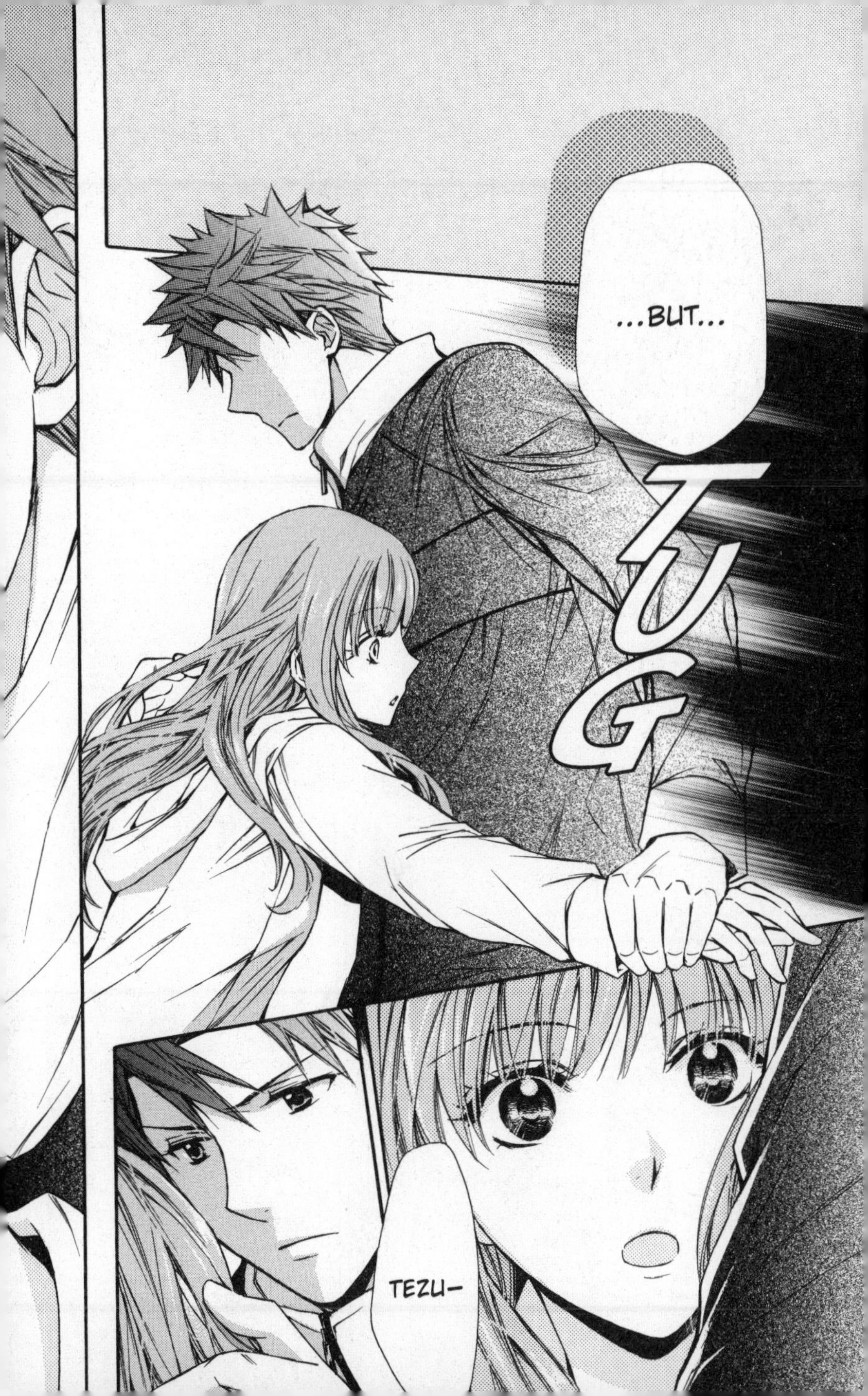
...BUT...
TUG
TEZU-

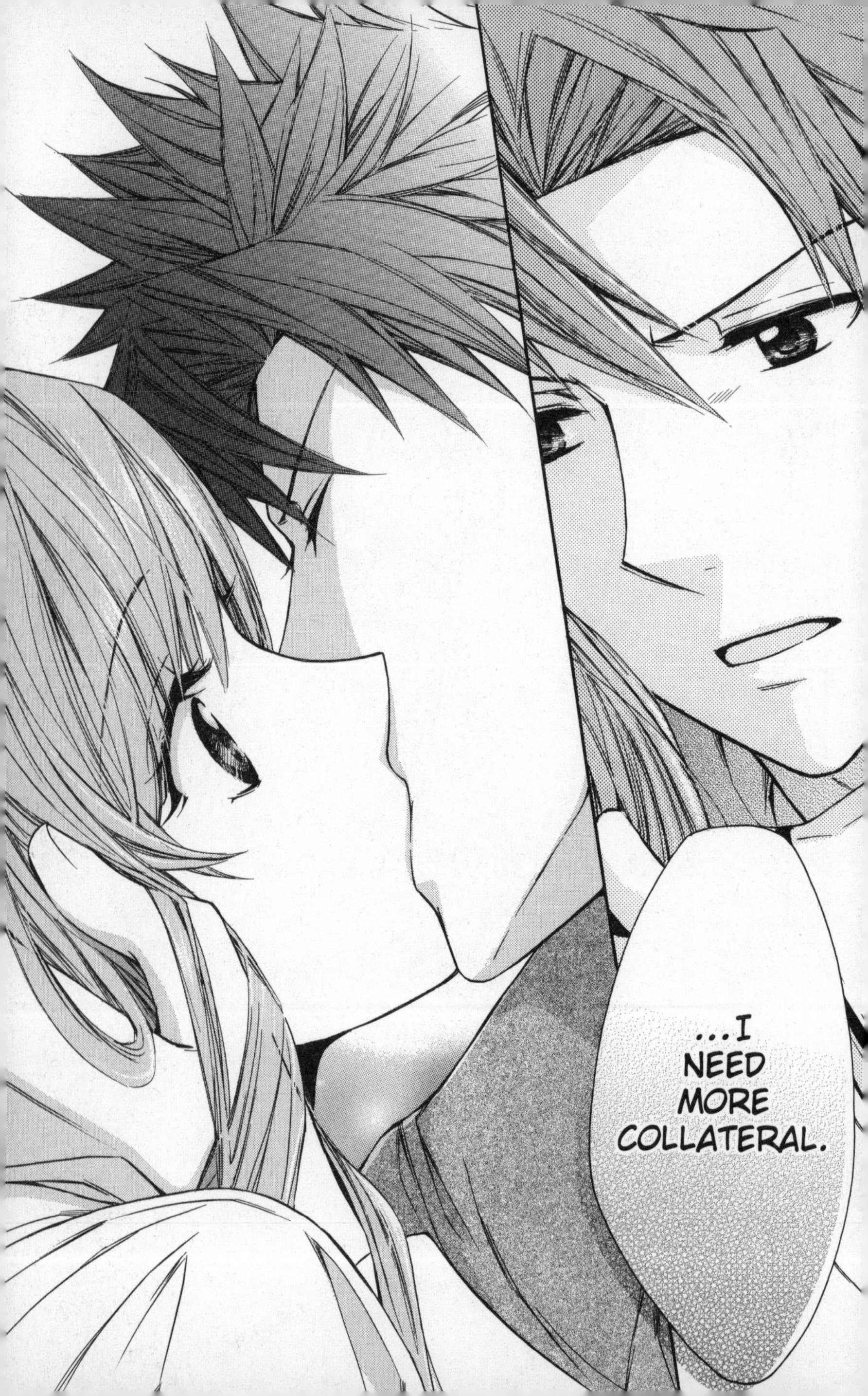
...I NEED MORE COLLATERAL.

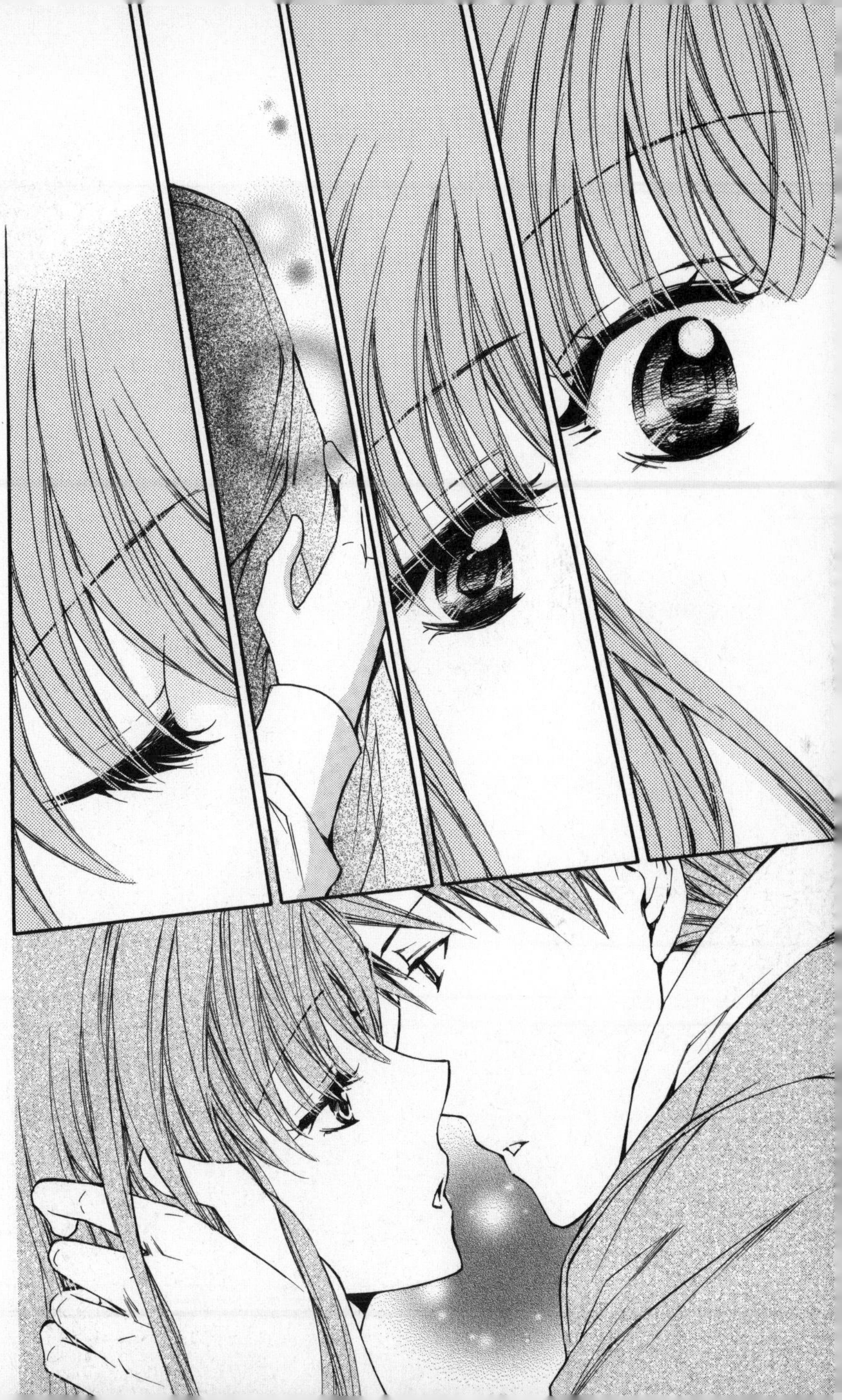

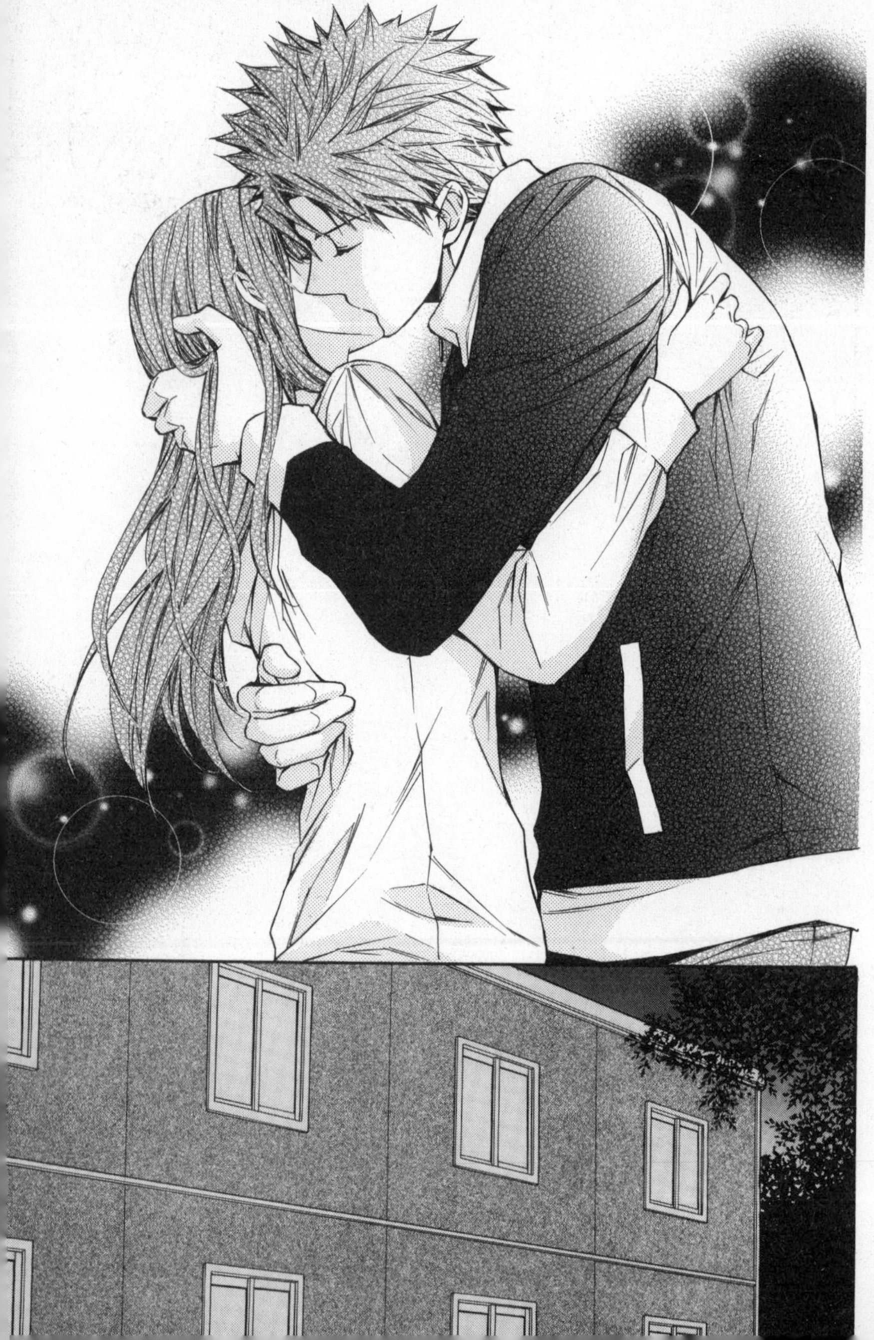

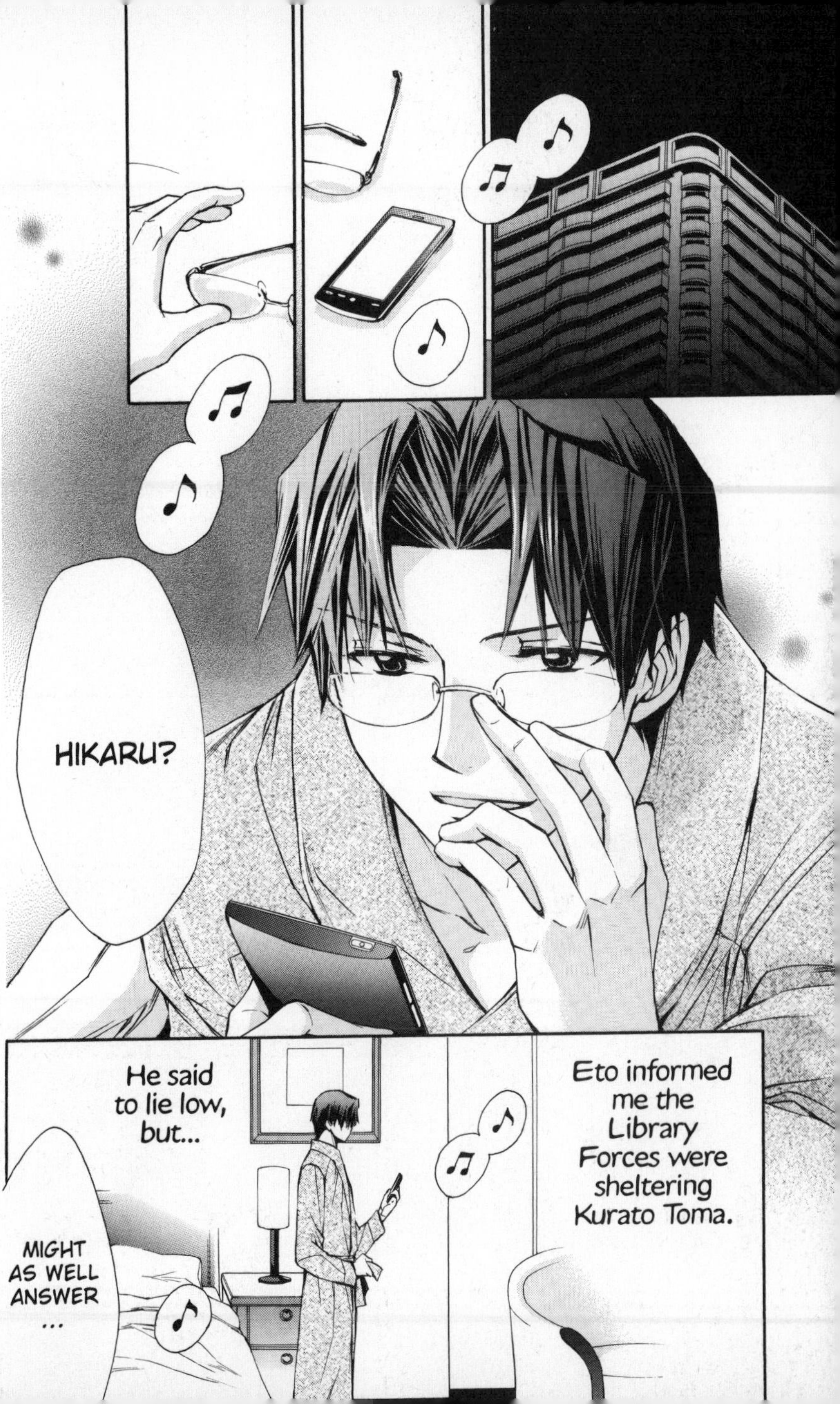
HIKARU?
Eto informed me the Library Forces were sheltering Kurato Toma.
He said to lie low, but...
MIGHT AS WELL ANSWER ...

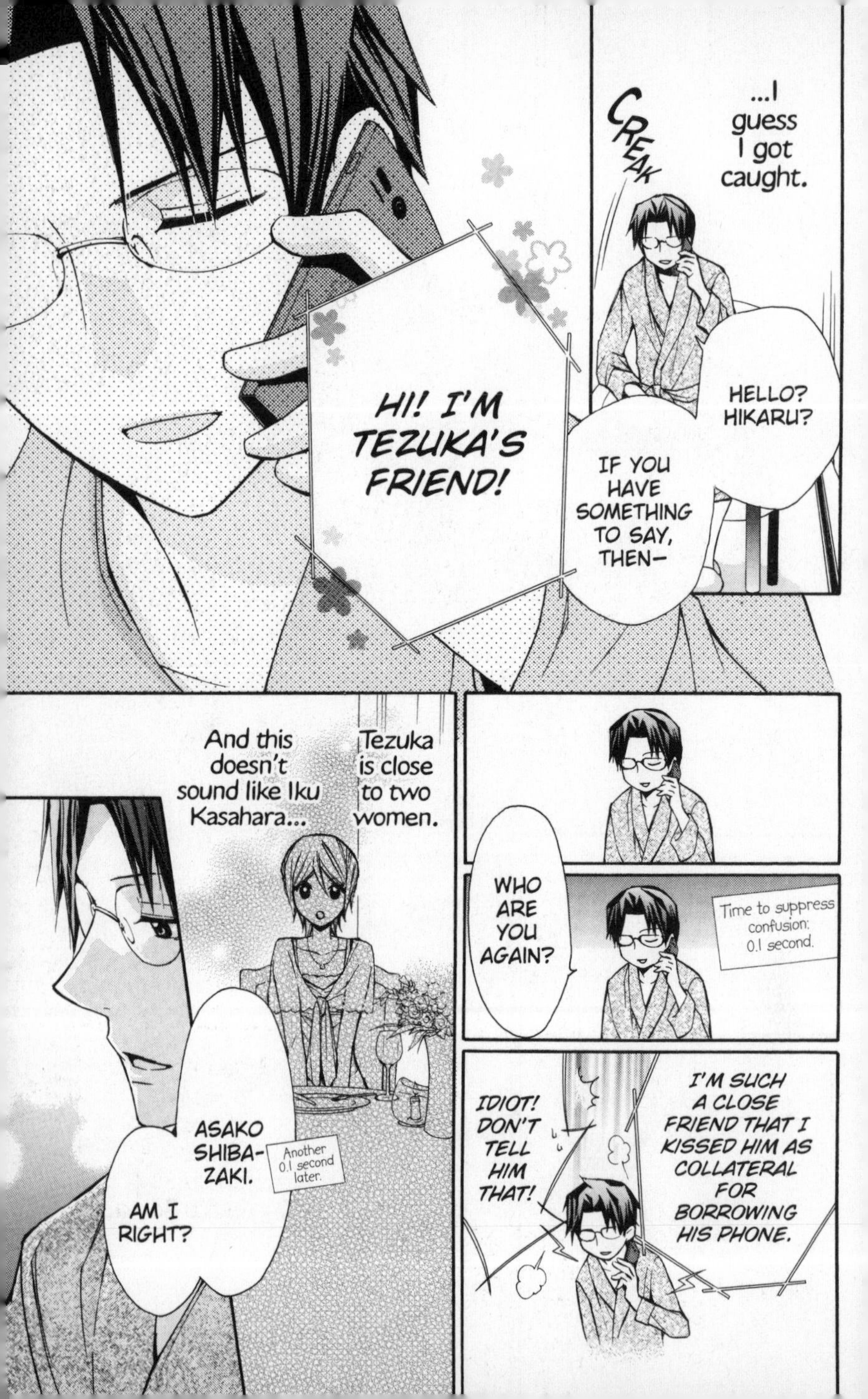
...I guess I got caught.
CREAK
HELLO? HIKARU?
IF YOU HAVE SOMETHING TO SAY, THEN—
HI! I'M TEZUKA'S FRIEND!
WHO ARE YOU AGAIN?
Time to suppress confusion: 0.1 second.
I'M SUCH A CLOSE FRIEND THAT I KISSED HIM AS COLLATERAL FOR BORROWING HIS PHONE.
IDIOT! DON'T TELL HIM THAT!
Tezuka is close to two women.
And this doesn't sound like Iku Kasahara...
ASAKO SHIBA-ZAKI.
Another 0.1 second later.
AM I RIGHT?

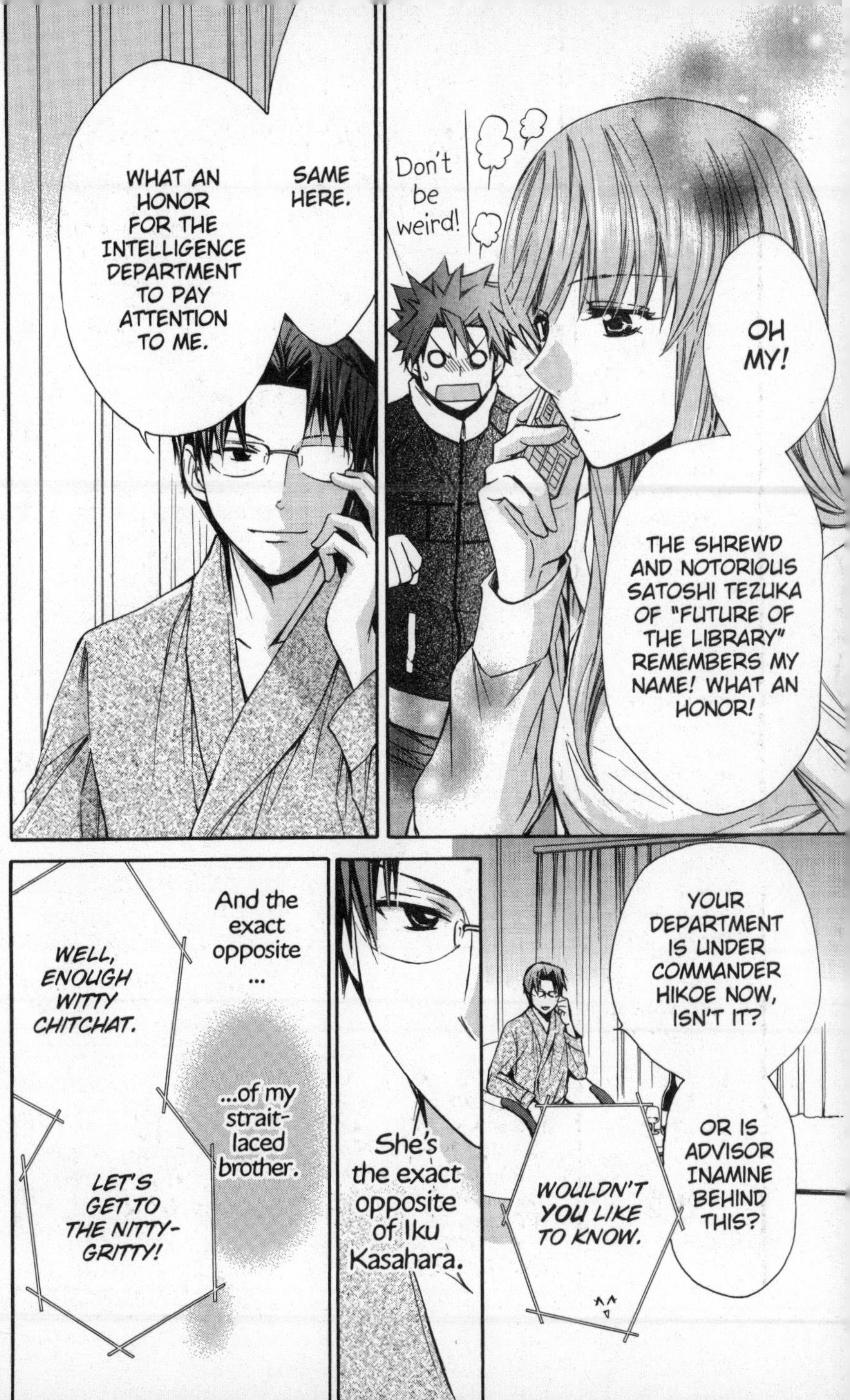
OH MY!
THE SHREWD AND NOTORIOUS SATOSHI TEZUKA OF "FUTURE OF THE LIBRARY" REMEMBERS MY NAME! WHAT AN HONOR!
Don't be weird!
SAME HERE.
WHAT AN HONOR FOR THE INTELLIGENCE DEPARTMENT TO PAY ATTENTION TO ME.
YOUR DEPARTMENT IS UNDER COMMANDER HIKOE NOW, ISN'T IT?
OR IS ADVISOR INAMINE BEHIND THIS?
WOULDN'T YOU LIKE TO KNOW.
She's the exact opposite of Iku Kasahara.
And the exact opposite ...
...of my strait-laced brother.
WELL, ENOUGH WITTY CHITCHAT.
LET'S GET TO THE NITTY-GRITTY!

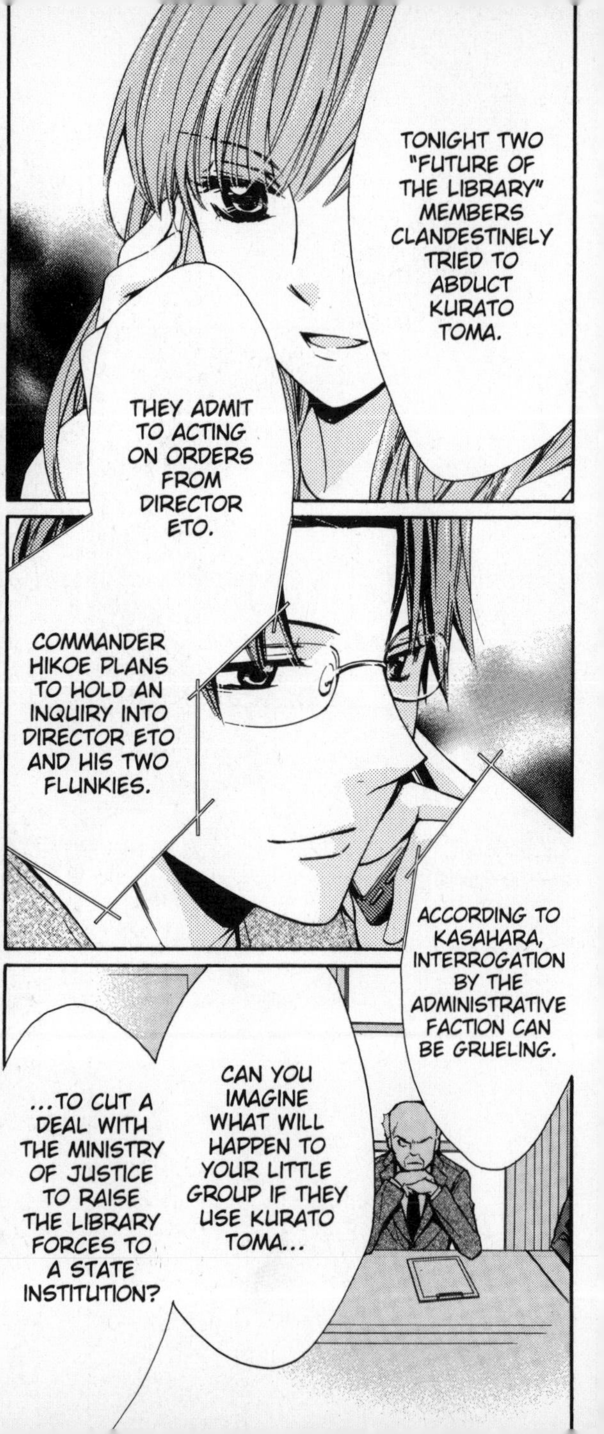
TONIGHT TWO "FUTURE OF THE LIBRARY" MEMBERS CLANDESTINELY TRIED TO ABDUCT KURATO TOMA.
THEY ADMIT TO ACTING ON ORDERS FROM DIRECTOR ETO.
COMMANDER HIKOE PLANS TO HOLD AN INQUIRY INTO DIRECTOR ETO AND HIS TWO FLUNKIES.
ACCORDING TO KASAHARA, INTERROGATION BY THE ADMINISTRATIVE FACTION CAN BE GRUELING.
CAN YOU IMAGINE WHAT WILL HAPPEN TO YOUR LITTLE GROUP IF THEY USE KURATO TOMA...
...TO CUT A DEAL WITH THE MINISTRY OF JUSTICE TO RAISE THE LIBRARY FORCES TO A STATE INSTITUTION?

4

Talking about movies...I went to see *The Avengers* in 2012 without knowing much about the superheroes who appear in it. And I recently watched all of the Marvel movies starring characters from that movie, including *Ironman 3*. Wow... Superheroes are awesome!! I love every last one! And after watching all the other movies it was even more emotional to watch *The Avengers* again. It must take an incredible amount of talent and brains to create such amazing entertainment!

I can't wait to see *Avengers 2* and *Thor 2*!

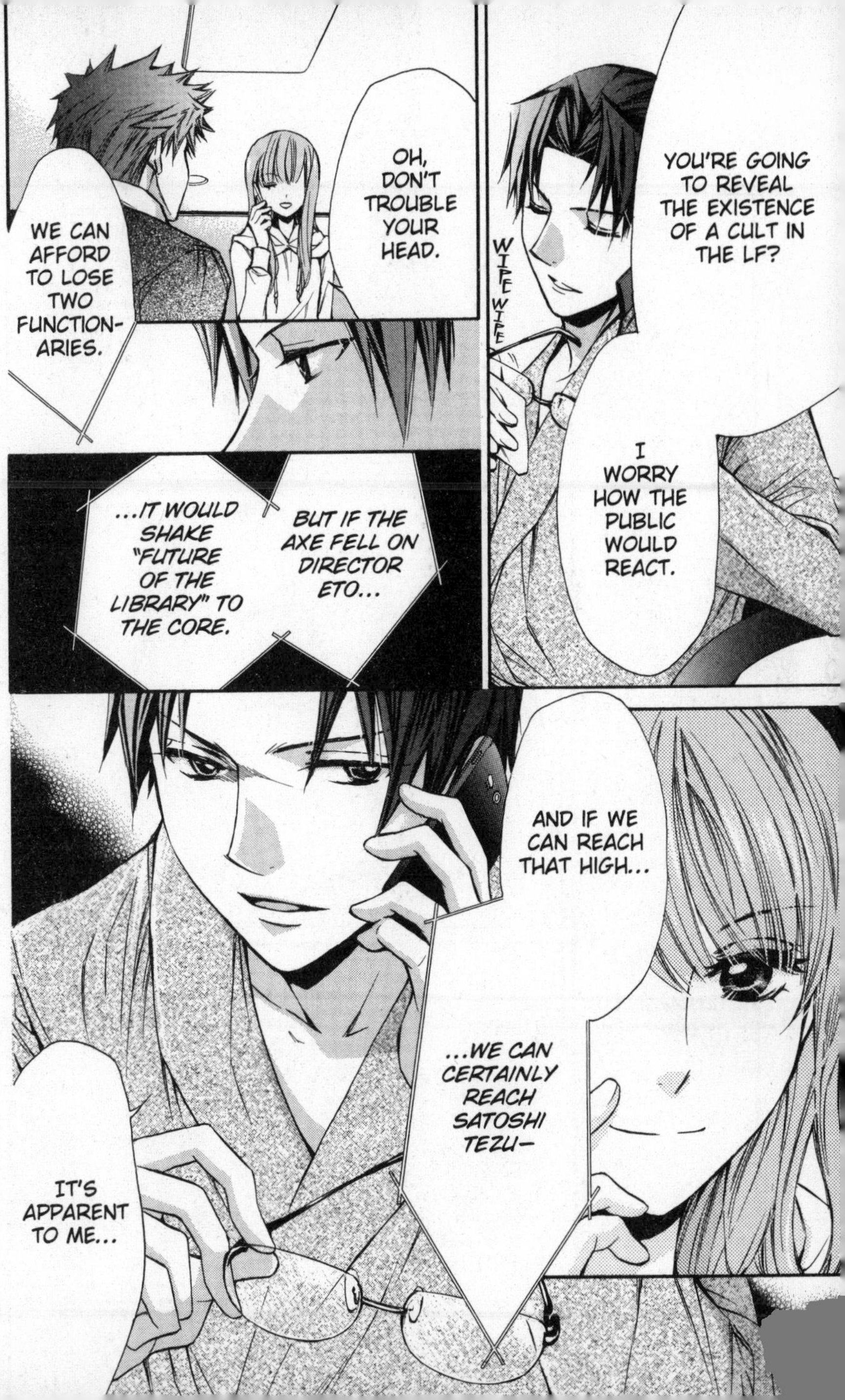
YOU'RE GOING TO REVEAL THE EXISTENCE OF A CULT IN THE LF?
WIPE WIPE
I WORRY HOW THE PUBLIC WOULD REACT.
OH, DON'T TROUBLE YOUR HEAD.
WE CAN AFFORD TO LOSE TWO FUNCTION-ARIES.
BUT IF THE AXE FELL ON DIRECTOR ETO...
...IT WOULD SHAKE "FUTURE OF THE LIBRARY" TO THE CORE.
AND IF WE CAN REACH THAT HIGH...
...WE CAN CERTAINLY REACH SATOSHI TEZU-
IT'S APPARENT TO ME...

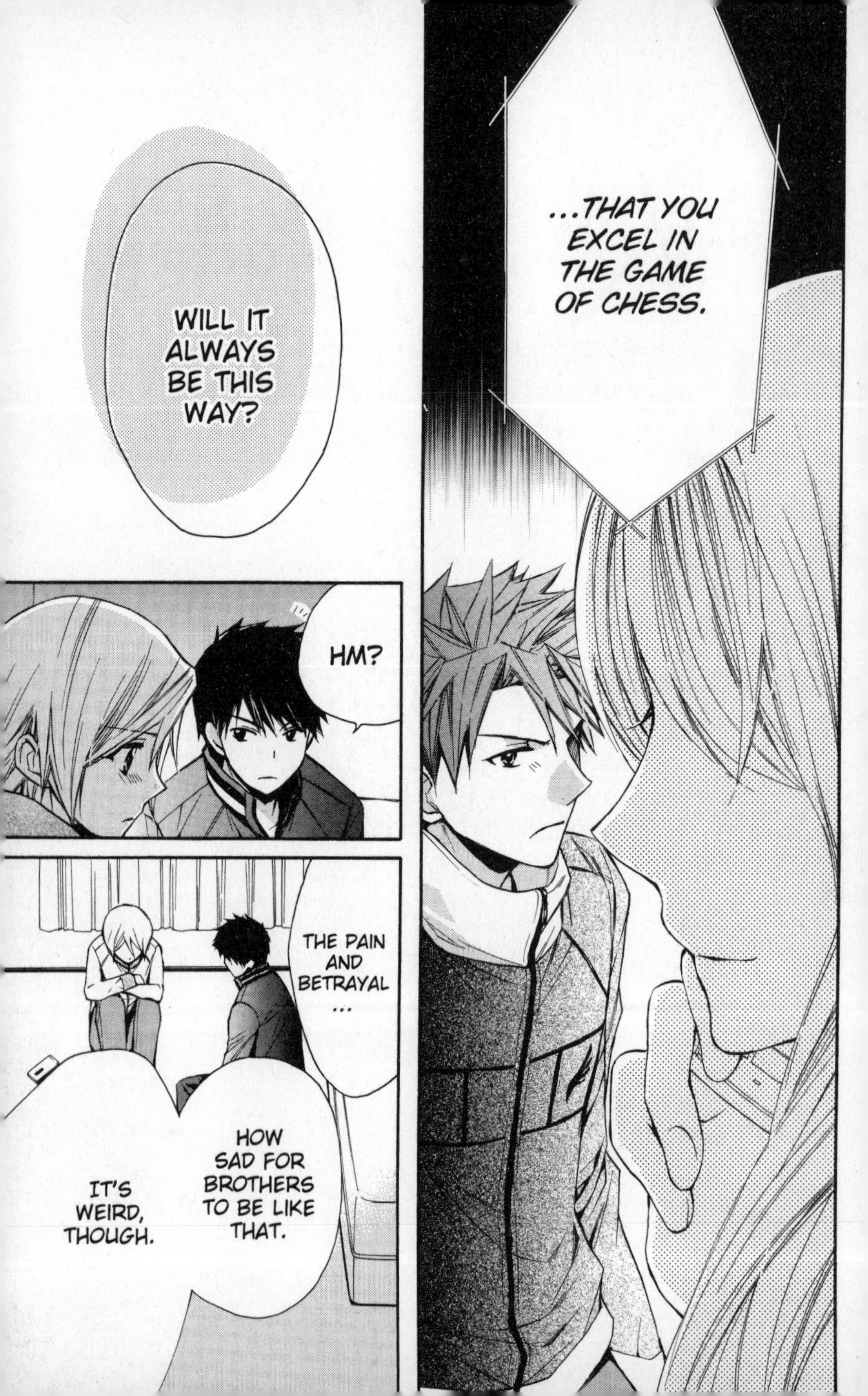
...THAT YOU EXCEL IN THE GAME OF CHESS.
WILL IT ALWAYS BE THIS WAY?
HM?
THE PAIN AND BETRAYAL...
HOW SAD FOR BROTHERS TO BE LIKE THAT.
IT'S WEIRD, THOUGH.

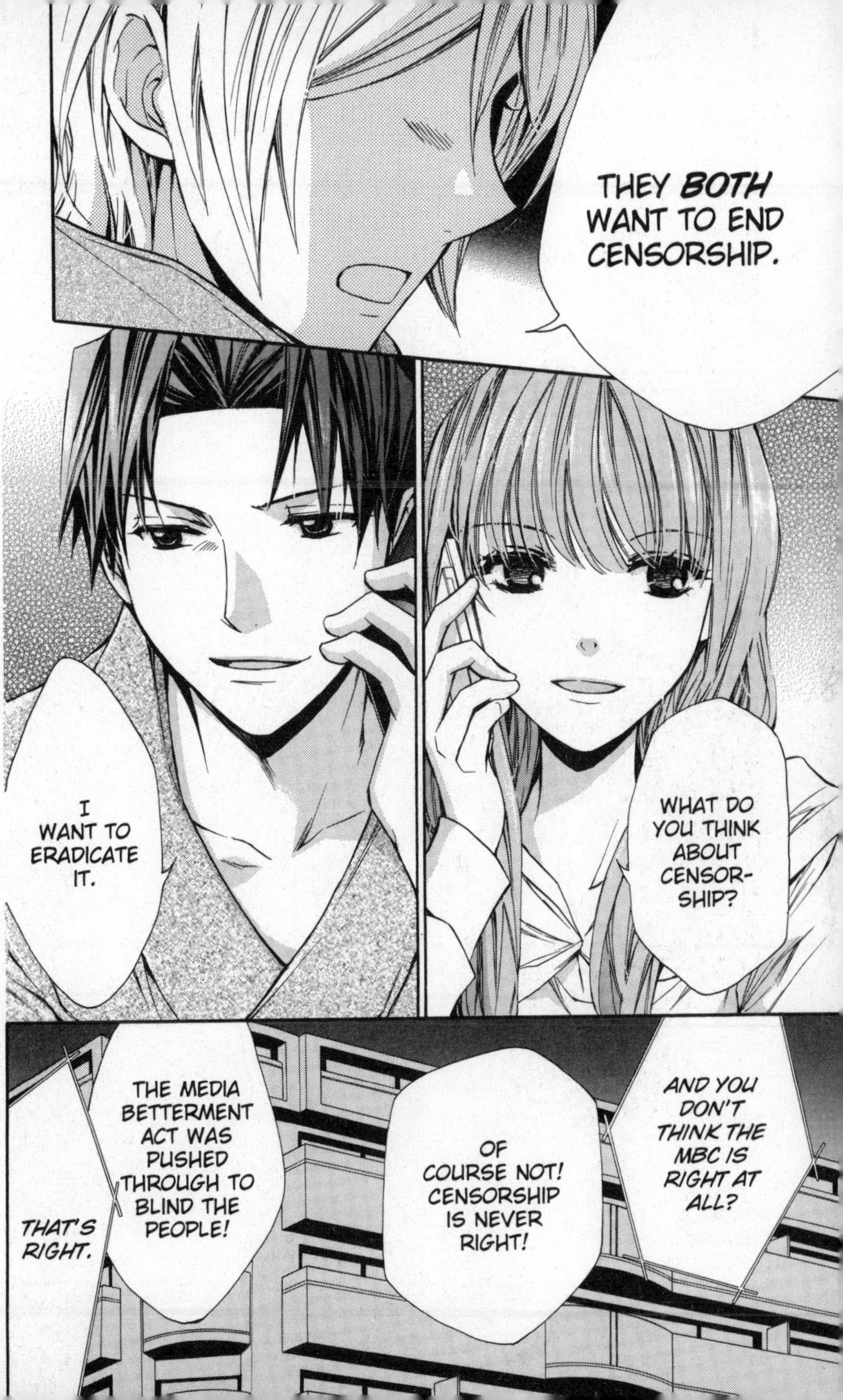
THEY **BOTH** WANT TO END CENSORSHIP.
WHAT DO YOU THINK ABOUT CENSOR-SHIP?
I WANT TO ERADICATE IT.
AND YOU DON'T THINK THE MBC IS RIGHT AT ALL?
OF COURSE NOT! CENSORSHIP IS NEVER RIGHT!
THE MEDIA BETTERMENT ACT WAS PUSHED THROUGH TO BLIND THE PEOPLE!
THAT'S RIGHT.

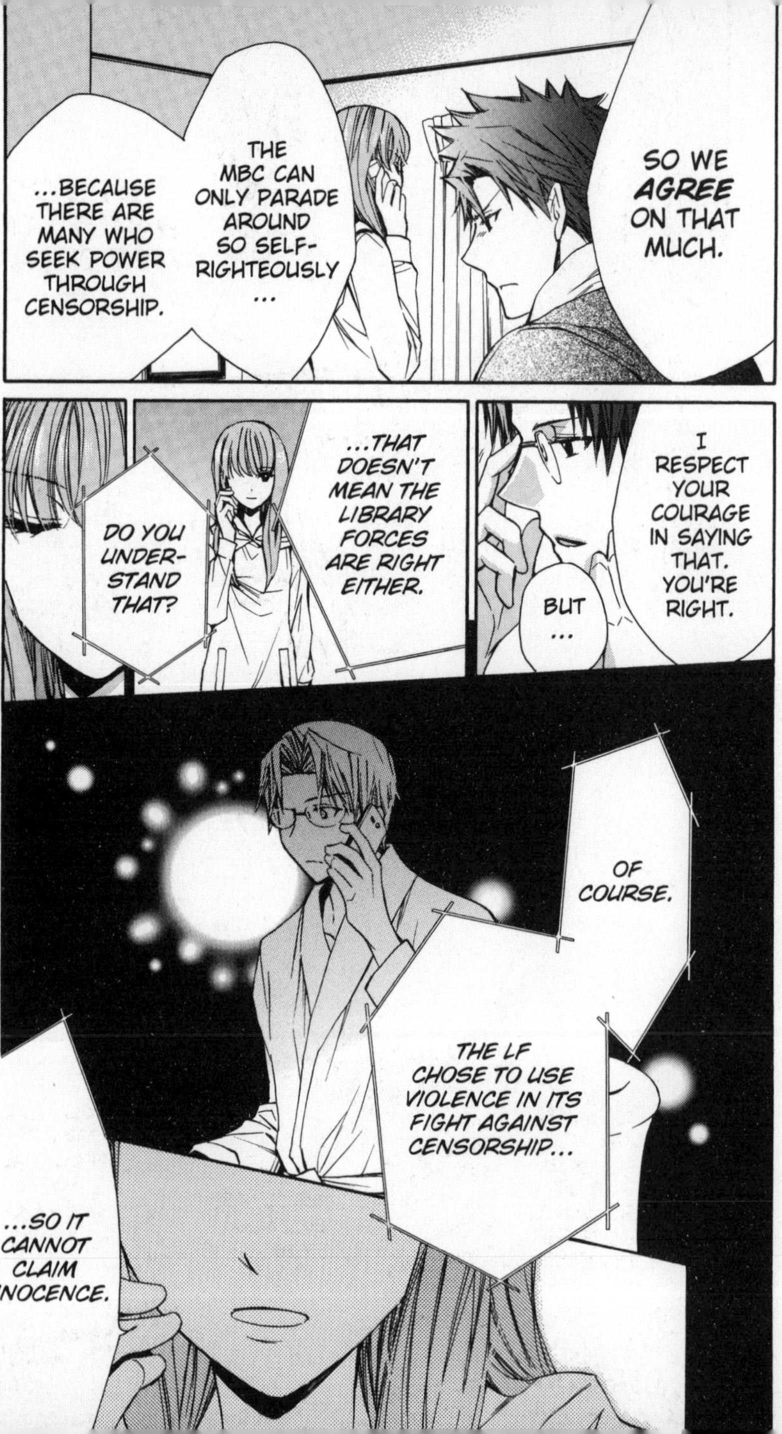
SO WE AGREE ON THAT MUCH.
THE MBC CAN ONLY PARADE AROUND SO SELF-RIGHTEOUSLY...
...BECAUSE THERE ARE MANY WHO SEEK POWER THROUGH CENSORSHIP.
I RESPECT YOUR COURAGE IN SAYING THAT. YOU'RE RIGHT.
BUT...
...THAT DOESN'T MEAN THE LIBRARY FORCES ARE RIGHT EITHER.
DO YOU UNDER-STAND THAT?
OF COURSE.
THE LF CHOSE TO USE VIOLENCE IN ITS FIGHT AGAINST CENSORSHIP...
...SO IT CANNOT CLAIM INNOCENCE.

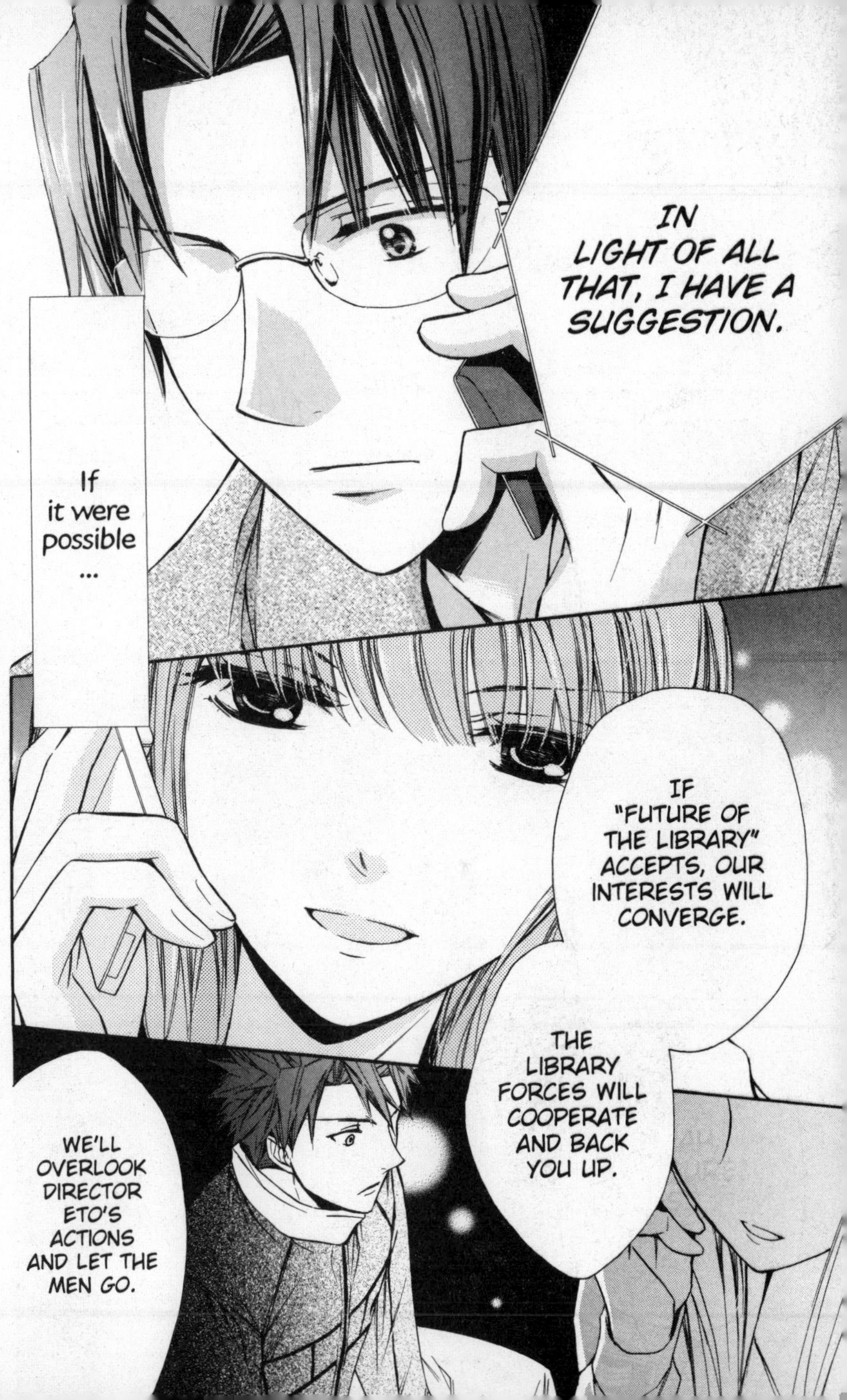
IN LIGHT OF ALL THAT, I HAVE A SUGGESTION.
If it were possible ...
IF "FUTURE OF THE LIBRARY" ACCEPTS, OUR INTERESTS WILL CONVERGE.
THE LIBRARY FORCES WILL COOPERATE AND BACK YOU UP.
WE'LL OVERLOOK DIRECTOR ETO'S ACTIONS AND LET THE MEN GO.

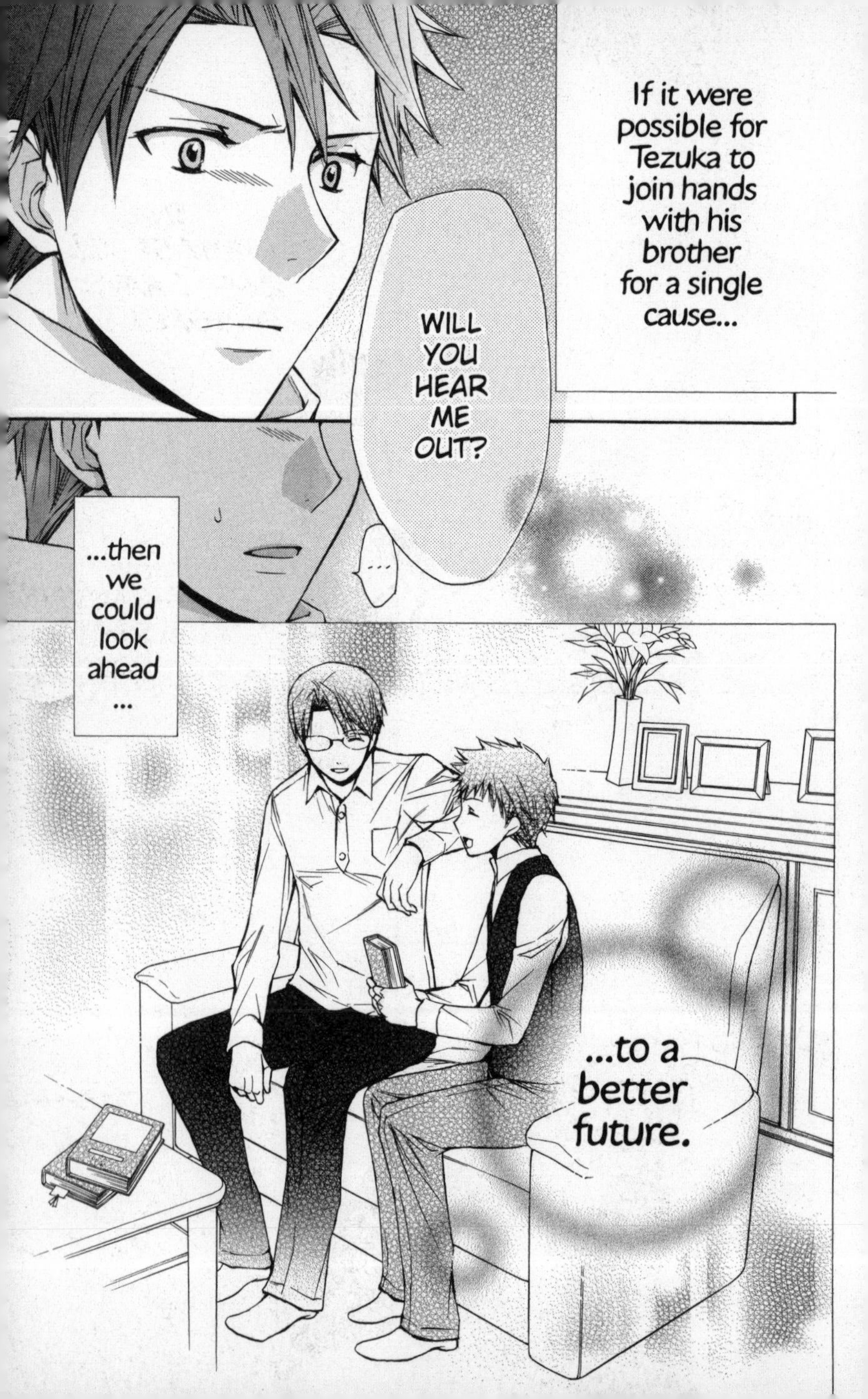
If it were possible for Tezuka to join hands with his brother for a single cause...
WILL YOU HEAR ME OUT?
...
...then we could look ahead ...
...to a better future.

Lifetime Secret

In order to avoid the eyes of "Future of the Library," Kurato Toma moved to a guest room in the women's barracks. Instructor Dojo secretly accompanied him as a guard.
Did anyone see you? Were you nervous?
Um...
I was fine.
Come to think of it...
Komaki said there's a special item for cases like this.
No, there isn't!
GRAAH
Don't shout...
Urgh...
There's no such thing...
Here, Dojo.
Take this just in case.
Party wig (task force gear)
He was almost discovered...
SWUF
And I certainly didn't use it!
?

"Atsuko" simply isn't pretty.

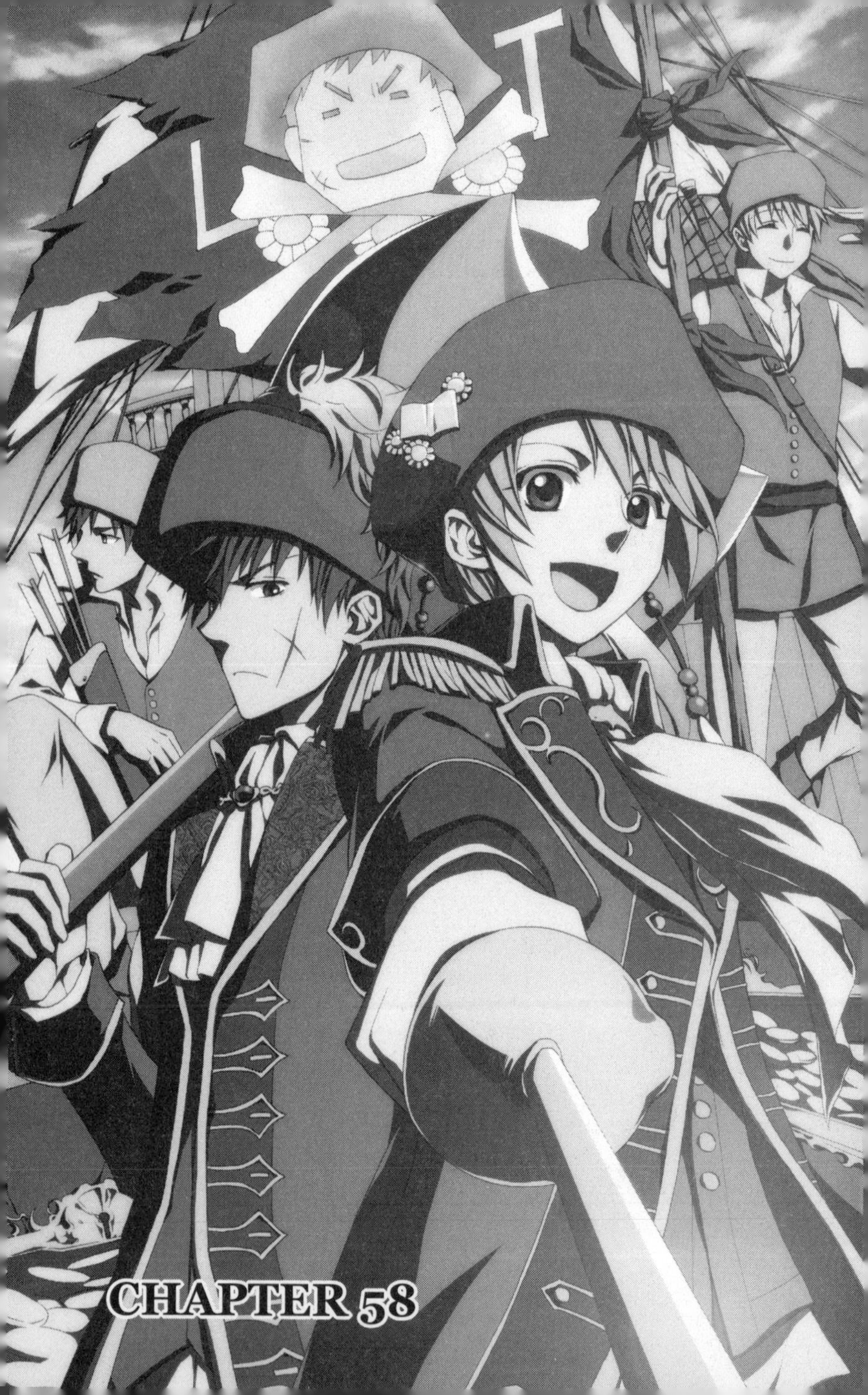
CHAPTER 58

The Endless Gen● Pose

Commander Hikoe, Chapter 55, page 19.

Commander Hikoe, Chapter 56, page 22.

Commander Hikoe, Chapter 57, page 25.

Commander Hikoe sometime in the future.

The way he folds his hands is slightly different.

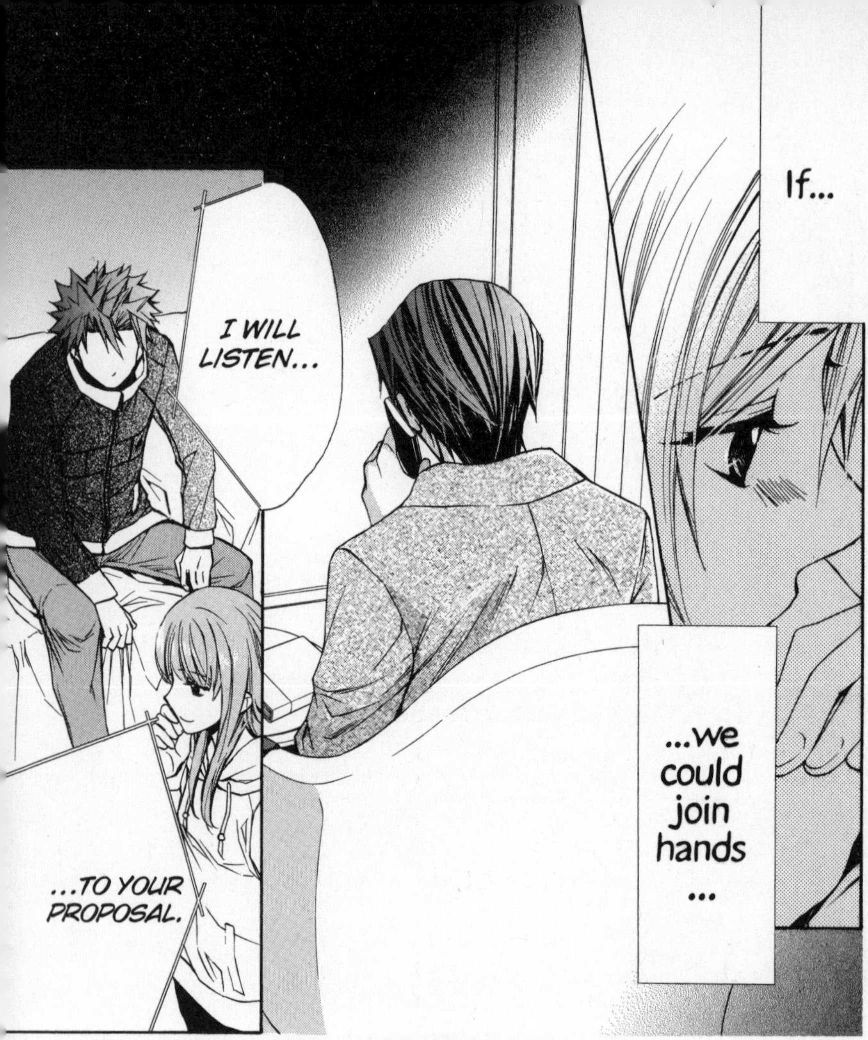
If...
...we could join hands...
I WILL LISTEN...
...TO YOUR PROPOSAL.

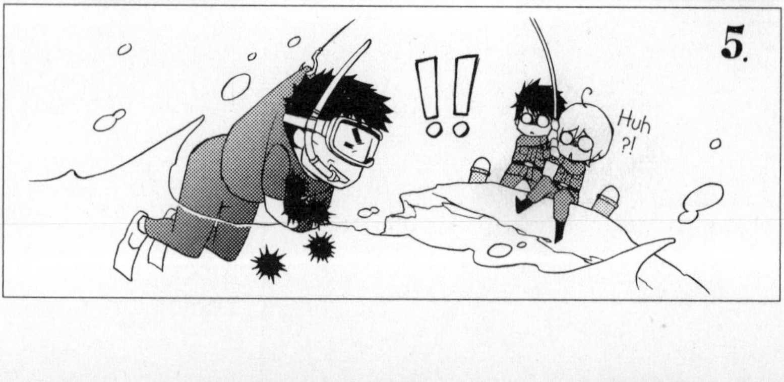
5.
!!
Huh?!

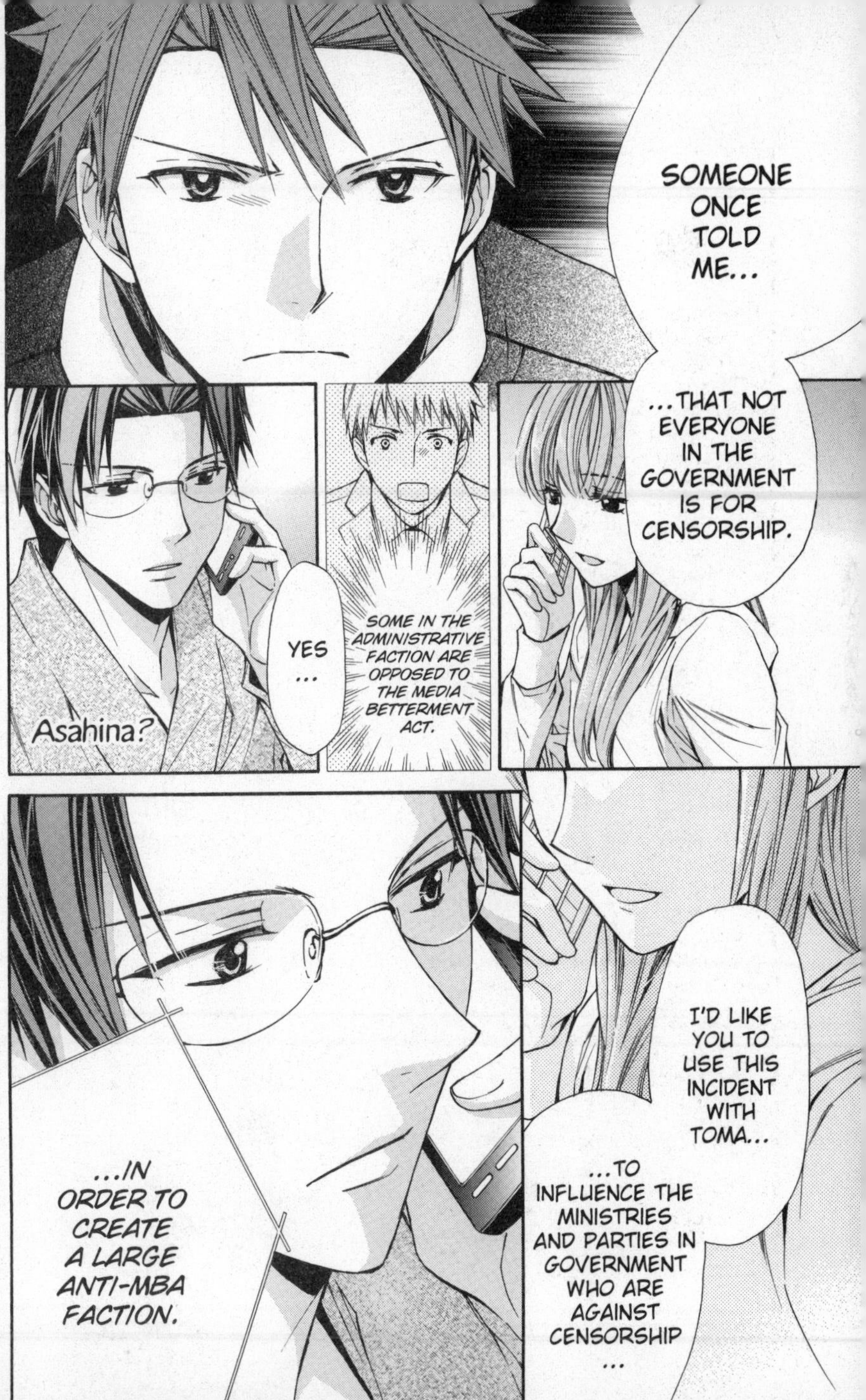
SOMEONE ONCE TOLD ME...
...THAT NOT EVERYONE IN THE GOVERNMENT IS FOR CENSORSHIP.
SOME IN THE ADMINISTRATIVE FACTION ARE OPPOSED TO THE MEDIA BETTERMENT ACT.
YES ...
Asahina?
I'D LIKE YOU TO USE THIS INCIDENT WITH TOMA...
...TO INFLUENCE THE MINISTRIES AND PARTIES IN GOVERNMENT WHO ARE AGAINST CENSORSHIP ...
...IN ORDER TO CREATE A LARGE ANTI-MBA FACTION.

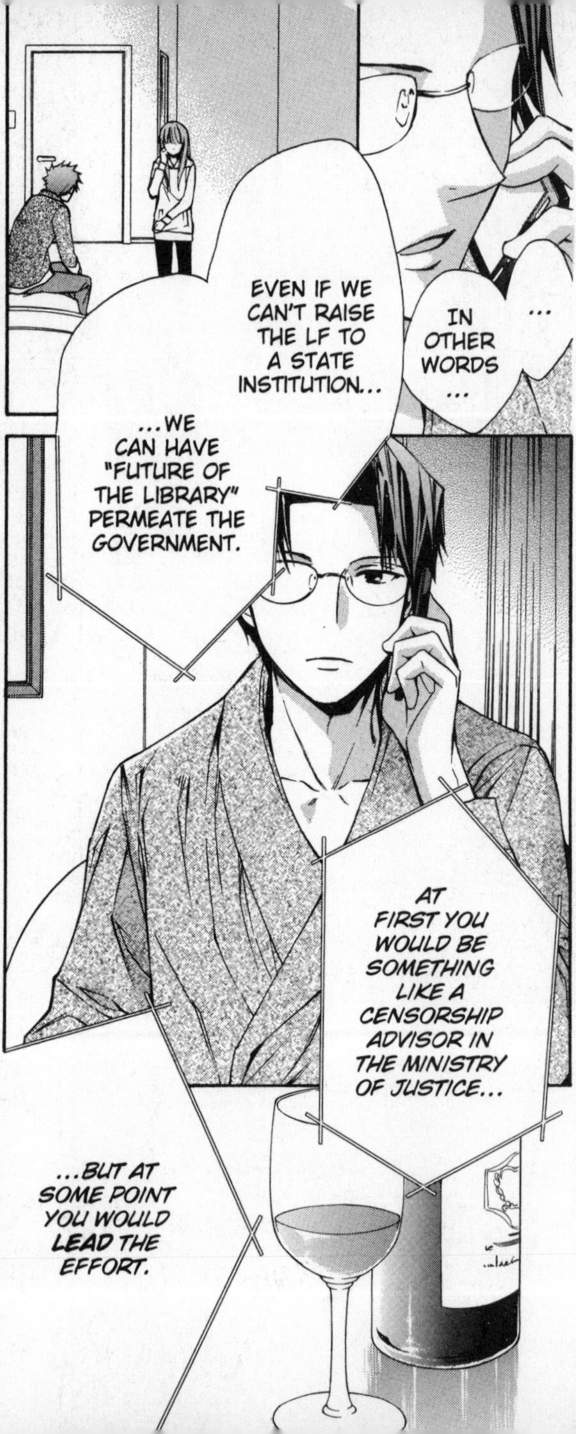
...
IN OTHER WORDS...
EVEN IF WE CAN'T RAISE THE LF TO A STATE INSTITUTION...
...WE CAN HAVE "FUTURE OF THE LIBRARY" PERMEATE THE GOVERNMENT.
AT FIRST YOU WOULD BE SOMETHING LIKE A CENSORSHIP ADVISOR IN THE MINISTRY OF JUSTICE...
...BUT AT SOME POINT YOU WOULD LEAD THE EFFORT.

5

Here's more about movies. Not only do I like *The Avengers*, but I also like other superhero movies like *Batman Begins* through *The Dark Night Rises*, all three of the original *Spider-Man* movies and *The Amazing Spider-Man*. As a *Library Wars* fan, I like to watch *The Amazing Spider-Man* dubbed in Japanese. Including superhero movies, I like flashy movies that make you say, "This is entertainment!" My tastes are pretty easy to peg when it comes to movies. I also thought *Wreck-It Ralph* was awesome. It was way too much fun!! I like Japanese movies, too!

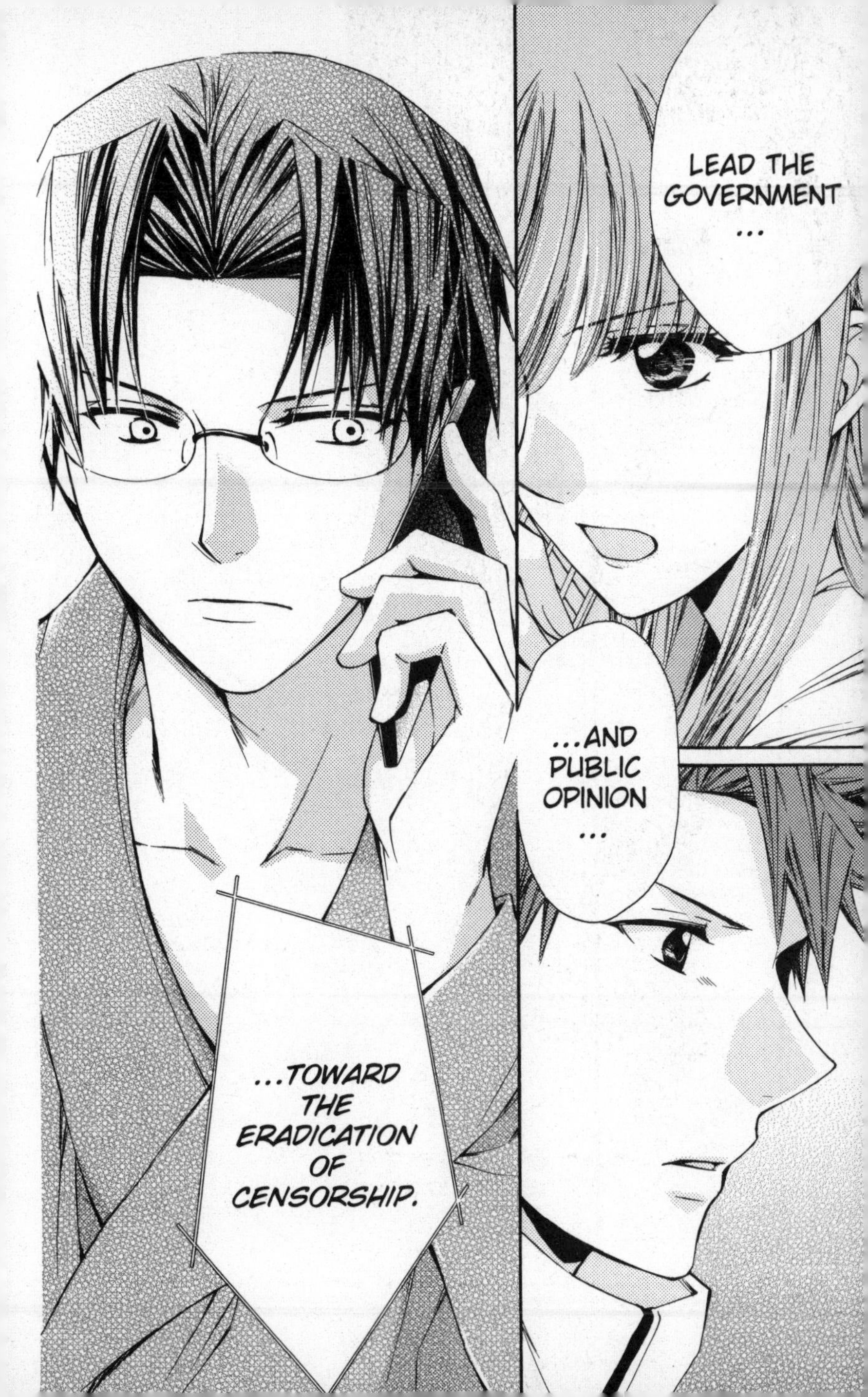
LEAD THE GOVERNMENT ...
...AND PUBLIC OPINION ...
...TOWARD THE ERADICATION OF CENSORSHIP.

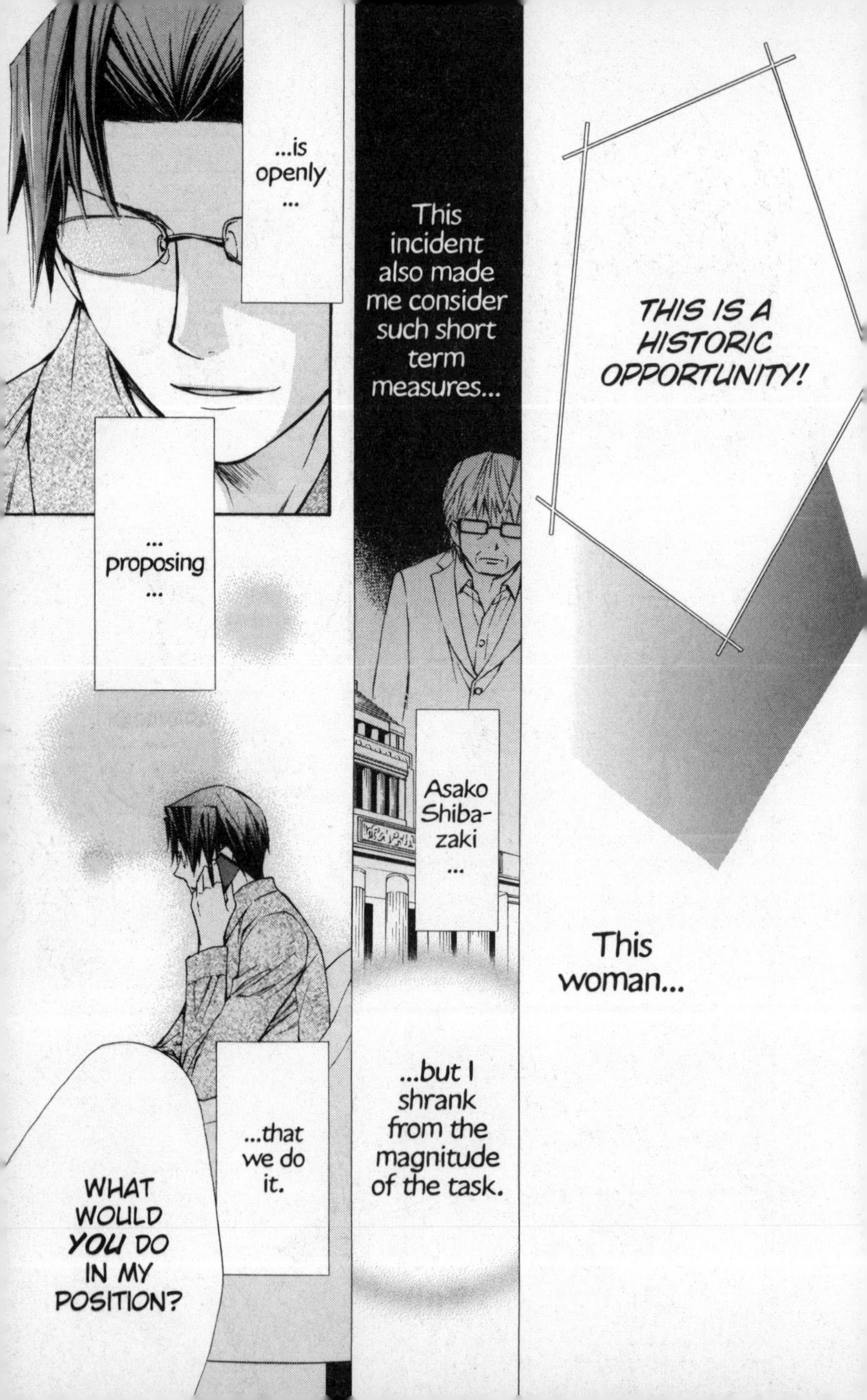

THIS IS A HISTORIC OPPORTUNITY!
This woman...
This incident also made me consider such short term measures...
Asako Shiba-zaki ...
...but I shrank from the magnitude of the task.
...is openly ...
... proposing ...
...that we do it.
WHAT WOULD YOU DO IN MY POSITION?

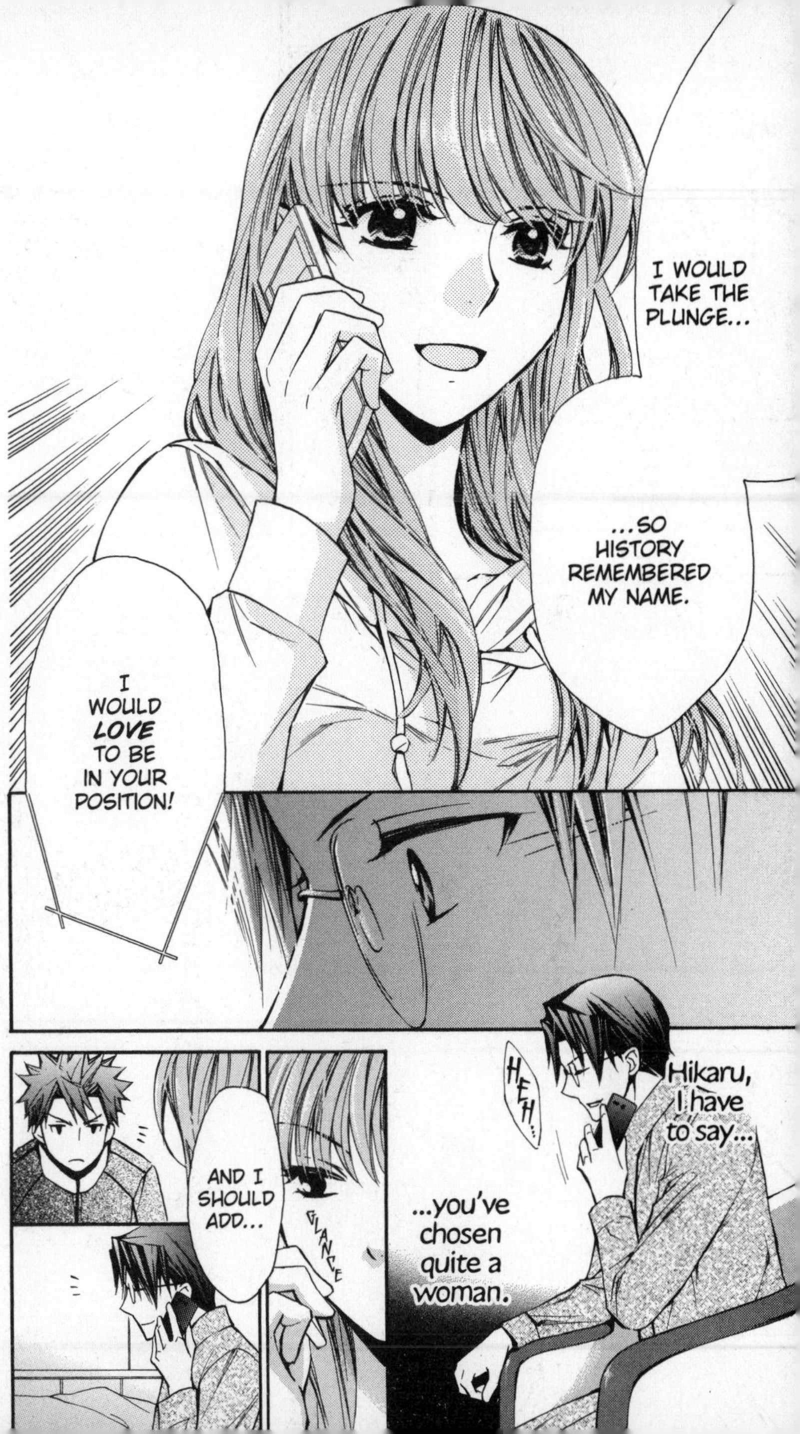
I WOULD TAKE THE PLUNGE...
...SO HISTORY REMEMBERED MY NAME.
I WOULD LOVE TO BE IN YOUR POSITION!
Hikaru, I have to say...
HEH...
...you've chosen quite a woman.
AND I SHOULD ADD...
GLANCE

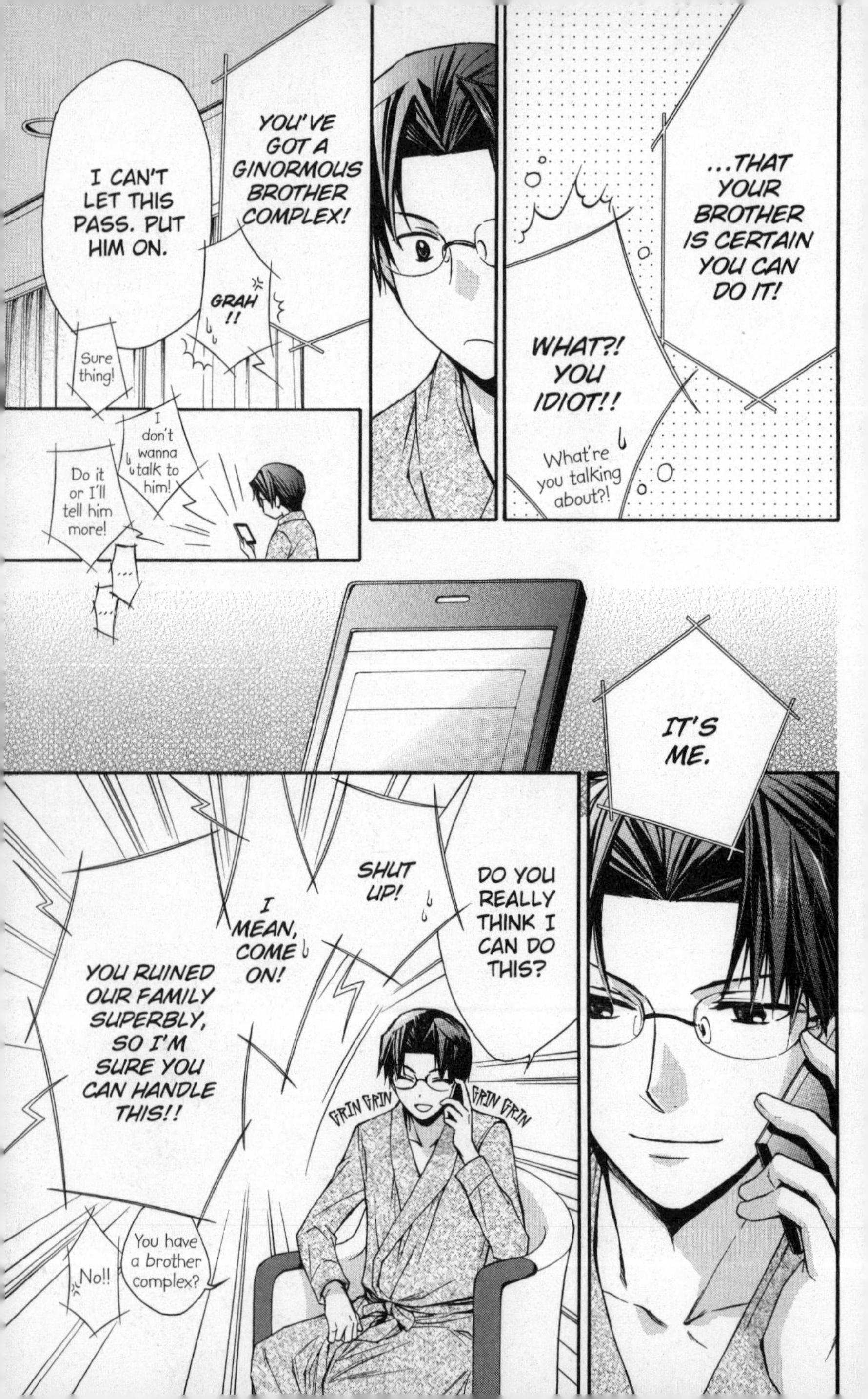
...THAT YOUR BROTHER IS CERTAIN YOU CAN DO IT!
WHAT?! YOU IDIOT!!
What're you talking about?!
YOU'VE GOT A GINORMOUS BROTHER COMPLEX!
GRAH!!
I CAN'T LET THIS PASS. PUT HIM ON.
Sure thing!
I don't wanna talk to him!
Do it or I'll tell him more!
...
...
IT'S ME.
DO YOU REALLY THINK I CAN DO THIS?
SHUT UP!
I MEAN, COME ON!
YOU RUINED OUR FAMILY SUPERBLY, SO I'M SURE YOU CAN HANDLE THIS!!
GRIN GRIN
GRIN GRIN
You have a brother complex?
No!!

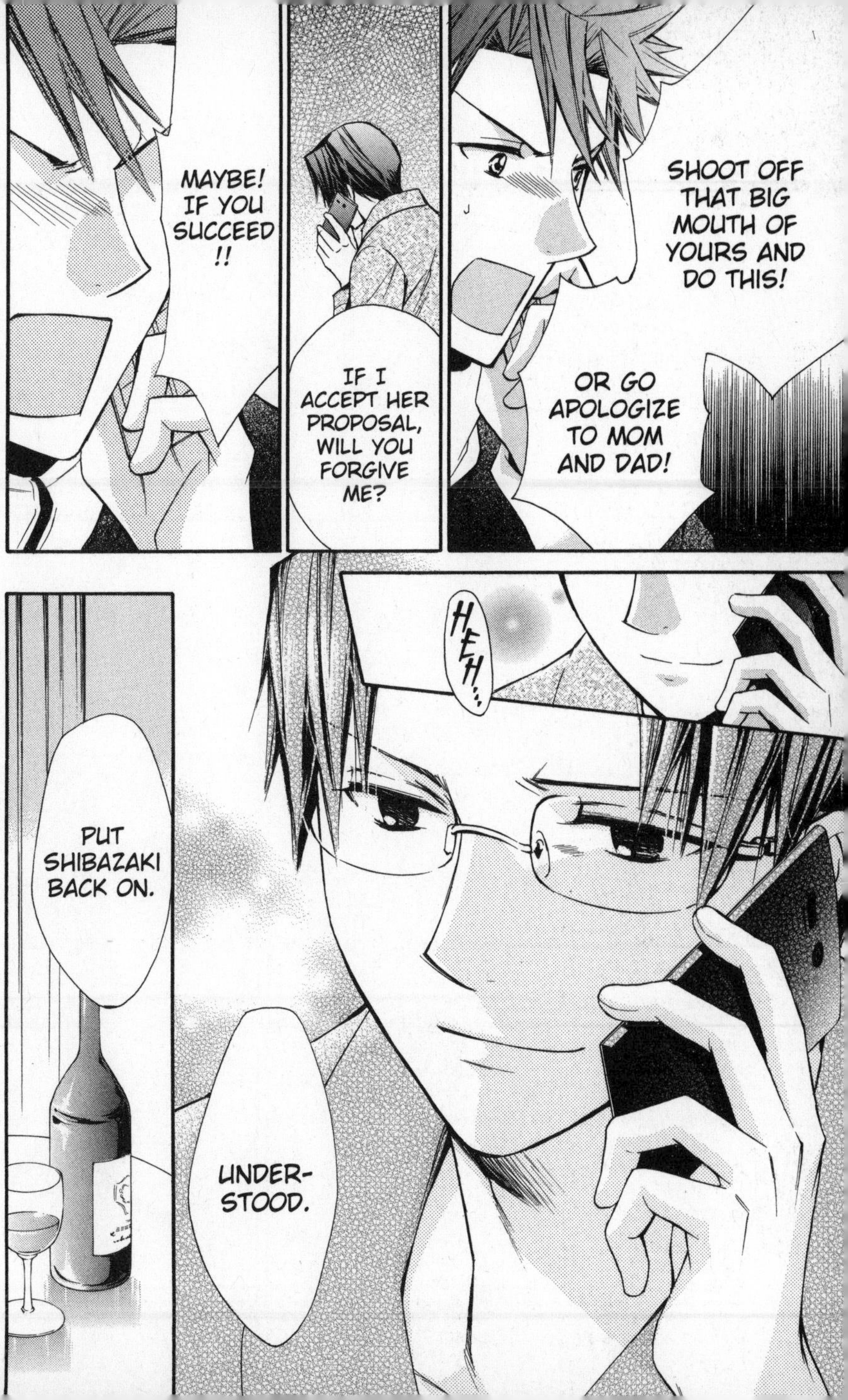
SHOOT OFF THAT BIG MOUTH OF YOURS AND DO THIS!
OR GO APOLOGIZE TO MOM AND DAD!
IF I ACCEPT HER PROPOSAL, WILL YOU FORGIVE ME?
MAYBE! IF YOU SUCCEED !!
HEH..
PUT SHIBAZAKI BACK ON.
UNDER-STOOD.

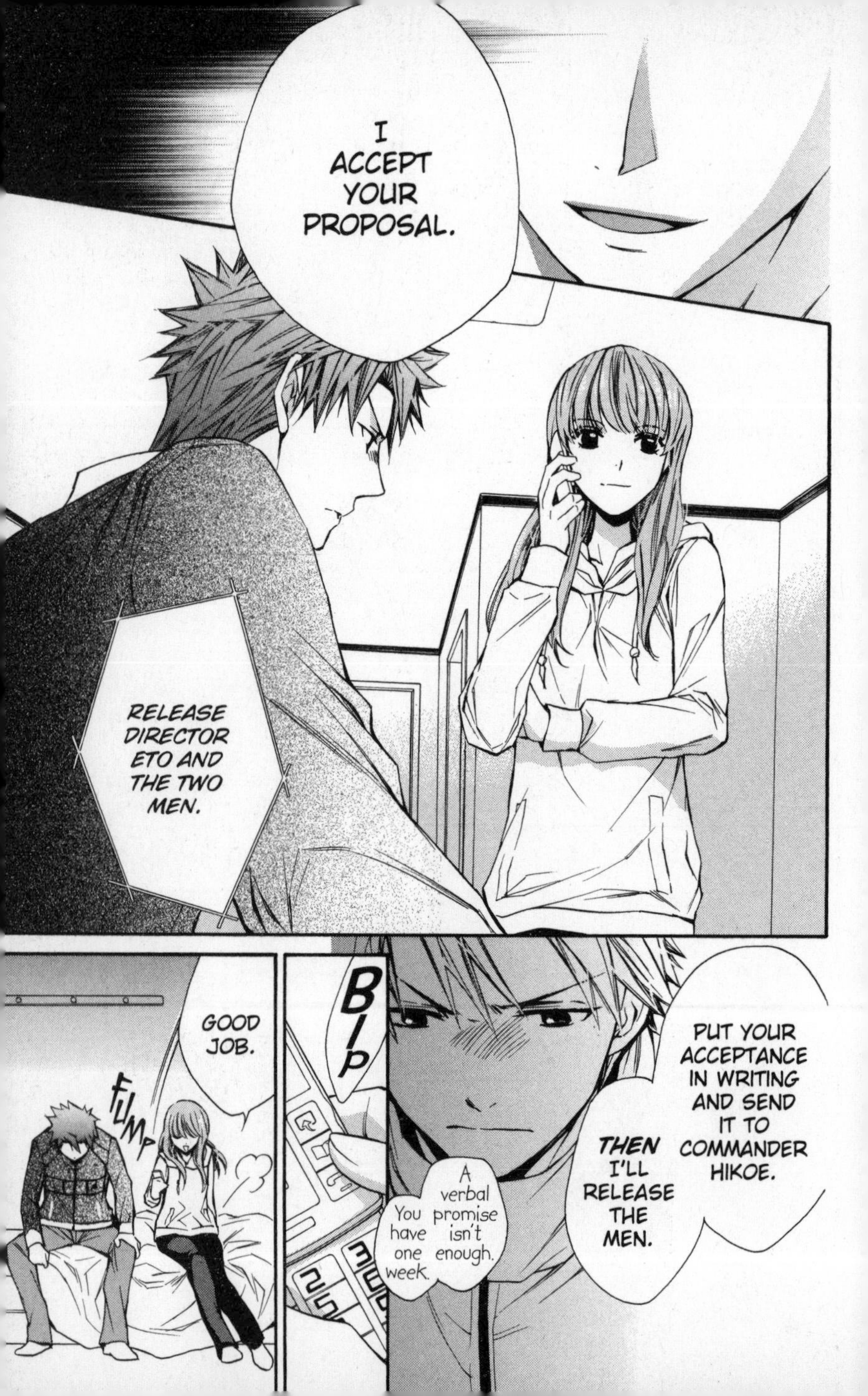
I ACCEPT YOUR PROPOSAL.
RELEASE DIRECTOR ETO AND THE TWO MEN.
BIP
PUT YOUR ACCEPTANCE IN WRITING AND SEND IT TO COMMANDER HIKOE.
THEN I'LL RELEASE THE MEN.
A verbal promise isn't enough.
You have one week.
GOOD JOB.
FUMP

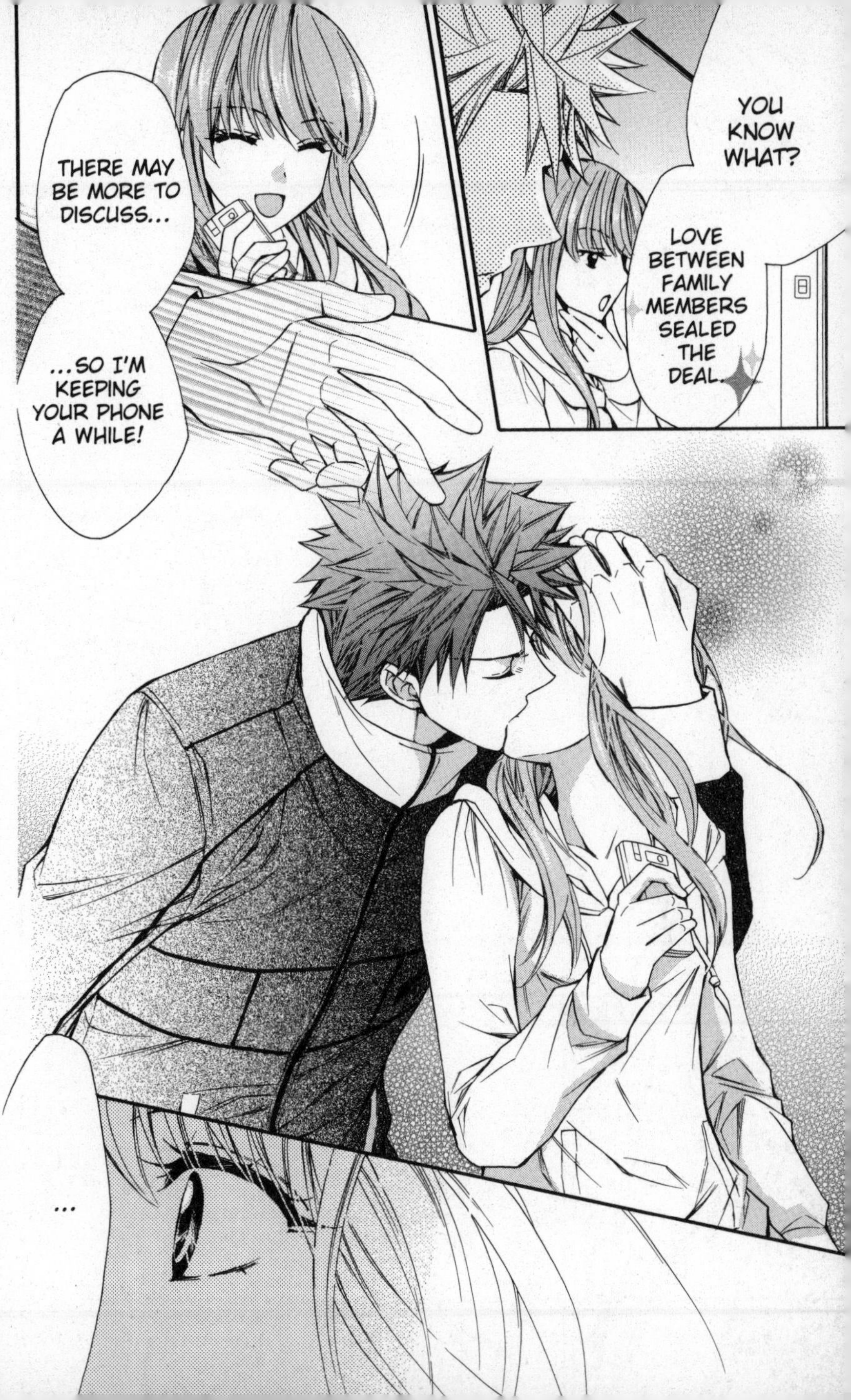
YOU KNOW WHAT?
LOVE BETWEEN FAMILY MEMBERS SEALED THE DEAL.
THERE MAY BE MORE TO DISCUSS...
...SO I'M KEEPING YOUR PHONE A WHILE!
...

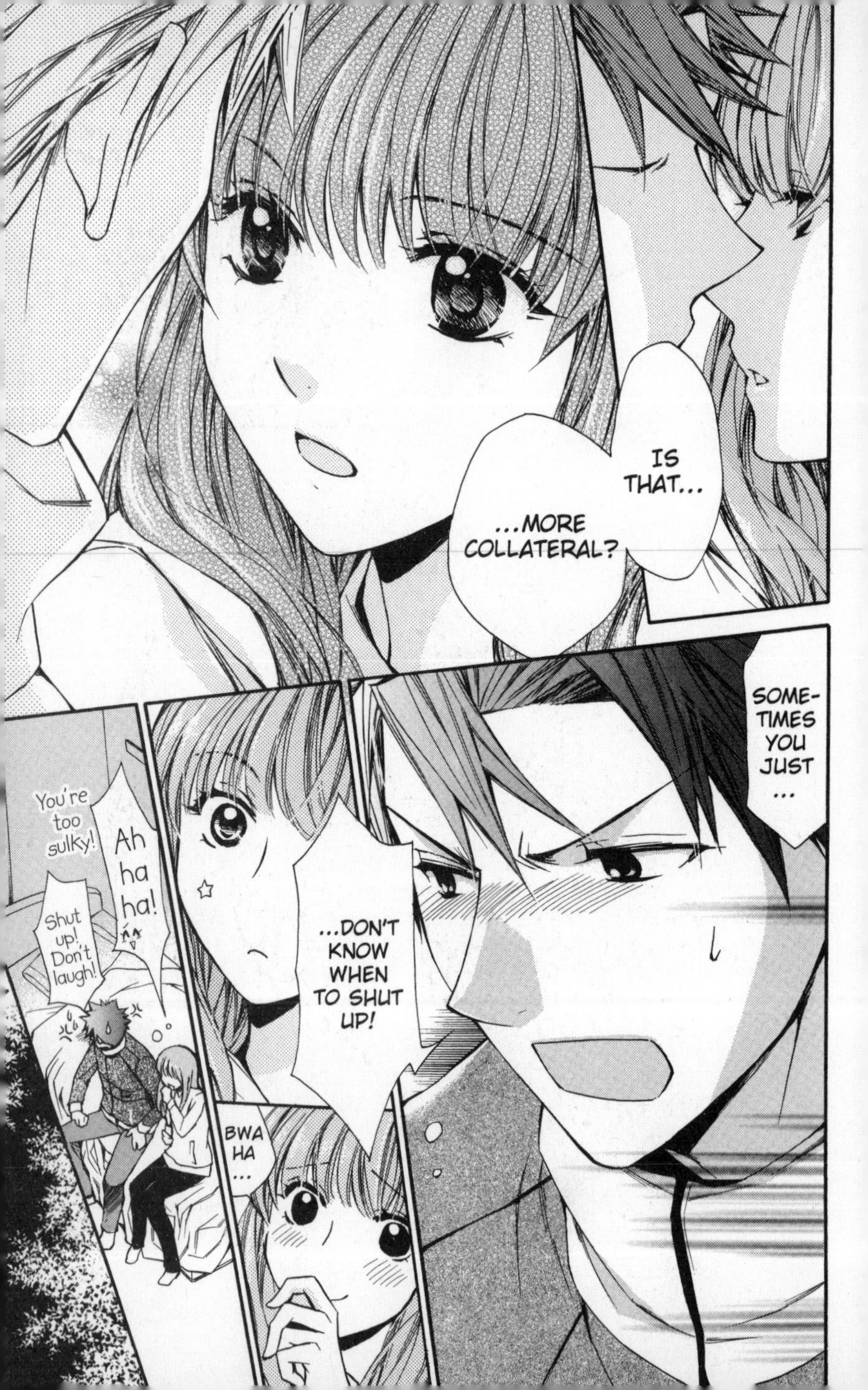
IS THAT...
...MORE COLLATERAL?
SOME-TIMES YOU JUST ...
...DON'T KNOW WHEN TO SHUT UP!
BWA HA ...
Ah ha ha!
You're too sulky!
Shut up! Don't laugh!

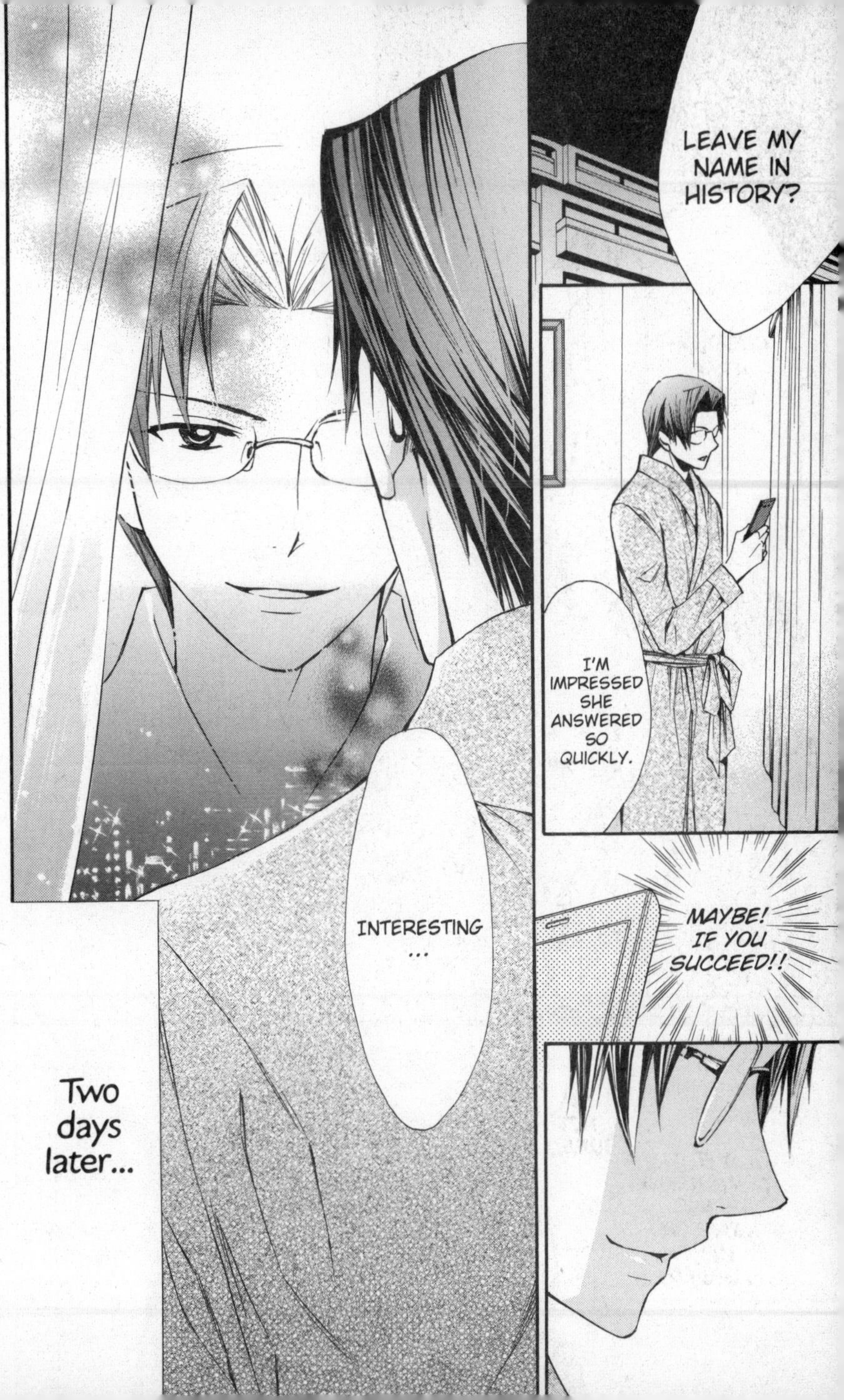
LEAVE MY NAME IN HISTORY?
I'M IMPRESSED SHE ANSWERED SO QUICKLY.
MAYBE! IF YOU SUCCEED!!
INTERESTING ...
Two days later...

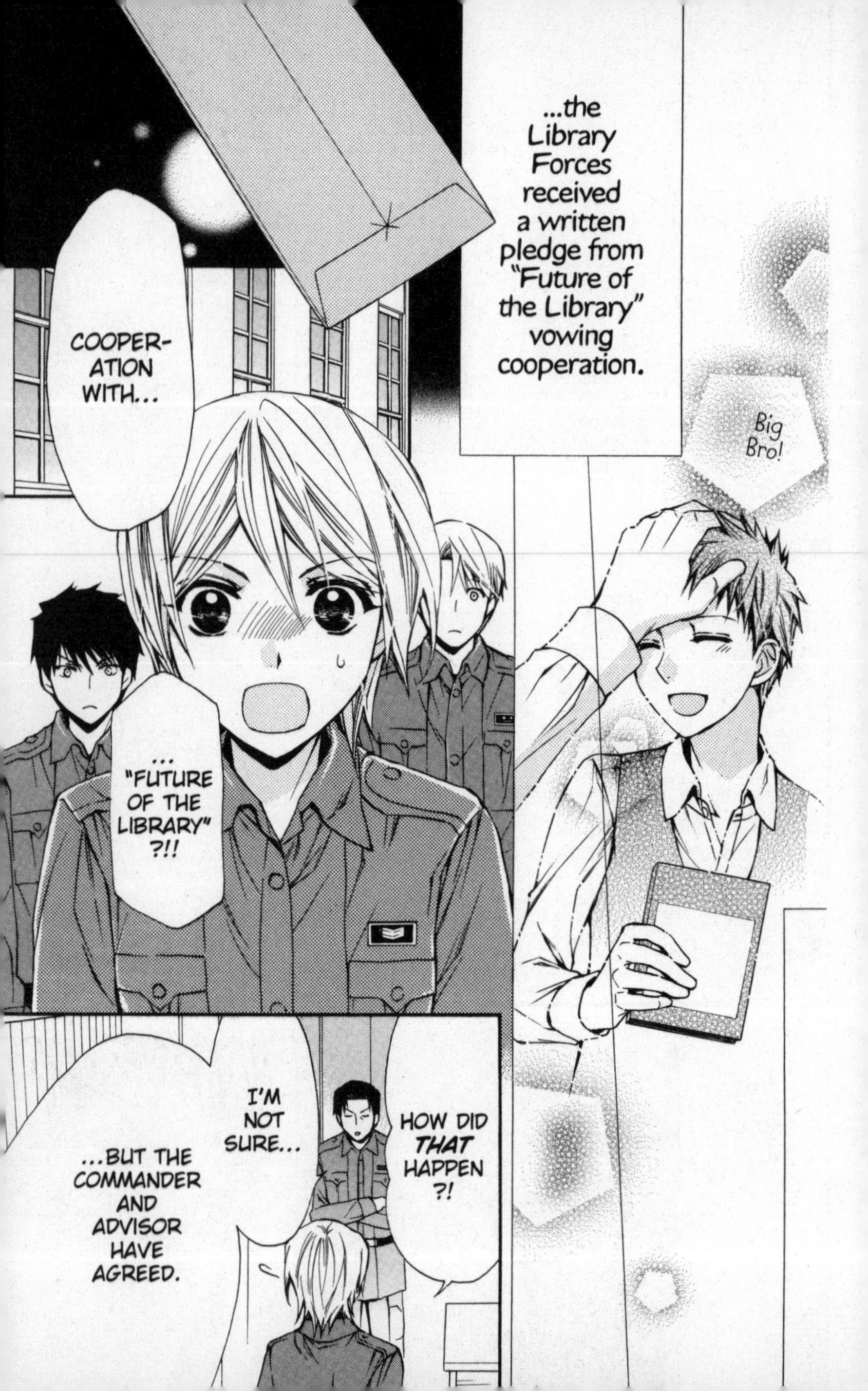
...the Library Forces received a written pledge from "Future of the Library" vowing cooperation.
Big Bro!
COOPER-ATION WITH...
... "FUTURE OF THE LIBRARY" ?!!
HOW DID *THAT* HAPPEN ?!
I'M NOT SURE...
...BUT THE COMMANDER AND ADVISOR HAVE AGREED.

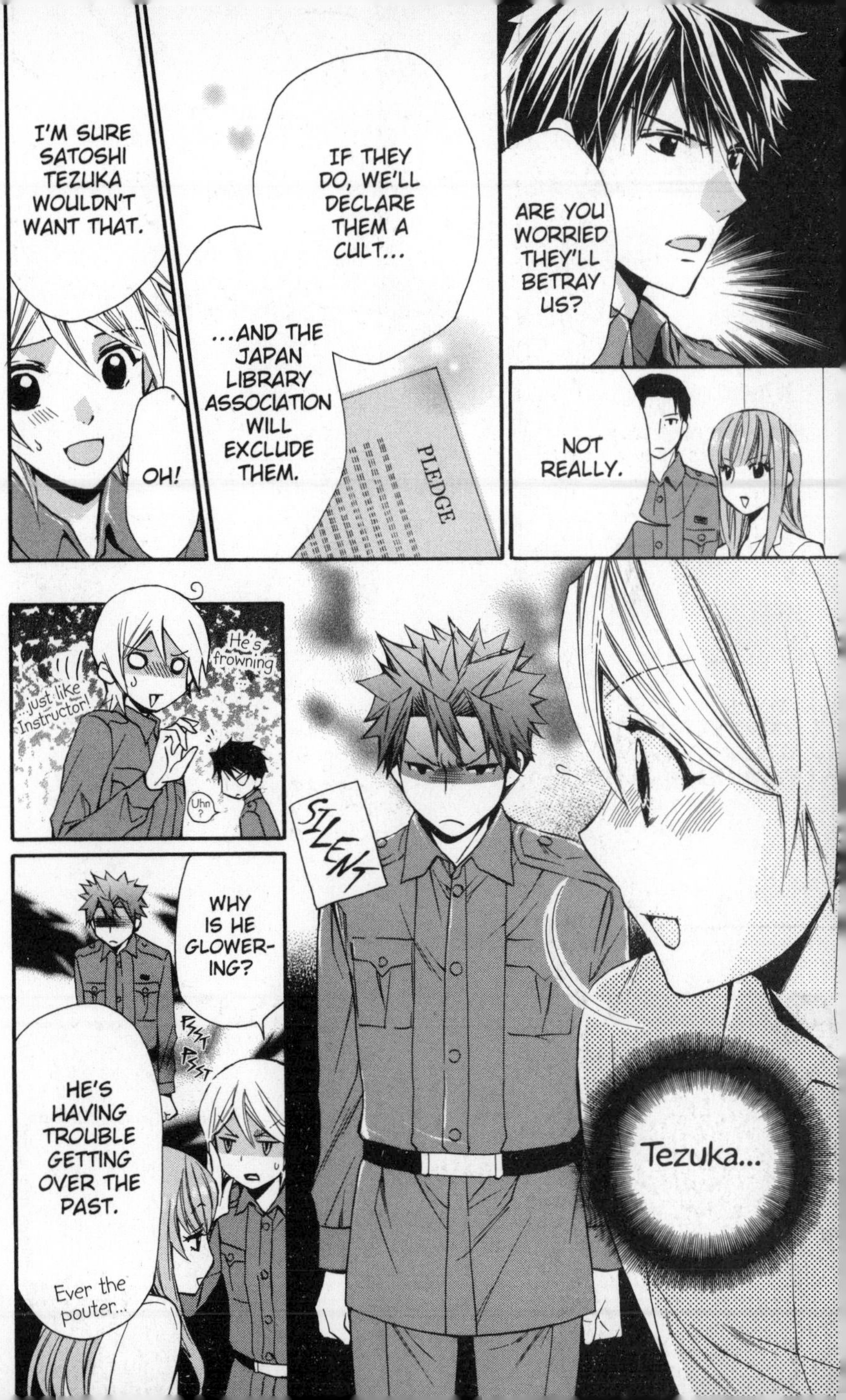
ARE YOU WORRIED THEY'LL BETRAY US?
NOT REALLY.
IF THEY DO, WE'LL DECLARE THEM A CULT...
...AND THE JAPAN LIBRARY ASSOCIATION WILL EXCLUDE THEM.
PLEDGE
I'M SURE SATOSHI TEZUKA WOULDN'T WANT THAT.
OH!
Tezuka...
SILENT
He's frowning...
...just like Instructor!
Uhn?
WHY IS HE GLOWERING?
PSST PSST
HE'S HAVING TROUBLE GETTING OVER THE PAST.
Ever the pouter...

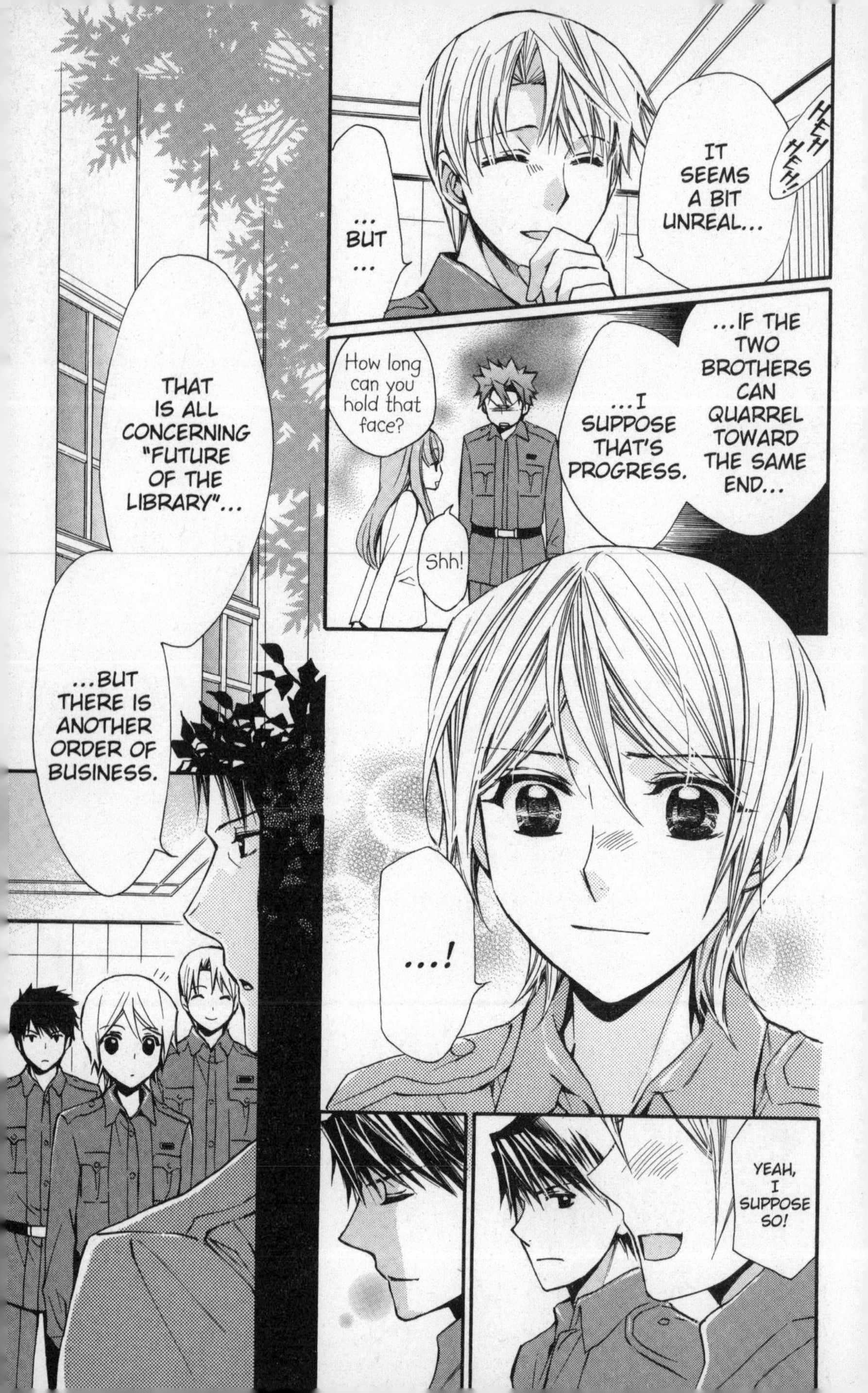
HEH HEH!
IT SEEMS A BIT UNREAL...
...BUT...
...IF THE TWO BROTHERS CAN QUARREL TOWARD THE SAME END...
...I SUPPOSE THAT'S PROGRESS.
How long can you hold that face?
Shh!
...!
YEAH, I SUPPOSE SO!
THAT IS ALL CONCERNING "FUTURE OF THE LIBRARY"...
...BUT THERE IS ANOTHER ORDER OF BUSINESS.

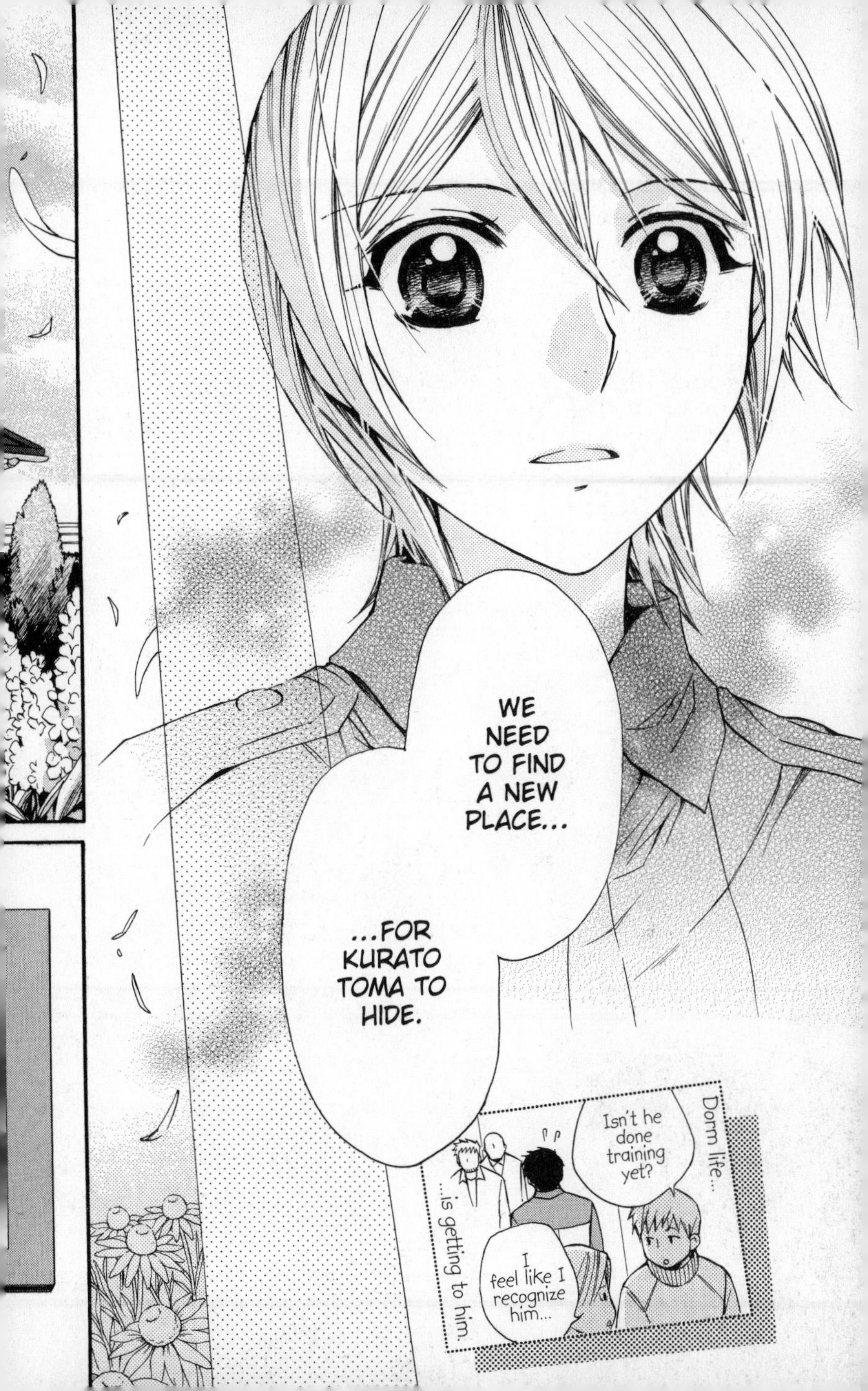
WE NEED TO FIND A NEW PLACE...
...FOR KURATO TOMA TO HIDE.
Dorm life...
Isn't he done training yet?
I feel like I recognize him...
...is getting to him.

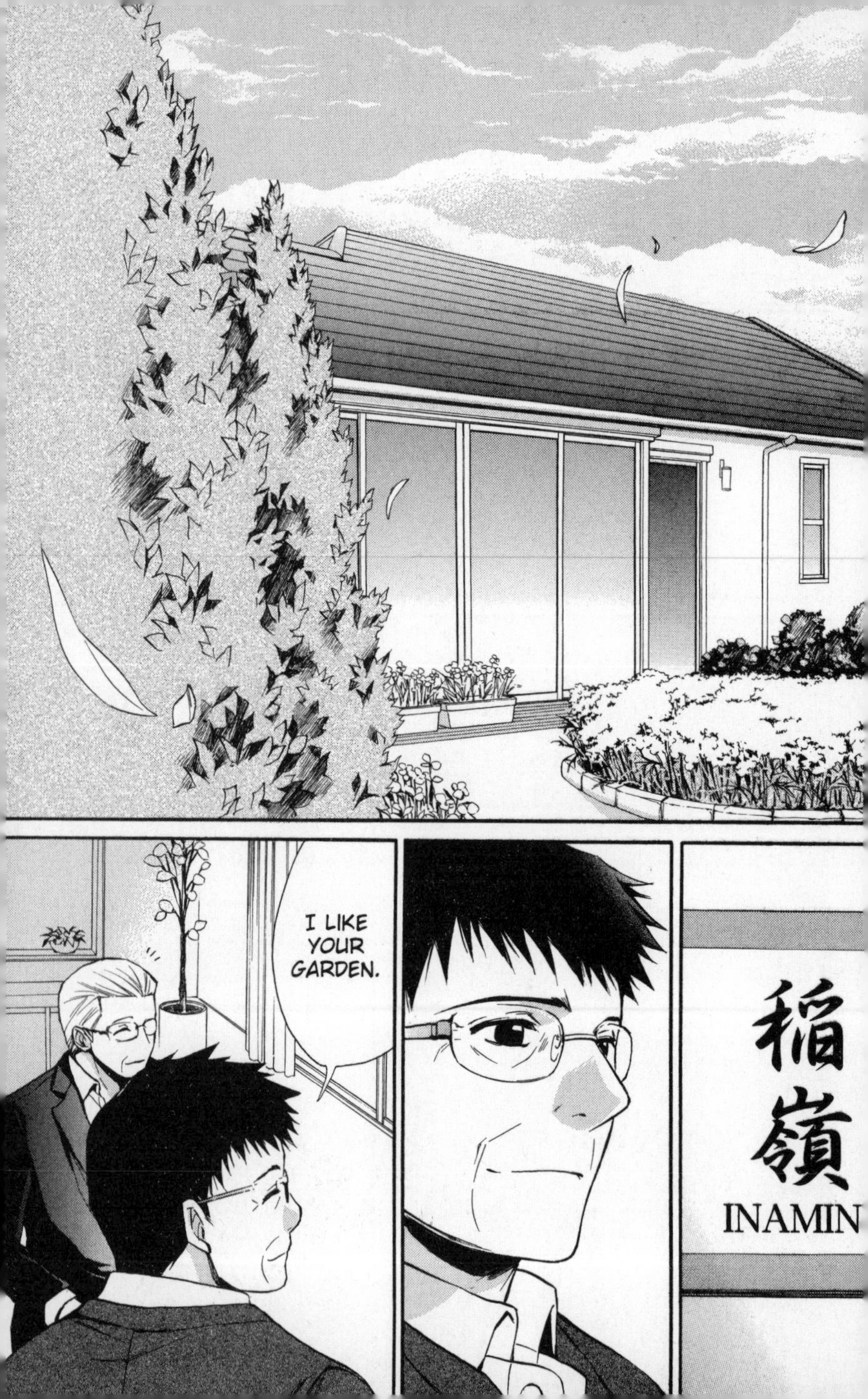
稲嶺
INAMIN
I LIKE YOUR GARDEN.

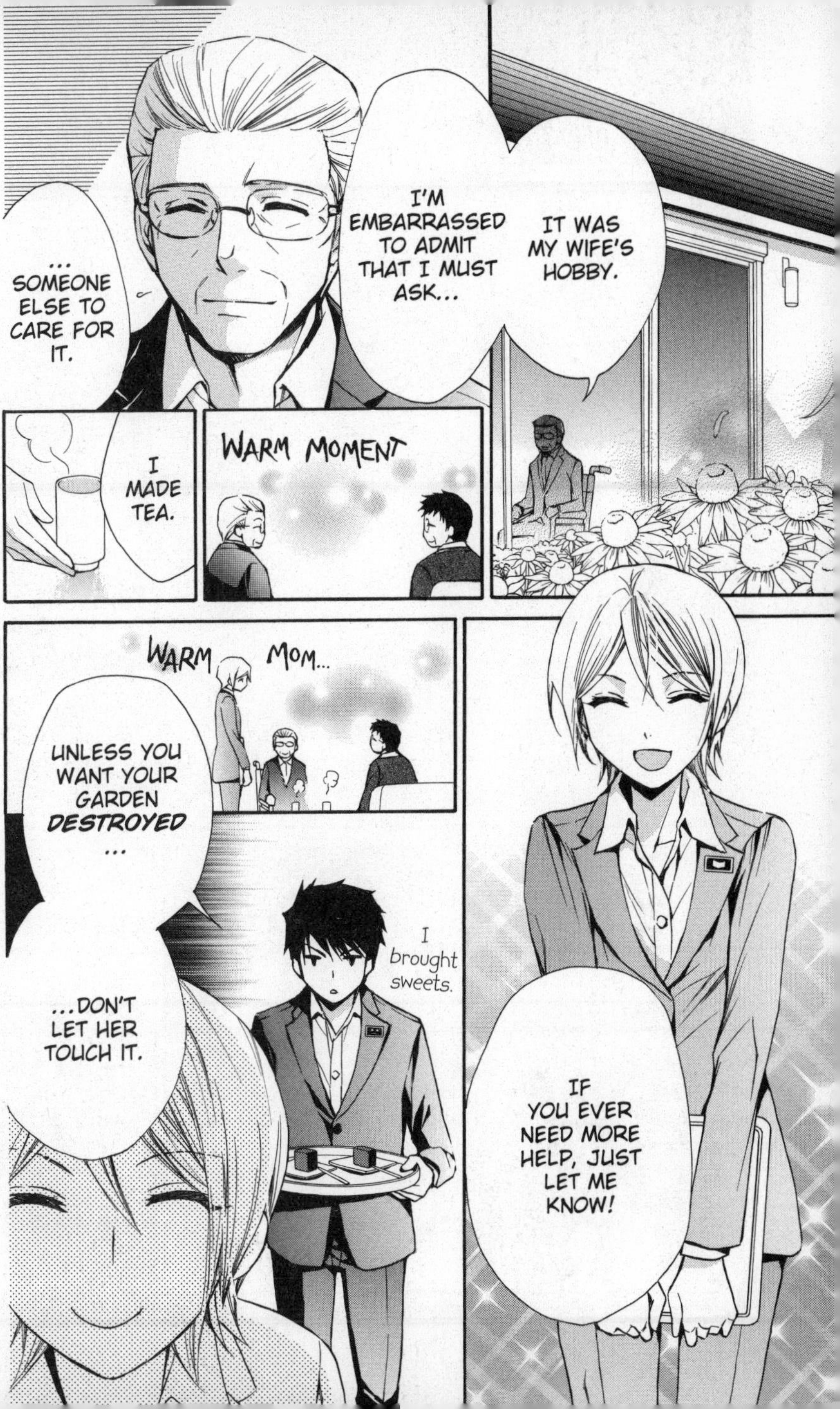
IT WAS MY WIFE'S HOBBY.
I'M EMBARRASSED TO ADMIT THAT I MUST ASK...
...SOMEONE ELSE TO CARE FOR IT.
WARM MOMENT
I MADE TEA.
IF YOU EVER NEED MORE HELP, JUST LET ME KNOW!
WARM MOM...
UNLESS YOU WANT YOUR GARDEN DESTROYED ...
I brought sweets.
...DON'T LET HER TOUCH IT.

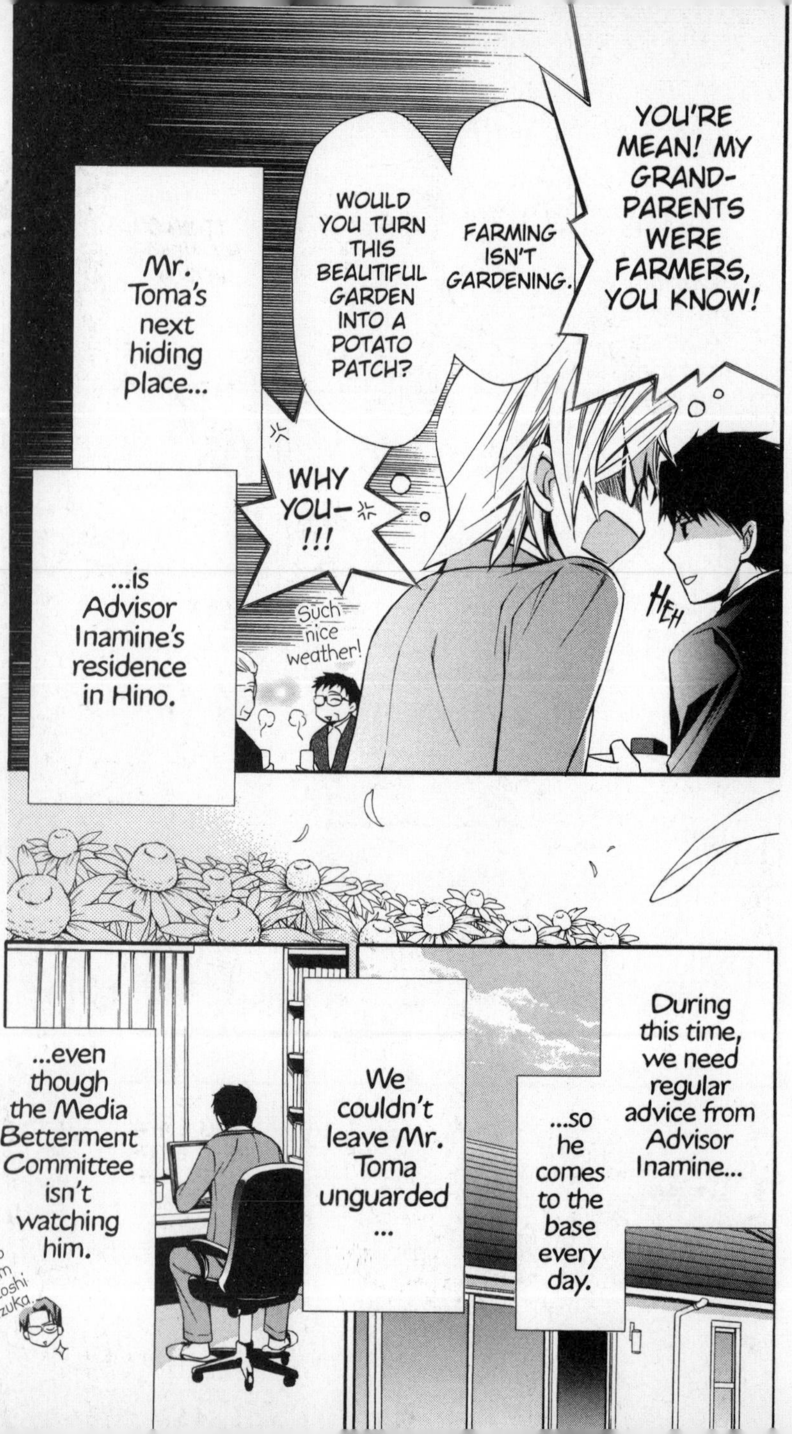
YOU'RE MEAN! MY GRAND-PARENTS WERE FARMERS, YOU KNOW!
FARMING ISN'T GARDENING.
WOULD YOU TURN THIS BEAUTIFUL GARDEN INTO A POTATO PATCH?
Mr. Toma's next hiding place...
HEH
WHY YOU—!!!
...is Advisor Inamine's residence in Hino.
Such nice weather!
During this time, we need regular advice from Advisor Inamine...
...so he comes to the base every day.
We couldn't leave Mr. Toma unguarded...
...even though the Media Betterment Committee isn't watching him.
*Info from Satoshi Tezuka.

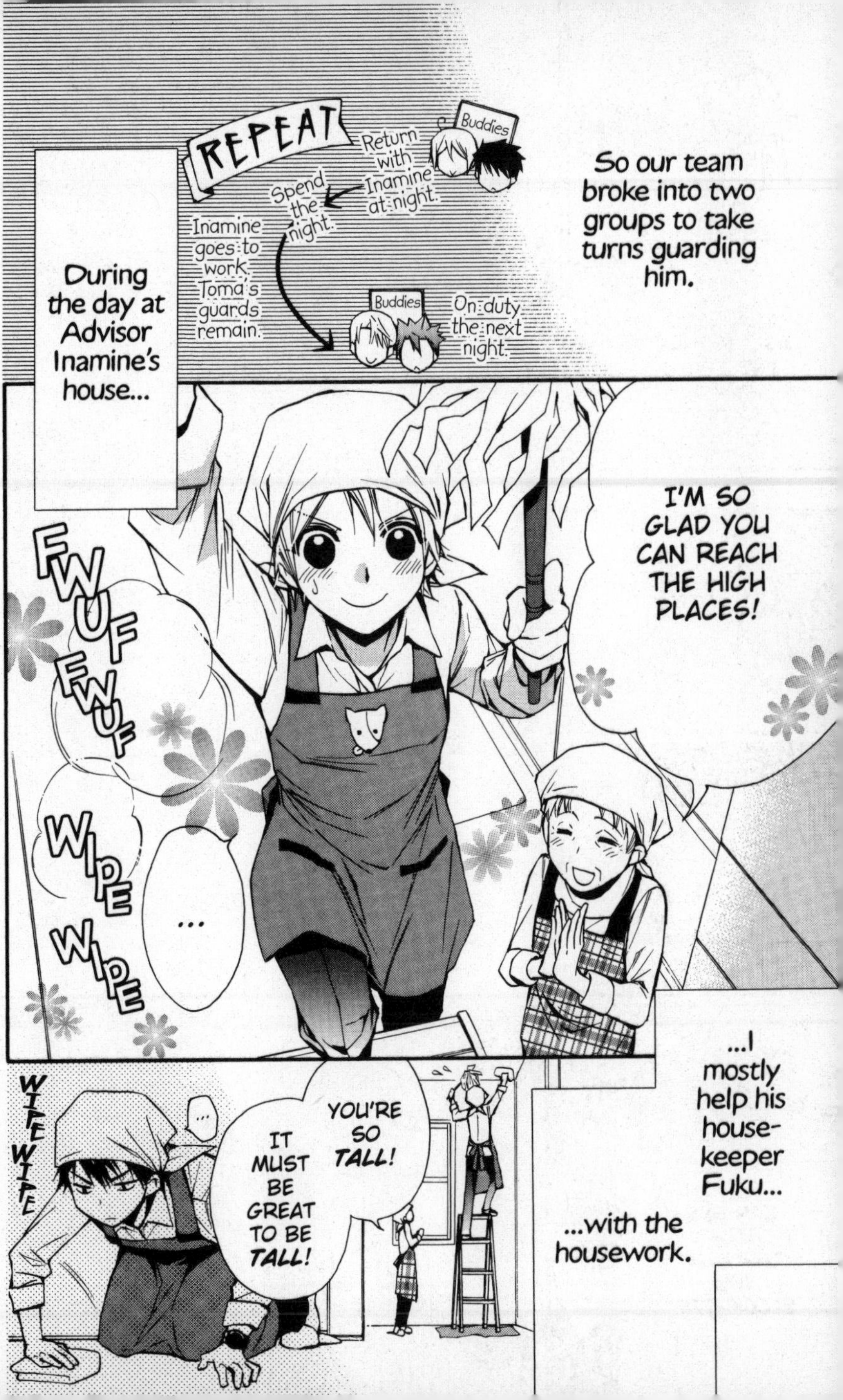

So our team broke into two groups to take turns guarding him.
REPEAT
Buddies
Return with Inamine at night.
Spend the night.
Inamine goes to work. Toma's guards remain.
Buddies
On duty the next night.
During the day at Advisor Inamine's house...
I'M SO GLAD YOU CAN REACH THE HIGH PLACES!
...
FWUF FWUF
WIPE WIPE
...I mostly help his housekeeper Fuku...
...with the housework.
YOU'RE SO TALL!
IT MUST BE GREAT TO BE TALL!
...
WIPE WIPE

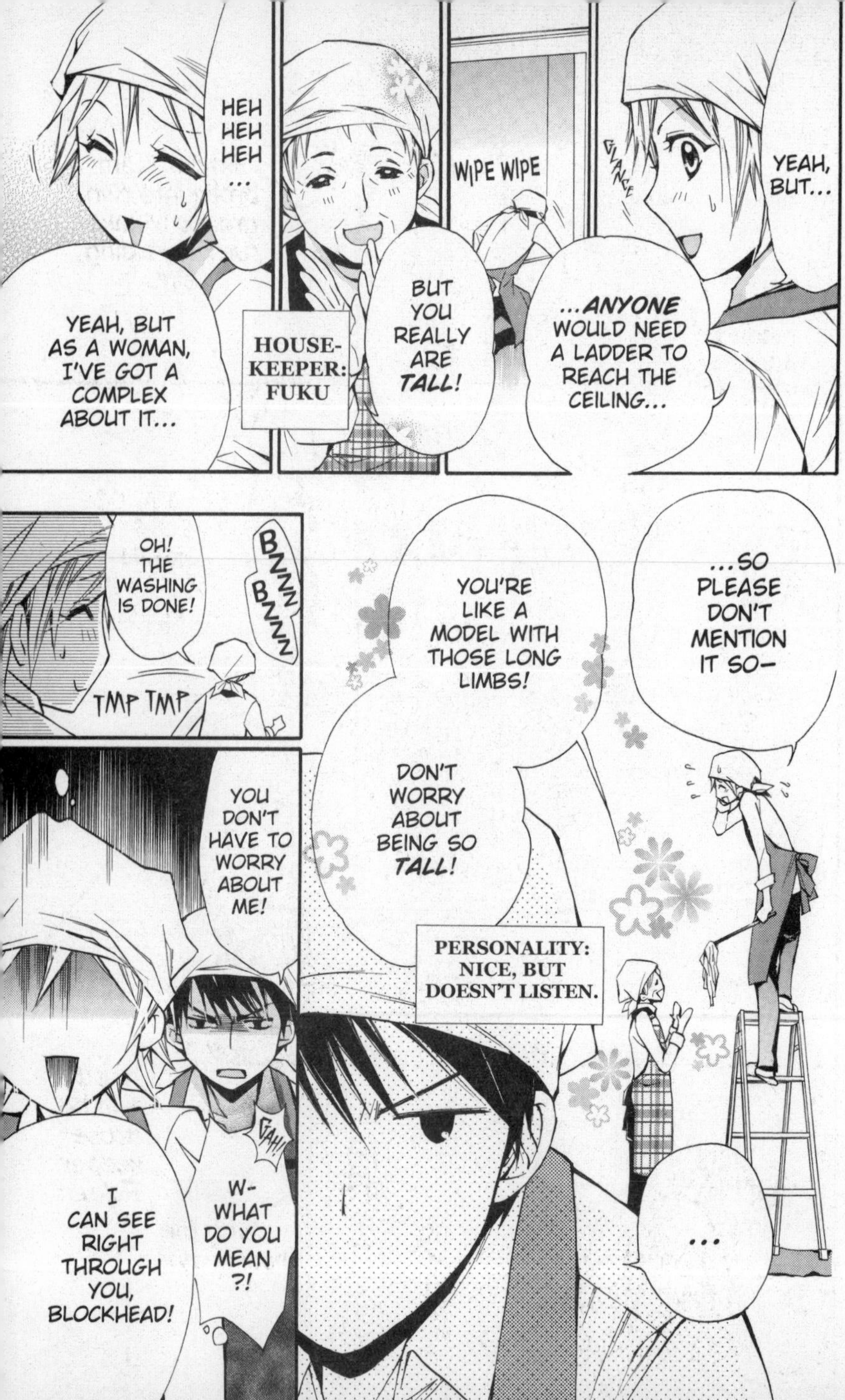
YEAH, BUT...
GLANCE
...ANYONE WOULD NEED A LADDER TO REACH THE CEILING...
WIPE WIPE
BUT YOU REALLY ARE TALL!
HOUSE-KEEPER: FUKU
HEH HEH HEH ...
YEAH, BUT AS A WOMAN, I'VE GOT A COMPLEX ABOUT IT...
...SO PLEASE DON'T MENTION IT SO—
YOU'RE LIKE A MODEL WITH THOSE LONG LIMBS!
DON'T WORRY ABOUT BEING SO TALL!
PERSONALITY: NICE, BUT DOESN'T LISTEN.
...
OH! THE WASHING IS DONE!
BZZZ BZZZ
TMP TMP
YOU DON'T HAVE TO WORRY ABOUT ME!
GAH!
W-WHAT DO YOU MEAN ?!
I CAN SEE RIGHT THROUGH YOU, BLOCKHEAD!

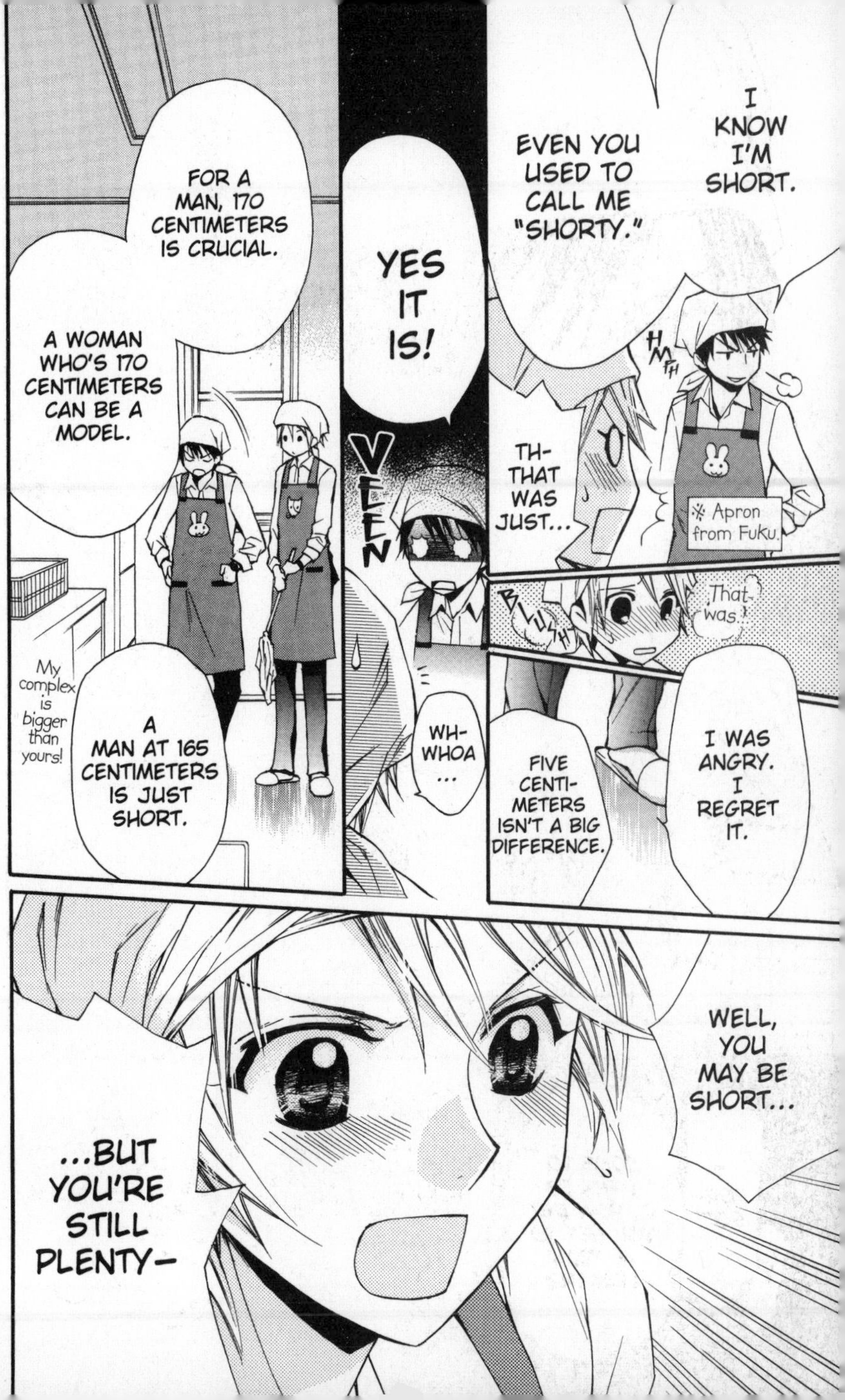
I KNOW I'M SHORT.
EVEN YOU USED TO CALL ME "SHORTY."
HMPH
TH- THAT WAS JUST...
※ Apron from Fuku.
BLUSH
That was..
I WAS ANGRY. I REGRET IT.
FIVE CENTIMETERS ISN'T A BIG DIFFERENCE.
YES IT IS!
VEEN
WH- WHOA ...
FOR A MAN, 170 CENTIMETERS IS CRUCIAL.
A WOMAN WHO'S 170 CENTIMETERS CAN BE A MODEL.
A MAN AT 165 CENTIMETERS IS JUST SHORT.
My complex is bigger than yours!
WELL, YOU MAY BE SHORT...
...BUT YOU'RE STILL PLENTY—

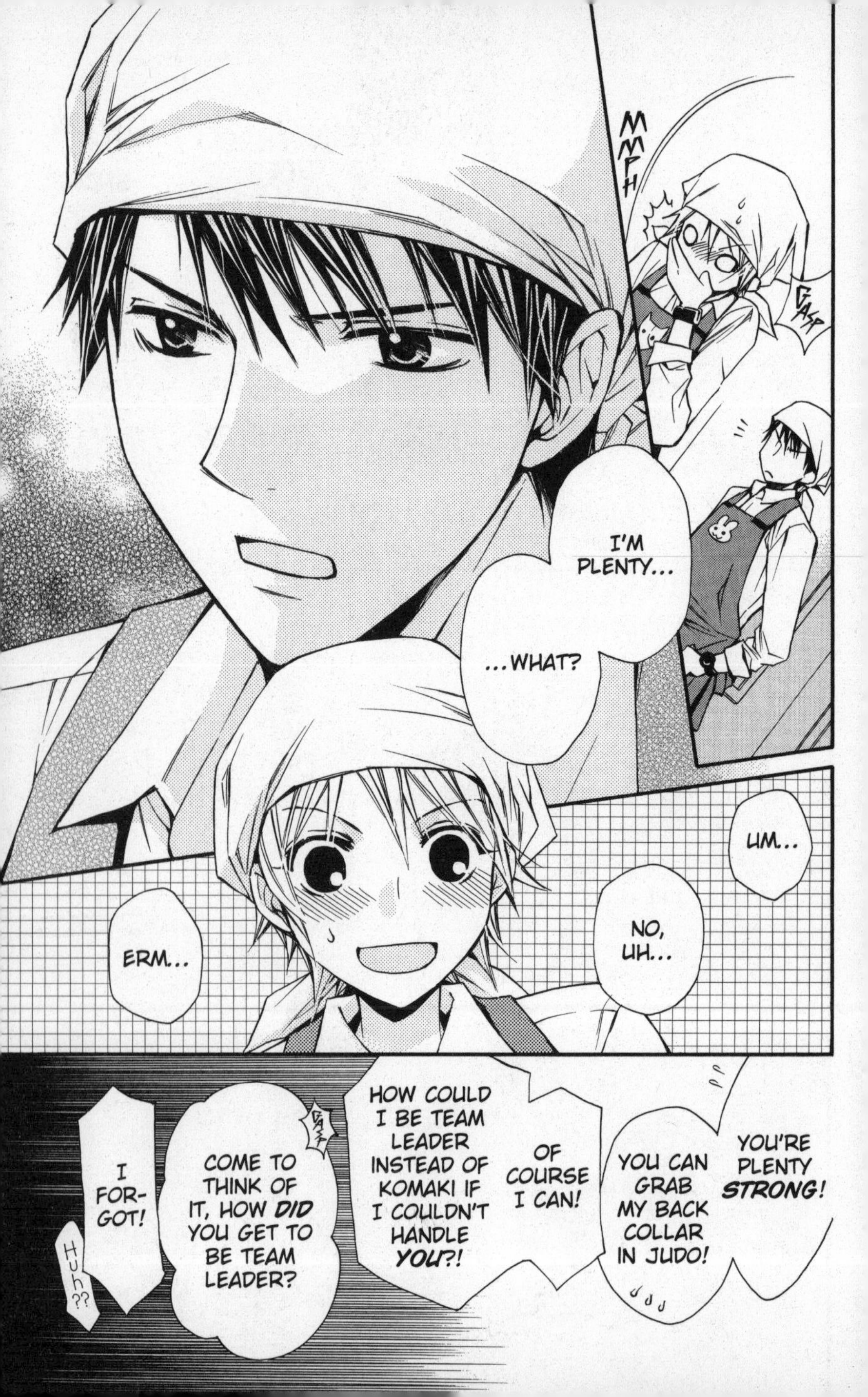
MMPH
GASP
I'M PLENTY...
...WHAT?
UM...
NO, UH...
ERM...
YOU'RE PLENTY **STRONG**!
YOU CAN GRAB MY BACK COLLAR IN JUDO!
OF COURSE I CAN!
HOW COULD I BE TEAM LEADER INSTEAD OF KOMAKI IF I COULDN'T HANDLE ***YOU***?!
GASP
COME TO THINK OF IT, HOW ***DID*** YOU GET TO BE TEAM LEADER?
I FORGOT!
Huh??

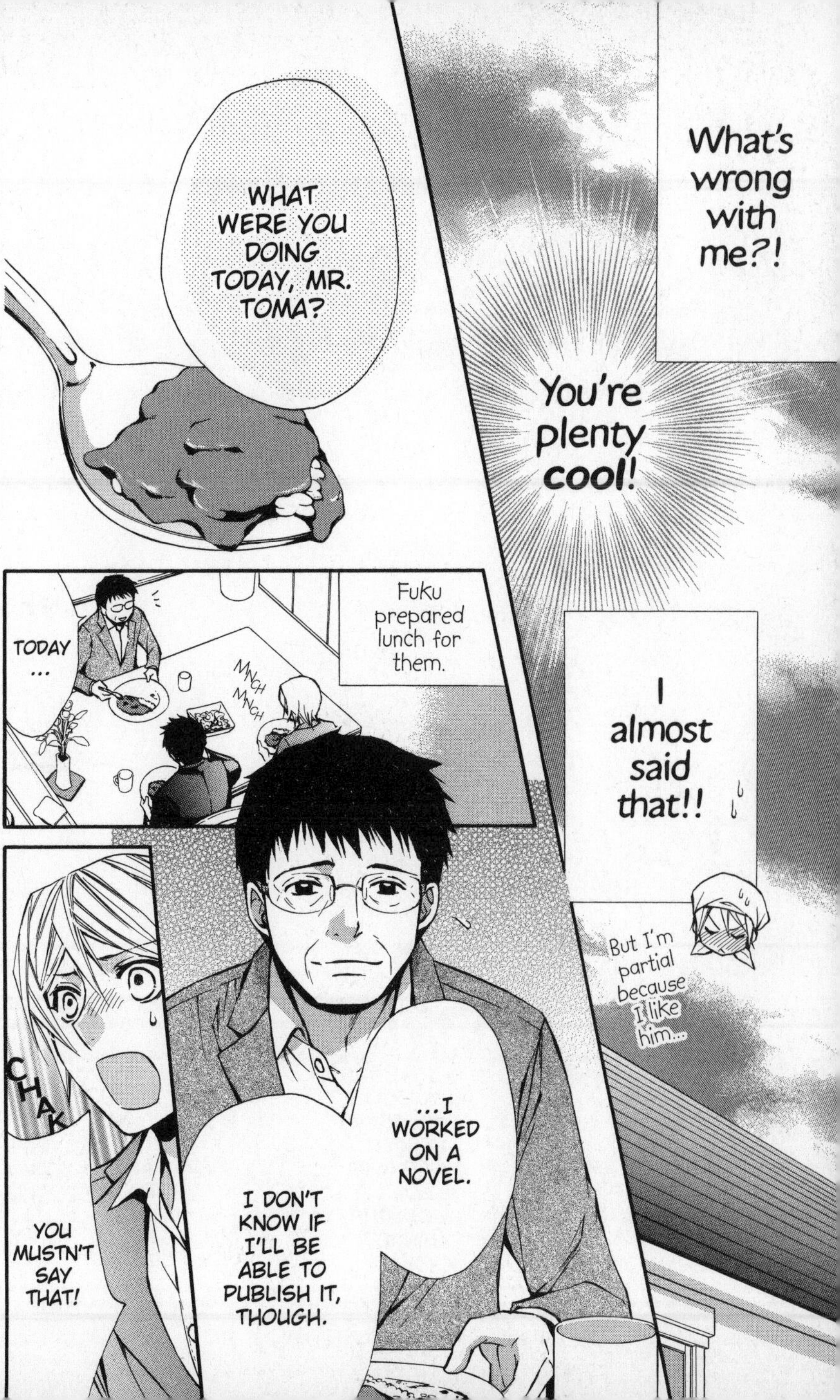
What's wrong with me?!
You're plenty cool!
I almost said that!!
But I'm partial because I like him...
WHAT WERE YOU DOING TODAY, MR. TOMA?
Fuku prepared lunch for them.
MNCH MNCH
TODAY ...
...I WORKED ON A NOVEL.
I DON'T KNOW IF I'LL BE ABLE TO PUBLISH IT, THOUGH.
CHAK
YOU MUSTN'T SAY THAT!

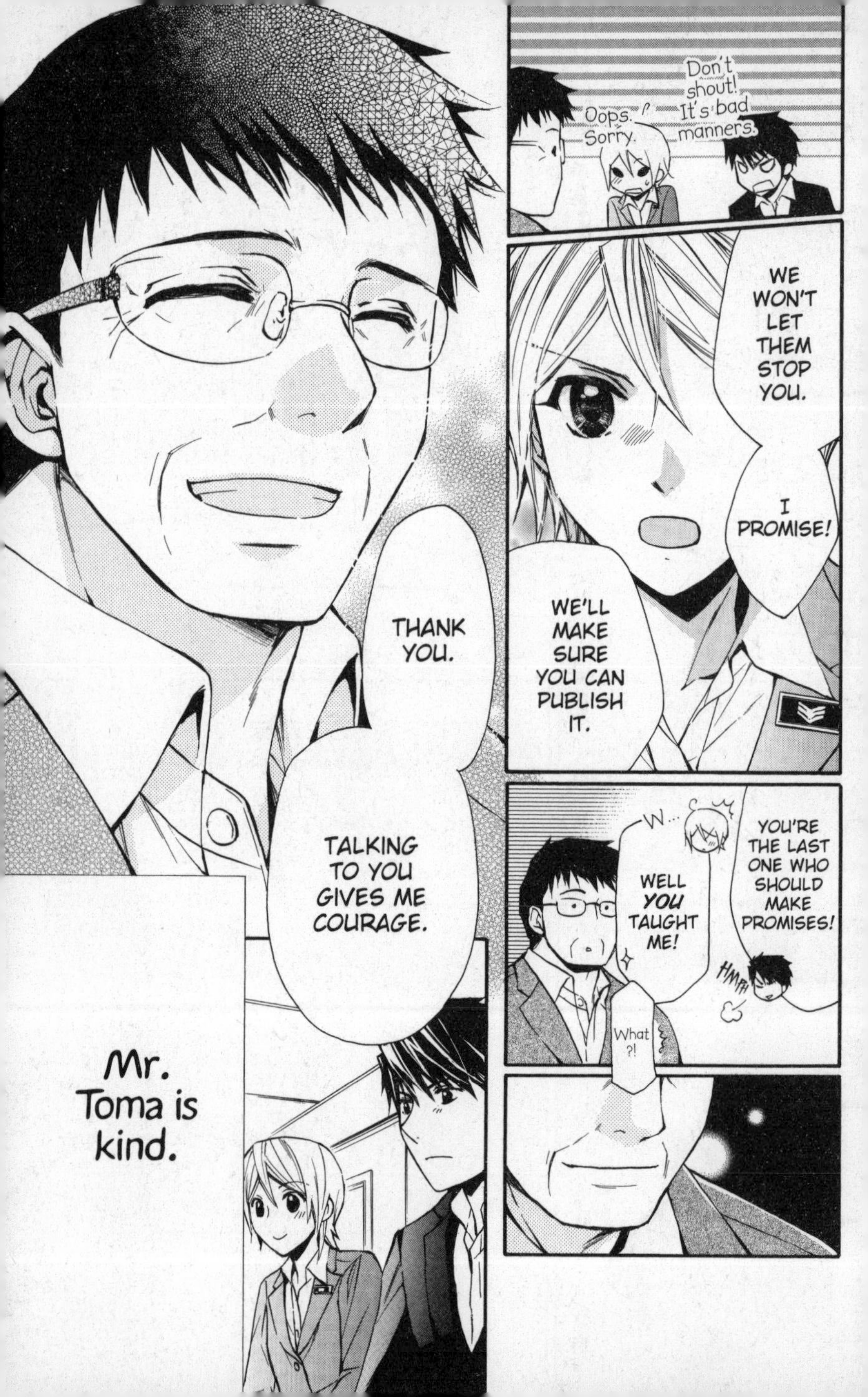
Don't shout! It's bad manners.
Oops. Sorry.
WE WON'T LET THEM STOP YOU.
I PROMISE!
WE'LL MAKE SURE YOU CAN PUBLISH IT.
YOU'RE THE LAST ONE WHO SHOULD MAKE PROMISES!
HMPH
W...
WELL *YOU* TAUGHT ME!
What?!
THANK YOU.
TALKING TO YOU GIVES ME COURAGE.
Mr. Toma is kind.

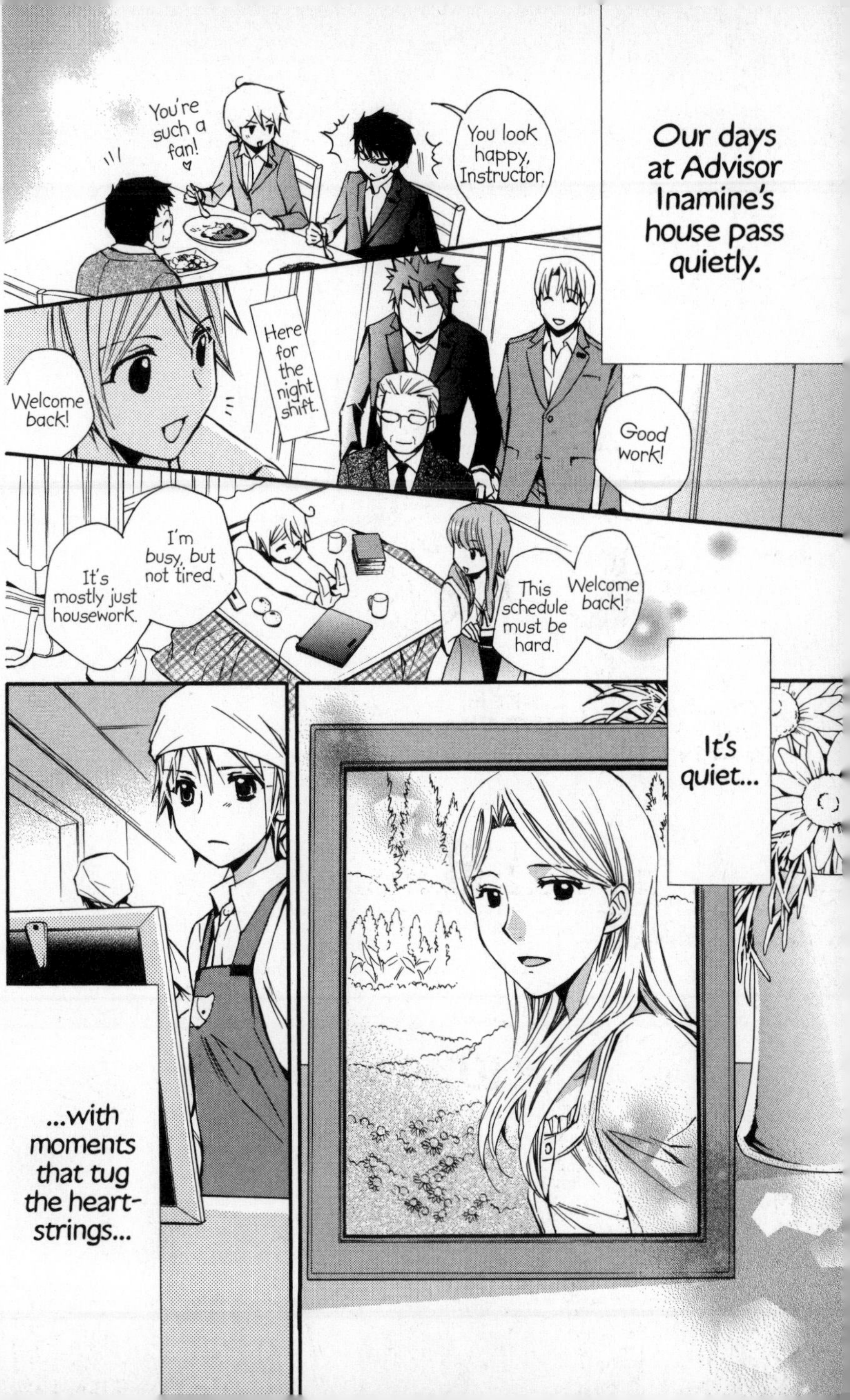
Our days at Advisor Inamine's house pass quietly.
You look happy, Instructor.
You're such a fan! ♡
Good work!
Here for the night shift.
Welcome back!
Welcome back!
This schedule must be hard.
I'm busy, but not tired.
It's mostly just housework.
It's quiet...
...with moments that tug the heart-strings...

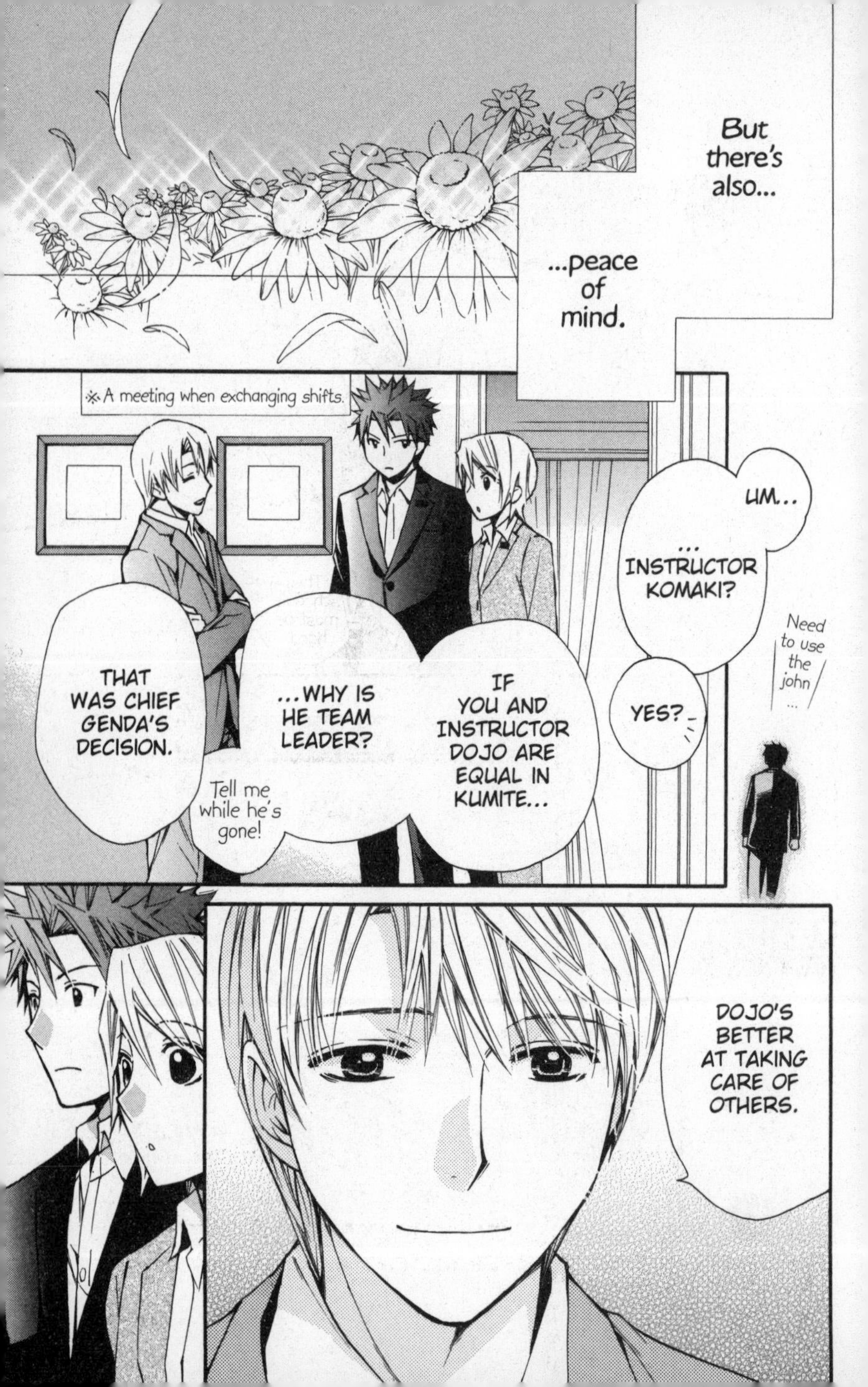
But there's also...
...peace of mind.
※A meeting when exchanging shifts.
UM...
...INSTRUCTOR KOMAKI?
Need to use the john...
YES?
IF YOU AND INSTRUCTOR DOJO ARE EQUAL IN KUMITE...
...WHY IS HE TEAM LEADER?
Tell me while he's gone!
THAT WAS CHIEF GENDA'S DECISION.
DOJO'S BETTER AT TAKING CARE OF OTHERS.

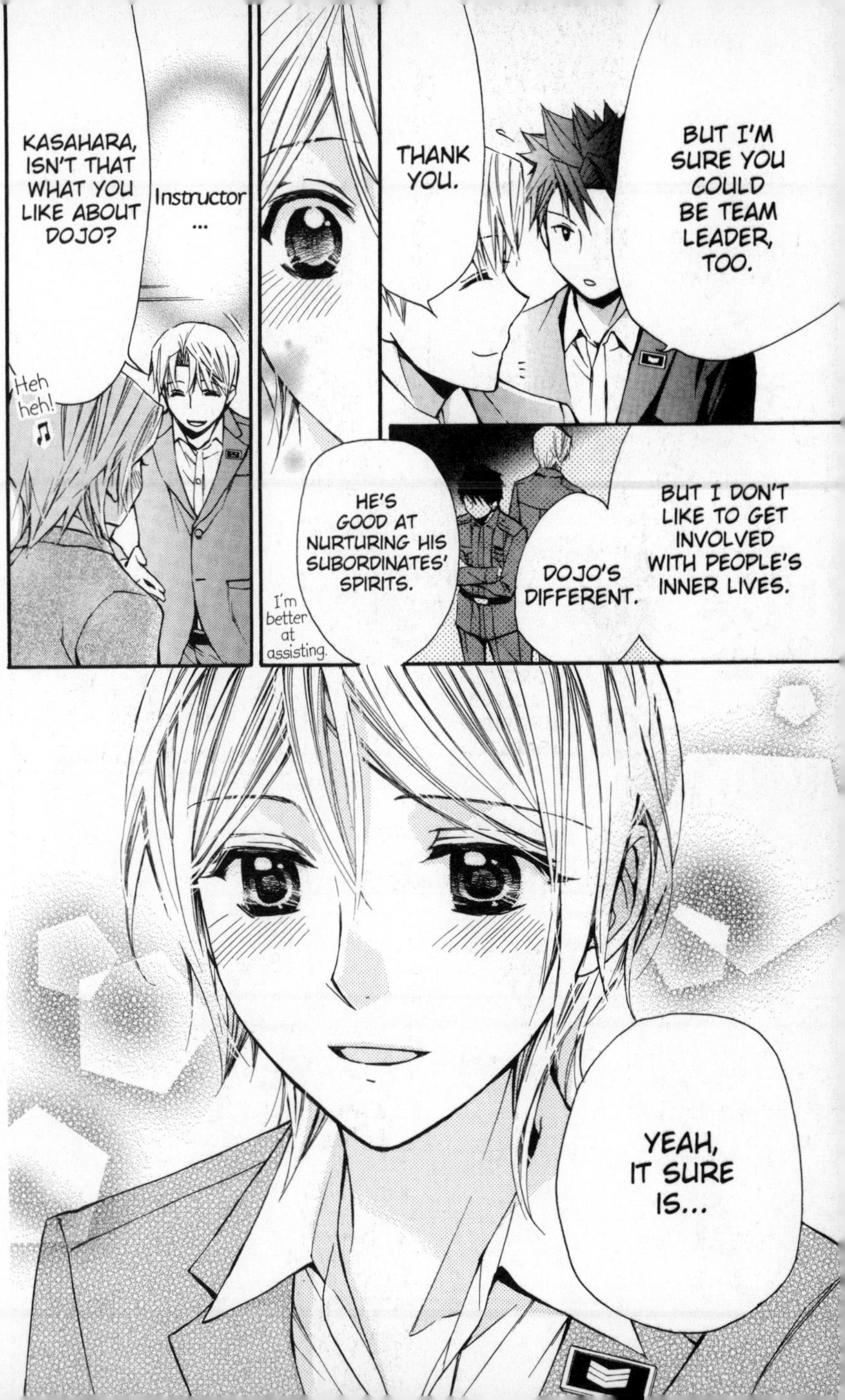
BUT I'M SURE YOU COULD BE TEAM LEADER, TOO.
THANK YOU.
BUT I DON'T LIKE TO GET INVOLVED WITH PEOPLE'S INNER LIVES.
DOJO'S DIFFERENT.
HE'S GOOD AT NURTURING HIS SUBORDINATES' SPIRITS.
I'm better at assisting.
Instructor ...
KASAHARA, ISN'T THAT WHAT YOU LIKE ABOUT DOJO?
Heh heh! ♫
YEAH, IT SURE IS...

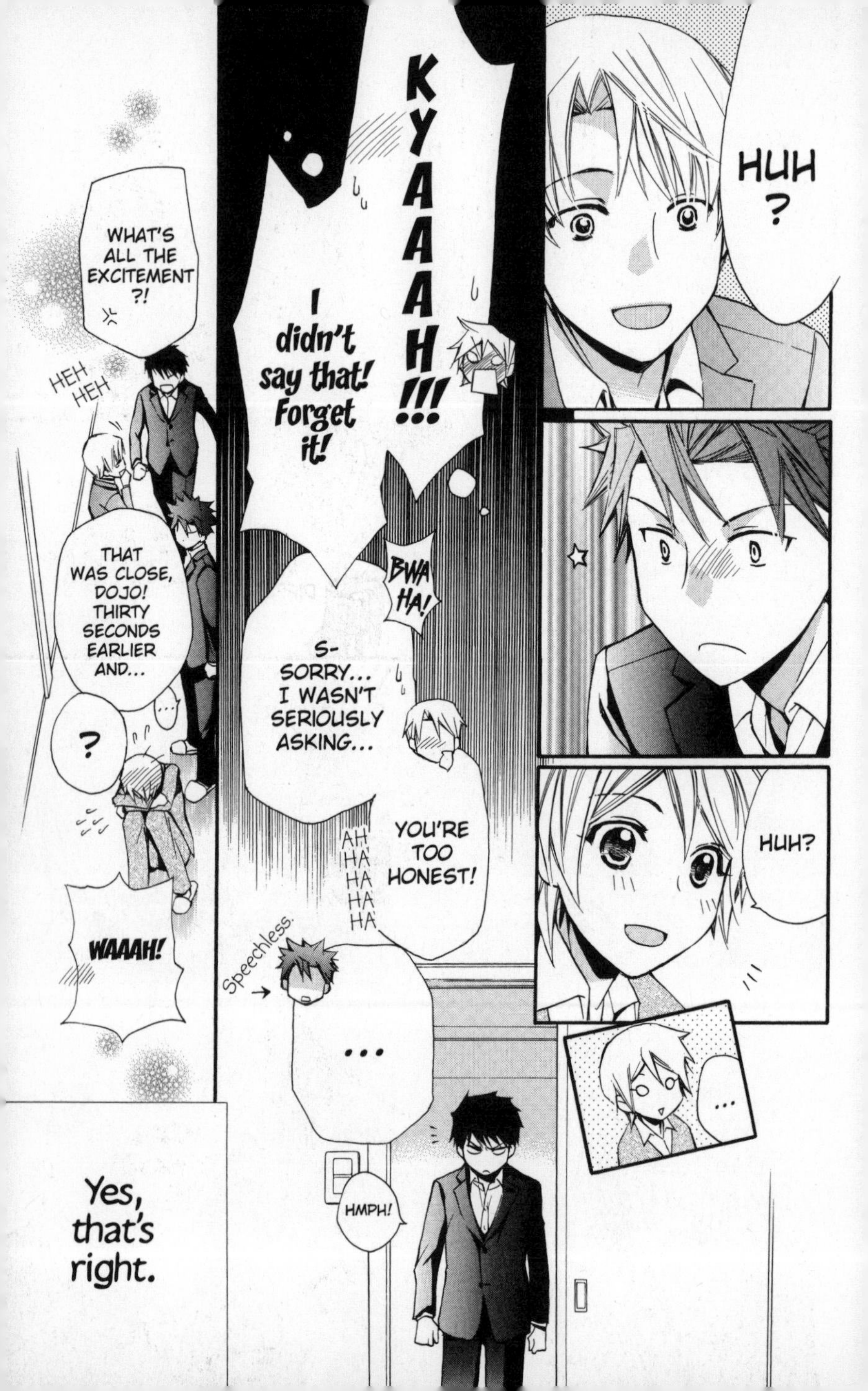
HUH ?
HUH?
...
KYAAAAH!!!
I didn't say that! Forget it!
BWA HA!
S- SORRY... I WASN'T SERIOUSLY ASKING...
YOU'RE TOO HONEST!
AH HA HA HA HA
Speechless.
...
HMPH!
WHAT'S ALL THE EXCITEMENT ?!
HEH HEH
THAT WAS CLOSE, DOJO! THIRTY SECONDS EARLIER AND...
...
?
WAAAH!
Yes, that's right.

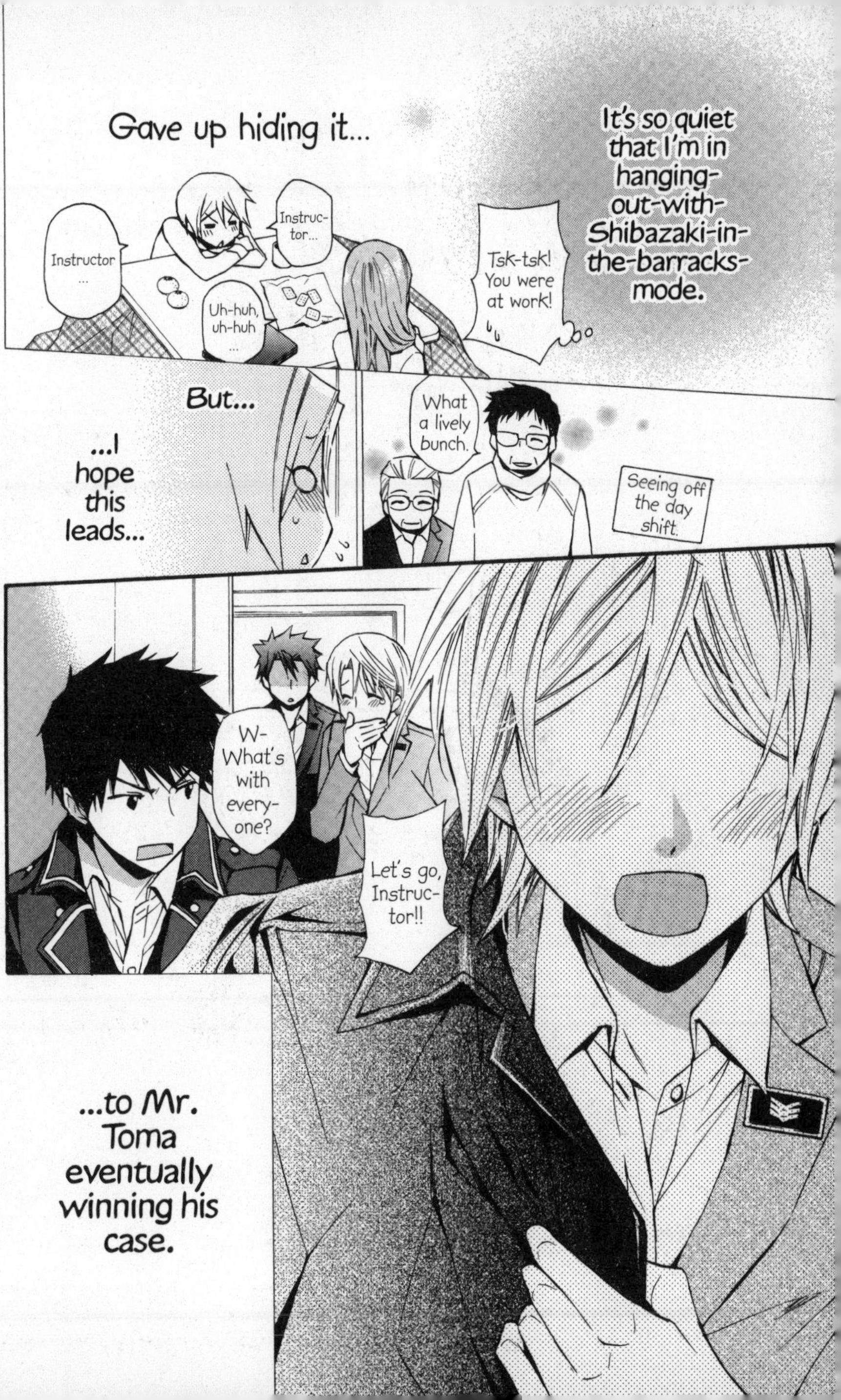
It's so quiet that I'm in hanging-out-with-Shibazaki-in-the-barracks-mode.
Tsk-tsk! You were at work!
Instruc-tor...
Gave up hiding it...
Uh-huh, uh-huh...
Instructor...
Seeing off the day shift.
What a lively bunch.
But...
...I hope this leads...
Let's go, Instruc-tor!!
W-What's with every-one?
...to Mr. Toma eventually winning his case.

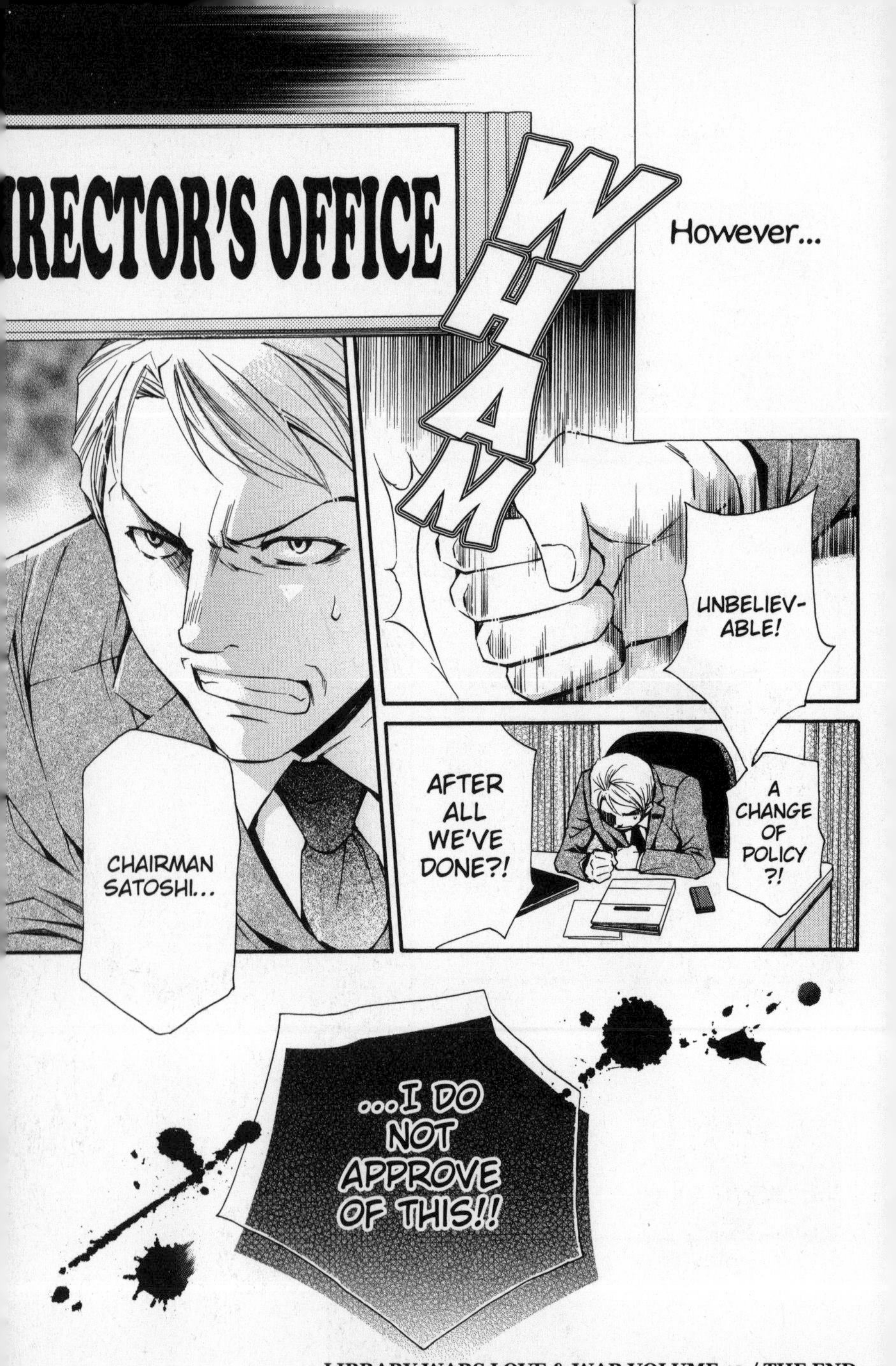
However...
WHAM
IRECTOR'S OFFICE
UNBELIEV-ABLE!
A CHANGE OF POLICY ?!
AFTER ALL WE'VE DONE?!
CHAIRMAN SATOSHI...
...I DO NOT APPROVE OF THIS!!

I'll Pull Myself Together in a Pinch, So Gimme a Break Right Now

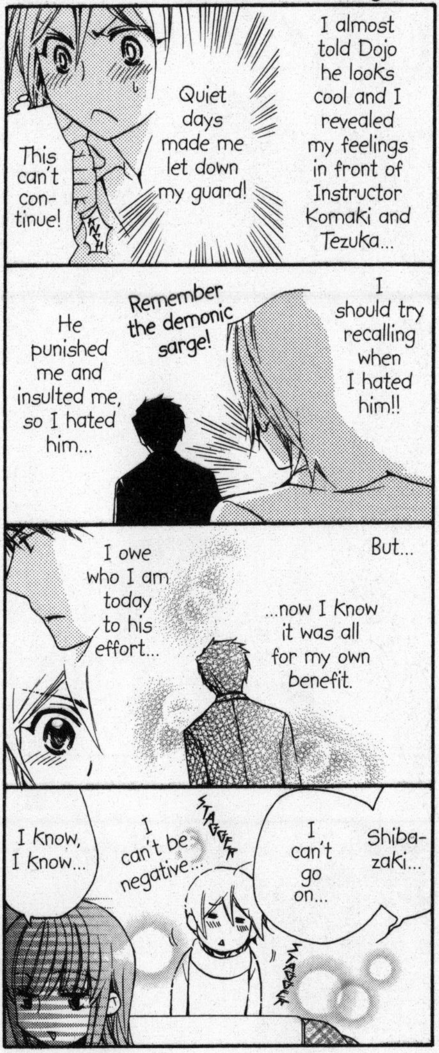

I almost told Dojo he looks cool and I revealed my feelings in front of Instructor Komaki and Tezuka...
Quiet days made me let down my guard!
This can't continue!
I should try recalling when I hated him!!
Remember the demonic sarge!
He punished me and insulted me, so I hated him...
But...
...now I know it was all for my own benefit.
I owe who I am today to his effort...
Shiba-zaki...
I can't go on...
STAGGER
STAGGER
I can't be negative...
I know, I know...

But I do my work!

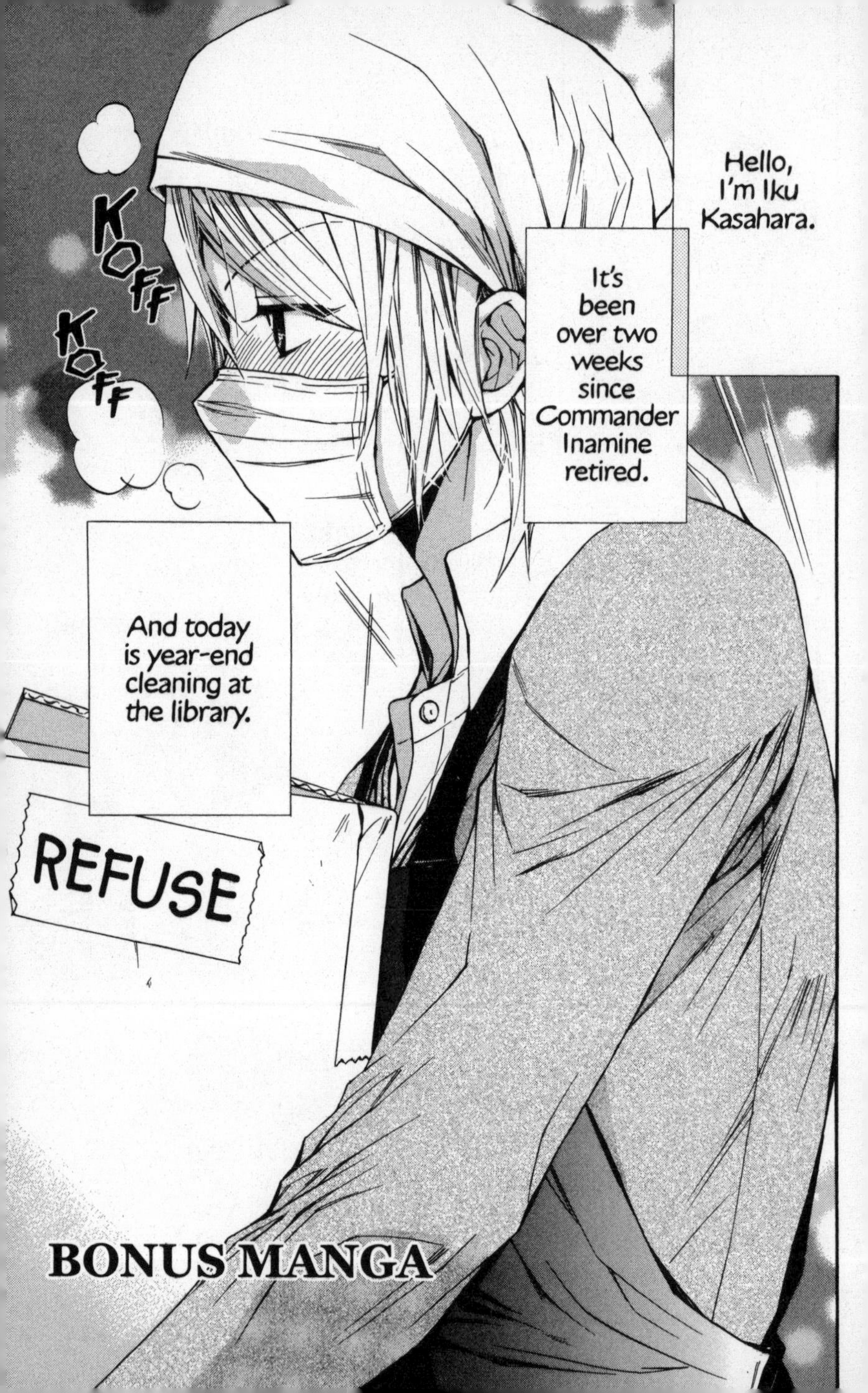
Hello, I'm Iku Kasahara.
It's been over two weeks since Commander Inamine retired.
KOFF KOFF
And today is year-end cleaning at the library.
REFUSE
BONUS MANGA

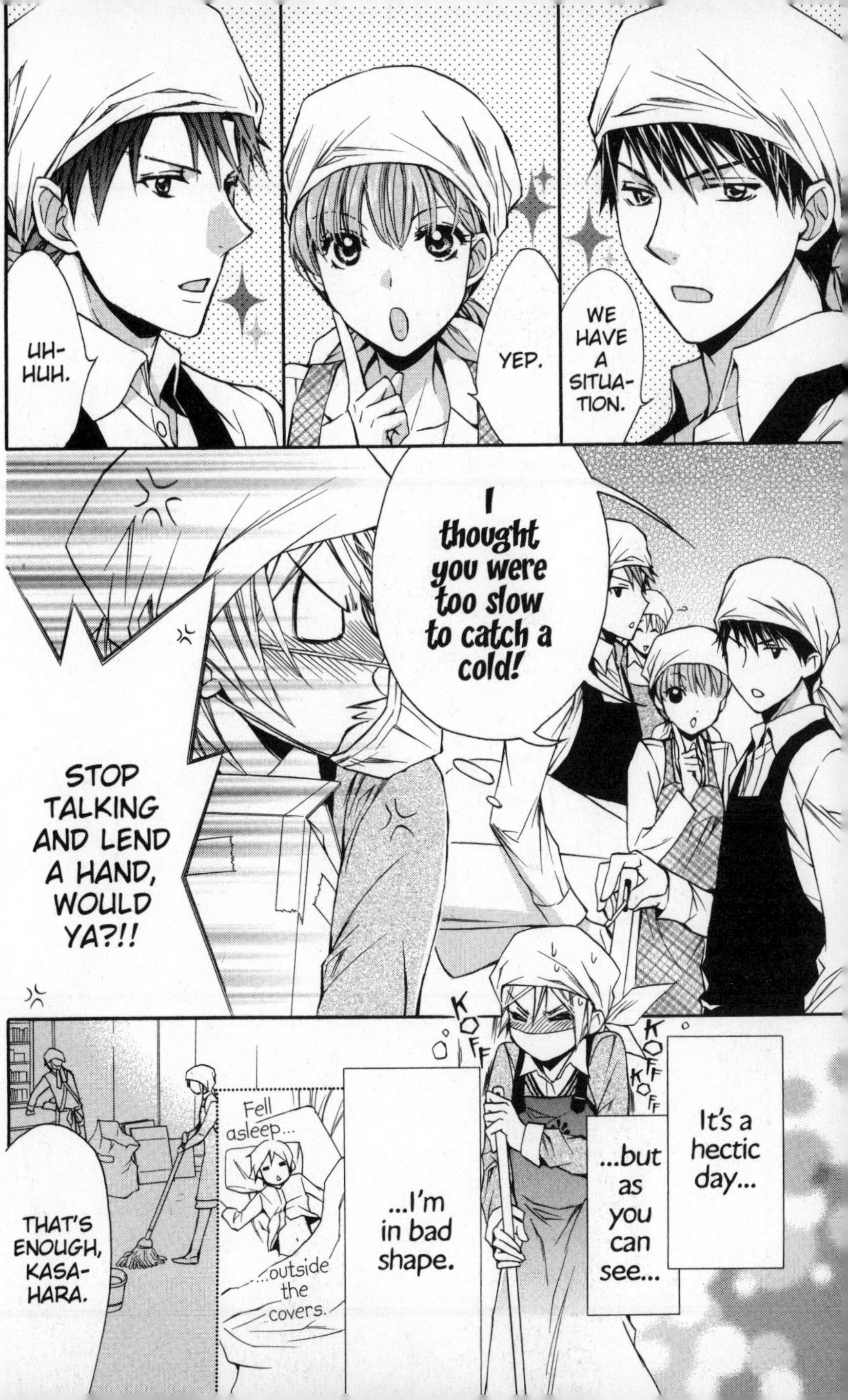
WE HAVE A SITUATION.
YEP.
UH-HUH.
I thought you were too slow to catch a cold!
STOP TALKING AND LEND A HAND, WOULD YA?!!
It's a hectic day...
KOFF
KOFF
...but as you can see...
KOFF
...I'm in bad shape.
Fell asleep...
...outside the covers.
THAT'S ENOUGH, KASA-HARA.

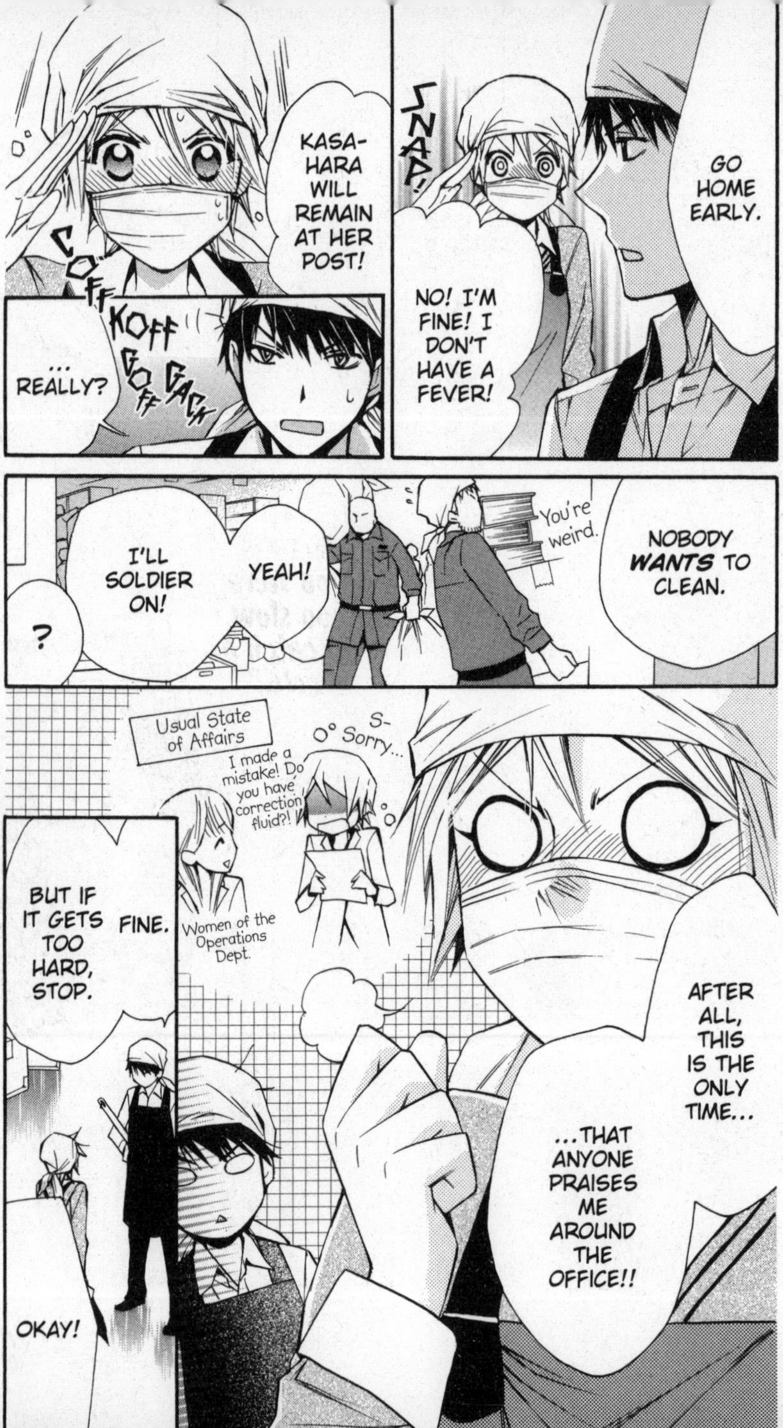
GO HOME EARLY.
SNAP!
NO! I'M FINE! I DON'T HAVE A FEVER!
KASA-HARA WILL REMAIN AT HER POST!
COFF
KOFF GOFF GACK
...REALLY?
NOBODY *WANTS* TO CLEAN.
You're weird.
YEAH!
I'LL SOLDIER ON!
?
S- Sorry...
I made a mistake! Do you have correction fluid?!
Women of the Operations Dept.
Usual State of Affairs
AFTER ALL, THIS IS THE ONLY TIME...
...THAT ANYONE PRAISES ME AROUND THE OFFICE!!
FINE.
BUT IF IT GETS TOO HARD, STOP.
OKAY!

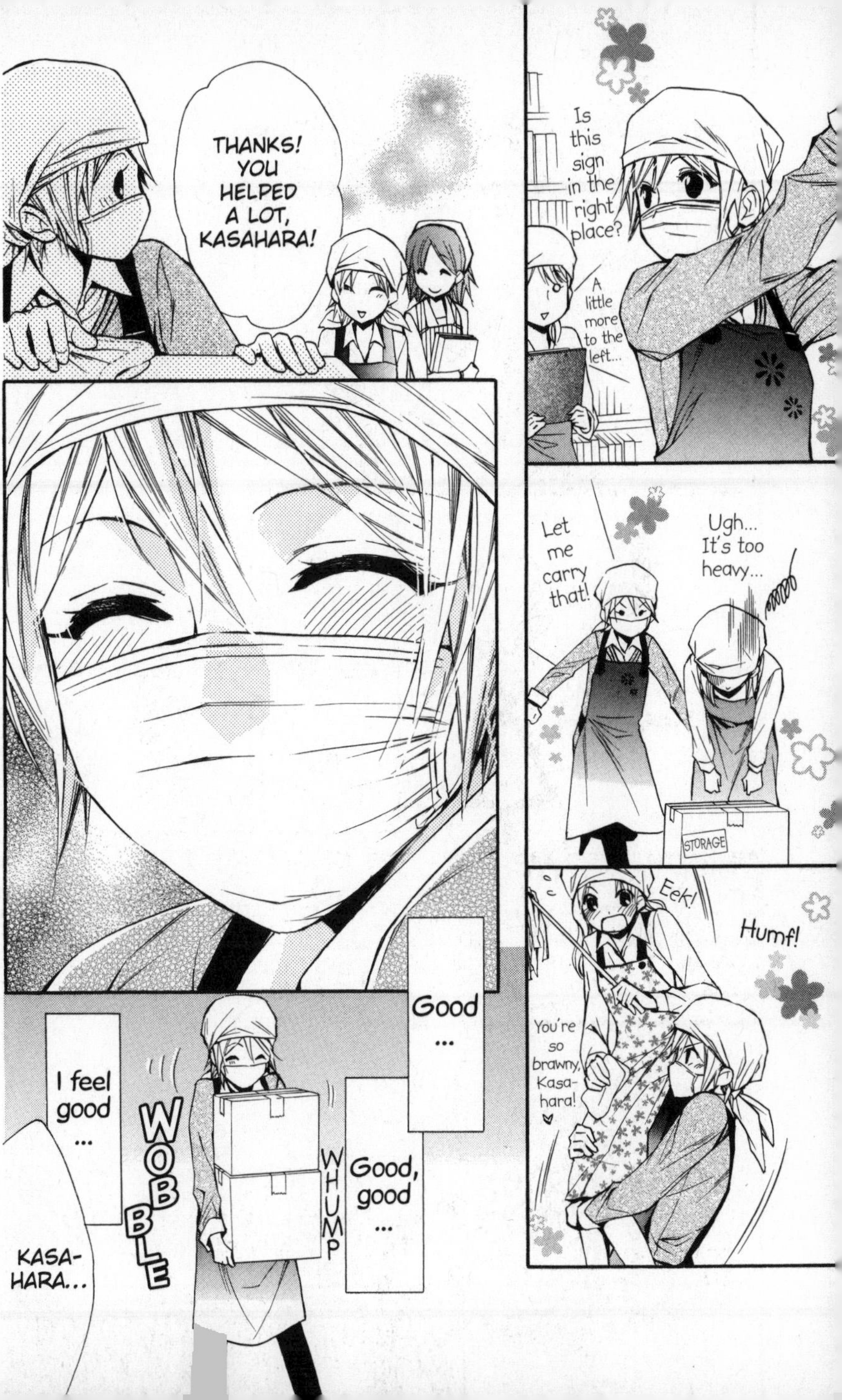
Is this sign in the right place?
A little more to the left...
Ugh... It's too heavy...
Let me carry that!
Eek!
Humf!
You're so brawny, Kasa-hara!
STORAGE
THANKS! YOU HELPED A LOT, KASAHARA!
Good ...
Good, good ...
WHUMP
WOBBLE
I feel good ...
KASA-HARA...

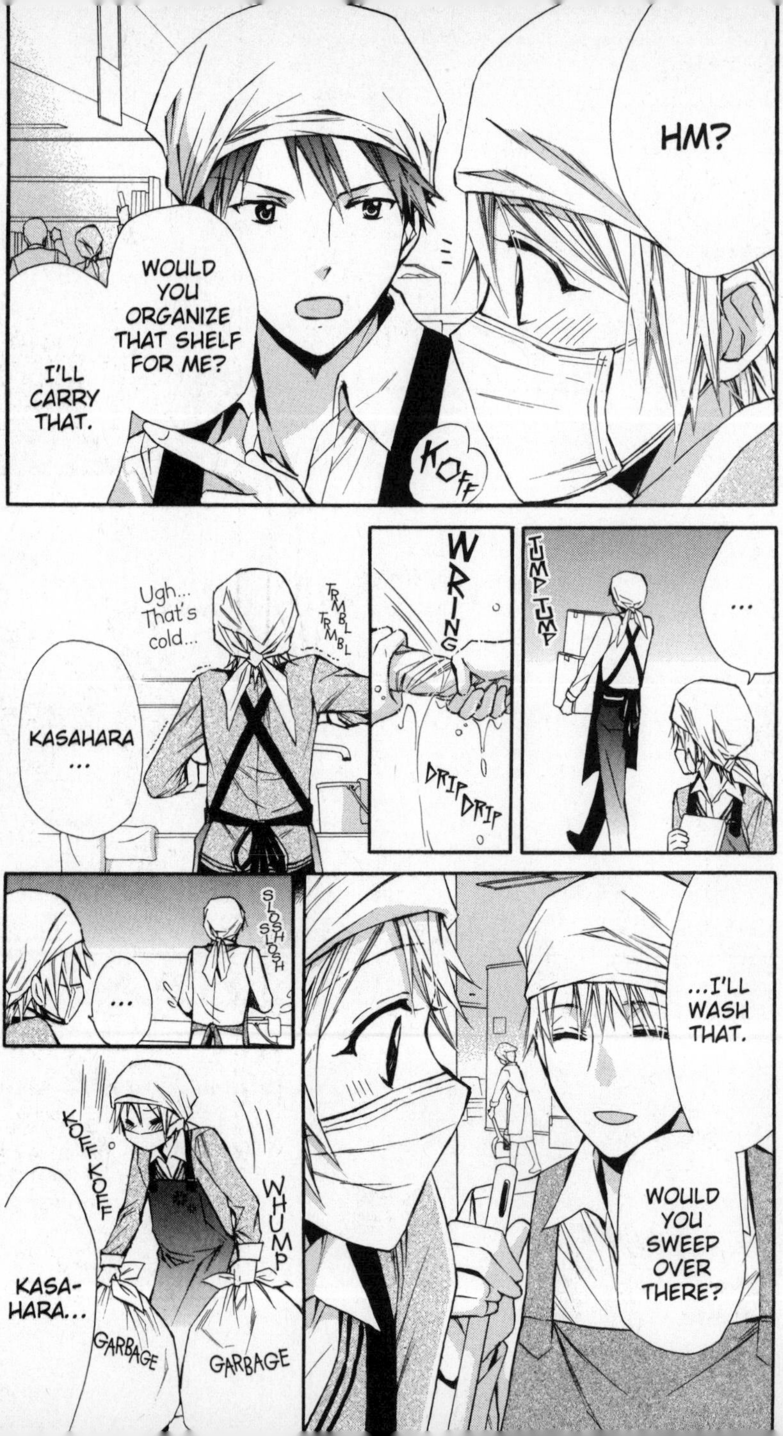
HM?
WOULD YOU ORGANIZE THAT SHELF FOR ME?
KOFF
I'LL CARRY THAT.
...
TUMP TUMP
WRING
DRIP DRIP
TRMBL TRMBL
Ugh... That's cold...
KASAHARA ...
...I'LL WASH THAT.
WOULD YOU SWEEP OVER THERE?
SLOSH SLOSH
...
WHUMP
KOFF KOFF
KASA-HARA...
GARBAGE
GARBAGE

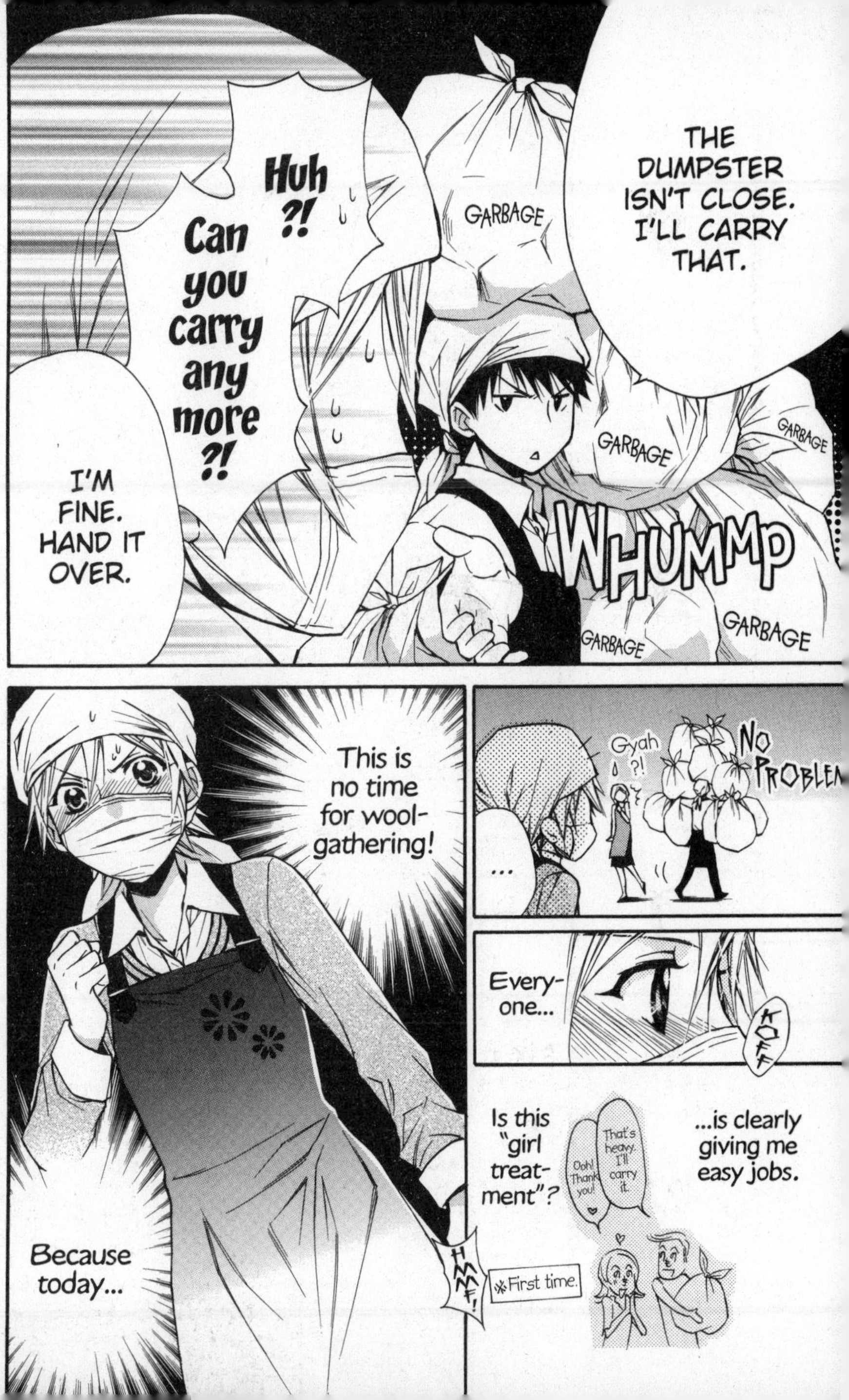
THE DUMPSTER ISN'T CLOSE. I'LL CARRY THAT.
GARBAGE
Huh ?!
Can you carry any more ?!
GARBAGE
GARBAGE
I'M FINE. HAND IT OVER.
WHUMMP
GARBAGE
GARBAGE
NO PROBLEM
Gyah ?!
...
Every-one...
KOFF
...is clearly giving me easy jobs.
That's heavy. I'll carry it.
Ooh! Thank you!
Is this "girl treatment"?
※First time.
This is no time for wool-gathering!
HMMF!
Because today...

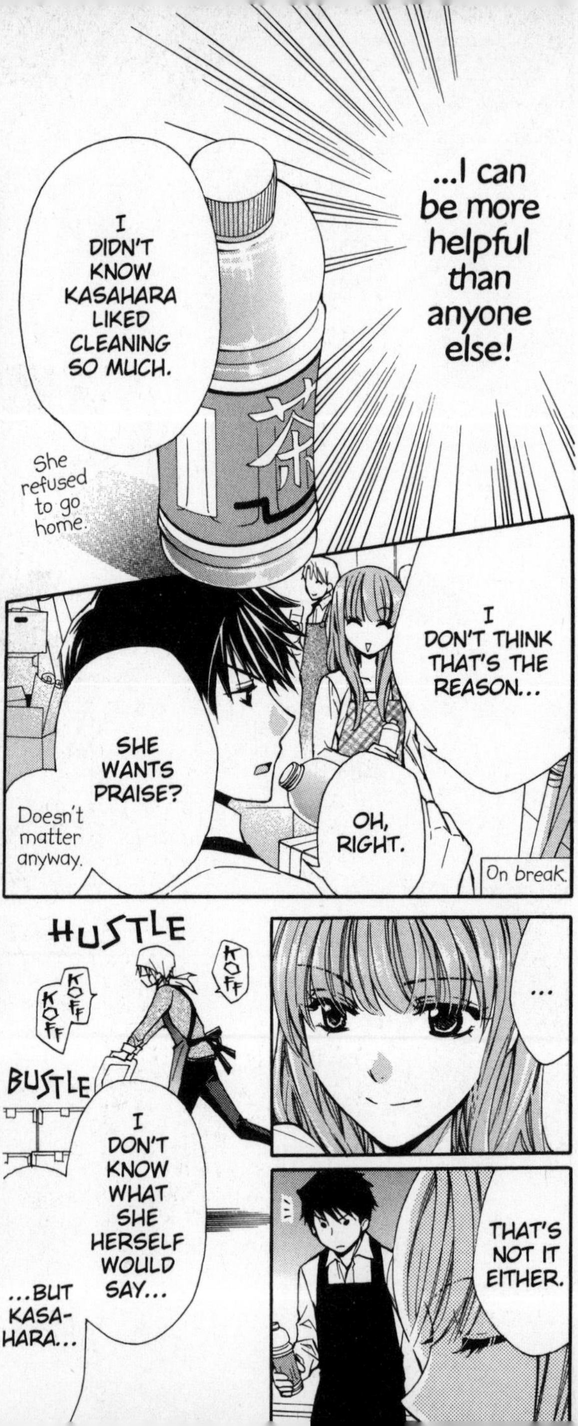
...I can be more helpful than anyone else!
I DIDN'T KNOW KASAHARA LIKED CLEANING SO MUCH.
She refused to go home.
I DON'T THINK THAT'S THE REASON...
SHE WANTS PRAISE?
OH, RIGHT.
On break.
Doesn't matter anyway.
...
HUSTLE
KOFF
KOFF KOFF
BUSTLE
THAT'S NOT IT EITHER.
I DON'T KNOW WHAT SHE HERSELF WOULD SAY...
...BUT KASAHARA...

6

This is the final sidebar! Thank you for reading all this way! I bet readers of the novels were like "???!!!" I put in that bit about "not enough collateral"! I was moved by that scene myself as a reader, so... I'm not sure I portrayed the scene very well. But I'm really happy to have made it this far. And I'd be even happier if you continue to warmly look over me from now on! Bye!

Special thanks are at the back of the book.

Kiiro Yumi

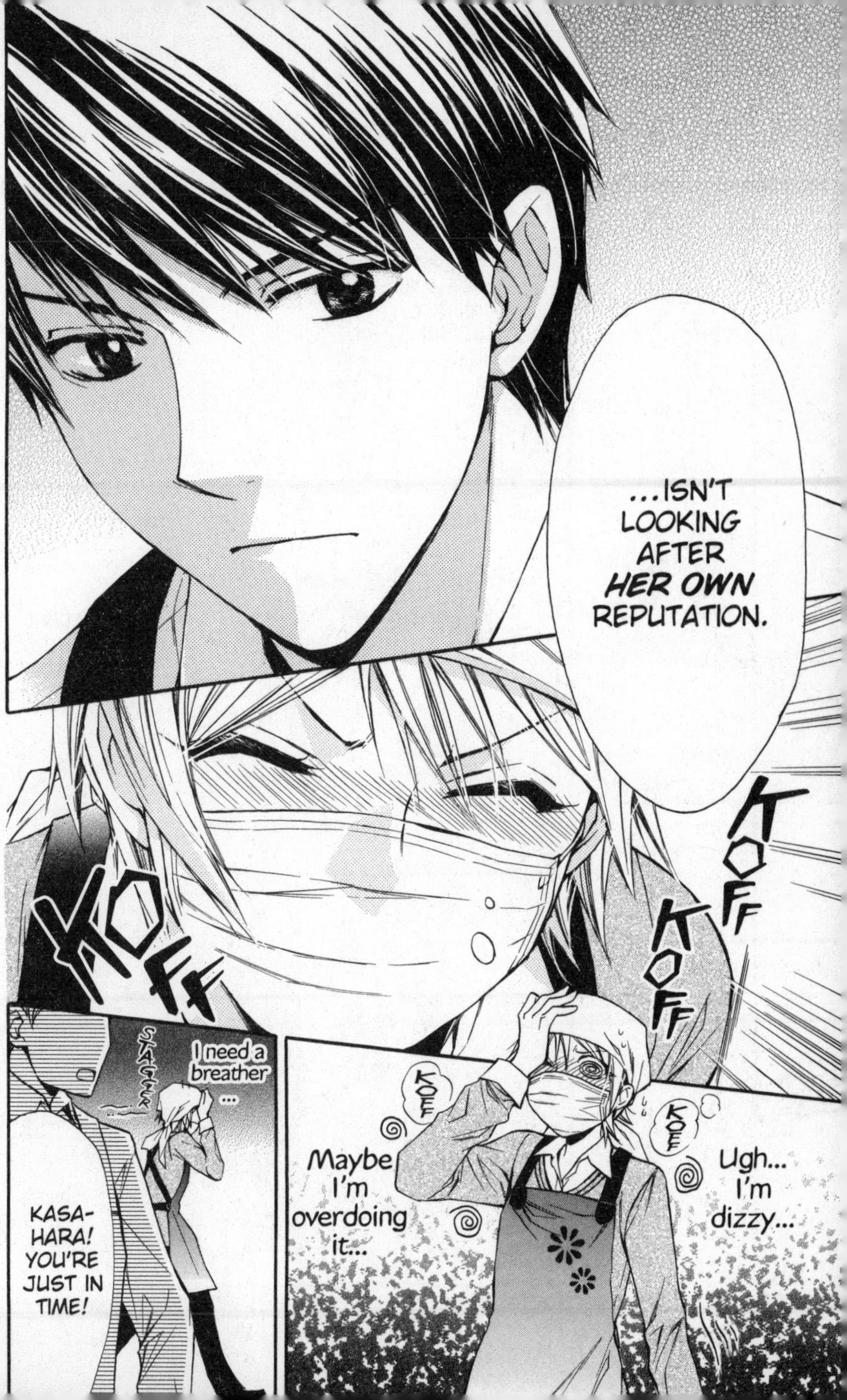
...ISN'T LOOKING AFTER HER OWN REPUTATION.
KOFF
KOFF
KOFF
KOFF
Ugh... I'm dizzy...
KOFF
Maybe I'm overdoing it...
I need a breather ...
STAGGER
KASA-HARA! YOU'RE JUST IN TIME!

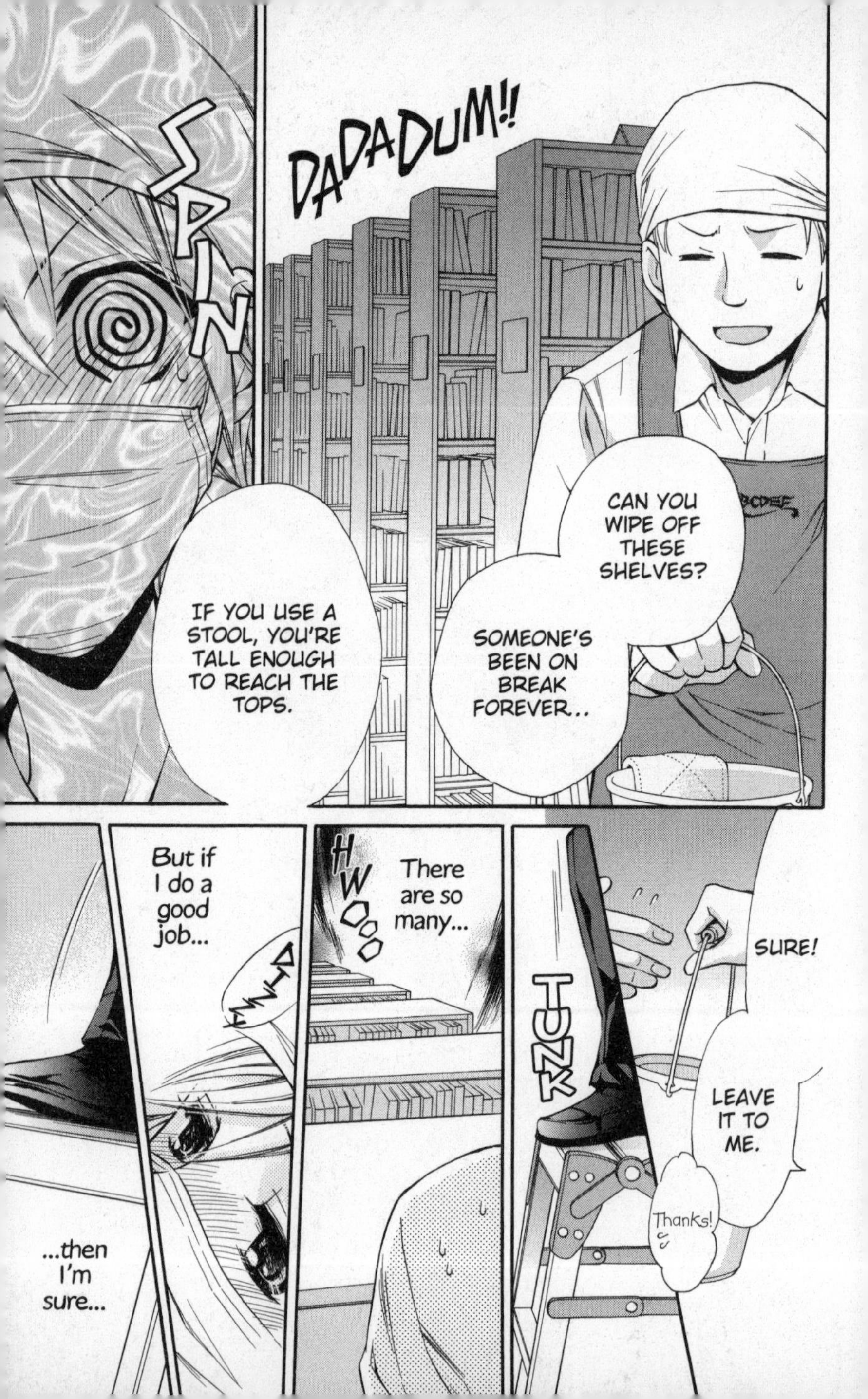
DADADUM!!
CAN YOU WIPE OFF THESE SHELVES?
SOMEONE'S BEEN ON BREAK FOREVER...
IF YOU USE A STOOL, YOU'RE TALL ENOUGH TO REACH THE TOPS.
SPIN
SURE!
LEAVE IT TO ME.
Thanks!
TUNK
There are so many...
HWOOO
But if I do a good job...
...then I'm sure...

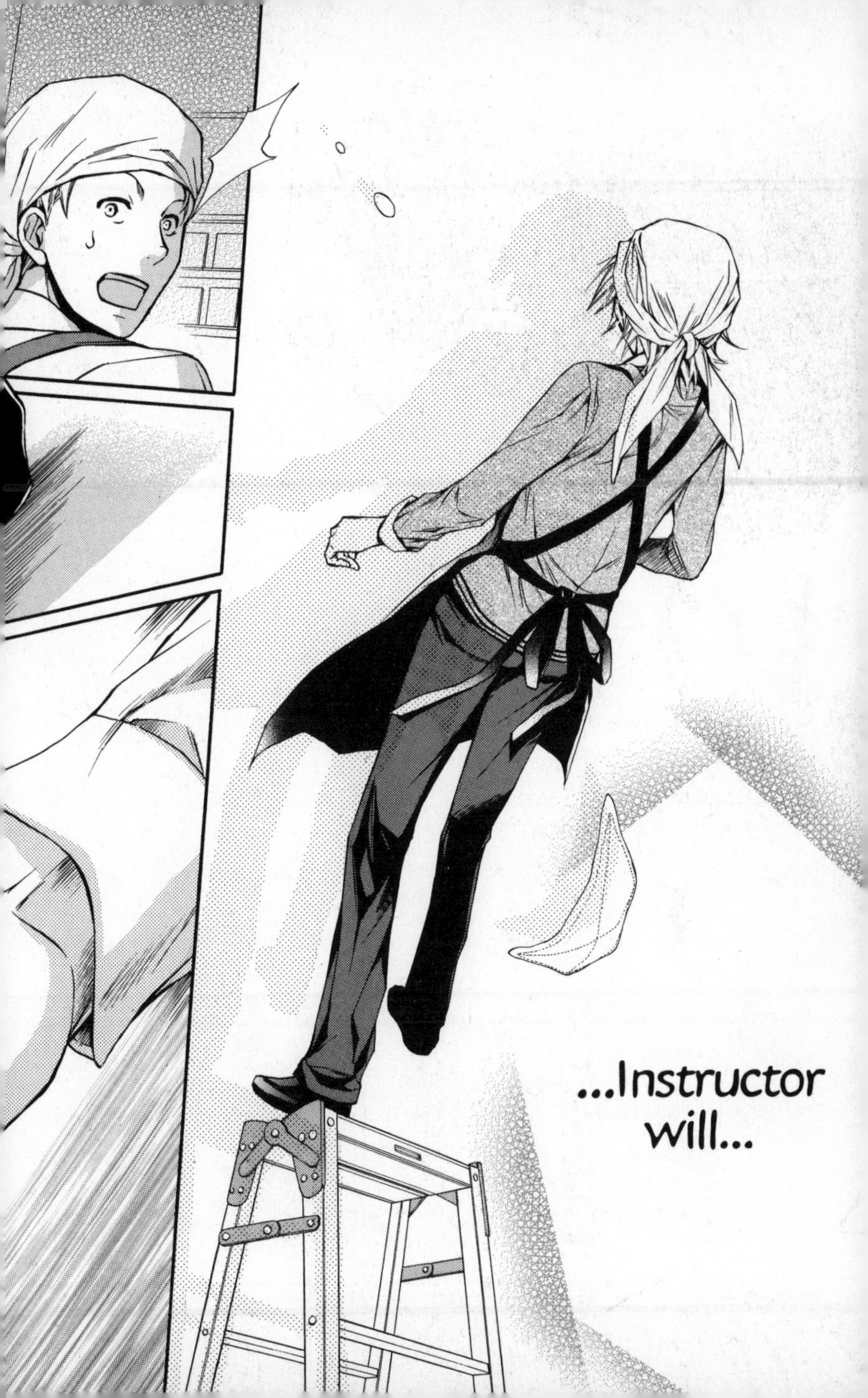
...Instructor
will...

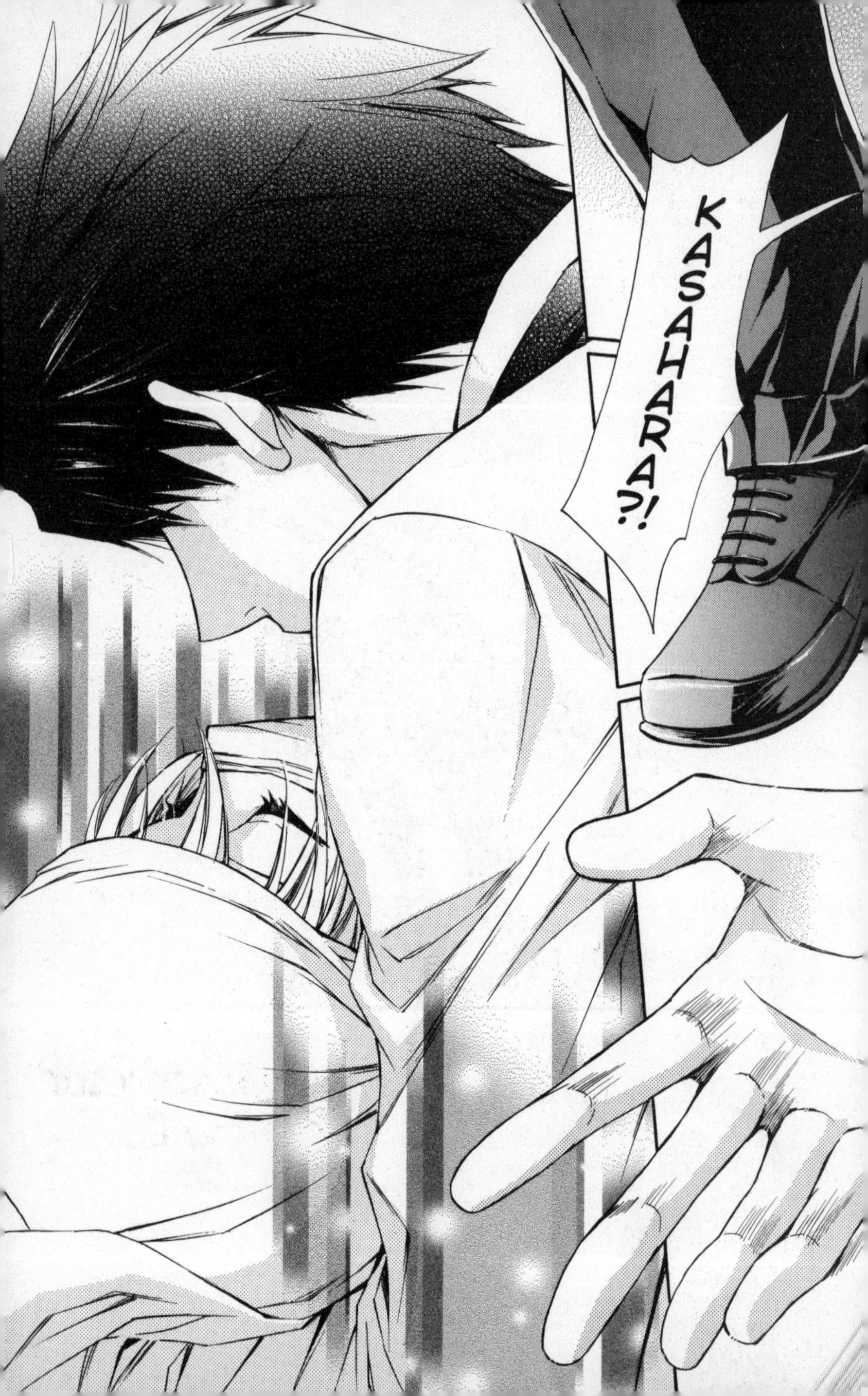
KASAHARA?!

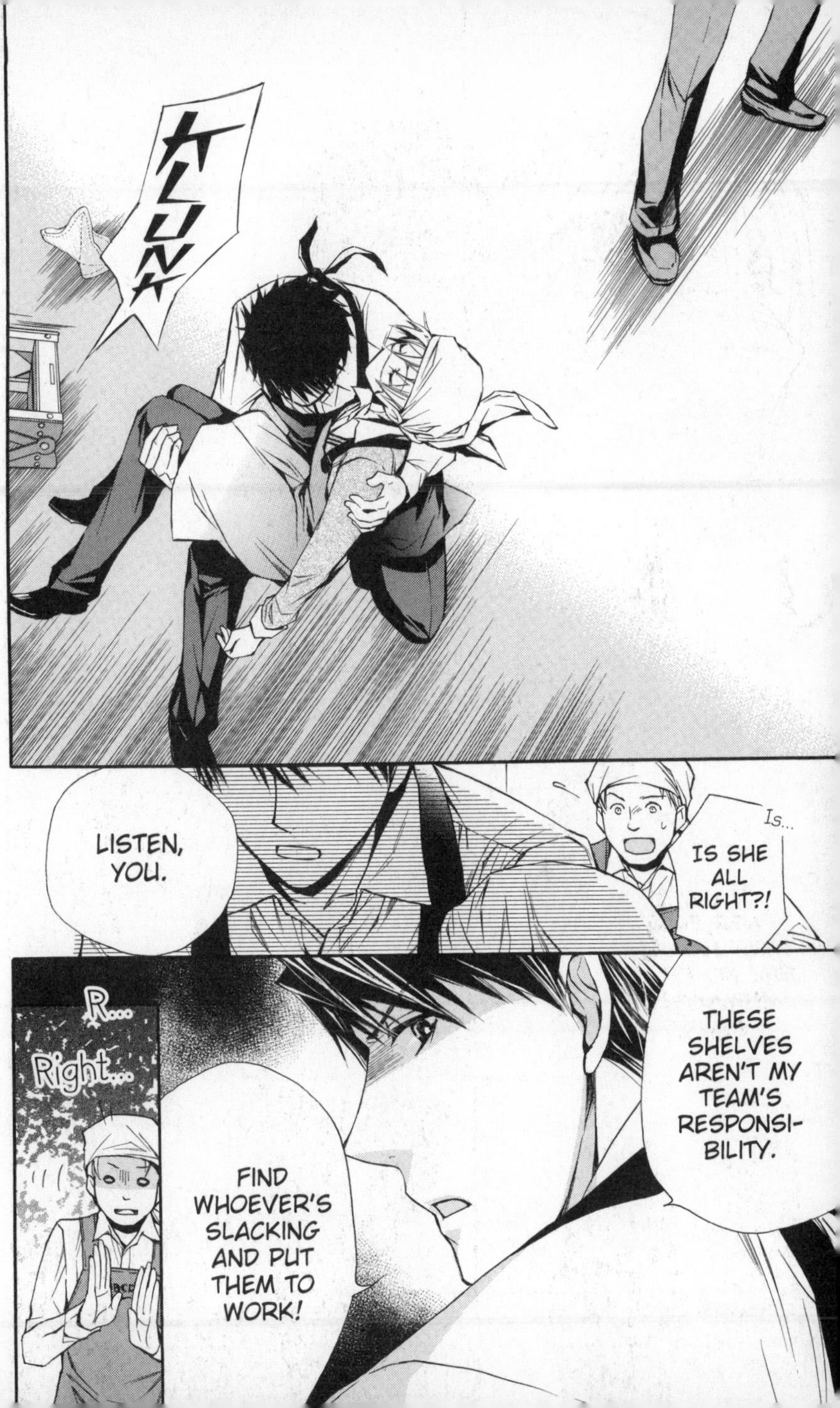
KLUNK
Is...
IS SHE ALL RIGHT?!
LISTEN, YOU.
THESE SHELVES AREN'T MY TEAM'S RESPONSI-BILITY.
FIND WHOEVER'S SLACKING AND PUT THEM TO WORK!
R...
Right...

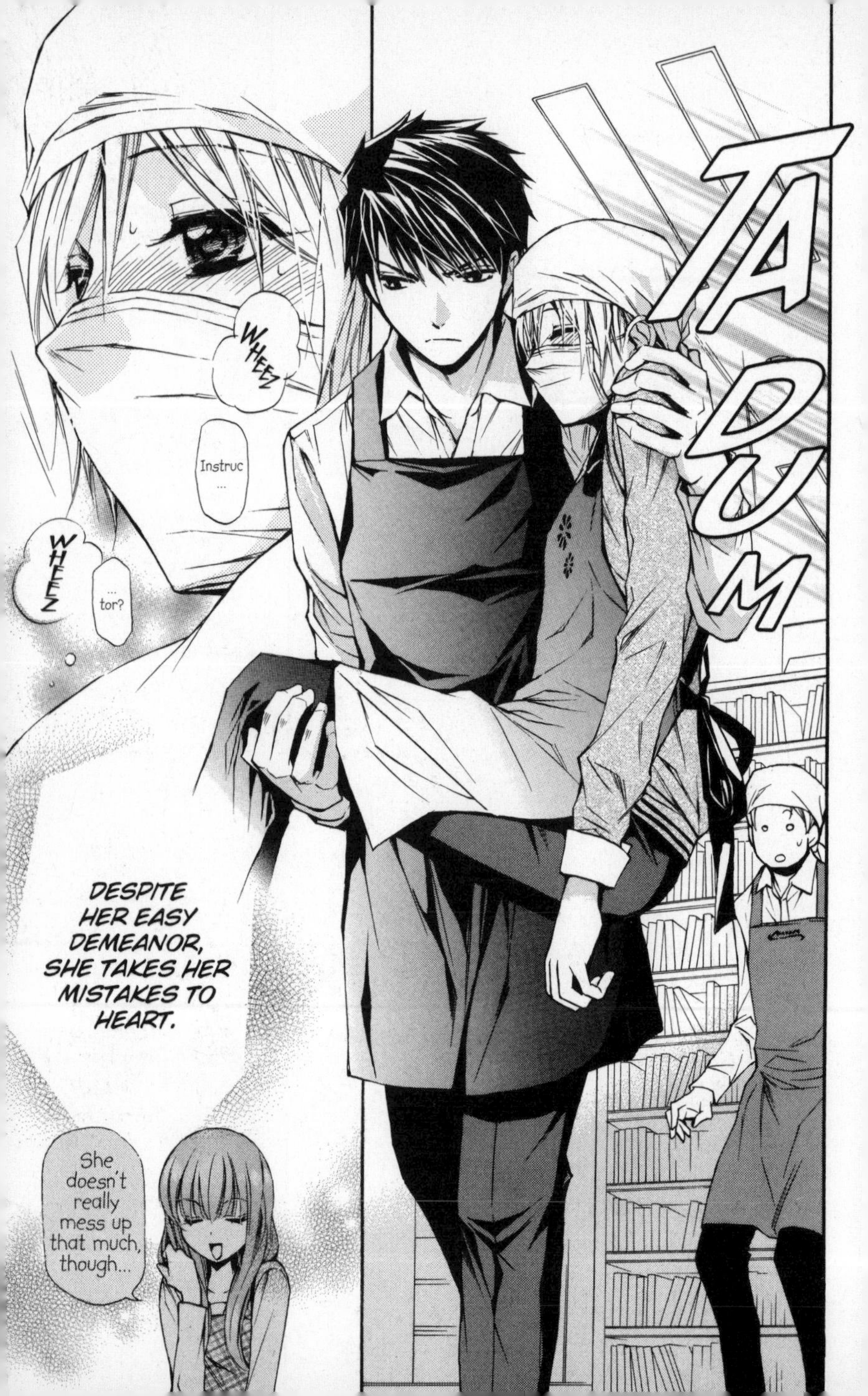
TADUM
WHEEZ
Instruc ...
WHEEZ
... tor?
DESPITE HER EASY DEMEANOR, SHE TAKES HER MISTAKES TO HEART.
She doesn't really mess up that much, though...

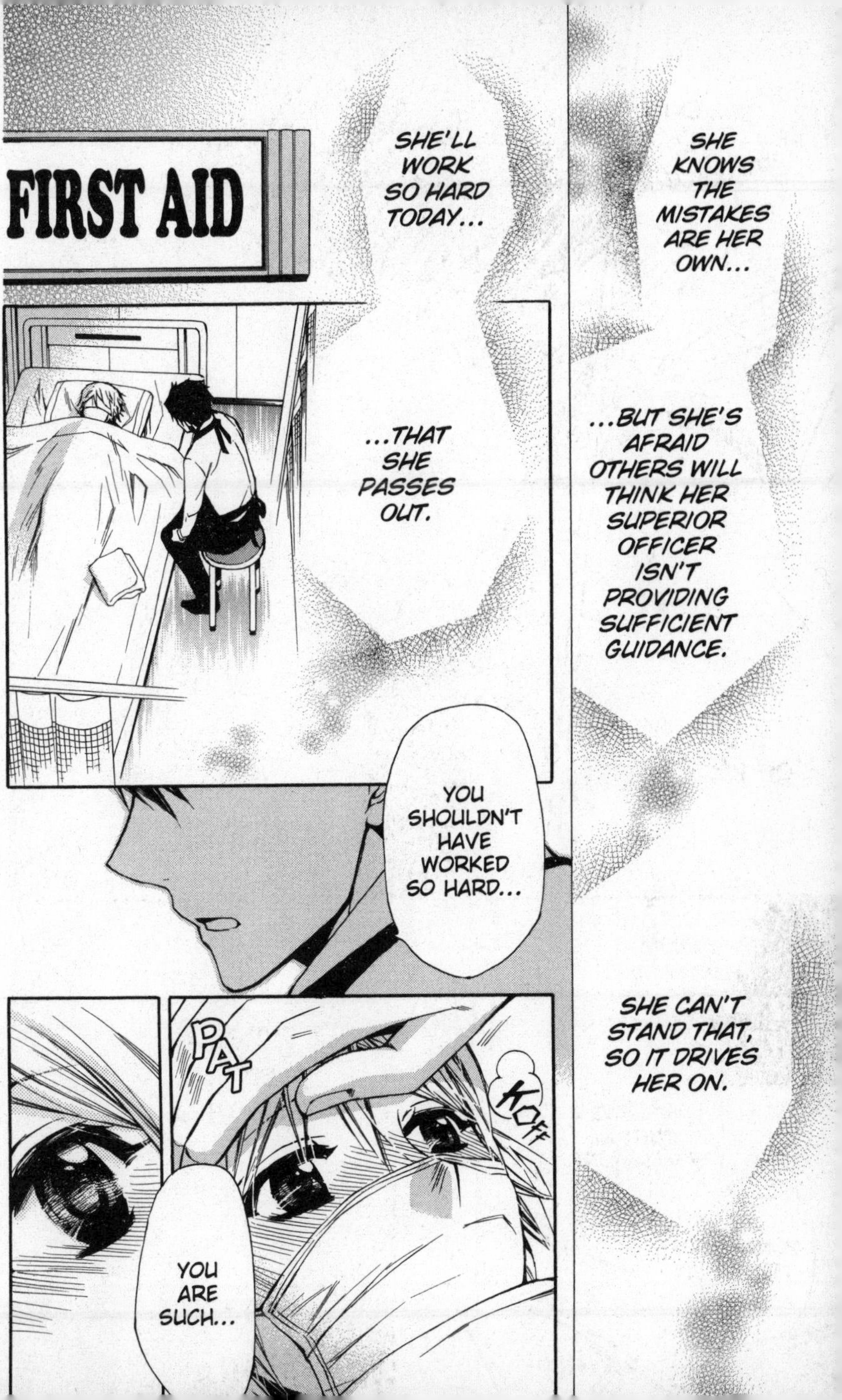
SHE KNOWS THE MISTAKES ARE HER OWN...
...BUT SHE'S AFRAID OTHERS WILL THINK HER SUPERIOR OFFICER ISN'T PROVIDING SUFFICIENT GUIDANCE.
SHE CAN'T STAND THAT, SO IT DRIVES HER ON.
FIRST AID
SHE'LL WORK SO HARD TODAY...
...THAT SHE PASSES OUT.
YOU SHOULDN'T HAVE WORKED SO HARD...
KOFF
PAT
YOU ARE SUCH...

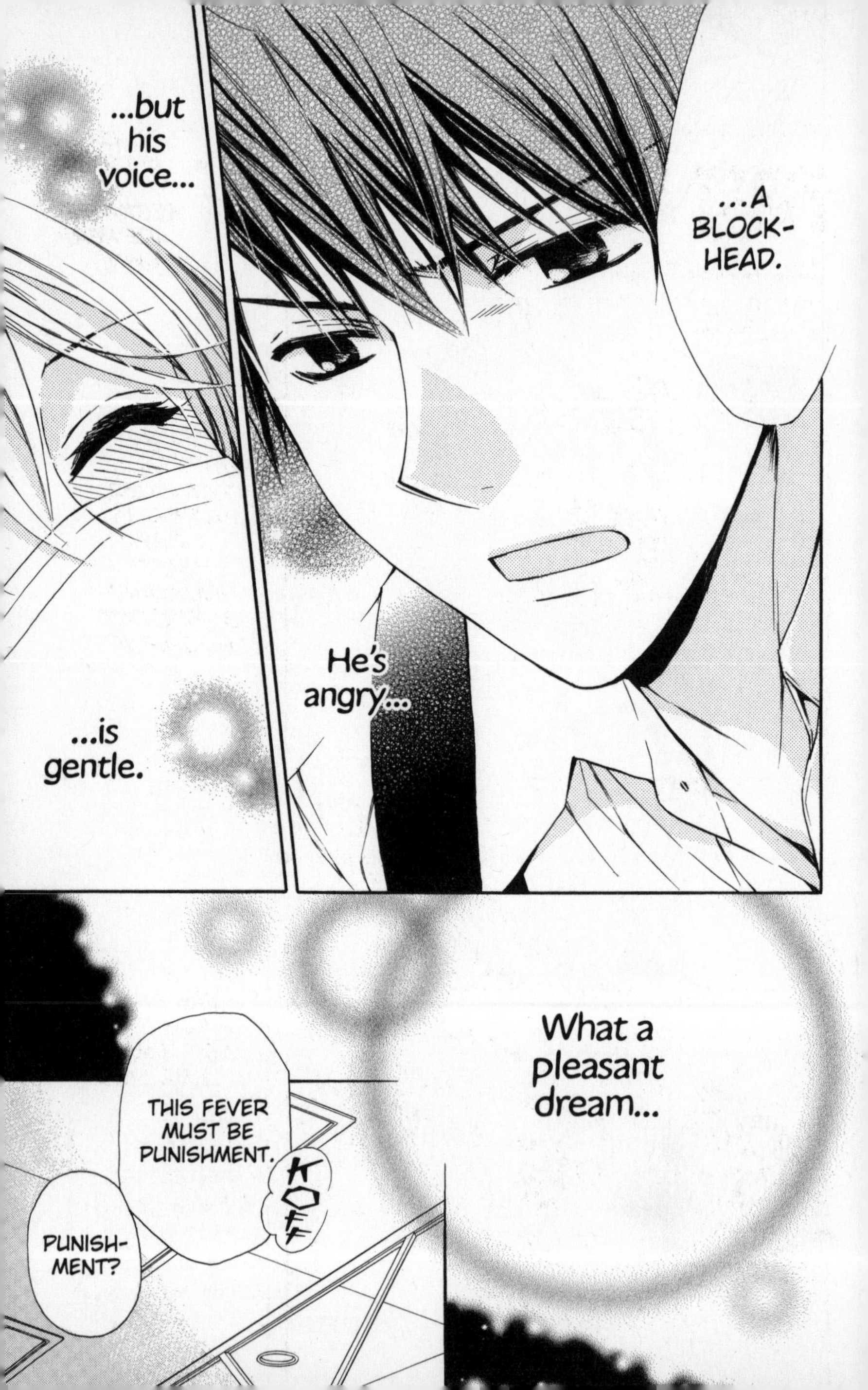
...A BLOCK-HEAD.
He's angry...
...but his voice...
...is gentle.
What a pleasant dream...
THIS FEVER MUST BE PUNISHMENT.
KOFF
PUNISH-MENT?

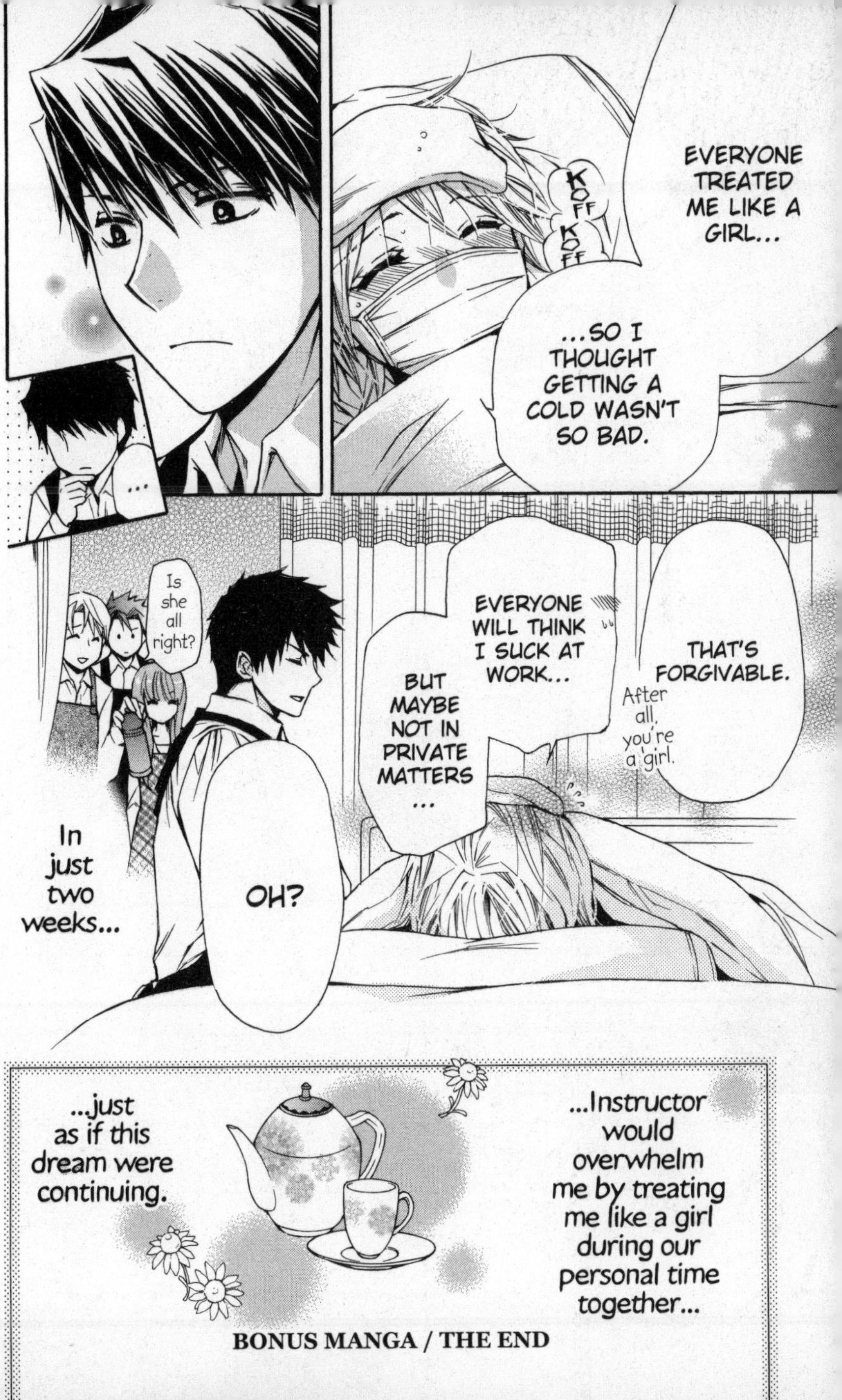
EVERYONE TREATED ME LIKE A GIRL...
KOFF KOFF
...SO I THOUGHT GETTING A COLD WASN'T SO BAD.
...
THAT'S FORGIVABLE.
After all, you're a girl.
EVERYONE WILL THINK I SUCK AT WORK...
BUT MAYBE NOT IN PRIVATE MATTERS...
OH?
Is she all right?
In just two weeks...
...Instructor would overwhelm me by treating me like a girl during our personal time together...
...just as if this dream were continuing.
BONUS MANGA / THE END

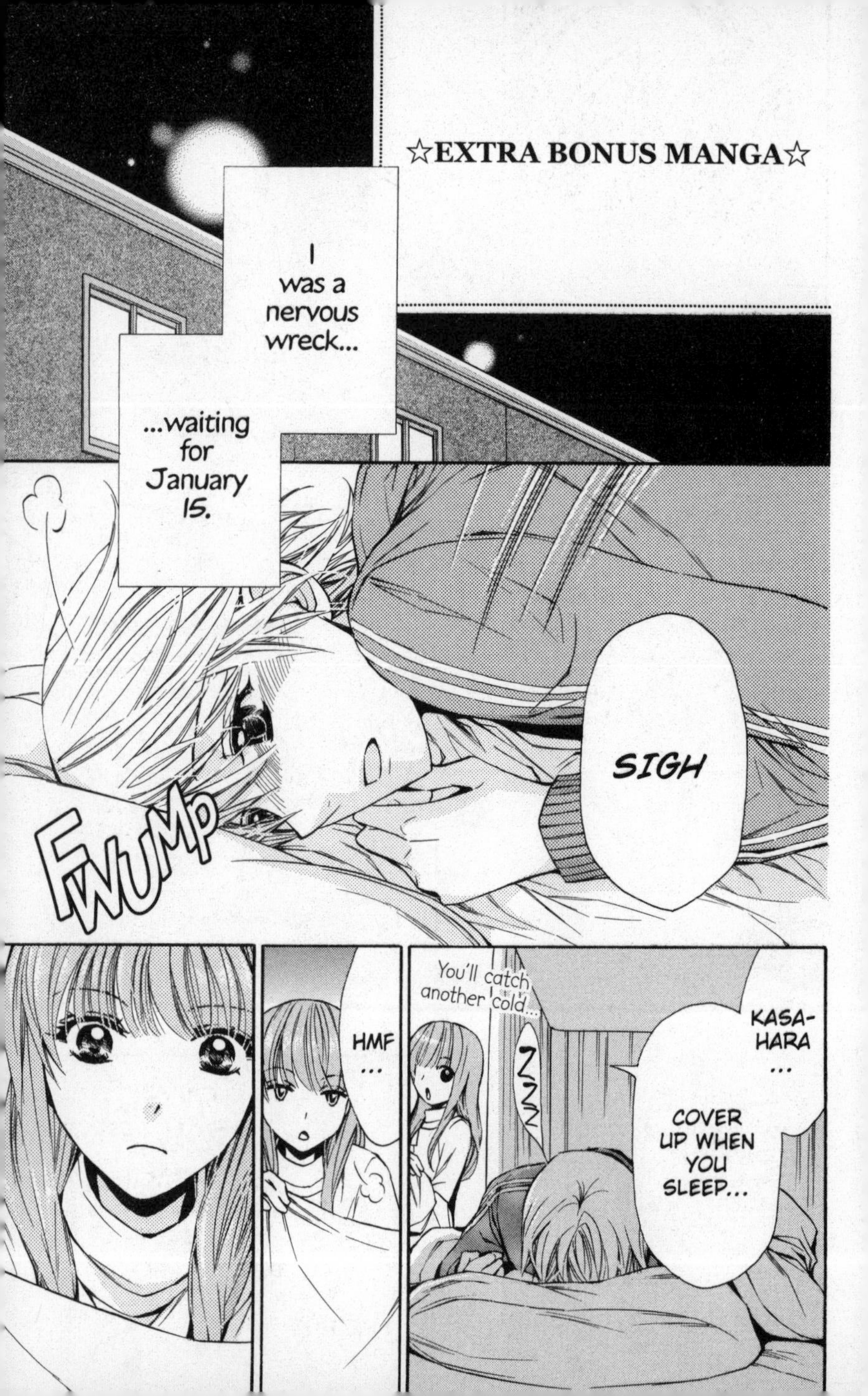
☆EXTRA BONUS MANGA☆
I was a nervous wreck...
...waiting for January 15.
SIGH
FWUMP
KASA-HARA...
COVER UP WHEN YOU SLEEP...
You'll catch another cold...
ZZZ
HMF...

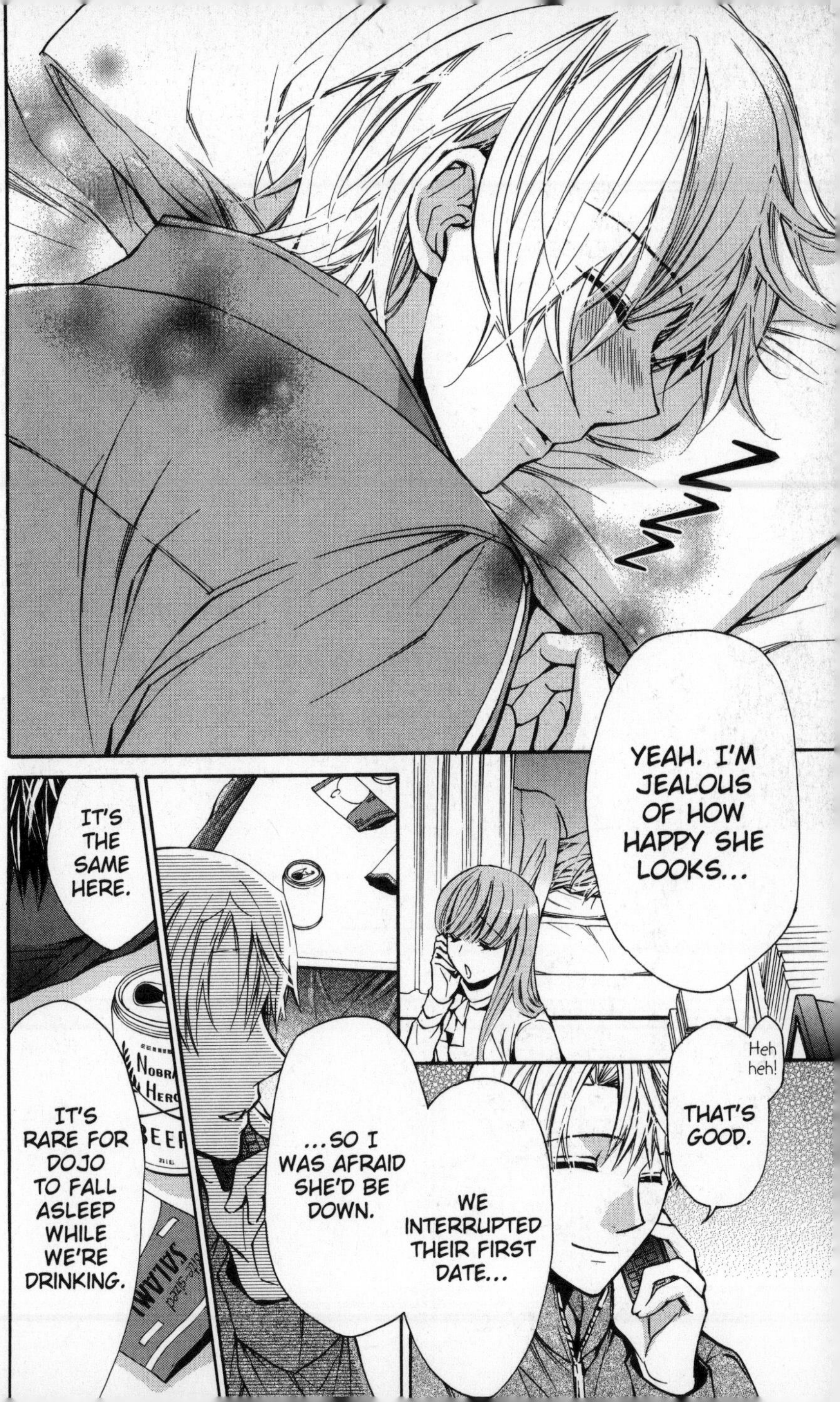
YEAH. I'M JEALOUS OF HOW HAPPY SHE LOOKS...
Heh heh!
THAT'S GOOD.
WE INTERRUPTED THEIR FIRST DATE...
...SO I WAS AFRAID SHE'D BE DOWN.
IT'S THE SAME HERE.
IT'S RARE FOR DOJO TO FALL ASLEEP WHILE WE'RE DRINKING.

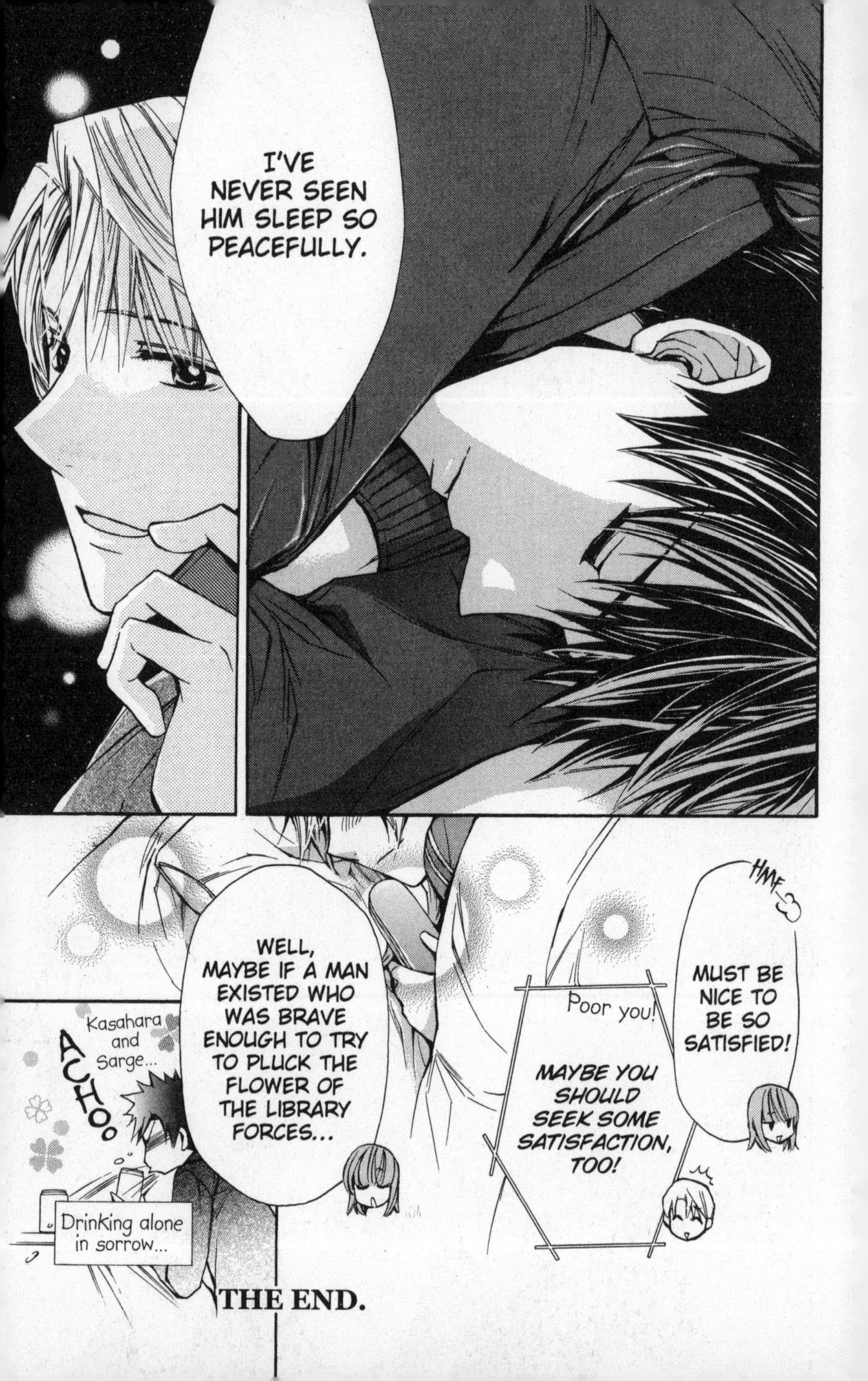
I'VE NEVER SEEN HIM SLEEP SO PEACEFULLY.
HMF
MUST BE NICE TO BE SO SATISFIED!
Poor you!
MAYBE YOU SHOULD SEEK SOME SATISFACTION, TOO!
WELL, MAYBE IF A MAN EXISTED WHO WAS BRAVE ENOUGH TO TRY TO PLUCK THE FLOWER OF THE LIBRARY FORCES...
Kasahara and Sarge...
ACHOO
Drinking alone in sorrow...
THE END.

Special Thanks!!

Ms. Arikawa
Ms. Arikawa's editor (ASCII Media)

★

Mamada, Murakami, Aoki

★

My family

★

My editor, the *LaLa* Editorial Department

★

Everyone who makes this series possible.

★
★

Thanks so, so much!

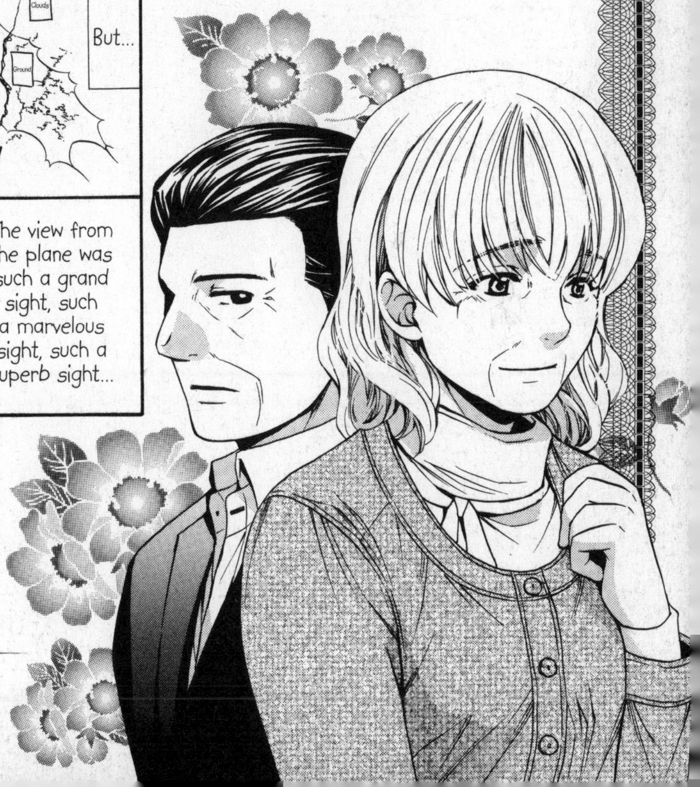

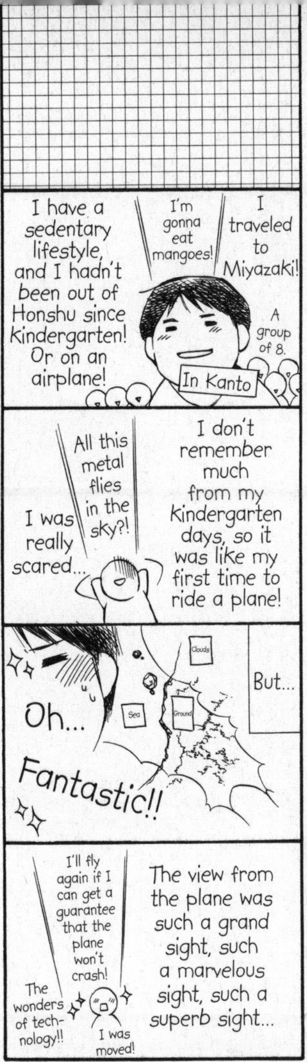

I traveled to Miyazaki!
I'm gonna eat mangoes!
A group of 8.
I have a sedentary lifestyle, and I hadn't been out of Honshu since kindergarten! Or on an airplane!
In Kanto
I don't remember much from my kindergarten days, so it was like my first time to ride a plane!
All this metal flies in the sky?!
I was really scared...
But...
Clouds
Sea
Ground
Oh...
Fantastic!!
The view from the plane was such a grand sight, such a marvelous sight, such a superb sight...
I'll fly again if I can get a guarantee that the plane won't crash!
The wonders of technology!!
I was moved!

The organizer was my friend! Thanks!

I like high places.

Hope to see you again next volume!

Kiiro Yumi won the 42nd *LaLa*
Manga Grand Prix Fresh Debut
award for her manga *Billy
Bocchan no Yuutsu* (Little Billy's
Depression). Her latest series
is *Toshokan Senso Love&War*
(*Library Wars: Love & War*),
which runs in *LaLa* magazine
in Japan and is published in
English by VIZ Media.

Hiro Arikawa won the 10th
Dengeki Novel Prize for her
work *Shio no Machi: Wish on My
Precious* in 2003 and debuted
with the same novel in 2004.
Of her many works, Arikawa is
best known for the *Library Wars*
series and her *Jieitai Sanbusaku*
trilogy, which consists of *Sora
no Naka* (In the Sky), *Umi no
Soko* (The Bottom of the Sea)
and *Shio no Machi* (City of Salt).

library wars

Volume 12
Shojo Beat Edition

Story & Art by **Kiiro Yumi**
Original Concept by **Hiro Arikawa**

ENGLISH TRANSLATION John Werry
LETTERING Annaliese Christman
DESIGN Amy Martin
EDITOR Megan Bates

Toshokan Sensou LOVE&WAR by Kiiro Yumi and Hiro Arikawa
© Kiiro Yumi 2013
© Hiro Arikawa 2013
All rights reserved.
First published in Japan in 2013 by HAKUSENSHA, Inc., Tokyo.
English language translation rights arranged with HAKUSENSHA,
Inc., Tokyo.

Printed in Canada

Published by VIZ Media, LLC
P.O. Box 77010
San Francisco, CA 94107

10 9 8 7 6 5 4 3 2 1
First printing, September 2014

www.shojobeat.com   www.viz.com